*The Gorgon's Gaze: German Cinema, Expressionism, and the Image of Horror* is an interdisciplinary study of recurrent themes in German cinema as it has developed since the early twentieth century. Focusing on pertinent films of the pre– and post–World War II eras, Paul Coates explores the nature of expressionism, which is generally agreed to have ended with the advent of sound cinema, and its persistence in the styles of such modern masters of film as Orson Welles and Ingmar Bergman. In considering the possibility of homologies between the necessary silence of presound cinema and the widespread modernist aspiration to an aesthetic of silence, Coates relates theories of the sublime, the uncanny, and the monstrous to his subject. He also reflects upon problems of representability and the morality of representation of events that took place during the Nazi era.

In *The Gorgon's Gaze*, Coates purposefully draws on a variety of methodologies in order to offer a model for the writing of cultural history. Arguing that the implicit complexity of cinema defies unilateral analysis, he builds a deliberately shifting, open-ended argument intended to accommodate elements from philosophy, sociology, film studies, comparative literature, psychoanalysis, and anthropology.

# THE GORGON'S GAZE
German Cinema, Expressionism, and the Image of Horror

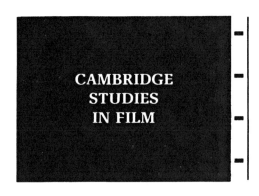

CAMBRIDGE
STUDIES
IN FILM

OTHER BOOKS IN THE SERIES

# THE GORGON'S GAZE

German Cinema, Expressionism, and the
Image of Horror

PAUL COATES
*Associate Professor of English, McGill University*

The right of the
University of Cambridge
to print and publish
all kinds of books
was granted by law
in 1534.
The University has printed
and published continuously
since 1584.

CAMBRIDGE UNIVERSITY PRESS
CAMBRIDGE
NEW YORK   PORT CHESTER   MELBOURNE   SYDNEY

CAMBRIDGE UNIVERSITY PRESS
Cambridge, New York, Melbourne, Madrid, Cape Town, Singapore, São Paulo

Cambridge University Press
The Edinburgh Building, Cambridge CB2 8RU, UK

Published in the United States of America by Cambridge University Press, New York

www.cambridge.org
Information on this title: www.cambridge.org/9780521384094

First published 1991
This digitally printed version 2008

*A catalogue record for this publication is available from the British Library*

*Library of Congress Cataloguing in Publication data*
Coates, Paul, 1953–
The gorgon's gaze : German cinema, expressionism, and the image of horror /
Paul Coates.
    p.   cm. – (Cambridge studies in film)
Filmography: p.
Includes bibliographical references (p.   ) and index.
ISBN 0-521-38409-5
1. Motion pictures – Germany – History.   2. Expressionism.
3. Monsters in motion pictures.   4. Film noir.
I. Title.   II. Series.
PN1993.5.G3C64   1991
791.43′0943 – dc20   90–14998

ISBN 978-0-521-38409-4 hardback
ISBN 978-0-521-06336-4 paperback

KENT:                    Is this the promised end?
EDGAR:   Or image of that horror?
          – *King Lear*, Act V, sc. iii, lines 264–5

# Contents

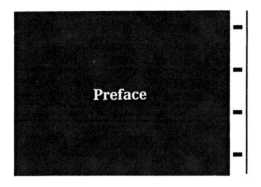

Preface

This book situates itself on the border of comparative literature and film studies. In recent years film studies has devolved into a somewhat insular possession, jealously guarded by its first colonists – if one can conceive of it as a country, it is a France whose capital is Metz – the generation that set up university film programs in the late sixties. Having once been compelled to fight clear of literature departments to secure their own existence, film programs are often averse now to recognition of the links between filmic and literary texts. Given film's status as the executor of the *Gesamtkunstwerk's* testament, film studies once promised to become an open forum for reflection upon the separate arts and cultural domains. Instead, once-exciting theories have been deprived of their speculative status and frozen into an orthodoxy that needs to be challenged in the name of the very theorists it takes as canonic: A Barthes or a Benjamin would surely have been appalled by his work's cooptation by the academy. All too often complacent orthodoxy speaks of difference and excludes anything that differs. If the study of film is to escape the confines of a terminology whose rigor is now a straitjacket perversely worn to indicate membership of an elite, it must recognize that to speak of Theory rather than theories is to pursue the fata morgana of an impossible totalization; whereas in fact the project of totalization would be better served by a multiplicity of perspectives, which alone would do justice to the overdetermined event and fulfill the goal of subverting arbitrary (because monologic) authority. Thus *The Gorgon's Gaze* drifts quite deliberately between separate domains: philosophy, sociology, psychoanalysis, literary theory, German studies, Polish studies, and, of course, film theory itself. If it has loose ends (in imitation perhaps of the Medusa's head that lends it its title?), this is quite intentional.

The book does not have a single subject, but rather several, which overlap and separate themselves in a shifting montage. Of the three terms listed in my subtitle – German cinema, expressionism, and horror – each has equal weight. This is not a book "about German cinema," but one about the relationship between the three terms of the subtitle and the title, which refers to the freezing powers of the look. Since it is also a meditation on the nature and legacy of expressionism, which is generally agreed to have ended about the time of the advent of sound cinema, its themes include the exile and partial persistence of expressionist habits of mind in several of the great styles and modern masters of cinema, such as film noir, or Welles and Bergman. Consideration of the possibility of homologies between the necessary silence of presound cinema and the widespread modernist aspiration to an aesthetic of silence feeds, in turn, into the subsidiary question of the degree of compatability of "high" and "low" cultural forms, of Adorno's *Bilderverbot* and the problematic representation of the Other in the horror film. The book thus intersects with such areas as the theory of the sublime, the uncanny, and the monstrous, and construes "horror" both historically and anthropologically: the horrific as perennial (Evil; the undead) and as the horror that attaches to this century's events in German history. For the Western culture of the late twentieth century the central image of horror is the concentration camp, which recurs in the iconography of both mass and high culture as an object of fascination (often fetishistic or kitsch-laden), a memory of the determining event of the current world order, and a fearsome image of the bankruptcy of our culture. If that culture is the home that is home no longer, it is, of course, the uncanny.

To consider the uncanny in the context of German cinema is inevitably to reflect upon the representability, and the morality of representation, of the events of the Nazi years, particularly within the German-speaking countries themselves. It is to ask whether or not anti-Semitism is present embryonically even in the 1913 *Student of Prague (Der Student von Prag)*, the founding work of German film history; how calculated are the omissions of Edgar Reitz's *Heimat*; how useful a term is *Vergangenheitsbewältigung* (can and should this be translated as "coming to terms with the past"?); and what form of *Trauerarbeit* (the work of mourning) can best do justice to the dead? (This book will argue that the most adequate response is found in Margarethe von Trotta's *Marianne and Juliane [Die bleierne Zeit]*). Is the refusal to engage in mimetic reconstruction of evil events a valid method of indicating the degree to which they defy the imagination (the proclaimed tactic of *Shoah*), or does Lanzmann's own mode of interviewing unwittingly place him too in the ranks of the persecutors? How willing are cultures and individuals to concede that monsters lie within their borders? This book will suggest that if one defeats the Medusa by directing a mirror against her, one simultaneously becomes blind to one's own monstrous status as the murderer of an alterity – usually feminine – demonized by one's own projections.*

* It is clear that the Medusa is a demonized, pathological image of female otherness; a lesser form of demonization occurs however in much early writing on cinema spectatorship, which tends to cast the female in the role of ideal viewer (hence Kracauer terms his collection of sketches of the film industry's melodramatic schemata *The Little Shop-Girls Go to the Movies*). The meaning of this tendency varied from critic to critic, but included as two primary components a masculinist disdain for the putative feminine incapacity for sustained reasoning – for Bovaryisme – and a terror of the unmanning effects of the physical passivity film watching enforces, a passivity that may be experienced as a prelude to rape. The male's alienation from the anima, into whose darkness he fears to descend and which he identifies with art and with the womb, seems to have been part of the depth psychology of the tendency. It is of course still alive and well: *Heimat* shows us Maria and Pauline at a Zarah Leander film, and in Syberberg's *Karl May* the writer's wife and secretary watch a Méliès movie in a kinetoscope while he is abroad. (Creating images of Paradise seems to be the prerogative of the male artist; Syberberg shows no interest in the possibility that the occultism of the women is a less lucrative form of May's own Utopian fabulism.)

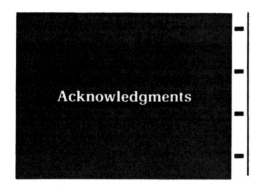

Acknowledgments

This book may be read (as a brief perusal of its notes and index will demonstrate) as an extended colloquy with three people in particular: T. W. Adorno, Siegfried Kracauer, and Thomas Elsaesser. The nature of my concurrence, disagreement with, and modification of their work will be apparent from my text; here I would simply like to acknowledge my indebtedness to them as partners in the dialogic process. Other partners were the students in the German cinema seminar I gave at McGill in 1989, so I would like to thank Antony, Caroline, Dave, Dominique, Jennifer, John, Kirsten, Renee, Richard, Scott, and Stephen for the stimulus of their presence and their heroic willingness to sit through films of exorbitant length. I must also thank Professor Edward Mozejko, whose kind invitation to speak at the University of Alberta prompted the formulation of early versions of two of these essays. Additional thanks are due to the McGill Comparative Literature Department, which provoked and endured two early versions of other essays.

"The Cold Heaven of the Blue Angel" first appeared in *Social Discourse,* and a version of the analysis of *A Short Film about Killing* in *Sight and Sound.* Part of "Three Faces of the Other in the Horror Film," parts of Appendixes I and V, and the analysis of *Welcome to Germany* first appeared in the October 1989, June 1989, June 1988, and October 1988 issues of *The World and I,* a publication of the Washington Times Corporation. Divergences from the published versions serve in the main to rescind unilateral editorial emendations.

My final chapter's excerpt from Julia Kristeva's *Powers of Horror,* copyright © 1981 Columbia University Press, is used by permission. I am grateful to Jerzy Giedroyc and the Instytut Literacki for permission to quote in my own translation an excerpt from Jarosław Marek Rymkiewicz's *Umschlagplatz.*

All translations, unless otherwise attributed, are my own.

Finally, I would like to thank the Montreal branch of the Goethe Institute for its generous supply of Syberberg films and material; Syberberg-Film, for the loan of a video copy of *Our Hitler;* the McGill

English Department, for a summer research grant that solidified the base upon which this book arose; and all those people in West Berlin who have been of particular help – Dr. Christa Vogel, the staff of the Stiftung Deutsche Kinemathek, and Dr. Karsten Witte.

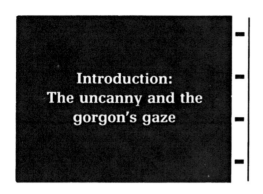

# Introduction:
# The uncanny and the
# gorgon's gaze

The world becomes uncanny when it is perceived as no longer simple substance, but also as shadow, a sign of the existence of a world beyond itself, which it is nevertheless unable fully to disclose. The uncanny sign is not allegorical, for it only *suggests* the presence of another world. Such suggestivity may seem to render it akin to the symbol, but it is in fact neither symbol nor allegory; it lacks both the transparency of the allegory and the positivity of the symbol. It is frustrated allegory, negative symbol.*

The uncanny world is a world of conspiracy. It is experienced as such by the modernist imagination, with its fascination by – and anticipation of – total systems. In his famous essay "The 'Uncanny,' " Freud may have noted sardonically his own lack of an instinct for its perception, but he is nevertheless himself enough of a modernist – sufficiently interested, like the great modernist novelists, in the creation of a personal encyclopedic system – to be able to cite an experience of the uncannily that itself uncannily resembles the accounts Hofmannsthal or Mann[†] give of passage through Venice, that labyrinthine deathly city of alienated desire:

* The following passage from Böll's *Billiards at Half-past Nine* casts an interesting light on the uncanny. In it Fähmel's secretary longs for "Leben. Nicht diese makellose Ordnung, nicht diesen Chef, der makellos gekleidet und makellos höflich war – und ihr unheimlich; sie witterte Verachtung hinter dieser Höflichkeit" [Life. Not this impeccable order, not this boss, who dressed impeccably and was impeccably polite – and made her feel uneasy; she sensed contempt behind the politeness] (*Billard um halbzehn*, DTV, Munich, 1987 [1959]). (*Unheimlich* has as its dictionary meaning "uncanny.") One sees here how the *unheimlich* involves a sense that reality is a deceptive façade. (Might not this render film particularly uncanny – for its sets really are unreal, while it is projected onto a wall *behind which* something else may indeed be happening?) I will be returning to Böll's novel in my final chapter.

† The resemblance between Freud's Italian town and Mann's Venice is intriguing, for one of the forms of the uncanny world of conspiracy is the Venetian carnival (a profoundly un-Bakhtinian carnival): During a conspiracy, faces become masks. One of the most powerful uncanny works of recent years is Dennis Potter's *The Singing Detective*, in which *every* face is a series of masks, which the work employs a quasi-Freudian analysis to lift: mother, whore, Lili Marleen, and one's wife are all interchangeable, as are

Once, as I was walking through the deserted streets of a provincial town in Italy which was strange to me, on a hot summer afternoon, I found myself in a quarter the character of which could not long remain in doubt. Nothing but painted women were to be seen at the windows of the small houses, and I hastened to leave the narrow street at the next turning. But after having wandered about for a while without being directed, I suddenly found myself back in the same street, where my presence was now beginning to excite attention. I hurried away once more, but only to arrive yet a third time by devious paths in the same place. Now, however, a feeling overcame me which I can only describe as uncanny, and I was glad enough to abandon my exploratory walk and get straight back to the piazza I had left a short while before.[1]

The uncanny experience of movement in circles itself reflects the uncanniness of the modernist evocation of the totality the circle symbolizes (cf. Eliot's crowd of people walking round in a ring in "The Waste Land"). It becomes clear that the modernist theme of temporality is linked to a perception of the uncanny, which establishes itself as time is abolished and one becomes trapped in the moment. Freud's provincial Italian town, with its suspended time, is out of De Chirico.* If this collapse of temporal succession is a concomitant of the post-Romantic regression to the talismanic immediate experiences of childhood, it is also the movement of psychoanalysis itself, to which the compulsion to repeat is as central as it is to the quoted passage. Psychoanalysis reveals itself to be a machine for the creation of the uncanny – a possibility Freud himself entertains only whimsically,[2] as if seeking to obscure the degree to which his newly founded discipline really *is* uncanny. One can understand why he should wish to do this: The Jew's decipherment of the hidden structures of German life could itself be demonized as part of the international conspiracy against the Germanic. And so, in his essay on the uncanny, Freud addresses to Hoffmann the reproaches he fears may be directed against himself: It is Hoffmann's "Der Sandmann," not

father, a scarecrow, and Hitler; the detective, meanwhile, tries to recover a lost God (and father) by becoming himself the author and the one who devises and uncovers mysteries. It is hardly surprising that Potter's work is steeped in the conventions of film noir, which emanates an atmosphere of conspiracy. For more on film noir, and on its two primary male protagonists, the detective and the lover (protagonists amalgamated in Potter's Philip Marlow), see "*The Big Sleep* and the little dreamer" in Chapter IV.
* Freud defines the uncanny as, among other things, the return of superstitious mental habits once surmounted, be it in the individual or in humanity in general. This is surely a definition of what he himself would find uncanny: the bending of the line of progress into a circle. (It is the circularity of his movement within the Italian red-light district that bothers him, not the possibility of an unconscious desire to remain in the presence of the painted ladies.) He accords only cursory mention to the return of the dead, deeming it gruesome rather than uncanny, even though his preferred definition of the uncanny as the manifestation of that which should have remained hidden fits precisely the appearance of a revenant. Even as his intellectual curiosity and desire for inclusiveness cause him to consider the relationship between the uncanny and the dead, his distaste for the supernatural causes him almost simultaneously to nip the theme in the bud.

Freud's essay, that "leaves us in bewilderment."[3] May this not also be the reason why Freud seems to repress the most brilliant section of his essay, relegating to a long footnote his analysis of the mutability of character in Hoffmann's story,[4] in order to mitigate the sense of the uncanniness of a psychoanalytic interpretation that sets everything in motion? Was it any accident that psychoanalysis, that uncanny remedy for the uncanny, was devised by a member of a race whose own *Heim* – the German-speaking area – was to become *unheimlich* later in the century?

If the uncanny world is the domain of conspiracy, it manifests itself whenever the fragmentation and incoherence that characterize twentieth century everyday life are suddenly reversed, in a moment of dialectical shock, to yield intimations of a world of enigmatic power and powers, a world with a *plot*. This uncanny world, some of whose most powerfully inscrutable images are to be found in the works of Kafka, Welles, Lang, and Rivette, is the fruit of projection, as becomes apparent from two works from the same moment of the midsixties, Pynchon's *Crying of Lot 49* and Antonioni's *Blow-Up*. I will not dwell on Pynchon's book here, having commented on it at some length elsewhere,[5] but will concentrate upon *Blow-Up*.

*Blow-Up* begins in utter fragmentation, in the infinitely divisible world of photography. The uncanny enters it as the conspiracy the photographer cannot name, for he does not know the identities of the two people he photographs in the park. The scenario is the very Freudian one of the primal scene, whose hidden insistence beneath the reality of consciousness creates the atmosphere of the uncanny that pervades the windblown park. In the primal scene the son watches mother and father make love, which is experienced as an aggression against the mother. (The uncanny aspect of love is intimated.) Antonioni's film embodies the son's reaction-formation of a fantasy in which the father is separated from the mother, whom the son is allowed to appropriate on the grounds of her relative youth (the man in the park is much older than the Vanessa Redgrave character, who, stripped to the waist in the photographer's flat, is associated with the teenage girl who appears thus the moment before Thomas asserts his sexual power over her and her friend). The father is killed by the camera's shots, which are metaphorically identical with those of the gun hidden in the bushes. The corpse that is still there when Thomas visits the park by night may well be a phantasm, a projection.* It is still there, in a sense, because the father's corpse

* Robin Wood has advanced a powerful, if testy, riposte to the argument that the corpse in the park is a hallucination; he fails to realize, however, that the corpse in the photograph and the one *still* present in the park when Thomas visits it are images of vastly different probability. (The former is probable, the latter highly improbable.) His argu-

is always present in the mind's eye and conscience of the son, the Fury that convicts him of the guilt of the survivor. Why does Thomas fail to take his camera to the park at night, where its impartial gaze might confirm the reality he thinks he has glimpsed through blowing up the pictures he took by day? Night is of course the sphere of the invisible, the unconscious. Thomas cannot realistically have expected to find the corpse still in the park – his own photographs of it having been threatened at birth. Does he not in fact visit the park as the criminal's double, to make sure the corpse is *not* there? As the criminal's double (camera as a gun with a silencer) Thomas has become superfluous. His disappearance in the final frame matches that of the corpse, marking his own transformation into corpse. The prelude to this metaphorical death is the death of his art: His photographs have become uncanny, not so much because they reveal a

ment gains in credibility by addressing itself primarily to the film's daytime events. It deserves quotation in full:

I know intelligent people who deny that there is a murder at all, except in Thomas's fantasy. This theory seems to me chiefly interesting in its unwitting confirmation of the universality of the film's theme – that we are all in danger of losing our grasp of objective reality – but it had better be answered briefly. It takes two forms: (a) Everything that happens in the park, everything involved in the mystery, is fantasy; (b) only the body is fantasy – the rest really happened, but Thomas misinterpreted his pictures and then hallucinated the corpse. The chief argument underlying the former seems to be that no-one but Thomas sees Vanessa Redgrave or the body, or notices the photographs (which are hanging up during the scene with the teenage girls). It quickly reveals its full absurdity if one just pursues it logically: The murder is fantasy, Vanessa Redgrave is fantasy, Thomas's photographing of them is fantasy, the park (perhaps) is fantasy; then the developing and printing of the photos is fantasy; the pictures hanging round the walls during the romp with the teenagers is fantasy, the theft of the photos is fantasy, the print the thieves leave behind is fantasy. No psychological theory of fantasy-making could possibly cope with all that, and it obviously makes no artistic sense whatever. The latter objection also (but less decisively) destroys the far more interesting second hypothesis. At the end of the film Thomas hallucinates the sound (at least) of a tennis ball hit by a racquet. This hallucination is the film's logical climax, and marks a decisive stage in the character's evolution; consequently, for him to have had a far more extreme hallucination much earlier would entirely destroy the film's logic. (Wood, in Ian Cameron and Robin Wood, *Antonioni* [Studio Vista: London, 1970], p. 131).

One notes the omission in Wood's account of the very important nocturnal encounter with the corpse. This encounter is improbable in the extreme, causing one to suspect the cooperation of fantasy in the image's generation: Why should the photographs testifying to the murder be stolen, while the corpse itself – a far more material, less grainily ambiguous, piece of evidence – is left in the park? It seems that Wood's argument (b) ought in fact to be subdivided into (b) and (c): (b) would run "Thomas misinterpreted the pictures," a statement it is relatively easy to refute; while (c) – "Thomas . . . then hallucinated the corpse" – is far harder to contravert. Assigning the corpse to the realm of fantasy does not destroy the logic of the film's conclusion: It retains force – though a different force from the one ascribed it by Wood – as the moment at which nocturnal delusion invades the day. The unreality of some of the other nighttime scenes (e.g., the incredibly catatonic rock concert, which is not "badly staged" but deliberately alienating) does indeed suggest that fantasy plays a part in the generation of the corpse's presence in the dark (though *not* throughout the film). The fantasy in question can be explicated in Oedipal terms, as the sign of Thomas's scopophiliac desire to assure himself that the father figure – the prime obstacle to the beckoning, but mysteriously elusive female image (Vanessa Redgrave) – truly is dead.

corpse as because they are now less akin to photographs (with the time-honored function of furnishing objective evidence) than to works of abstract art. Again, the sense of the uncanny is linked to the reversal of time: Photography becomes uncanny as it dissolves into the painting whose realistic functions it once appropriated – as the utmost realism uncannily discloses its hidden affinity with abstraction.

Thomas's projection, like that of the paranoiac, is a reaction to exclusion: exclusion from the primal scene. Paranoia counters the sense of exclusion by asserting one's actual presence everywhere in the world, as the object of its designs and hidden principle of its unity. It may seem as if all there is is the world, as if the world is all that is the case. But what if there *is* a plot after all? The artwork is virtually compelled to entertain this hypothesis, since it has a plot itself. However apparently random it may seem to be, it will always display a unifying principle, become a fingerprint of sorts. In perceiving a plot in the world, it projects its own constitution onto it. Its alibi for so doing is epistemological uncertainty: Pynchon's Oedipa Maas cannot know whether her ex-lover Pierce Inverarity has sought a vengeful afterlife by planting clues calculated to foster obsession within her. Pynchon's work is exemplary, because it examines the preconditions for the emergence of the projections it simultaneously employs. Nevertheless, it is also possible for the artist to succumb to the projection, transforming his fiction into a myth in order to aggrandize the status of his art. This is, I think, a clearly pathological and compensatory move. It can be seen to occur in Tarkovsky's *The Sacrifice,* whose willed decision to take signs for wonders (to inflate a private dilemma into a cosmic one) is the source of its utter falsity. The film itself becomes uncanny: It may look like art, but in actuality it aspires to the condition of myth.

Freud's essay on the uncanny accords great prominence to Schelling's definition of the experience: " '*Unheimlich*' is the name for everything that ought to have remained . . . hidden and secret and has become visible."[6] Schelling's words may be rewritten to define the uncanny moment as one in which the other emerges within the same. Thus Jung notes its appearance as the male approaches the anima, "the woman in man";[7] it is also present in the revelation of the man within the woman, and androgyny in general (see the remarks on Dietrich in Chapter I, "The cold heaven of *The Blue Angel*"). The male monopoly of power in most societies may have lent prevalence to the tendency to identify the uncanny with the emergence of the woman within the man – this is the hidden subject of "The Fall of the House of Usher" – but the opposite transformation is equally uncanny. Thus the moment of the uncanny punctuates a transformation, and the sense of the uncanny is widespread in a society that perceives itself to be in transition. Occurring while the transformation is still incomplete, it forces one to hold one's breath, as one's wonder over which reality will prevail, the old or the new, gives way to a suspicion of the imminence of negative revelation. The uncanny moment of modernity is interposed between residual feudal or agrarian cultures and emergent industrial ones. A later uncanny moment can be seen in the cinema of the twenties, corresponding to the imminence of totalitarianism in the thirties. It is present in the films of the period in the form of the dissolve or superimposition. As one scene emerges through another, it indicates that nothing is substantially itself; in the society governed by Identity, a separate identity is denied to all its component parts. The superimposition or dissolve can be described as the intervention of the principle of System – as the takeover bid of a prospective monopoly. If a sense of the uncanny is again prevalent in the late eighties (often being theorized in terms of the pervasiveness of a quality termed the postmodern), it is a result of a repression of one's awareness of the interdependence of almost everything in an increasingly integrated world economic system. People are clearly unwilling to admit the uncanny insight of psychoanalysis and Marxism: that "their" reactions are not really "theirs" at all. The more strident the official proclamations of individual rights, the greater the individual's actual subjugation, and the more uncanny (and consequently the more likely to be repressed) the recognition of where one actually stands.

The uncanny action is inherently displaced: Deeds apparently committed in the present reveal themselves to be inappropriate repetitions of past actions. An adherent of Bergson's theory of comedy might deduce from the lack of fit between behavior and environment that such actions are comic in effect. But although works of would-be horror are indeed often unwittingly comic, the uncanny clearly is not. The prototype of the uncanny action is given by Benjamin when he describes Baudelaire waving his pen to stab a path through the invisible city crowd. Such action has more of the heroism of modern life than the comic. Because modernity has rendered us all displaced persons, no safe place is available from which to mock an action as inappropriate. Moreover, the atmosphere of the uncanny generally accompanies a growth in the power of the person or object one perceives as uncanny; its threat to overwhelm us is no laughing matter.

Consideration of the threat posed by the moment of the uncanny ought to prompt one to reflect on the nature of the relationship between the uncanny and the monstrous. The uncanny is not the monstrous or horrific. While the moment of the uncanny lasts, the Other has not yet been externalized; its location is not out there but *here*, in the blind spot that is the self's place vis-à-vis itself. The process of the projection of the Other has begun, but has not yet been completed. Consequently, one cannot be sure of its presence. Reality may seem to mean more than itself – to have become "possessed" – but one cannot yet be certain of this. Events are off-key, but not yet utterly discordant. And so the observer has to seek confirmation from others. Büchner's Lenz asks Oberlin, "Can't you hear that terrible screaming men call silence?"[8]

Büchner's great short story "Lenz" is worth dwelling on at greater length here; its role in this introduction will in fact resemble the one played by "Der Sandmann" in Freud's theorization of the uncanny. Büchner's work pungently establishes the relationship between the sense of the uncanny and the defamiliarization of the family. Its usefulness is enhanced by the self-consciousness of Büchner's fusion of novella and case study, which anticipates the practices of psychoanalysis itself, thereby undermining the superior position psychoanalysis habitually assumes vis-à-vis the texts it explicates.

In the moment of the uncanny the apparently familiar reveals its unfamiliarity: The *heimlich* melts into the *unheimlich*. The sense of the uncanny is one of entrapment, as one grasps that one's failure to penetrate the essence of the apparently human being or seemingly friendly situation has allowed the Other to gain power over one. If Freud – echoing Schelling – saw the uncanny as the coming to light of that which should have remained concealed, the secret that discloses itself is the true identity of the ostensibly familiar being or situation, which is now sufficiently strong and in control to be able to discard all pretense. The familiar is of course the family itself. To leave the context of Büchner for a moment, it is interesting to note the experience of Frances Farmer, as documented in the film *Frances*. Frances mistakes her mother's feelings for her for love and becomes aware too late that they are founded upon hatred. One is unprepared to combat an enemy secreted within one's own family. The family is not interested in the welfare of its individual members, but in perpetuating itself. The realization that home is not really home but *unheimlich* is what drives Lenz – like so many other Romantic writers – into exile from it.

Büchner's story begins on January 20, with Lenz crossing a mountain range. The paratactic, sometimes verbless sentences indicate the lack of relationship that pervades his world and can only be overcome by a monumental effort of synthesis (mimicked by a breathtakingly long descriptive sentence that recalls a virtuoso tracking shot) that then leaves him drained. Lenz is engaged in a journey from an earthly father, whose bourgeois ambitions he repudiates, to a spiritual one: On entering the mountain valley of Waldbach, he will live with the pastor Oberlin. His flight from the world outside is the result of the uncanny fissure in language caused by the splitting of the word "father" from its referent. Although Lenz has realized that the word connotes threat as well as goodness and security, the word has such power over him that he is seeking to recover its old meaning and referent elsewhere, through the substitute father who will then become "the true father."

Throughout Büchner's story Lenz's actions are "inappropriate," for he lives amid afterimages generated by a sense of loss. His situation resembles that of Baudelaire, as described by Benjamin, repeating shocks in an effort to domesticate them. For Baudelaire the primary shock appears to have been the loss of the mother to his stepfather: The images of women in black in "À Une Passante" or "Le Cygne" reflect the son's feeling that the mother should have continued to mourn the dead father rather than remarry (and so betray the poet); the son is mortified to discover that the father's death does not free the mother for himself alone, since the father returns in the form of the stepfather. In the case of Lenz the trauma appears to have been far more complex, and hence all the more difficult to manage: It is a compound loss of self, of father, of lover, and of God.

As he crosses the mountains, Lenz imagines that he can suck the whole universe into himself; but in doing so he shrinks it into a point as small as the one he himself occupies. If Lenz can swallow the universe, then he can be everywhere. Hence processes of association can permit him to identify a series of different figures, primarily female ones, with one another. During the absence of Oberlin, the pastor who has taken him into his care, Lenz hears the maid singing: "Auf dieser Welt hab ich kein Freud, / Ich hab mein Schatz, und der ist weit." ["In this world I have no joy at all, / But my sweetheart, and he's away"].[9] The song evokes multiple echoes in Lenz's mind. It can refer to the distant Oberlin, for instance. Lenz consciously correlates it with his lost lover, Friederike Brion; and although Madame Oberlin cannot possibly know Friederike's fate, Lenz enquires of her after it. He identifies with the desolate maid, though for him the distant sweetheart is female. He sees the distance as unbridgeable, and will later accuse himself of having murdered a girl whose remoteness is that of death. When he makes the accusation, he is no longer sure of the identity of his victim. Speaking to Madame Oberlin of Friederike, he says, "Doch kann ich sie mir nicht mehr vorstellen, das Bild läuft mir fort." ["And yet I can no longer picture her, the image runs away from me."][10] Because the vagueness of her image allows her to be assimilated to other people, Lenz can reproach himself with having murdered the sick girl from Fouday, whose name was also Friederike, and whom he failed to wake from the dead. When speaking to Kaufmann of his aesthetic ideals, he had voiced a wish to be a Medusa's head so as to freeze a scene with two girls, preserving it from such loss. The wish now returns to haunt him: To desire to hold unchanged one of the ever-

mutable forms of beauty is to desire its death, its transformation into
an unresistant thing. Lenz may see his attempt to raise the dead girl
as an effort to undo damage he himself has already done. But the attempted expiation fails. Lenz describes Friederike to Madame Oberlin
as having been like a child, as was he himself:

Ganz Kind; es war, als wär ihr die Welt zu weit: sie zog sich so in sich zurück,
sie suchte das engste Plätzchen im ganzen Haus, und da sass sie, als wäre
ihre Seligkeit nur in einem kleinen Punkt, und dann war mir's auch so; wie
ein Kind hätte ich dann spielen können.

[She was wholly a child; it seemed as if the world were too wide for her, she
was so retiring, she would look for the narrowest place in the whole house,
and there she'd sit as though all her happiness were concentrated into one little point, and then I thought so too; then I could have played like a child.][11]

Her reduction of herself to a minuscule point is reiterated in the gesture with which Lenz distills the universe into himself. To compel an
adult into the frame of a child is, however, as constricting as it is
idyllic:

Jetzt ist es mir so eng, so eng! Sehn sie, es ist mir manchmal, als stiess ich
mit den Händen an den Himmel; o, ich ersticke!

[Now I feel so hemmed in! So restricted! You see, sometimes I feel my arms
colliding with the sky; oh, I'm suffocating!][12]

Regression to childhood turns the world into the coffin of the adult;
the ingestion of the universe deprives one of the space in which to
live, of air to breathe. To be content with one's place, as Lenz says
Friederike was, is to be feminized to the point of death. And so the
male is doubly suffocated: by his enclosure in the silent position patriarchy assigns to the female, and by his identification with the death
he too has wished upon her. In seeking to heal the dead girl, Lenz is
attempting to recover Friederike, and to heal himself, the wounded
child. Identifying with Oberlin also, his voice as he instructs her to
rise is the voice of God. But it is not that of God the Father (and here
the identification with Oberlin collapses) but that of God the Son.
Since Lenz would rather cast himself as child than as father, his momentary adoption of the fatherly role of Oberlin the healer is false and
is bound to fail. So does his attempt to heal himself by taking the advice of the father figure (Oberlin) and praying to God when unable to
sleep.

As Lenz's mental deterioration approaches its nadir, one encounters
the following fascinating sentence:

Wenn er allein war, war es ihm so entsetzlich einsam, dass er beständig laut
mit sich redete, rief, und dann erschrak er wieder, und es war ihm, als hätte
eine fremde Stimme mit ihm gesprochen.

[When he was alone he felt so horribly lonely that he constantly talked, called out to himself in a loud voice, and then again he was startled, and it seemed as though a stranger's voice had spoken to him.][13]

Büchner's own sentence has the uncanny duality of the event he describes. Is Lenz ascribing his own voice to another; or does he, after hearing his own voice, then hear that of another person? In identifying with a healer who is both father figure (Oberlin) and son (Christ) Lenz has split his own voice in two. His disturbance deepens as he applies to language the freezing tactic previously used for the look of things:

Im Gespräch stockte er oft, eine unbeschreibliche Angst befiel ihn, er hatte das Ende seines Satzes verloren; dann meinte er, er müsse das zuletzt gesprochene Wort behalten und immer sprechen.

[In conversation he frequently stuttered, an indescribable fear possessed him, he had lost the conclusion of his sentence; then he thought he must hold on to the word he had last spoken, say it again and again.][14]

Fear freezes language. The stammer is generated by the Medusa's head's turn in the direction of language. The concluding word is avoided by the man unwilling to look death in the face. (One notes the crucial organizing importance of the last word of the sentence in German syntax; everything tends toward it.) The stammer repeats an arbitrarily chosen word as one repeats one's own name, fearful of losing one's identity; the very arbitrariness of the obstructive word itself embodies the arbitrariness of one's identity once one has swallowed the whole universe, and so become identical with everything within it. It is surely significant that as Lenz's desires for apocalypse grow more intense – at the start of the story he simply wished to invert himself; now he wishes to turn houses upside down – a new name should appear for the first time, that of Satan.

Es war ihm dann, als existiere er allein, als bestünde die Welt nur in seiner Einbildung, als sei nichts als er; er sei das ewig Verdammte, der Satan.

[Then it seemed to him that he alone existed, that the world was only a figment of his imagination that there was nothing but he himself, and he the eternally damned, Satan.][15]

Büchner's critique of aesthetic idealism here encompasses philosophical Idealism. Like Lenz, Idealism extends into adulthood the child's belief in the omnipotence of thoughts. The Lenz who accuses himself of murder mistakes thinking the deed for doing it; it is a confusion abetted by the Christian belief that to think evil is virtually equivalent to its commission. Like a child, Lenz conceals his impotence through overcompensation. Büchner aligns Lenz with a Satan who is the tormented child his father cannot – or perhaps will not – save.

For Lenz, the father is a trinity: Oberlin, the pastor whom he doubtless addresses as father, the physical parent, who wants him to come home to provide support, and God the Father. Lenz finds repose with Oberlin because he mediates between the earthly and the heavenly father; his very name – with its reference to the above (*Ober-*) – connotes transcendence, the divine superiority that exists *to serve*: One recalls the "*Ober!*" wherewith a waiter is addressed in German. Just before leaving Waldbach, Lenz presents himself as the prodigal son, kneeling before Oberlin and placing his head on his lap. As Kracauer noted,[16] the gesture was a frequent one in Weimar cinema, where the lap was that of a woman, and the underlying wish one for the womb's security. For Lenz the father figure is there to stop him from falling forward, as he had done while crossing the mountains at the start of the story. Lying down is an embrace of Mother Earth that is associated with death.

"Lenz" includes many references to home and to the *heimlich*. In the end, as one would expect, the *heimlich* becomes *unheimlich*. As the story nears its end, *heimlich* loses its association with home, thereby indicating the collapse of Lenz's search for a second home, and assumes its other meaning of "secretly," as the following passage shows. Lenz has to be watched:

Sein Begleiter war ihm endlich lästig, auch mochte er seine Absicht erraten und suchte Mittel, ihn zu entfernen. Sebastian schein ihm nachzugeben, fand aber heimlich Mittel, seinen Bruder von der Gefahr zu benachrichtigen, und nun hatte Lenz zwei Aufseher, statt einen.

[His companion began to be a burden to him; also perhaps he guessed his intentions, and now tried to get rid of him. Sebastian seemed to give in to him, but found secret means of informing his brother of the danger, and now Lenz had two keepers instead of one.][17]

Although *unheimlich* is a recurrent word in the text, up to its end it is applied to phenomena outside Lenz: the moonlight on the face of the sick girl, the darkness. Lenz's fate is sealed when the adjective fits himself – when he looks at Oberlin "mit unheimlichen Augen" [with uncanny eyes].[18]

Near the story's end Lenz is described as having become "doppelt" (double). The splitting of self from itself at this moment is also Büchner's own separation from Lenz: He abandons the doomed vessel, leaving his story a fragment. The double is of course a key image in the repertoire of the uncanny; I do not intend to investigate it closely here, for the reader can find an ongoing examination of the image's meanings in my other critical works.[19] At one point in "Lenz," however, Büchner is virtually identical with, doubled in, his protagonist, who enunciates his aesthetic creed in colloquy with his friend Kaufmann. Lenz's rejection of the doctrine that Greek art offers ideal forms for imitation is due to his identification of idealism with the petrification of life; and yet the Medusa's head that freezes the élan vital is his own chosen metaphor for his own aspiration to realism based on love. Clearly Lenz's relationship with Greek culture is far less polemically simple than it would seem to be. It is in fact an uncanny one. There is a deep elective affinity between the Greek gods, the uncanny, and Greek and German dialectic. The Greek gods are the most uncanny of all deities, since their close resemblance to mortals renders it on occasions impossible to perceive their divinity. One may think it no accident that the Greeks devised the dialectical form of thinking, which is inherently uncanny in its demonstration of the identity of apparently different things. (The identity of "Socrates" and "Plato" in the Socratic dialogues was the uncanny first fruit of the method Plato took from his mentor.) Dialectic is linked to the process of secularization: Gods and objects are no longer simply themselves and hence are not to be trusted. In rejecting eighteenth-century idealism Lenz rejects the resignation of an ideology that could locate beauty only at an unattainable distance. Lenz's own stated ideals are nearer in time and place: Shakespeare, Flemish painters, Goethe. His form of Romanticism is shot through with a longing intensified by an intuition that the ideal and the real might be brought into congruence. Consideration of the fates of Lenz and Hölderlin – who may have identified the ideal with the Greek city-states but who yearned for its reestablishment in the present – allows one to interpret the absolute eighteenth-century distinction between reality and ideal as a way of protecting oneself from the devastation of shattered hope. Strongly though Lenz disavows the Greek ideal, it returns as the repressed: Its rejected beauty returns wrathfully as the Medusa's head, the Medusa being, as Tobin Siebers has shown, the hidden double of Athene.[20] The moment at which Lenz states his wish to be the Medusa is a disturbing indication of the madness and magical thought underlying his conscious commitment to realism. It also suggests that Lenz's identification with a series of women *petrifies* him as a male and makes him wish to turn the arresting gaze back on the women whose beauty once froze him:* Speaking

---

* If Odin has sacrificed an eye in order to obtain knowledge, then whichever Norn bears it at any one time partakes of the power of the ruler of the Gods: Like Medusa, she has absolute sway over life and death. Odin's loss of the eye with which the triform image of the female (a degraded image of the White Goddess) is then able to see resembles Adam's loss of the rib from which woman was fashioned. The one-eyed person is often perceived as possessing the evil eye, which radiates envy. It may be read as the envy of the one-eyed for those who have two. (In a sense – a fantastic sense – the camera's envy of the human being.) But the myth of Medusa seems rather to suggest that the evil eye is borne by a woman envious of male privilege – of the phallus. (This reading would be borne out by the Medusan coiffure of Alex in the recent *Fatal Attraction* – her aspirations to masculinity, and the lawlessness of that aspiration, being apparent in her name [a-lex] and her final appropriation of the phallic knife of *Psycho*'s Norman Bates.) Her

of how he saw two girls seated on a stone braiding their hair, he remarks, "Man möchte manchmal ein Medusenhaupt sein, um so eine
Gruppe in Stein verwandeln zu können, und den Leuten zurufen."
["Sometimes one would like to be a Medusa's head, so as to be able to
transform such a group into stone and show it to people."][21]

Lenz speaks of reality as composed of an unending loveliness he
would like to arrest in a series of scenes. The world he posits is the
almost endlessly divisible one made available by the film camera.
Lenz's remarks reveal the dangerous, uncanny underside of photographic realism: the sense that humanity is engaged in recording the
world so as to be free to destroy it. His words betray the madness he
seems to have firmly under control as he propounds his Bazinian aesthetic of love. The taking of a photograph involves a projection inward
of the world into a black box, on the basis of which a projection out-
ward becomes possible (the screening of the film); and this rhythm
whereby images are ingested and then projected is very like that of the
story's opening sequence, in which Lenz first feels he can absorb a
world that has become very tiny, and then finds it overwhelming him,
as if the photograph has been blown up during the projection, like a
Brocken apparition. There seems in fact to be a profound correlation
between the invention of photography in the nineteenth century and
the Romantic preoccupation with projection. Thus in early nineteenth-
century fiction one begins to encounter descriptions of persons whose
characteristics have impregnated their environment; some of the best
examples are provided by Balzac, who draws conclusions from a Romanticism he simultaneously parodies by showing that the faculty of
projection need not simply be employed in the presence of nature to
generate a sense of the Sublime, but can also be used by misers who
identify libidinally with their world by treating their possessions as
extensions of themselves. Perhaps the best example, however, is Poe's
"Fall of the House of Usher." The protagonist of Poe's story is a man
who arrives in an environment into which somebody else's mind has
already been projected. The fact that that mind already "possesses"
the house is the source of its *Stimmung* (a word that, like *unheimlich*,
coincides with its opposite, for it indicates that something *stimmt
nicht*, is "off-key"); it is hardly surprising that the building is compared to a head. A sense of the uncanny besets the observer who
walks through the materialized form of another's mind. Poe's spiritual-
ism is itself uncanny in its *materialism*. Like the picture in "The Oval

gaze is ironically castrating, transforming the whole body of the male opposite her into a
stiff member. In identifying with her, Lenz both feminizes himself and identifies with the
castrating father who frustrates his efforts at relationships. Like the Norns, this father is
triform: God, the physical parent, and Goethe, the symbolic father figure who also loved
Friederike Brion and whose desire Lenz imitates.

Portrait," the house has become uncanny by drawing life from its in-habitants. This linkage of self and environment is cemented by the growth of photography. The lengthy exposure times of the first films occur as the glue that links the person to his or her surroundings grows hard. The photograph implies a necessary relationship between person and environment. Even when an environment appears to be empty, it is in fact predicated upon the individual who is absent from it, the cameraman who takes the place of Berkeley's God. In the photo-graph the world becomes the fetish form of an absent individuality, the mind of the person who has just left the environment. This feature of photography is exploited powerfully in the films of Antonioni, and has become a mannerism in the hand-held camera of the horror film, its jerkiness saturating an empty scene with the presence of a dis-turbed mind. If the basic mechanism of fetishism is "I know this is so, but...," then the viewer of a photographed scene is locked into an un-canny symbiosis with the look of the camera, which is both his and not his. His own double, he is present in the past moment and its sur-vivor, enjoying the twofold pleasure of identification and detachment. The cameraman has been for him the Perseus who slew Medusa by mirroring her.

## Postscript: "Lenz," Herzog, and the freak

Writing elsewhere, I have likened the paratactic world of "Lenz" to that of the films of Werner Herzog.[22] The link is most apparent in *The Mys-tery of Kaspar Hauser* – which takes as its epigraph Lenz's remark on the screaming men call silence – rather than in *Woyzeck*, as one might otherwise expect. Indeed, *Woyzeck* can be interpreted as involving a subtle aesthetic mistake in the casting of Klaus Kinski, rather than Bruno S., as Woyzeck – an error that marks the onset of a certain arbi-trariness in Herzog's films. The germs of Herzog's later collapse may, however, be discernible even in *The Mystery of Kaspar Hauser*, which is in a sense a fusion of "Lenz" and *Woyzeck*. In depriving Kaspar of the noble appearance attested to by contemporaries, Herzog clearly subordinates the "Lenz" element to the *Woyzeck* one. At moments Her-zog's work seems to approach the revival of metaphysics through an immersion in the immediately physical advocated in the philosophy of Adorno:

Aber damit dies Allgemeine, das Authentische an Prousts Darstellung, sich bildet, muss man hingerissen sein an dem einen Ort, ohne aufs Allgemeine zu schielen.[23]

[But the formation of this generality, of that which is authentic in Proust's pre-sentation, requires that one be overpowered by the one spot without casting furtive glances at the general.]

The frequent intense lengthy concentration on certain landscapes in Herzog's films can suggest the working of just such a spell. And yet at moments the metaphysics of the immediate is betrayed, and the metaphysical achieves the *Reader's Digest* air noted by Pauline Kael,[24] as Herzog relinquishes the effort to immortalize the instant and dreams instead of general archetypes beyond the present (e.g., Kaspar's dream of the valley of the windmills). Such visions of the distant indicate the utopian character of the Adornian program: The here-and-now cannot satisfy, and the prolonged gaze in its direction is not one of mystical unity but an obtuse one whose real focus is inner, with the inward eye. To be under the spell of nature is to experience the sublimity Schiller describes:

Der moralisch gebildete Mensch, und nur dieser, ist ganz frei. Entweder er ist der Natur als Macht überlegen, oder er ist einstimmig mit derselben. Nichts, was sie an ihm ausübt, ist Gewalt, denn eh es bis zu *ihm* kommt, ist es schon *seine eigene Handlung* geworden.[25]

[The morally cultivated man – and only such a man – is quite free. Either he is superior to nature through power, or he is in agreement with it. Nothing it imposes upon him is violence, since before it reaches *him* it has already become *his own action*.]

Schiller fails to see that this experience of the sublime is founded upon a masochistic identification with the aggressor that anticipates recompense through itself becoming the aggressor at a later date. The masochism will express itself sadistically when freed from the yoke of submission. This is precisely what happens in Herzog's work, whose prolonged stare seeks to discomfort both viewed and viewer, both the figure before the camera and the audience. The final interchangeability of sadist and masochist within Herzog himself is recognized in the casting of Klaus Kinski in the Bruno S. role of the victimized Woyzeck.* This casting, however, destroys the dialectic between the two, causing the evaporation of the possibility of narrative, which depends upon opposites. When they fuse, the story ends. What follows – what has followed in Herzog's career – is empty repetition.

The dominant image in this system of repetitions has been that of the freak, though as his popularity has grown, he has been less in-

---

* In "Werner Herzog: Tarzan Meets Parsifal" (*Monthly Film Bulletin*, May 1988), Thomas Elsaesser justifies the casting of Kinski as Woyzeck, rather than Bruno S., with the dubious assertion that they "are brothers underneath the blundering and blustering egos: the two sides of Kaspar Hauser" (p. 132). Any kinship between the two is not intrinsic, however, but emerges retrospectively following this casting, which in fact destroys the basis of Herzog's aesthetic system. The commitment to titanic singularity in his earlier work had entailed a rejection of such doubling. And impressive though Kinski is in the part, Woyzeck – excellently described by Paul Rosenfeld as "a fine but incomplete and defenseless individual in an unspiritual society," a man whose individuality is "half-awakened" (*Musical Impressions* [London: Allen & Unwin, 1970], p. 83) – is surely closer to Bruno S. than to the Kinski Herzog associates with deranged power.

clined to jeopardize it by using real freaks. Herzog's pursuit of the freakish may be likened to that of Diane Arbus, as defined by Susan Sontag:

The camera is a kind of passport that annihilates moral boundaries and social inhibitions, freeing the photographer from any responsibility toward the people photographed. The whole point of photographing people is that you are not intervening in their lives, only visiting them. The photographer is super-tourist, an extension of the anthropologist, visiting natives and bringing back news of their exotic doings and strange gear. The photographer is always trying to colonize new experiences or find new ways to look at familiar subjects – to fight against boredom. For boredom is outside rather than inside a situation, and one leads to the other. "The Chinese have a theory that you pass through boredom into fascination," Arbus noted. Photographing an appalling underworld (and a desolate, plastic overworld), she had no intention of entering into the horror experienced by the denizens of those worlds.[26]

The work of each is played out between "boringness and freakishness," which are linked in Herzog's case by the lengthiness of the camera's stare and the frontality that moralistically eschews striking angles and hovers between nostalgia for nineteenth-century photography and the exhibition of a specimen. Herzog's superstardom on U.S. campuses thus has roots akin to those of Arbus's fame:

This look that is not (mainly) compassionate is a special, modern ethical construction: not hardhearted, certainly not cynical, but simply (or falsely) naïve. To the painful nightmarish reality out there, Arbus applied such adjectives as "terrific," "interesting," "incredible," "fantastic," "sensational" – the childlike wonder of the pop mentality.[27]

It is the faux naïveté of the sophisticate of sensation, whose primary intent – as Sontag notes – is to "render history and politics irrelevant ... by atomizing it, into horror."[28] Sontag displays an ambiguous fascination with the work of Arbus, which renders her queasy but nevertheless impresses her as a sign of the times: "Arbus's work is a good instance of a leading tendency in high art in capitalist countries...."[29] Such ambivalence can be reduced by comparing the function of fearsome images in the work of an Arbus or Herzog with the role played by famine and concentration camp photographs in Margarethe von Trotta's *Marianne and Juliane* (*The German Sisters / Die bleierne Zeit*). Where the former, tourists disguised as anthropologists, are collectors of horrors, the latter is *visited* by images that are the inescapable legacy of the postwar German family, though they are signally absent from Herzog's work, perhaps because the German family, and the questions of continuity associated with it, is also. Von Trotta is not seeking out images for stimulation or the construction of a quasi-metaphysical, quasi-sociological case against modern reality in general; these images seek her out. And so her attitude to them is one of anguish rather than mindless wonder: She does not mistake the message of the medium – alienation – for that of the specific work the medium carries. Whereas Arbus and Herzog are connoisseurs of a chaos removed to a safe distance, Von Trotta bridges distance with an identification that is deeply uncomfortable, for it opens one to the pain of the other. (It is clearly not identification in the sense castigated by a knee-jerk Brechtianism.) It can even be argued that whereas Herzog's procedure is photographic, thus validating the comparison with Arbus, Von Trotta's is filmic. Like Thomas in *Blow-Up,* Herzog avails himself of the photographer's privilege of separating people from the context of narrative temporality; arranged in tableaux, they are castaways after the storm of history. Whereas Herzog's characters are heroic icons of isolation, both beast and god, those of Von Trotta are burdened by traumatic pasts, struggling to reach a future.

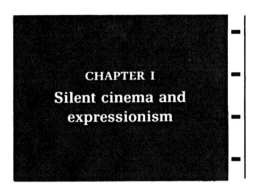

CHAPTER I
Silent cinema and
expressionism

## Realism, totalitarianism, and the death of silent cinema

The received accounts of the development of the arts during the past 150 years speak of a movement from realism to modernism, and thence to postmodernism. This schema is often extrapolated to the history of cinema, which is said to replicate, in speeded-up, time-lapse form, the history of the other arts. The model implies a history that proceeds in dialectical fashion, with the inherent shortcomings of one form calling forth another to correct it and that a successor, and so on. Each stage constitutes an organic response to – an answer to the lack in – the preceding one. But what if this is not the case in cinema? What if one is dealing with mechanism rather than organism, with a history that has been dictated by violence rather than anything even vaguely resembling necessity? Thus sound cinema is not the answer to silent cinema; it is qualitatively *different* from it. Silent cinema does not die a graceful, biologically ordained death but is destroyed by a catastrophe. The same applies to monochrome in the sixties. It seems to me, moreover, that cinema does not begin with realism but with modernism, with an alienation of our everyday experience of reality that is then dispelled by the coming of sound, with its enhancement of realism – sound's advent being part of the international fascist and socialist realist backlash against modernism. (A backlash is less a necessary response than a counterrevolution.) If the silence of silent cinema enabled it to tap material from below the level of linguistic rationalization (as in the "incoherent texts" of the early Lang) sound entered – accompanied by "realism" – to end this chaos. It did so as the tyrant whose assertion of order founds a society in which *Gleichschaltung* is valued above imagination. This fact alone should have rendered Kracauer more suspicious of the apparent healthiness of realism. It was certainly one of the reasons why many other German intellectuals protested against the imposition of sound. Sound film is centrally controlled, the fitting instrument of the dictatorship it helped usher into power.

Silent films seldom let one know the exact words characters employ in their dialogues. The intertitles rarely give them in full, and they cannot often have been supplied by the lantern-lecturer whose commentaries accompanied the very earliest silent works. It thus seems as if silent cinema is not fully integrated into language (a fact which may pose problems for the linguistically oriented analyses of semiology; one notes that most of these analyses have been of *sound* films). If the meanings of the filmic situations are codified nevertheless by the conventions used within them, is the presence of such conventions tantamount to a presence of language?* What is the effect of this partial absence of language? It is surely an experience akin to that of the operagoer who has failed to study the libretto before attending the performance. (The fact that this analogy is possible is surely a symptom of early cinema's aspirations to resemble opera, to become the *Gesamtkunstwerk*.) But since no libretto is available to the filmgoer, may not he or she feel excluded by the inevitable lack of knowledge of the full story, despite the insistent musical accompaniment that seeks to silence the demand for speech by turning the film's scenes into the tableaux of a dream play? If the viewer could then feel strangely *cheated,* this was what rendered Von Stroheim's confidence man so pregnant an icon of early cinema, with the audience reconciled to his duplicities by seeing them inflicted upon the rich and foolish.

According to Lacan's famous definition of the unconscious, it has the structure of a language. The formulation may reveal the limit of Lacan's loyalty to the Freud whose close exegete he claims to be. For Freud, the unconscious manifests itself initially in disturbances of speech and then, when the disturbance becomes extreme, language breaks down – rendering the "talking cure" ineffectual – as the body alone continues to "speak," in the metaphorical sense of producing signs that are susceptible of interpretation. It can be argued that this symptomatic body speech – which is speech in a foreign language – is privileged by a silent cinema whose own speech is experimental, often uncodified, and baffling. It has not yet hardened into a *system* of representation.†

The efforts of the advocates of psychomime to attach one meaning to each gesture attempted to dispel the potential ambiguity of the image by transforming it into a tautologous duplication of language; Eisenstein's assimilation of the photograph to the ideogram tended in

* Is the notion of "the code" a bridge that will allow one to pass from convention to language, or is such passage possible only because the term is slippery enough to permit theoretical sleight of hand?
† I would also argue that it is not the introduction of certain camera angles in the second decade of this century that establishes classic realism as a system firmly in place but the coming of sound, which qualitatively alters the nature of the filmic experience.

the same direction, some of whose absurd effects were trenchantly mocked at the time by the Polish film theorist Karol Irzykowski.[1] It can also be argued that the unsystematic speech of silent cinema reappears, once the hegemony of the narrative economy of classic realism has expired, in the cinema of the mid-fifties, where, paradoxically, it serves as an enhancement of realism in the psychological sense: in the stammerings of Brando or Dean, or in the silences of Antonioni's films. As Bela Balázs put it, writing in the twenties of the wordless soliloquy of the face: "In this silent monologue the solitary human soul can find a tongue more candid and uninhibited than in any spoken soliloquy, for it speaks instinctively, subconsciously. The language of the face cannot be repressed or controlled."[2] Nor can it be subordinated easily to a narrative. Neither director nor actor can control the face completely, though the former may seek to do so, to sterilize its otherness, by typecasting, through the allegorical use of pantomime, or by associating the actor with a particular type of role – the tactic of classic Hollywood. The impossibility of translating facial signals into unequivocal messages was to lead in the end to an attempt to distract attention from the visage, through the addition of sound. It destroyed the aura of the equivocal consummately exploited in the Kuleshov effect. Ambiguity had been held at bay up to that point by a theatrical rhetoric of gesture and music, but the hooves of the cavalry were mercifully *audible* in the distance. If the emergence of cinema itself can be read as a tactic to repress the inherent ambiguity of the photograph by inserting it into a context, sound cinema draws the logical conclusion by rendering uncertainty residual.

As I suggested above, it is this ambiguity that renders Von Stroheim – particularly in the role he plays in *Foolish Wives* – so fascinatingly disturbing a figure. The hero of the world in which bodily signs have been alienated from their contexts is the confidence man. In *Foolish Wives* Von Stroheim plays a bogus Russian count in exile in a grand villa on the French Riviera, using counterfeit money and attempting to compromise and blackmail the wife of a visiting American millionaire. The counterfeit exile is of course a professional actor – a hypocrite – and so the work toys exhibitionistically and reflexively with the possibility of exposure, whose reward would be masochistic pleasure. Von Stroheim's stiff strutting has an air of existential risk: His own "Von" was an affectation. He has a safety net nevertheless: He can tell the truth about himself on the precondition, and in the knowledge, that it will be taken for fiction. Light effects and reflections in the plate glass of the immense hotel Von Stroheim had custom built for the film embody the deceptiveness of surfaces dislocated from depths. In a chiaroscuro world the self is secreted partly in darkness. Thus there are the flashings of the count's teeth, the whites of his eyes, his enormous

white cigarettes, or the astonishing scene – cross-hatched with light
and shadow by blinds long before such images had become a film
noir cliché – of the count's transactions with the counterfeiter Ventucchi. During this scene Ventucchi threatens to kill anyone who seeks to
seduce his daughter. At the end of the film the Count Karamzin is foolish enough to attempt this. He climbs to the daughter's window, past
the image of a saint. Such images often appear in the vicinity of the
seducer in his seduction scenes – thus one has the monk who enters
during the storm or the crucifix in the tower where Karamzin makes
his second attempt on the virtue of Andrew Hughes's wife. Stroheim
may be exploiting popular mythology's association of potency with the
odor of sanctity in the figure of Rasputin, another Russian. The seduction attempt is rendered more piquant by the tangible memorials of
the norms the seducer is transgressing, while impotent envy is as-
suaged by the reminder that a force is ready – albeit presently immobile – to discomfit him, as the monk's arrival curtails the seduction in
the peasant's hut. Karamzin is killed off-screen by Ventucchi and, in
an astonishing scene, stuffed down a manhole. (Stroheim's intended
ending, showing an octopus scoffing the remains, was deleted by the
studio-imposed editors.) Like the death of many a confidence man,
however, that of Karamzin is illusory, being simply the negative aspect
of his transformation and reincarnation. For Stroheim is resurrected in
the coda – taking a bow in propria persona as he lowers the curtain –
when we see Andrew Hughes and his chastened wife reading in bed a
book called *Foolish Wives* by none other than Erich Von Stroheim. It
is as if his own confidence man's status as a master of many parts
(the next role is writer) is an insurance policy against anticipated ejec-
tion from the directorial seat. The couple may rejoice in evasion of the
count's clutches, but the book that is his alter ego has captivated them
all the same. And so, by implication, Von Stroheim's film has cap-
tured us. His one-man culture industry, intolerant of interruptions in
consumption, passes us on to its next product – the new form of the
shape-changing fetish – the book of the film. If Ventucchi survives
Karamzin, it is because the master counterfeiter who is Von Stroheim
himself outlives his creation. One fake count dies, but another (the
count-erfeiter) lives on in the next frame in the hall of mirrors. Dis-
persed between two places, both before the camera and behind it,
present as director even when absent as actor, and present as writer
even in the director's absence, he makes his getaway. (A strategy that
would later be repeated by Welles, who was also obsessed by the process of forging identities.) If forgery involves duplication, then film,
the art form most adept at exact reproduction of the appearance of
reality, becomes the most apt for deception. The obsessive concern for
naturalistic detail of the Von Stroheim of the film histories becomes

the strategy of the forger. "Naturalist" is merely the identity that best dissimulates his investment in illusion. In the vortex of the film's self-reference, "Von Stroheim" becomes as dangerous and illusive as Melville's confidence man. The confidence man overcomes chaos by creating it. He is, as it were, a fascist leader with no party, for he has absorbed the crowd that would otherwise have followed him. So although it was canny of Syberberg to consider Von Stroheim at such length in *Our Hitler*, he was sadly blind to the elective affinities between his martyred Austrian hero and the demon-doll Austrian villain. Meanwhile, the Americans may seem to have eluded the confidence man, but he is a deeply American figure: The American leaves the old self in the Old World; he is reborn as performing self, existential master of situations. *Foolish Wives* is Von Stroheim's dream of repeating in Europe the confidence trick he worked in America. The U.S. Syberberg must surely be at work on *Stroheim – A Film from America*.

The difference between "silent" and sound cinema may be likened – *toutes proportions gardées* – to the psychoanalytic distinction between psychosis and neurosis. Whereas in neurosis language continues to be present, albeit buckling under the strain of trauma, in psychosis it dissolves into indecipherability. The comparison should not be pressed too far, however, for it implies a greater "health" in sound cinema than in the silents, and obscures the possibility that sound cinema demonstrates the psychology of the cunning psychotic, whose excellent mimicry of normality is too good – too thoroughly stripped of the everyday neuroses we all share – to be true. Sound cinema's closer adjustment to reality indicates that the price of apparent health is conformism. It may therefore be more politic to rephrase the distinction in terms of the opposition between poetic, metaphorical communication and the clarity of denotation of prose. Sound as it were streamlined the filmic system to carry unambiguous messages, mobilizing the audience to take up well-defined ideological positions during the thirties. Recent cinema, by way of contrast, is fascinating, maddening, and confusing, for it mixes the two strands. It has perceived the limitations of classic narrative, but is unable to return to the conditions of silent cinema. Its implicit viewer is not a fixed entity but a fluctuating duality, oscillating between the two poles of the master contradiction of society – between speech and silence, the eloquence of the rulers and the disenfranchised wordlessness of the oppressed.

Balázs's comments on speech in silent cinema include a paradoxical passage of great suggestivity, which is worth quoting at some length. He is writing of Mikhail Romm's version of *Boule de Suif* (*Pyshka*):

In this silent film Romm did in fact achieve many pictorial and dramatic effects which would have been impossible in a sound film.

The story is well-known, but will bear repetition: a little Parisian tart, escaping in a bus from the Prussians with a number of other passengers, is demonstratively treated with contempt by her fellow travellers, who, while quite willing to eat generously proffered food, keep her at arm's length in all other respects. The bus is held up by a Prussian patrol and the officer commanding it refuses to allow the fugitives to proceed unless the little cocotte spends the night with him. Two nuns who form part of the strictly virtuous company are the most zealous in trying to persuade the reluctant prostitute to comply with the Prussian officer's demands. Under the pelting rain of their words the little streetwalker bows her head. [ ... ] The incessant, irresistible cataract of the words, their cruel, determined, unbearably violent insistence is much more convincingly shown by the *visible*, rapid ceaseless motion of the lips than could even be conveyed by making *audible* the same, or slightly varied, arguments repeated over and over again.[3]

Balázs's argument is paradoxical, and it may well be that even he is not fully convinced (whence his adjectival insistence), that he has used legerdemain (if something is to be "shown," as he puts it, the visible is inevitably privileged by the choice of verb), or that he has misdescribed the scene's effect (the nonaudibility of the nuns' words can be a sign of contempt, since it suggests their speech is not worth giving). Nevertheless, the passage provides suggestive testimony to the way in which the absence of spoken words enables one to concentrate intensely upon the visual image. The conjunction of silence with a cataract of words can suggest Beckett: The modernist sense of the negativity and ritualistic hollowness of language is, here, implicit in the form of silent film. It seems hardly accidental that silent cinema and modernism were born, and died, at the same time. Here the systematic doubt of language found in the period's works of high culture is echoed in the form of popular culture: To the working class and immigrant audiences of early cinema, words are less trustworthy than looks; as in the music hall, one of their own number speaking eloquently is a spectacular comic freak. For if cinema can be said to isolate the signs of behavior from their contexts, the experience it embodies in its early days is that of the immigrant – the man who fails to understand the language of his new American homeland or the peasant lured to the big city: of the working class, whose semiliteracy welcomes the illustrations to the intertitles. The interval between the birth of silent cinema and the introduction of sound may be interpreted as a "period of grace" during which the immigrant was allowed to assimilate the language at – and in – his leisure. Whence the speed of growth of the film industry in the United States – by immigrants and for immigrants, it expressed their sense of the simultaneous volubility and silence of the world. Early film does not only exclude the spoken word because the technology does not yet exist; the technology does not yet exist because it is not yet required. The absence of the spoken word deliberately avoids rubbing in the immigrant's nonpossession of the language. Language is the patrimony of the rulers (as Bernstein would say: of the speakers of "the elaborate code"), who are like the nuns in *Boule de Suif*, using it to maintain one in a position of degradation or suffering. The silence of Romm's film identifies with the silence of the cocotte. The browbeaten, isolated individual is able to "speak" only through silent gestures. (This may well render Büchner's Woyzeck the first cinematic hero.) Silent cinema is utopian in its bracketing of the social structures inscribed in every intonation of every language: All men will be equal only when they are silent together, as before God. The silent film's longing for the utopia in which language no longer matters finds it prefigured whenever the body speech and physical prowess of the working class speak louder, through the on-screen actions of its surrogates (the slapstick artist in Hollywood, the outraged sailor in Eisenstein), than the unheard words of command the ruling class employs. And yet the utopia is ambiguous, maintaining the working class in an alienation from speech that reinforces its powerlessness. The coming of sound may mark the end of immigration, the beginning of a process of nationalist American consolidation that is the milder, more democratic form of the totalitarianism of thirties Germany, Italy, or the Soviet Union, but it can also be said to expose the audience to an eloquence it can freely assimilate in the shame-free darkness of the auditorium, where the mechanisms of identification encourage one to translate passive competence in the language into active performance. The leading characters of the early sound films all have exemplary accents. To identify with them is to transcend – to betray – one's class.

This identification can be read in psychoanalytic, as well as social, terms. It is strikingly akin to the process Lacan terms the passage from the Imaginary to the Symbolic. The moment of the Imaginary – an earlier moment still – parallels the birth of cinema itself. The Imaginary, to quote Fredric Jameson:

swarms with bodies and forms intuited in a different way, whose fundamental property is, it would seem, to be visible without their visibility being the result of the act of any particular observer, to be, as it were, already-seen, to carry their specularity upon themselves like a color they wear or the texture of their surface.[4]

Similarly, the objects and characters of a film are visible even in an empty auditorium. The passing of the silents marks a movement from the Imaginary order to the Symbolic realm of language. It was widely felt to involve a dilution of the "specifically cinematic." The transition to the linguistic sphere was as painful to the collectivity, particularly the collectivity of actors, as it often is to the individual. In *The Wild Child* (*L'Enfant sauvage*), Truffaut would identify the transition with the necessary pain of socialization; and yet one can see Truffaut's own nostalgia for the cinematic past – the decimated forest – in his use of monochrome, and a regret for silent cinema in particular in his recourse to the Griffithian iris-in and iris-out. One may rightfully mourn the possibilities of variable framing of which Griffith was the pioneer who had no successor. A Werner Herzog, meanwhile, will seek to undo the process. His Kaspar Hauser – a mystical version of Woyzeck – withdraws into the visionary darkness whence he came, his frustration by speech marvelously embodied in the half-pugnacious, half-puzzled acting of the semiliterate Bruno S. Herzog further revokes the process of socialization by presenting Kaspar as a rocklike peasant, rather than the beautiful youngster over whom contemporaries marveled. Herzog's adoration of German silent cinema is apparent in his reverence for Lotte Eisner, one of the few keepers of the flame of expressionist cinema for the New German Cinema of the late sixties; it was to culminate in his reenactment of Murnau's *Nosferatu*. The identification with Murnau nevertheless has the self-conscious quality of a symbolic deed; Herzog's "innocent eye" is in fact *faux naïf,* deliberately oblivious of his chosen prototype's enormous sophistication. And so the identification undermines itself. For if, as Jameson notes, the Imaginary is the realm of binary oppositions (silent film is founded on the opposition of black and white that determines its optics and justifies its expressionism and melodrama by setting it apart from "the real"), Herzog's *Nosferatu* erodes that binarism by rendering the vampire a sympathetic figure. In other words (Jameson's), "verbalization itself superposes a Symbolic relationship upon the Imaginary fantasy."* A similar process seems to have debilitated the last films of Tarkovsky. There is after all no going back to the purity wherewith the visual was present in silent film. Knowledge that this is the case renders recent cinema perpetually uneasy; its mixture of language and silence, verbal speech and body speech, persists in a tension that refuses resolution. The result is not the best of both worlds but a gnawing sense of double exclusion.

* Jameson is describing one of Melanie Klein's therapies aimed at equipping the child to manipulate verbally symbols that up to that point had bewitched him simply as images. It is perhaps worth noting in this context that one of the prerequisites of the birth of cinema seems to have been the privileging of the child's vision by the Romantic Movement, which allowed authors to focus a novel's point of view in a child. It is indeed a question of *viewing*, of the "rawness" of the child's experience of events he is unable to name as yet.[5]

## Seeing through Hitler

In his *Theory of Film*, Bela Balázs remarks on the difficulty of lying convincingly to the camera: "If someone wants to tell a lie and is a capable liar, his words will serve him almost to perfection. But his face has areas over which he has no control." This is because "the expression of the whole face cannot cover up the expression of its details, if these details belong to a different, more profound truth." If the camera is indeed difficult to lie to, it is by virtue of its impassivity: The liar cannot be sure whether or not he has persuaded it. Unlike the traditional lie, which need be effective only at one time and place, the lie that fools the camera has to be a superlie, capable of convincing many people many times over. May it have been Hitler's awareness of the difficulty of achieving the Big Lie that caused him to choreograph his performances so carefully, and to concentrate on radio instead? Like Balázs, he seems to have believed that "the art of reading faces was about to become the very useful property of the masses, thanks to the silent film."[6] Thus the introduction of sound in the thirties helpfully disturbs the audience's concentration on the potentially revealing image. A demonic ruse of history protects the image of Hitler from ridicule as non-Aryan. Could it be that no one saw through Hitler because the addition of the voice – and the multiplication of the forms of the Führer's manifestations achieved thereby – dispelled the audience's incipient mastery of the image, placing it at the mercy of its manipulators? That people failed to *see through* Hitler simply because they were too busy *listening* to him?

## Notes on *Faust, Caligari,* and *The Student of Prague*

### The implicit spectator of Weimar cinema

Thomas Elsaesser has speculated that the implicit spectator of Weimar cinema derived pleasure from the masochistic narratives he encountered by categorizing their protagonists as his doubles. As he observed them, "The valorization of vision would fundamentally seem to transform the perception of anxiety into a pleasurable experience":[7] It is identification with the unfettered camera, the instrument of vision, that serves to transform pain into pleasure. But quite apart from the elided question of the position of the female spectator, the explanation is unsatisfactorily general: The Metzian model of primary identification with the apparatus, employed by Elsaesser here and elsewhere, provides no basis for distinguishing the specific constitution of the spectator of Weimar cinema from that of filmgoers from other cultures and periods. In fact, given the prevalence of *Schadenfreude* and scapegoating in Weimar cinema, it would seem to be less a cinema of identification, assimilable to the models of "classic cinema" that have gained wide acceptance in recent years, than one of cruelty: a training ground, even, for the passive contemplation of the victimization of others in the following decade.* Masochism, meanwhile, could be discerned in the filmmakers themselves. What pleasure, other than a masochistic one, could Heinrich Mann have derived from the degradation of his *Professor Unrat* into *The Blue Angel* (*Der blaue Engel*)?† In a perhaps magical effort to avert the actual realization of their fears by realizing them first themselves on screen, they created scenarios of their own humiliation at the hands of femmes fatales, who act on society's behalf to strip the intellectual of all power. The baby names of Lulu or Lola reflect the regression of their contemplators, who fear that German women will avenge their oppression – not on the real oppressors, but on the only figures weaker than themselves, the (mostly Jewish) intellectuals.

* *Schadenfreude* is generally felt by the adherent of authority who witnesses the comeuppance of someone he perceives as disorganized or unprepared. It seems to me that scenarios drawing on *Schadenfreude* become more common after the midtwenties, displacing the earlier expressionist structure of feeling of identification with the victimized individual. *The Blue Angel* or *M* identify with the victimizer as well as the victim. It is instructive, for instance, to compare the criminals' attitude to the child murderer in *M*, with the following passage from the memoirs of Rudolf Hoess, commandant of Auschwitz:

A man who had many previous convictions for indecent assault had enticed an eight-year-old girl into a doorway in Berlin, and there assaulted and strangled her. He was sentenced by the court to fifteen years' imprisonment. On the same day he was brought to Sachsenhausen for execution.

I can see him now as he stepped out of the truck at the place of execution. Grinning cynically, he was an evil and vicious-looking, middle-aged individual, a typical asocial. The Reichsführer SS had ordered that this professional criminal be shot straight away. When I informed him of his fate, his face turned a sickly yellow and he began whining and praying. Then he screamed for mercy, a repulsive sight. I had to have him bound to the post. Were these immoral creatures frightened of what they might find on "the other side"? I can see no other explanation for their behavior.[8]

*M* places a powerful plea for mercy in the murderer's mouth, but its open ending shows its inability to determine which side to come down on: The judges of the final image have the inscrutable mystery of the courts in Kafka. It is piquant to place the Hoess quotation alongside Syberberg's *Our Hitler*, which gives the murderer's monologue to an SA man; and Hoess's mention in the same breath of the Reichsführer SS and the fear of what lies "on the other side" become all the more piquant when one remembers that Himmler's masseur in Syberberg's film reflects that, if a man's deeds in this life come to meet him when he dies, what kind of deeds will his master encounter following *his* demise?

† T. W. Adorno offers an acid comment on this negative alchemy. Adorno's note on the title change contains an extremely compressed theory of expressionism as a movement that reveals both the "demonic masks" of the bourgeoisie and the experience of helplessness the bourgeois banishes from his awareness (p. 654). One may wonder, however, whether, in likening the "enlightening magic" of Heinrich Mann's original to that of Wedekind's *Frühlings Erwachen*, Adorno is prompted unconsciously by – and even justifying unwittingly – the film's kidnapping of the figure of Lulu. (Cf. my pairing of Lulu and Lola in "Lulu, Lola, and male masochism.")[9]

It is intriguing to consider the symbolic figures who populate the poetry of Rilke – the greatest German poet of the era of early German cinema – as in fact filmic in nature. If the angels are unable to distinguish between the living and the dead, and the unrequited lovers are reconciled to the unattainability of the objects of their devotion, are not these also the characteristics of the filmgoer? The motif of self-sacrifice was not Rilke's exclusive property, but was to be fatally appropriated in Nazi ideology. It can be argued even that the framed narratives of Weimar cinema themselves involve sacrifice – the sacrifice of one narrative to another. The implicit reader of the high culture of Rilke becomes uncannily similar to the low mimetic form of cinema's ideal viewer – a resemblance that suggests that the Nazi equalization of high and low had some logic, as well as an enormous amount of violent *ressentiment,* behind it. Perhaps the image of the SS man reading Rilke is not the total paradox it is assumed to be. Without wishing to suggest that Rilke is in any clearly identifiable way "responsible" for the Nazi order, may it not be – *pace* Kracauer – that he is as much so as that easy scapegoat of mandarins, Weimar cinema?

## Caligari, *Kracauer, and the demonic fun fair*

The demonic fun fair is a central motif in expressionist cinema. For the bourgeois intellectual the fair has the attraction of the forbidden Other, a precapitalist form of exchange – the liberation Bakhtin identified with popular carnival. In the case of cinema, however, the relationship is more complex and dialectical since fairgrounds were among the first sites of film exhibition, while the mountebank conjurer's spirit of Méliès had been one of cinema's prime animators. Merely to be a filmmaker in the era of the *Kinodebatte* was a potential source of humiliation for an intellectual. The quest for humiliation seems to have been part of the general ethos of many German-speaking filmmakers, instilled by the encounter with petty bureaucracy that befalls even Dr. Caligari himself. Outside Germany Von Stroheim displays it by virtually inviting Universal to make a whipping boy of him. Cinema is the domain of the declassed – whence the strenuous theoretical insistence that montage could impose redemptive form on the untidy rawness of life. The fun fair is demonized by a would-be intellectual cinema seeking to escape its own vulgar origins. Such a cinema denounces a rival – the popular form of cinema also represented by Hollywood, the American invader – that is simultaneously its own double. Yet the experience of the fair, of course, also provides German modernist art with one of its main structuring devices: the episodic stroll from booth to booth in a non-linear, decentered space. It is the walk of Benjamin's flâneur, transported from the phantasmagoria of a dream of

nineteenth-century Paris. The itinerant cabaret is merely an outrider of
the fair – Lola Lola, the bride of Caligari. If *The Blue Angel* rehearses
the fascist mockery of the intellectual, it also embodies the modernist
fantasy of victory over the patriarchal bourgeois stuffiness represented
by Unrat. The contradictory attitude to the fair found among Weimar
intellectuals is perhaps best exemplified in Kracauer. Writing of the
fair in *The Cabinet of Dr. Caligari* (*Das Kabinett des Dr. Caligari*), he
describes it as the antidote proposed by Mayer and Janowitz – the
scriptwriters – to the authoritarianism of Caligari, and yet fails to perceive its ambivalence: After all, *it is Caligari's home.* The ambivalence
typifies the bourgeois attitude to magic: Desirous of something for
nothing, one yet fears the magic that effects this miracle, for it demonstrates the existence of forces beyond the ken of commonsense
philosophy. May not such fears have prompted Goethe's enormous delay in bringing Faust and Mephistopheles together? Profoundly un-
Bakhtinian, Kracauer notes that "the fair is not freedom, but anarchy
entailing chaos."[10] The bourgeois objection to the fair (*Ordnung muss
sein!*) evinces the very split personality Kracauer himself castigates in
the Social Democrats – thereby confirming the accuracy of his diagnosis of the Weimar left of which he was part. It is, of course, that of the
would-be revolutionary who believes in *Kultur.**

*Faustian man*

The image of Faust has haunted both the Germans' imagination and
the world's imagination of the German. Hans Schwerte writes of the
image of "Faustian Man" as the fruit of an ideology, or, in the language of the time, a *Weltanschauung*, which saw its high-water mark
between 1870 and 1918 and involved Faust's reduction to a symbol of
titanic German national destiny – one which traduced the sense of the
Goethean work that had helped make Faust so well worth appropriation.[11] Schwerte overlooks the degree to which the myth itself solicited
its own misreading. His denunciation of the discourse of "the Faustian" as a misinterpretation of Goethe's work represses the drama's
own ambiguity. For if the process is to be described as the removal of

---

* The final interwar incarnation of the demonic funfair may well be the one that concludes *Hitlerjunge Quex* (*Unsere Fahne Flattert Uns Voran*; 1933). Hitler-youth Quex,
pursued by communists whose whistle-signal recalls the criminals of *M*, stumbles into a
shooting gallery and bumps into a clockwork drummer, activating its mechanism and
thereby betraying his presence. His very decision to secrete himself in a shooting gallery
stresses his vulnerability, his status as target. The animation of the inanimate clockwork
drummer politicizes the uncanny. If the funfair is demonized by the Nazis here it is primarily because of the flimsiness and unpredictability of the shelter it affords, though one
may imagine that they would further have disapproved of so dangerously unregimented
and unstructured a form of leisure (a relic of the *Systemzeit*).

the tragic from Goethe's poem – and it is thus that Schwerte characterizes it – then it had surely already been inaugurated by Goethe's addition of Part II, and Faust's redemption. At a time when even the state
designated "Germany" failed to encompass all the German-speaking
peoples, it was hardly surprising that the archtransgressor of boundaries – Faust as Prometheus – should have become the period's hero
with a thousand masks; and the fact that the very formation of "Germany" involved the overstepping of borders lent a deadly rationale to
Hitler's annexations – he himself being the Austrian who conquers
Berlin and then generalizes that conquest into the German subjugation
of yet further states.

Although Schwerte sees the ideology of "Faustian Man" entering its
decline in 1918, it persists strongly throughout the twenties, its prestige augmented by Spengler, who prepares the German conquest of Europe by presenting what earlier ideologists had deemed "typically
Germanic" as "typically Western" instead – and receives its first fundamental challenge in Wilhelm Böhm's *Faust der Nichtfaustische*
(*Faust the Non-Faustian*, 1932–3). It is thus hardly surprising that the
pervasive, frequently disguised hero of Weimar cinema should be the
Faust whose status as "mad scientist" renders him "archetypically
German," with the madness of the Romantic and the scientist's technological obsessions. His symbiosis with Mephistopheles reflects the "in-
feriority complex" of the underdeveloped nation state, which can only
recognize its own identity when it is confirmed by the recognition of
another.[12]

The Faust myth may have provided Klaus and Thomas Mann with a
metaphor for the events of the Weimar and Nazi years, but it was in
the cinema that it underwent the full gamut of its transformations.
Cinema itself could be interpreted as a Faustian creation. The Wagnerian formulation of the theoretical possibility of the *Gesamtkunstwerk* was a displacement into the aesthetic sphere of the political
desire for a synthesis of the German-speaking peoples into a single
nation-state, the displacement a sign of Wagner's own transposition of
his early politics into the aesthetic key. Both cinema and the German
nation-state had long been merely theoretical constructs. Thus the
Faustian overreachers of early German cinema symbolize a fear of the
demonic origin of the magic (the "magic" of technology, for instance)
that facilitates the rapid synthesis of diverse states into one super-
state, varying art forms into a superart. As Thomas Mann reproached
the legend and the poem with the failure to link Faust to music – a
failure his *Doktor Faustus* would make good – cinema was to go one
further by linking him to the *Gesamtkunstwerk*, the name "Wagner"
magically connecting Goethe's poem to the late-nineteenth-century's
dreams of pomp. The common denominator in the metamorphoses of

Faust in early German cinema is the master–slave relationship, which follows the dialectic delineated by Hegel. The transformations of Faust begin with Balduin in *The Student of Prague,* proceed through *The Cabinet of Dr. Caligari,* in which Caligari is the Mephisto figure, concluding in explicit evocation of the myth in Murnau's *Faust.* Mephistopheles here stands for the authority to which all German classes – not just the petit bourgeoisie – submit, on the assumption that it will fulfill their deepest longings. One notes the degree to which Hitler's language owed its success to its absorption of all the dominant elements in the German ideology of its time, a synthesis of left and right signaled in the term "National Socialism."* The splitting or doubling that this relationship involves – the drama that, in Goethe's *Faust,* follows the collapse of the unified lyric I (a breakdown presaged in "Zwei Seelen wohnen, ach! in meiner Brust") – establishes the self as a hierarchy that replicates and reinforces the social hierarchy. One of the primary gains of the demonization of desire through its association with Mephisto is to allow Faust to disclaim responsibility for the deeds he commits.† In Murnau's work, Mephistopheles often goes ahead of him, both shadow and scout. This disavowal is part of "the German complex" diagnosed by the Mitscherlichs; it thus antedated World War II instead of emerging afterward, as *The Inability to Mourn* argues.[14] Such a disavowal had been the slender bridge across which Faust had scuttled to salvation at the end of the second part of Goethe's drama. (In envisaging the damnation of Faust, Berlioz is a Frenchman securely contemplating the perdition of the German.) The separation between the self and its actions that granted the German-speaking peoples "credible deniability" was to be institutionalized by cinema, which permits one to view the magical, derealized spectacle of oneself acting. The viewer confronted with the absent scene becomes,

---

* Utz Maas comments on this synthetic tendency in the language of National Socialism. This fusion of opposites is also found in the Nazi aesthetic, as described by Saul Friedländer, which combines kitsch, and the sense of belonging it generates, with an experience of danger, the prerequisite of combat readiness; thus the feverishness of the *Blitzkrieg* mentality indicates a fear that one's project is threatened. The "short-circuit" Friedländer describes in *Kitsch und Tod* (p. 21) occurs between kitsch and existentialism. The paradigmatic combination of the two – as Adorno has demonstrated in *Jargon der Eigentlichkeit* – is to be found in the philosophy of Heidegger.[13]
† Mephistopheles' status as Faust's double is implicitly conceded by Faust himself when he terms him a "kalte Teufelsfaust" (literally, "cold devil's fist"). Faust's speech at this point is dreamlike in its repression to the status of casual detail of what is in fact the key to his drama. In a sense that key fact is unspeakable both to him and to the drama: to admit his identity with Mephistopheles (who is "a part of the part" in another sense than the one *he* admits – a split-off part of the part that is Faust) would terminate the play, collapsing everything back into the lyric with which it began. (There is a profound preoccupation in German thought with the entry into language of the unspeakable – a preoccupation related to its concern with *Innerlichkeit* [inwardness]. It may also have something to do with the ease and frequency with which German creates compound nouns – as it were, irruptions from a private language into the public sphere.)

like Faust, briefly in thrall to the otherworldly. Thus Syberberg is justified
in a sense in reading Hitler as "a film from Germany" – though the oppressive length of his demonstration of this thesis belies the fact that
what rendered the Nazi régime most filmlike was the relative *brevity* of its
omnipotence. The most potent pleasure cinema offered – then as now –
was that of irresponsibility. The displeasure that accompanied it was
that of envy, an emotion that could nevertheless be recycled into the economy of pleasure as masochism – an attitude that may even be encoded in
the hypnotic dynamics of the verb placement in German sentences, which
forbid one to "walk out" on a message. For if the screen world was a world
elsewhere, and one's presence there partook of godlike invisibility, it also
involved exclusion, a persistent sense that one had been passed over –
most dramatically, passed over by the light cutting through the darkness
above one's head. The German demand for a place in the sun was perhaps one for a position before the arc lights. Cinema provided a space for
the unfolding of a colonial impulse denied actual triumphs. But the
merely negative, imaginary status of this space fed a poisonous *ressentiment*. It is rendered all the more corrosive by continual deflection from its
object: The constant use of narrative framing devices in early Weimar cinema is a Kafkaesque imitation of the functioning of the state bureaucracy,
referring the question of the text to a higher instance, which usually overturns the sense of the subordinate text and sometimes destroys it entirely.* This higher instance is the conservative one of the reality
principle.

*Faustian narcissism and desire*

Partway through Murnau's *Faust* we find its hero, an old man, in despair. He has sought demonic powers as a way of relieving the plague
afflicting his native town, but the onlookers' horror at his retreat from a
cross borne by a dying girl has driven him back to the solitude of his
study, where he consigns his books to flames and prepares to take poison. As he looks into the poison, the image of a young man appears
in it, and Mephisto identifies it as Faust's youth. It can be enjoyed
again, Mephisto persuades. Janet Bergstrom describes the moment as
follows:

Because the young man is said to represent his own youth, Faust's desire is
designated by the narrative as natural, rather than as the result of a sexualized
seduction. Desire for the young Faust is represented as being even more indi-

* Kracauer was to argue that the appended ending of *Caligari* defused the subversive
potential of what had gone before by reclassifying it as the maunderings of a madman
i.e., it overturns the sense of the preceding text; I would be more inclined to read it as
introducing an ambiguity that destroys the notion of sense completely, leaving one in a
state of vertigo.

rect by the fact that Mephisto, the mediator, is necessary to Faust's temptation. That the temptation is sexual is made clear by the first act Mephisto performs after endowing Faust with the young man's body: he presents a diaphanous vision of a woman, almost naked in transparent veils as the pleasure Faust's youth is entitled to. The young man eagerly accepts. Thus, the woman's body is presented (very briefly) as sexuality, and in a way that directs our narrative interest away from the sight of the young Faust himself. Her sexuality is presented as the work of the devil, as entrapment, for Faust will sign his soul away a few scenes later to avoid interrupting this first gratification of his sexual appetite. Given all this narrative and stylistic machinery, the viewer is left to enjoy the beauty of the young Faust without thinking twice.[15]

Powerful though Bergstrom's analysis is, her contention that we enjoy the young Faust's beauty without thinking twice is false, and depends on severing the image's links with the surrounding narrative. The emergence of the image of the young Faust is far from being unequivocally positive, since it involves responsibility's submerging in the pleasure principle, the superego's defeat by the id. The superimposition of beauty upon poison is anything but unambiguous, so that when the creation of the swooning image of the young Faust is followed by the materialization of a veiled female image at the center of the screen, the manner in which this new image solicits our attention – and since it is both centrally placed and in the process of coming into focus, it makes a double demand on our attention – acts in part as an alibi for, and in part as a diversion of, the potentially homoerotic feelings aroused by the exquisite young Faust. When Faust then visits Italy and seduces the Duchess of Parma with Mephisto's aid, his turbaned appearance renders him akin to Valentino – a problematic identification figure for the German audience.* Faust-as-Valentino proves a blind alley the text then abandons; it does indeed think twice about where it has gone to, growing skeptical of the value of unalloyed pleasure. Faust's melancholy leads him to long for the *Heimat* he finds magically unchanged upon reentry. Having oscillated between stern morality and pure pleasure, he seeks a synthesis of the two through a relationship with the Gretchen Mephisto derides as inferior to girls who would be only too happy to allow Faust his desires. Attraction to Gretchen may, however, be linked to homosexual desire; for if, as Jo Leslie Collier notes, the asexual madonna "is so perfectly feminine, and femininely perfect, that to have sexual intercourse with her could only be a sacrilege, a profanation,"[17] then desire for her also involves a will to her nonattainment, and may be diverted elsewhere – first recoiling back on the self, in the form of narcissism, and then flow-

---

* The problems Valentino poses both for traditional identification and for Laura Mulvey's theorization of the gendered spectator have been described incisively by Miriam Hansen.[16]

ing out toward another male (whence the doubling of Faust and Mephisto, which is disavowed yet present, like that between Harker and Nosferatu) – and may culminate in a fusion of the religious and the cinematic spectator. (If one deems this fusion unsuccessful, one may call it sentimentality.) Thus Gretchen, the "asexual madonna," is also a pre-Raphaelite image, and represents pubescence on the verge of awakening. Faust is able to persuade himself that his love for her is innocent, for it is in fact Mephisto who precipitates the disaster, preceding Faust like a shadow, slandering Gretchen so Valentin will rush home to discover her in Faust's arms, and then stabbing Valentin in the back, but the elaborate parallels between his lovemaking with Gretchen and Mephisto's pursuit of her aunt suggest Faust's self-image at this point is a rationalization. Pilloried, cast out in the snow, then brought to the stake as the putative murderess of her child, Gretchen calls out to Faust, her face covering the landscape, and he defies Mephisto and renounces the pact. As he does so, he lifts his right arm in a manner imitative of the angel who challenged Mephisto to corrupt Faust at the film's outset. At this point Faust's beauty – which previously had seduced the old Faust and perhaps also the viewer – is sublimated beyond sexual pleasure to the realm of the angelic. When Gretchen stands amid the burning flames and recognizes her young lover in the wizened old form Faust has resumed, the hallucinations of her earlier scenes become insight. The image of the young Faust is rescued from the Devil's mirror and reprojected from the eyes of his lover. Given the degree to which Murnau's work anticipates Dreyer's – here *Day of Wrath* (*Vredens Dag*) in particular – and the degree to which Dreyer's own is a throwback to Hawthorne's, it is hard not to recall the ending of *The Scarlet Letter*.

In identifying love as the redemptive power, Murnau's film may seem to be simply mawkish, but it is at least attempting to fill a logical gap in Goethe's work, which leaves it unclear why Faust should be saved. Continual striving appears to render one redeemable – but Goethe's irrationalism fails to supply any goal toward which Faust may be said to be striving. Indeed, its apparent glorification of action without content – "Im Anfang war die Tat" – can have chilling implications. It is as if genius may expect to be saved, regardless of its deeds. Goethe's amoralism is deeply worrying, and does indeed foster the "removal of guilt from the tragedy" ascribed to a later, ideologically tainted period by Schwerte. Its germ can be found much earlier, in Goethe's work itself.

In this context – the context of guilt in German history – one of the most intriguing and enigmatic aspects of Murnau's film becomes its depiction of the old Faust. When he raises his books above his head in triple invocation of Mephistopheles, he recalls images of Moses;

when he recoils from the crucifix and is stoned, it is almost as if a Judaic punishment is being applied to the Jew who abhors the cross. In the light of the film's date of release – 1926 – its eschewal of the anti-Semitic potential inherent in some of these images is commendable, and can be contrasted with the manner in which the 1926 *Student of Prague* activates the neutralized anti-Semitic elements of the 1913 version. (For more on *The Student of Prague*, see the next section.) Instead the film draws on the chiaroscuro iconography of the late Rembrandt, who accorded enormous and poignant dignity to the Jews he depicted. It even identifies the "Jewish" Faust as the moral one: The lineaments of the Book of Job shine through its surface. Nevertheless, its Hebraism is a pro-Jewishness that cannot speak its name – hardly surprising in the homosexual in whom social persecution has bred the habit of chronic indirection.*

## Hoffmann's Italian children

To take the Faust myth as the point of origin of German cinema is oneself to mythologize. Consideration of other works can help indicate the arbitrary nature of assigned origins. Thus, in the final two sections of these notes, I will be taking E. T. A. Hoffmann as my founding father, rather than Goethe, even though I will be beginning with Goethe's Italian journey. For a German–Italian axis existed long before the one cemented by Hitler and Mussolini, one established by Goethe's *Italienische Reise*. For Goethe, Italy was "das Land, wo die Zitronen blühn," its palaces a living equivalent of the lost Grecian world so many other German poets mourned. Yet there seems to be a dark side to Italy, just as there was one to the ideal Grecian world;

* The genesis of anti-Semitism is of course too vast and extensively researched a topic to be addressed properly here. I would merely like to make a few comments intended to suggest avenues of inquiry beyond the obvious ones. Sartre has argued that the anti-Semite "seeks only what he has already found" (*Anti-Semite and Jew*, p. 19). (I will for the sake of convenience ignore the irony whereby Sartre's reification of "the anti-Semite" echoes the latter's objectification of "the Jew.") One corollary may well be that anti-Semitism attempts to destroy the Jew in order to remove a reminder of lack in general. For the Germans this lack was surely first and foremost one of national identity. The strength of Jewish identity must have seemed all the more mocking by virtue of its maintenance despite the Diaspora. Germans, meanwhile, lived adjacent to one another yet without unity. (On achieving unity, they exact revenge on the apparently mocking Jewish presence.) Sartre contends that anti-Semitism bears no relation to experience. In so doing he fails to grasp that the anti-Semite's irrational virulence may well be fueled by a sense of the growing inadequacy of his inherited stereotypical ideas in the shifting modern world of assimilation, where nationality is becoming increasingly elusive. Anti-Semitism is thus a rearguard action against epistemological uncertainty, an effort to reattach names to the things that have shed them. In religious terms, meanwhile, anti-Semitism is readable as a coded form of rebellion against God, which may appear as Nazi paganism or as the Christian denial of Christ's Jewishness – the means whereby the Christian himself crucifies Christ.

and if the underside of the latter was to be intuited by Hölderlin and expounded by Nietzsche, that of the former becomes apparent in E. T. A. Hoffmann's "Story of the Lost Reflection," which presents Italy as the site of Erasmus Spikher's loss of his mirror image. Similarly, in "The Sandman" Nathanael associates the sandman, the bogeyman said to pluck out bad children's eyes, with the Italian seller of eyeglasses, Coppola. It is a name to conjure with, for something similar (Cipollo) appears in Thomas Mann's *Mario and the Magician* – his analysis of the hypnotic powers of a fascism that is a displaced image of National Socialism. The displacement is perhaps necessitated by artistic form (creating the distance that facilitates representation); by the fact that Italian fascism was more full-blown, having been of greater longevity, than national socialism; and by Mann's suspicion that the polarities of North and South upon which so much of his work rests are less firmly removed from one another than they might seem to be. Yet it can also be read as infected with the lack of self-knowledge that made national socialism possible. The tendency on the German left to speak of "fascism" rather than National Socialism may fall into this trap too. And even Victor Klemperer hovers on its edge, as he reflects on how *undeutsch* Hitler was and wonders whether National Socialism was a disease caught from Italy, before veering back to a recognition of its specifically German qualities. Located beneath Germany on the map, Italy can stand for its unconscious. It is simultaneously double and other. Which brings one to "Caligari," a name surely chosen for its resemblance to Cagliostro, and what Kracauer terms the "puzzling poster" announcing "You must become Caligari!"[18] – perhaps itself a message from the collective unconscious, instructing the Germany of 1919 to become fascist. Caligari's somnambulist also bears an Italian name, Cesare. An enigma and an irony concerning hierarchical relations are embodied in the subordination of one called Cesare – though this may well mean, as the surrealists would have said, that he is the emperor of the unconscious. The irony extends to the figure of Caligari himself, both persecuted outsider and figure of control. The motif of the outsider as dictator reminds one of Orwell's comment on the frequency with which authoritarian rulers come from the *edge* of their countries – perhaps because identity is most threatened there, and requires greater ferocity in its maintenance? Caligari is thus an image of the artist, anticipating Bergman's *The Magician* (*Ansiktet*): He is the one who controls the irrational, and so can become in the end a figure running an asylum – an uncanny image of the psychoanalyst as the scientist whose other name is artist. His extravagant cloak may recall Worringer's remark that in Gothic art drapery became an organism on its own.[19] Again this is Bergmanesque: Think of Death in *The Seventh Seal* (*Det sjunde inseglet*). If Cesare's garments hug the skin, it is because he is that organism once it has assumed independence: the shadow self, that ultimate item of threatening expressionist drapery, waxing much larger than its bearer as his hidden power (the phallus, a Lacanian would say) manifests itself.

Bespectacled, bearing an Italian name, Caligari recalls figures from "The Sandman," with its obsession with dead eyes. The diabolic controlling figure in *The Student of Prague* also has an Italian name, Scapinelli. Hence Hoffmann emerges as not simply the founding father by proxy of German cinema; *Caligari* and *The Student of Prague* become the recto and verso of "The Sandman." And why the debt to Hoffmann? Surely, among other things, because of the ambiguity of the latter's position in German literature, poised between the sensationalist and the respectable in the same way as the German intellectual interested in cinema in this century's earliest years.

More to the point, however, may be Hoffmann's interest in ambiguous sexuality, in transformation as the male's feminization. For if it can be argued that cinema fosters an ambiguous sexuality in its spectators – the putatively sadistic gaze of the male viewer rendered masochistic ("feminized") through subordination to another person's choice of angle and shot duration; its victimized females simultaneously empowered to scrutinize males in the dark – then it is understandable that the films commonly described as the foundation stones of German cinema (*The Student of Prague* and *The Cabinet of Dr. Caligari*) should both allude to a work that links loss of male sexuality to obsessive voyeuristic use of machines for looking: E. T. A. Hoffmann's "The Sandman." Freud, of course, read the story as an allegory of castration anxiety (the propensity for allegory in German thought is perhaps expressive of a will to power over the alien objects that exclude one) – but his master narrative can itself be translated into other narratives revolving around such themes as the student's lack of power (a lack that can be symbolized in its turn by castration – as in Lenz's *Hofmeister*) and the trauma of the German's subordination to the non-German (the Italian professor, the seller of eyeglasses). Exchange as sex-change may however be desired as well as feared. Nathanael's misdirection to Klara of his letter to Lothar is an index of his sexual confusion at the story's start; the fear of loss of one's eyes to the Sandman is a fear of becoming like Olimpia, with her dead eyes, or Klara, with her prosaic nature; while fear of loss of sexual identity underpins the transformation of Coppelius into Coppola, a loss of male identity (the feminine "a" replacing the male "us") that encodes a multiple degradation – from the German to the Italian, from the Latin to the Italian, and from the lawyer to the street vendor (loss of sexuality entailing loss of nationality and declassement). An exclusively Freudian analysis would fail to grasp the extent and multiplicity of humiliation.

Degradation, of course, involves a two-part movement and a repetition: Nathanael's relationship with Coppola duplicates his father's with Coppelius, and in each case transgressive desire issues in destruction. Since Coppola's name is reminiscent both of the Italian *coppo* (eye-socket) and the German *Kuppler* (procurer), it is hardly surprising that he should be the facilitator of voyeurism. Nathanael passes from the regime of conscious verbalization (letters), through that of unconscious verbalization (his poetry), to conclude under the regime of inarticulate sight. Meanwhile the "fremde Macht" (foreign power) that brings these disasters upon him is a mystified image of the narrator himself.*

In reading *The Student of Prague* and *Caligari* as the recto and verso of "The Sandman" I am of course simplifying. The actual genealogies of these works are far more complex and heteroglossic. In the case of *The Student of Prague*, for instance, it is possible to discern fault lines running across the text where one influence collides with another. Thus Scapinelli is related simultaneously to Hoffmann's Coppola ("The Sandman"), his devil ("The Story of the Lost Reflection") and Mephisto in "Faust." Hence one has the inconsistency in the narrative line when Scapinelli secures the student's reflection, as if it were Balduin's soul, and he himself the devil, and yet is not shown doing anything with it. It functions as it were independently of him, and he is perhaps simply the midwife who separates it from Balduin. Consequently the parallel with the devil's pact becomes incomplete, since Balduin does not enter the transaction in the knowledge that he is selling his soul; he is not Goethe's self-confident Faust but a dupe. And so the responsibility he bears for his double's actions is all the more cruel: He is the German as the victim of his own unconscious impulses. And also of his unconsciousness of the unconscious. Upon losing his reflection he shrugs his shoulders and says "hin ist hin" (what's gone is gone). There is no horror, little regret. Balduin imagines he can live without the soul his reflection connotes. His subsequent soullessness is then reflected in the double's stiff, automatic

---

* A similar multiform degradation informs Hoffmann's "Story of the Lost Reflection" (the near-prototype of *The Student of Prague*), whose protagonist Emmanuel Spikher loses his reflection in Italy. This loss is, of course, also amenable to Freudian reading as a cipher for castration (a punishment for sexual transgression that may itself stand for the effects of venereal disease). Analogous losses are suffered by Spikher's doubles, Peter Schlemihl and the hatless, cloakless narrator, whose continual flight is in essence an hysterical attempt to escape his own identity with Spikher (the latter's Giulietta as a version of the former's Julia; again one notes the dialectic of Latin and Italian names). In its deepest and darkest recesses the story suggests an ambiguous sexuality that is diabolic: the doubling of Giulietta and Dapertutto ("he saw Dapertutto stand up behind her") being the flickering manifestation of a Devil of variable shape and sex, who seeks to destroy the sexual specificity of those "he" encounters so as to render them like "himself." It is fitting that "the first German art film" should allude so strongly to this work: Early German films displace a fear of the unsexing properties of the cinematic form onto the content of the stories it relays.

movements. It was surely present even at the outset, however, in his fixation on wealth, to which he subordinates love (given his initial desire for "a rich heiress" one may doubt the sincerity of his love for Margit). It is as if he wants *both* the alternative solutions he had mentioned to Scapinelli: a win on the lottery *and* a rich heiress. Balduin's split – an image of the violence such beliefs do to the self – may also be a reflex of the film's own split nature. For Elsaesser, a split is apparent even in the first image (one that is doubled, presented later on in a different key, when the reflection's murder of the Baron has alienated Balduin from Margit's affections), with its dual focus on the melancholic foregrounded Balduin and the riotous student life, centered on Lyduszka, immediately behind him.[20] The film's split nature causes it to retain a supernaturalist machinery while simultaneously unplugging some of its components: God and Devil are absent; there is only Scapinelli. The Jewish and Christian worldviews are present only as enigmatic stumps, the dialectically adjacent images of Christ on the cross and the Jewish cemetery (image and word): In placing them at its center, incidentals to be passed over, the film as it were represses them. Its omission of the past that has brought Balduin to his initial straits is complicit with his own ability almost insouciantly to bid farewell to his reflection.

The awkwardness of the fit between Scapinelli and the archetype of the devil may prompt one to question the legitimacy of classifying him as diabolic – a question that brings him even closer to the Coppelius and Coppola of "The Sandman," who are devoid of evil intentionality and are simply misperceived by Nathanael. *The Student of Prague* is far more bourgeois a work than Goethe's *Faust*: The dream of supernatural powers is feared even as it is indulged, and the splitting of the image of the self indicates continual second thoughts. In this context it is worth noting how Murnau's version of *Faust* aligns the material with *The Student of Prague,* showing us an older Faust who contemplates his younger self: self as Other in an impossible space – the magical space of the cinema – double as Other. Elsaesser draws a useful parallel between Balduin's rescue of a horsebacked woman from the upper class to which he aspires, and the experience of the clerk in *Phantom,* who becomes obsessed with the woman in the carriage that knocks him down. The pairing of woman and horse may be read as a reiteration, in a different key, of the opening split, as the sign of a crisis in the male self-image. The horsebacked woman is in a sense a realistic double to the fantastic donor who is Scapinelli: Marriage to her would offer a feasibly realistic way of achieving what Scapinelli offers through magic. Scapinelli's appearance at the film's start stems from Balduin's fatalistic belief that real advance is impossible: He may have turned his back upon his girlfriend, but he cannot reach the woman to whom he aspires. And yet her image beckons: Although her horsebacked position means she looks down on him, her solitariness indicates her freedom – and hence her availability. She can even be paired with that which is lower: the student as the equivalent of the horse. Her freedom, however, is ambiguous: Available to suitors, she is also already paired with the horse, already satisfied sexually. Her liberty is that of the late-nineteenth-century bluestocking, and so her image represents the point at which this early-twentieth-century work departs from the medievalizing idealization of the Lady found in Romanticism. And so Balduin's discouragement over his prospects is also expressive of the early-twentieth-century male's doubts of his ability to hold the woman he loves. He will have to redouble his efforts – which means doubling himself – to have a chance.

The Student of Prague *and* Caligari

In 1913 the first version of *The Student of Prague* appears; in 1919, *The Cabinet of Dr. Caligari* is released. Taken together, the two films yield a double beginning for German cinema, the first two works at the outset of the standard histories. The double beginning is symptomatic of the difficulty of beginnings in general, the doubts that accompany them, the threat they pose to an authoritative voice that has not yet "got into its stride." A Hegelian might wish to add the 1926 *Student of Prague,* a synthesis in a sense of *Caligari* and the earlier version. The overlaps between the three works justify Kracauer's tendency to speak of Weimar cinema as collectively authored, though he then tends to lose the specific collectivity of authors in the larger collectivity of "the German soul." The contrasts however are equally important. The 1913 *Student of Prague* presents the fantastic in a real setting; indeed, its opening credits regale us with a list of all the noteworthy sights of which it will present views, appealing as much to spectators' interest in picture postcards from faraway places (the link between the fantastic and the exotic) – to the Lumière hemisphere of the cinematic brain – as to the magical Méliès side. *Caligari,* however, presents a world that is entirely internal: the same world found in the 1926 *Student,* which restages the Veidt–Krauss scenario of *Caligari,* though on this occasion Cesare's double is a real person rather than a lifeless doll.

A comparison of the 1913 and 1926 versions shows a passage from a world in which fantasy and reality are potentially distinguishable to one in which they have fused. In the earlier version the strong presence of outdoor scenes corresponds to the hope of an escape from self-obsession; Balduin's story begins outside, moving inside for the scene of narcissism in which the diabolic Scapinelli takes advantage of a victim whose self-sequestration – "I will be my own sole opponent," Balduin announces to the mirror – renders him easy meat, and many of its key incidents occur in the open air. It is in an interior, however, that the reflection is first lost and then, at the film's end, killed: the final killing of the double reiterating the earlier loss, in a different, more deadly key.* The exteriors are signposts to liberation: a Romantic liberation into nature, rather than an expressionist projection of the self; and Balduin's cry of "Ins Freie!" at the end is an attempt to discover a nature humanity has abolished. It has been replaced by the picture postcard and retains its old menace and integrity only at one place, the graveside where Balduin finally sits. To find this place, however, he has to identify with death, his own double. *Caligari* draws the logical conclusion and abolishes an exterior that in any case had been merely the mockery of nature. Prague is no longer "another world" for the Germans; its invasion in the late thirties is anticipated by the 1926 version's superimposition upon it of the *Caligari* problematic. With the loss of the sense of the other world as a place with as much right to exist as one's own – a sense destroyed by the Great War – German cinema also forfeits its links with Scandinavian cinema, which live out an eccentric and poignant afterlife in Murnau's work. In the 1926 version other worlds are simply screens upon which to project inner anguish. Hence although the 1913 version contains elements an anti-Semitism could mobilize – the use of the Jewish cemetery, Scapinelli's role as the provider of gold – the hints are not brought together to confirm a conspiracy; indeed, the narrative is full of loose ends, such as the figure of Lyduszhka, the slip of a girl whose catlike eros leavens the whole work in a part accorded prominence simply to showcase the athletic abilities of Salmonowa. (Imagine a film with Baryshnikov in which the great dancer did not dance!) Scapinelli's angular strangeness is far removed from the Jewish usurer. The 1913 *Student of Prague*, may be a story of self-enclosure, but it tries to open windows on the world outside. In *Caligari*, and in the 1926 version, those windows have been painted over. They know that the nature of the 1913 version was merely a daub on the glass.

## Lang, Von Harbou, and the female god: *Metropolis* and *Kriemhilds Rache*

Metropolis *and the double*

If the logic of the double and the Other pervades Weimar cinema, one of its most interesting and surprisingly little-investigated manifesta-

---

* Since suicide occurs as the accidental by-product of the murder of the Other, the film sees suicide as a means of preserving an ideal ego; essentially – as the remainder of the film's bias toward exteriors would suggest – there is no such thing as suicide, only *murder* deflected.

tions is in the cooperation of Fritz Lang and Thea Von Harbou. There
may be a copious literature concerning the Lang–Von Harbou films,
but there is precious little consideration of the give-and-take between
the two. This is perhaps less strange than it would at first seem: Their
separate labors have been fused – and confused – in the final prod-
ucts, the finished films. Criticism generally restricts itself to deploring
the sentimentality of the wife's screenplays,[21] though Patrice Petro appears at least to approve of Von Harbou's proabortion campaigns,
while passing over her explicitly National Socialist activities.[22] Given
the widespread critical derision of the *melodramatic* qualities of Von
Harbou's scenarios and Petro's own wish to remove prestige from the
male-directed genre of the fantastic and restore it to the melodrama,
one wonders why she has so little to say of Von Harbou. The reason is
surely that it would be bad tactics to associate onself too intimately
with a neo-Nazi lacking even the alibi of Riefenstahl's colossal talent –
together with the sheer difficulty of determining Von Harbou's actual
contribution. Too much speculation is involved in the enterprise.
Nevertheless, much could be done with Von Harbou – with the apocalyptic chaos of *Kriemhild's Revenge* (*Kriemhilds Rache*), for instance,
proving readable as a female subversion of the patriarchal patterning
of *Siegfried*, whose proto-Nazi transformation of people into objects to
be arranged in mass ornaments was lambasted by Kracauer. A feminist remapping of the terrain of Weimar cinema could indeed find useful sustenance in the Lang–Von Harbou relationship, for the existence
of Von Harbou's novel *Metropolis* allows one to postulate an ideal scenario from which the extant film diverges – apparent double, it proves
in the end unfaithful Other, particularly in the conclusion. This devia-
tion is not simply to be ascribed to the perceived American need to
reduce seventeen reels to ten – though it could be argued that the inherent impatience of the imaginary American viewer who prompted its
ghost-cutting corresponds to an attachment to Oedipal narrative forms
nourished by speed and suspense. Behind the Oedipal scenario whose
grid lends some shape to the film's current corrupt form – not that the
original can have been much less absurd – lies the novel's nostalgia
for matriarchy, sentimental feminism fused with Mariolatry, a crypto-
Catholicism that may have been shared by Lang as Austrian, or may
simply have been something he went along with. Nevertheless, there
are elements indicative of conflict. The figure of the robot, both feminine and phallic, may link the projects of both Lang and Von Harbou,
but by the end of the film it is apparent that a male principle has
triumphed over the Catholic deification of the maternal principle. The
final scene rubs salt in the fatally wounded scenario of Von Harbou's
novel. Where the film ends with labor–capital relations healed in the
meeting of three men on the cathedral steps, the novel closes with Joh

Fredersen on his knees before his mother, who hands him the letter Hel gave her to pass on to him in the event of his repentance. Echoing the Bible, Hel says in it that she will be with Joh to the end of his days. Freder is defined as fit to mediate because all features meet in his face, which recalls Hel, Joh, and Maria – but also the face of the crowd. It is a quasi-Jungian dream of integration. If the ending of Lang's film scrambles the novel's adoration of the matriarchal principle, it was perhaps only poetic justice that saw it drastically amputated for U.S. import. On seeing the mutilated version Lang reputedly vowed never to make a film in America. Manhattan, as it were, had the last laugh on the man who had tried to pour the old wine of Von Harbou's messianism into the tall new bottles of New York's skyscrapers. The disjointedness of the *Metropolis* we know, however, lifts its absurdity into the logic of a dream book instead. Félix Guattari has argued that silent cinema more closely approximates the language of dream and desire than does sound cinema: The very silence abstracts one from everyday life. *Metropolis* is perhaps the only multimillion(-mark) spectacle to bear out a contention that usually adduces low-budget surrealist and avant-garde film as evidence. Its discontinuities and absurdities – H. G. Wells termed it "the most foolish film," peeved perhaps by its traduction of the dystopian vision of his *Time Machine* – also create a kinship with the rock video. It is hardly extraordinary that it should have been raided for imagery by the British band Queen and transmogrified into a rock opera by Giorgio Moroder. Moroder justifies his version, clearly a labor of love, with an initial quotation from Lang, which ruefully notes that "I experience with my eyes, and never, or only rarely, with my ears." The film seeks to remedy this deficiency.* Nevertheless the synaesthetic power of the origi-

---

* Moroder falsely claims that the film has been "restored as close to its original conception as possible." The extent to which the film has been edited to conform to Hollywood reverse-field practices, noted by Thomas Elsaesser,[23] should not be exaggerated however. Elsaesser describes Moroder's version as a trimming of the original to accommodate it to Hollywood continuity editing, noting that a purist might object to this. Elsaesser himself does not object, but nevertheless here (and elsewhere in his work, e.g., "Film History and Visual Pleasure") posits a "German aesthetic" opposed to the norms of Hollywood kinetic efficiency. *Metropolis* offers only shaky ground for the construction of such a theory, for even pre-Moroder versions evince certain "American" editorial habits, indicating that Manhattan provided some of the inspiration for the film's form as well as its decor. (For instance, when a worker in the catacombs asks, "Where is our Mediator?" an implicit answer to the question is given by Maria's glance off-screen and the eyeline match with the kneeling, exalted Freder.) The occasional use of subjective camera – Maria screams at Rothwang's window, and the darting camera imitates Freder's inquisition of the building for the source of the noise; the dolly-in on her scarf on the ground reflects the ineluctable attraction it exerts upon him – also implies point-of-view editing. In *Metropolis* Lang's Americanization – like that of the Germany able to import large numbers of U.S. films following the inception of the Dawes Plan in 1924 – is already well underway. The relative innocence of earlier German silent cinema has vanished. Thus Moroder's version does not so much violate a "German aesthetic," which can be read as an

nal version's imagery is such that at points it may seem to enable one to hear with one's eyes, as Lotte Eisner notes: "In this silent film sound has been *visualised* with such intensity that we seem to hear the pistons throb and the shrill sound of the factory siren."[24] Even had it not added the statue of Hel or reconstructed Gyorgy's trip to Yoshiwara, Moroder's enterprise would have been justified as a way of posing the question of the relationship between silent film and its score. The film shuttles back and forth between three different applications of music: For much of the time, the music simply ticks over, preventing the sound track becoming empty between the narrative climaxes; it then dramatizes and underlines those high points through sung lyrics – arias as it were, interrupting the recitative – which are foregrounded as carriers of information virtually on a par with the images; while at other moments it propels the silent aesthetic in the direction of the sound one by mimicking the incidental noises a talkie would have provided – for example, the individual notes that accompany the robot's first steps. The shuttling movement corresponds to a sense that none of the proposed solutions is adequate in itself. The latter two in particular evince a temptation to use music merely illustratively and redundantly. Such redundancy may be verbal – for example, when we know that the false Maria is misleading the workers, we do not need the lyric's banal question "Is there a mask behind the face?" – or nonverbal – the notes marking the robot's steps. The problem would largely vanish however if the songs were of higher quality.*

Nevertheless, Moroder's choice of text was very canny, for its camp-laden, postmodern pastiche administers perverse poetic justice to a film that was itself to a large extent a pastiche of expressionism. If the

alternative to mainstream practices, but amplifies the American elements that have already infiltrated it. Moreover, Elsaesser ignores the problems involved in discussion of the editing of silent film, whose lack of the protection dialogue affords renders it vulnerable to cutters' caprice and souvenir clipping – for if a film has dialogue and is clipped, the result is verbal or narrative incoherence. It is consequently virtually impossible to know whether or not a particular silent film print accurately represents the *original work*.

* This problem of redundancy is frequently encountered by rock videos, whose images are often point-by-point illustrations of the song's lines. I would argue, in fact, that the most interesting sound tracks are those that eschew explication of the image and relate to it only obliquely: Thus the music is not subordinated to, and consumed by, the image, but interacts with it. In order to achieve this, the music must be of a caliber that makes it interesting even when separated from the film. (One regrets that the false Maria's unveiling was not paired with Madonna's "Like a Virgin.") And since the best musicians generally avoid the indignity of creating music that will occupy a merely subsidiary position, many films are let down by their music. This syndrome clearly vitiates Moroder's version: Most of its music, alas, is somewhat clumping. Perhaps only one sequence is truly successful, offering a hint of what might have been achieved: When tuxedoed men duel over the indifferent false Maria, the use of Freddie Mercury's "Love Kills" is haunting, accentuating the slow motion's aura of prehistoric male struggle.

presence of a certain postmodernism within a film of the modernist period seem problematic, it can be correlated with the way Lang uses Art Deco ornament and the utopian image of Americanization to rejuvenate a German modernism that is seen to be aging. In the process Lang becomes a trailblazer for the postmodern vulgarization of modernism, which could not reach the scale of the present-day before modernism had become part of official culture. The mania of pastiche is the eclectic opportunism that leaps from one ruined style to another. Pastiche depends on the existence of a gulf between itself and its material; it is thus unlike parody, which arises out of obsessive intimacy with a writer or work. Distance frees it to play with alternative modes of rendition. For Moroder the distance is furnished by history and culture; in Lang's own case there is a detachment from Von Harbou's ideas that may correspond either to a general anti-intellectualism or to a shrewd recognition of the vapidity of his wife's world-saving scenarios; it probably also prefigures their future divorce.* For many auteur-

---

* The opposition between Lang and Von Harbou personalizes the one between *Neue Sachlichkeit* and expressionism in the film, whose suspension between the two movements is insightfully pursued by Andreas Huyssen.[25] The effort to reconcile *Neue Sachlichkeit* with expressionism is part of the straining for totality that was to render the film so appealing to that future totalitarian, Adolf Hitler. The dream's pervasiveness may be seen in the frequency with which the word "totality" recurs in interwar German thought. The taint of ideology clinging to it prompts Adorno to term the whole the false. In the end, however, the totality's unattainability provokes self-destructive violence: If one cannot have everything, one would rather have nothing. Whence the Spenglerian dreams of apocalypse in Weimar cinema.

One of the most potent images of the totality in that cinema is that of the crowd. The themes of occult power and mass manipulation in Lang's silent films permit him a considerable degree of self-reflexivity in his twenties work, for as director he too employs the "magic" of film to transform one object into another – superimpositions and dissolves perform alchemy – and to stage-manage enormous crowds. If the protagonists of Lang's American films – which are far more conceptual in tone, as if wishing to chasten an excessive past indulgence of the eye at the expense of the mind, as if the removal of Von Harbou's fevered messianism had left Lang a mere technician, a newspaper reader – often seem to be hollow men, it is because the crowd they once spoke for as ventriloquist's dummies has evaporated. Lang left his audience behind in Germany: The American films often feel like plays staged in a deserted theater. Broken off from the crowd and its frenzy, the Lang protagonist is no longer fully animated. This renunciation was surely a long time coming, the culmination of a series of losses – including that of his wife – that began with his loss of an eye while filming *Dr. Mabuse*. The image of Lang with his monocle deserves to be as well-known a metaphor for the director's identification with the camera eye as the photograph of James Stewart pointing his lens at the opposite apartment in *Rear Window*. It is poignant that the dream of possessing many eyes should be associated with Lang's return to the Mabuse figure in his last film (*The Thousand Eyes of Dr. Mabuse* [*Die Tausend Augen des Dr. Mabuse*]). The threatened status of the eye is the source of the dream's power. Lang's wearing of a monocle is surely related to his obsession with single circles at the center of the image: with the view through the gunsight or down the empty tunnel in *Man Hunt*, with the empty plate on the table in *M*, with the circles that surround the robot Maria during the process of her animation in *Metropolis*, and so on. The empty circles are dead eyes: images of a feared blindness.

It has often been remarked that whereas in the films of Jean Renoir the frame is as

ists, eager to save Lang from the stigma of responsibility by lodging it with Von Harbou – a move made easier by the sexism of the early sixties auteurists – the divorce was present in the films long before it occurred in fact. Although one would not wish to see Von Harbou elevated into a second Riefenstahl – one is enough! – she ought not to shoulder the blame alone. The question of the degree of opprobrium each of the begetters of *Metropolis* ought to bear is indeed a vexed one. Sentimental and ideologically confused though it may be, it can hardly be seen as proto-Nazi, except in the sense that its effort to fuse opposites matches that of National Socialism; and Von Harbou's screenplay was far from being simply the shapeless mass of loose ends we know and perversely love.

A knowledge of Von Harbou's novel – which was coeval with the film* – allows one to project an original film that made somewhat more discursive sense. The father–son rivalry over Maria was part of an Oedipal contention for the mother and wife, Hel, whom Maria resembled. Their resemblance suggests that Hel's premature death had left the issue of ownership unresolved and still festering. When we see the angelic Maria preaching patience to the workers assembled in the catacombs, she appears before a jumble of diagonally arranged crosses. The diagonals are typically expressionist, of course, but the multiplicity of the crosses – in addition to suggesting a future form of religion that is a variant on the present one, which persists into the future as the repressed embodiment of the good – turns the catacombs into a stylized graveyard. Maria thus becomes Hel resurrected. And if Maria is the mother reborn, then Freder's strange knickerbocker garb

open as the river that beguiles him that of Lang is "closed." Hence in *M* the camera is often as immobile as the hidden murderer himself, who fears to stir: The frequent shots of empty spaces recall what Noël Burch has termed the "pillow-shots" of Ozu. The immobile camera plays dead – plays at being an early silent camera, in fact, as simultaneously the drifting sounds of off-screen songs, whistles, or shouts underscore its status as a self-conscious *sound* film. The circles that recur throughout the film justify the periodic immobility through the specter of totalization they summon up. To become fixated upon the circles, however, is to enter the position of the child murderer, to enter the maelstrom of obsession designated – as Kracauer rightly observed – by the spiral in the shop window. (The ruinousness of the spiral is underlined by the down-pointing arrow alongside it, which thrusts sexually.) In this window the untouchability of one's reflection reveals the unattainability of one's ego-ideal. As in Hitchcock's *Vertigo*, which also makes extensive play with spirals, sexuality is tied to the demise of consciousness in the orgasmic moment: This is why the child murderer can say he only discovers what he has done through reading of it subsequently. The vortex sucks one in by according the real the atemporal fascination of *the symbolic* – an important feature of the first German talkies, which thus bridge the gap between expressionist fantasy and the realism of the New Objectivity.
* Lotte Eisner notes (*Fritz Lang,* p. 90) that the novel was "possibly written before or during the shooting." It is also possible, of course, to read it as Von Harbou's effort to set the record straight by presenting her own preferred form of the narrative. At this late stage, when none of the figures concerned is available for interview, its temporal relation to the film is impossible to determine.

becomes explicable: It shows that he is still a child where she is concerned. Maria's preeminence is recognized only in the depths of society, that is, in the basement of the Fredersen consciousness. Freder's father Joh has the cold gaze that denies sexuality as it identifies with the law, and is generally termed "castrating"; his right hand tucked into his jacket suggests Frederick the Great or Napoleon, the strong independent leader.* The adoration extended to a girl named Maria, who stands before a multitude of candles that have a votive appearance, indicates the power wielded over the German Protestant imagination by the repressed image of the maternal Catholic religion, together with the fear that its return would mean an apocalypse in the present. (A psychoanalysis of Lang himself might wish at this point to emphasize his background in an Austria in which Catholicism was predominant; his arrival in Berlin matched that of Hitler, and may have been one reason why the latter was so taken with *Metropolis*; in each case coming to Berlin to achieve success may have involved a repression of Austrian predilections, whose possible pathological consequences could only be escaped as Lang escaped them, by superimposing upon the repression of the Austrian a repression of the Germanic in general – through departure for the United States.) In the midst of the incense of expressionizing crypto-Catholicism, Freder – who removes his headgear before Maria – is the son crucified for his effort to seduce the mother away from God the Father. Descending into the depths, he is like Christ harrowing Hell, though his is the inferno of his own desire; his spread-eagled arms on Gyorgy's machine are those of the Crucifixion; and "Father, father, I did not know that ten hours can be torture" clearly echoes Christ's death cry. If Protestantism is indeed linked to the work ethic, it is hardly surprising that Mariolatry should be rediscovered by a son whose only labor is his leisure.

The theatrical pain Freder suffers had of course become a cliché by the time of *Metropolis*. Originally it belonged to the expressionist problematic of the difficulty of individuation and of managing overmastering desire – essentially a desire to escape a world of destructive technology through return to the womb; behind all expressionism lies Wagner. Expressionist desire reaches febrilely for an astrally unattainable *Du* (Thou). In Freder's case, the Thou of the dead mother is resurrected in Maria; Von Harbou's decadent expressionism translates

---

* The concealed hand also relates him, of course, to Rothwang. (If technology is the extended arm of humanity, in Rothwang's case it extends *into* humanity, eating it away.) It is almost as if Joh is hiding his loss of a hand – sacrificed, in a sense, to his "right-hand man" Rothwang. The image is also a dreamlike pun upon the capital–labor relationship: The "hired hands" are hidden underground, and Fredersen may think he has them "in his pocket," but they are in fact recalcitrant to control. The right hand of the ruler does not know what the left hand of his subjects is doing.

unfulfillable wish into actuality. Expressionist language was a primal scream at one's isolated entry into this fierce world, whose hostility was not existentially given (not solely explicable in psychoanalytic terms), but was temporally localized as the German fathers' hatred of the sons they were to despatch to the trenches of World War I. Hence the film's allusions to Moloch are linked to the expressionist theme of child sacrifice (the danger the flood poses to the children). Maria's statement that "These are your brothers" shows Freder he is not in fact "the only son," as Von Harbou calls him; collective drama and family drama fuse, trivializing the former.

The Moloch that consumes the children is also the city itself – the Berlin that swallowed up so many peasants and others driven or drawn there by economic necessity. The jagged cityscape of *Metropolis* does not promise a new world – its meaning is the reverse of the Manhattan skyline that is said to have inspired Lang – but a consolidation of the power of the father. It is a power with which Lang identifies more than did Von Harbou: Where her religious allusions indicate a wish to flee into the timeless, Lang is fascinated by the overpowering spectacle of the modern sublime. The implicit power worship of much of his twenties work may further explain the appeal of *Metropolis* to the eighties, with its fetishization of the computer as a mode of access to total systems.

Where all power lies in the hands of the father, the son's identity is perilously brittle: Freder Fredersen is a helpless stammer repeating the name of the father. The father has power to steal identity, to create doubles. His son's name defines Freder as merely his father's replicant: Its echo of the nomenclature of Norse saga shows that the novelty of the future has been mortgaged to the patriarchal order that preys vampirically upon it. Fortunately, however, the father's power is itself dual in nature, despite the dwarfing of the cathedral that corresponds to the repression of the maternal in the name of a unitary male rule. Fredersen himself has a double in Rothwang, and between them the doubling passes out of control to create chaos. For who is really brain here and who hand? Rothwang is Joh Fredersen's right-hand man, and yet is ironically lacking one hand; and as mad scientist he is identified with the – albeit fevered – brain. Joh for his part may be the brain of Metropolis – and may also "lack a hand," since one often sees him with it tucked away in his coat – but his scheme for the rationalization of labor unleashes irrational disaster. The doubling stops only when a third term, Freder himself, is inserted between hand and brain. The feminization of Freder allows the patriarchal order to appropriate through him the female element it represses. For all the ostensible recognition of the power of the female, all we see in the final image are three *men*. (One may wonder under what pressure Von Harbou modified the ending of her novel, which shows Joh visiting his mother, a wise old woman figure, instead.) There is a sense nevertheless in which the mediator is not so much Freder as the robot, a blank sign that can be exchanged for a multiplicity of other signs; the most valuable one is Maria, and Joh determines that the android be given her features; she is most valuable as the double of Hel.

In Von Harbou's novel, there are in fact two robots: Freder is shown at the outset as the creator and owner of a machine that loves him jealously; he thus doubles Rothwang. The novel, indeed, is a labyrinth of doubles: Its true translation into the visual would have been bewildering in the extreme, for the fact that everyone is related to Joh Fredersen means that Freder's brothers are indistinguishable from him. One may read this as the fascist ideal of national unity intensified to the point at which it recognizes its own nightmarishness.* The robot links the crowd and the individual: It has the anonymity of the shuffling workers it is intended to replace, but it is also singular. The robot parodies the expressionist hero, both hyperanimated into superhumanity and drained into a mere personification by an Idea; it has the blank eyes of fanaticism. If the brusque gestures of the expressionist actor respond to electroshocks administered by the father, then the robot is the hero in his final stage of development, fully lobotomized, impervious to pain. This is the living death endured by Freder's brothers and lying in wait for Freder himself: the skull intercut with the image of the false Maria, leering lasciviously, that plagues him in his delirium.

The expressionist double is the individual who is one person in him/herself and another when in the crowd, borne along by a mob that externalizes repressed rebellious instincts. It is the doubling of rationality by myth described in Adorno's analysis of the archaic bedrock of apparent enlightenment: Joh Fredersen's planned rationalization of work by replacing the slaves with robots backfires into near-apocalypse, for his own reason has capitulated to myth in projecting onto the blank screen of the robot's face the countenance of the dead, unattainable Hel. Since Hel ruled the underworld in the Norse mythology echoed so assiduously by Von Harbou, it is appropriate that the reincarnation of the mother-wife be found in the lower depths. Below the weight of patriarchal oppression – one remembers the notoriously underprivileged status of German women – below the phallic assertiveness of the skyscrapers, the image of the feminine beckons. It has been repressed, of course, to allow the work ethic to tap the force of libido. In this sense Joh Fredersen is as much the slave of his enter-

* For Von Harbou the nightmare may be industrial male, not organic female, reproduction; Maria doubles Hel benevolently, and it is only the patriarchal doubling of Maria through the robot that renders the feminine fatal.

prise as are the automated blocks of workers. Hence the emergence of the false Maria, both hyperworker and sex doll, culminates in her erotic display to crowds she renders orgiastic. She triggers the release of normally sublimated libido; the flood is, as it were, a tremendous ejaculation from the skyscrapers. The determining force of archaic images is further apparent in the improbable medieval thatched cottage Rothwang inhabits beneath the vaulting skyscrapers. It is typical of the film's repression of some of the feminist elements in Von Harbou's novel that the architectural rival to the skyscrapers should not be the cathedral where Hel was wont to worship but the dwelling of a male. The pentangle on the door of Rothwang's house is a parapraxis, a blurred double of the Star of David: Momentarily, the film conjures up the specter of the Jewish mastermind of conspiracies, with the robot Maria a second Golem, death on her forehead.* In Von Harbou's novel the father–son rivalry over Maria echoes a youthful rivalry between Joh Fredersen and Rothwang for the love of Hel. Here, as elsewhere, the work's doubling mechanisms serve compensatory ends: Having lost the real Hel, Rothwang seeks to reanimate her. In Lang's film he seeks power over Maria through the persecutory flashlight that resembles a pointing camera. In an interesting self-referential touch that signals the depth of Lang's identification with the Mabuse-like scientific hero-villain, the grand unveiling of the false Maria resembles that of *Metropolis* itself, a prestige project whose opening night was attended by cabinet ministers and other dignitaries. Another moment of self-reference is also worth noting: As Maria recounts her version of the story of the tower of Babel, we see a group of men sitting around a tower, thereby revealing how the illusion of Lang's own metropolis was achieved – through the use of models. (And Eisner notes a parallel between the sobriety of Lang's office and that of Fredersen.)

The fascination and incoherence of *Metropolis* derive in part from its superimposition of a form of early twentieth-century feminism upon the characteristic sexual ideology of the late nineteenth century. Victorian sexual ideology – embodied in much of the work of Freud – requires a male quest for "a degraded erotic object."[26] In *Metropolis* this form of eros undergoes splitting and disavowal: The son is assigned a girl from the lower depths, but the degradation with which she is traditionally associated is dispelled by placing her sexualized double in the arms of the father. Since Maria is the double of Hel, this duplica-

---

* The pentangle is linked to Solomon in occult tradition; in her novel Von Harbou terms it "the seal of Solomon." Since the scenario hinges on the disparity between a father's values and those of his son, it is worth recalling that in the David–Solomon relationship the son rejected the father's values. In the Bible this rejection is presented negatively, as the cause of the disintegration of the kingdom of Israel. The loss of cohesion is perhaps anticipated in the fact that the pentangle has one less arm than the Star of David.

tion serves to cleanse the mother of contamination by the primal scene. The primal scene is disavowed, stripped of its primal quality by its staging, long after the mother's death, between the father and the erotically charged robot. Sexuality is denied by its separation from humanity – and so in essence the film endorses the "sublimation," that is, perversion, of eros into the work instinct. If the topography of the Madonna/whore split would lead one to expect to encounter an idealized Maria in society's upper reaches and an eroticized one in its lower depths, both the real and the false Maria are uncanny in their mobility. The slippage has been initiated by the mother's death, which has translated the ideal into the depths – the grave, Hel's natural abode. The crosses behind Maria suggest the neglected graveyard in which Freder seeks the repressed, forgotten maternal element. The true Maria's miraculous appearance in the upper world renews the crisis of the mother's death and activates the whole work. Meanwhile the false Maria is omnipresent, fomenting working-class frenzy one moment and inciting upper-class men in the Yoshiwara brothel the next. Maria in her guise of Madonna draws a working class unsexed by the machines that drain their libidinal energy; as mechanical whore, she represents the sexuality invested in the machine – Moloch as an enormous, full-breasted robot – and the possibility that its withdrawal from the work process will issue in chaos. The text seeks to persuade the working class to continue to invest its sexuality in the machine, for the release of libido would not generate more offspring but would in fact kill the children one already has. But although *Metropolis* concurs with Victorian ideology in opposing the vamp to the Madonna and mother, their dangerous resemblance shows that ideology to be on the verge of collapse. What makes the work finally regressive is its ultimate determination to distinguish between the two: Freder is there less as mediator than as the authority instinctively able to distinguish between the apparently identical. It is this ability that lends him his authority and legitimates his succession. His urge to distinguish between the two seemingly identical Marias is reinforced by the threat hanging over his own identity, as his name verges upon collapse into the-Name-of-the-Father. The watery imagery that accompanies the city's near apocalypse suggests the birth of the hero; in traversing it, Freder is born existentially into a status that is achieved rather than merely ascribed. As the robot dissolves into flame before the assembled crowd, its baptism of fire puts to death the alternative possibility of a female authority. It is no wonder the true Maria melts into the background on the cathedral steps: The feminine has been put in its proper place. The triple feminine – Maria, Hel, and the robot – gives way to a masculine trinity of father, son, and labor.

    *Metropolis* is a film of obsessive cross-cutting. Images of Freder scouring the cathedral for Maria alternate with shots of her trapped in Rothwang's house. (Only an altercation between Rothwang and his master – not shown in the extant versions – allows her to escape.) As Fredersen consults with Rothwang we see images of young Freder venturing into the catacombs. The double scenes correspond to the polarization of society. The mediator, however, is not Freder but the film itself, as it neatly ties together the oppositions out of which it arises and voices the desire for a unity of different people and places via Freder's point-of-view shots of distant scenes (Maria in Yoshiwara).

If expressionism is shot through with images of revolt against the father, *Metropolis* both unmasks the paternal order and consolidates it. This duality may be the fruit of its double authorship: Where Von Harbou's material is expressionizing, Lang's style is eclectic to the point of opportunism. The film bridges expressionism and National Socialism, linked to both but of neither camp. Son may revolt against father, and the latter's irrationality may be revealed by the near apocalypse he brings upon people who are in fact his sons, but in the end reconciliation prevails. And yet its very absurdity intimates the falsity of a resolution that is merely a wish fulfillment. The father having become white-haired overnight, the son can bide his time in the knowledge that mortality will not long delay his assumption of power. Labor and capital shake hands under the son's benevolent gaze. The instant whitening of the father's hair is the younger generation's successful revenge for its own suffering. It is the revenge fantasy whose contribution to the evolution of National Socialism Alexander and Margarethe Mitscherlich have described. If Fredersen's will to destroy his own people anticipates the Hitler of 1945, the manner of his son's assumption of power uncannily resembles that of the Nazi dictator: each subordinates himself to a father figure (Joh Fredersen, Hindenberg) who has in fact been reduced to a mere figurehead. The son's near annihilation during the Oedipal struggle is redefined retrospectively as the rite of passage necessary to determine his fitness to rule. The ending relegates Oedipal rivalry to the past; there are now only brothers, ready to unite perhaps for the conflict against the real enemies who lie without.

*The destroyer goddess:* Kriemhilds Rache

At the beginning of this essay I made fleeting mention of *Kriemhild's Revenge* (*Kriemhilds Rache*), to which I would like to return now. For although it was made immediately before *Metropolis*, it is appropriate to consider it after that film: Kriemhild can be viewed as a fusion of the two Marias, her visage a feeling mask, her body stiffened by passion to the hardness of the robot's, her gaze both awesome and ap-

palling. If the film's narrative pacing is epic in the sense in which
Auerbach wrote of Homer – the retarding element introducing past episodes one savors, rather than awaiting their end with the impatient
split attention that constitutes suspense – then this is because the
whole work unfolds under the aegis of the flashback. The second part of
*The Nibelungen* displays a realism and despair that burns off the airy
magicality of much of *Siegfried*. We are in a fallen world; there is no
suspense, for one has no desire to return from the past, which one
views with the inward gaze of which Kriemhild's closed or narrowed
eyes and agonized expression are the ciphers. The present world de-
cays when the sustaining image of the past itself crumbles from
within: When, in the midst of the film's final flashback, the blossoming
tree alongside Siegfried becomes a skull, and the allegorical world of
death is shown to have been ever-present. The tree's transformation
into a skull lifts the mask from Kriemhild's masklike face – eyes alone
burning at its center – to reveal her inner condition: 'My heart died
with my husband,' we are told at the end. Kriemhild is the military
Melencolia. If in *Kriemhilds Rache* – as many critics have noted – the
characters are less completely integrated into ornamental structures,[27]
this is because they are ready to generate such structures by themselves: All are *soldiers awaiting mobilization,* grouping for the final
battle of the *Götterdämmerung*. This is most stunningly and chillingly
the case when Rudiger enters the hall the Burgundians are defending
against the chaotic assaults of the Huns: The donning of armor turns
him into an honorary Burgundian – in terms of the film's subterranean
ideology, an honorary *German* – capable of mounting a more impressive challenge than the pitiably ragged and reptilian Huns. Canetti
would surely align Kriemhild's melancholia with that of the German
whose army was disbanded at Versailles; writing of the August of
1914 as "the period in which National Socialism was begotten," he remarks that for Hitler this was the "decisive experience, the one moment at which he himself honestly became part of a crowd. He never
forgot it and his whole subsequent career was devoted to the re-creation of this moment, but *from outside.* Germany was to be again as it
was then, conscious of its military striking power and exulting and
united in it." Hence to the postwar German, "the prohibition of the
army was like the prohibition of religion."[28] Kriemhild's impassive direction of waves of ineffectual Huns against the treacherous Hagen
surely helped provide the self-image Hitler was to adopt in his final
days, projecting himself as the leader frustrated by the weakness of a
German people he was finally to disown. The symbolic source of this
weakness can be located in the effects of the inflation of the twenties, of
which the loss of the treasure to Hagen is a coded image. Canetti
notes that treasure functions as a crowd symbol; in "men who live for

their money alone, treasure takes the place of the human crowd," thus "they are the successors of the mythical monsters who existed solely to guard, watch and cherish some treasure."[29] Consequently, Kriemhild's effort to slay Hagen replays Siegfried's conquest of the dragon. Her inability to recover the treasure corresponds to the final ineffectuality of the crowd she dispatches against Hagen – as if she lacked the resources adequately to arm them; in the end she kills him herself. Loss of the treasure renders Kriemhild as it were the impoverished widow of the Great War, sold into slavery. Her stiff mien breathes stoical endurance, playing dead until the time comes for the exaction of revenge. Foreshadowing of the Hitler of the last days, war widow, military Madonna: The figure of Kriemhild is heavily overdetermined. As the leader deprived of an army, her femininity is the result of that loss.

If Kriemhild can be described as inhuman by her brothers, it is because her life is allegorical: The death's-head stands for humanity's reduction to a single quality, revenge – monomania cauterizing the complexity of the fully human. It is this that renders her a religious image of stunning authority, the rays of power's sun focused on a single point as mere mortals shuffle all around her. Attila throws his cloak on the puddle before her, but she does not even deign to step upon it: She remains concentratedly immobile. Beside her even the fearsome king of the Huns becomes like a jester or even pet ape, his woebegone expressions anticipating King Kong. The gaze trained on a point in the distance belongs to a face that is a mask. It places the film under the sign of conclusion: "Once the mask is in position there can be no more *beginnings*," as "all transformation becomes difficult and, in the end, impossible";[30] even the emergence of a child in whom Siegfried seems to be reborn does not bind Kriemhild in love to Attila. He is merely the instrument of her revenge, paradoxically the most sympathetic figure in the film. Kriemhild's upright separation renders her the spiritualized essence of power: "Particularly impressive is a man who stands isolated by himself, facing many others, but somehow detached from them. It is as though he, in his single person, *stood for* them all."[31] In *Kriemhild's Revenge* Lang's static compositions become images of death, his circles signs of closure, his heroine the Medusa. (An image, perhaps, of the wife one has to divorce?)

## Lulu, Lola, and male masochism

In Weimar cinema, as in the philosophy of Nietzsche, a woman's power leads a man to reach for his whip and then for his knife. The impressiveness and threat of the greatest femmes fatales of the period – the Lulu of Louise Brooks and Dietrich's Lola Lola – derive from their "foreign" status. Brooks was an American, Lulu a class invader, and Dietrich foreign in one sense to Von Sternberg – she was a non-Austrian – and another to Unrat – Lola is of another class – and she was shortly to leave for Hollywood. The link between the two figures is cemented by Pabst's original intention of filming Heinrich Mann's novel after *Pandora's Box* (*Die Büchse der Pandora*), presumably with Brooks as Lola Lola. In a patriarchal Germany still smarting with the memory of a lost war and the diktat of Versailles, the femme fatale's linkage with the foreign allows her to function as a scapegoat, suffering in the place of invulnerable, victorious strangers.* Such women are all the more fearsome for representing a modernity identified with Americanism. This aspect of German ideology lives on in *Heimat* and the films of Wenders. Proscription of female sexuality allows sexual energy to return in "sublimated" – that is, perverted – form in the leader worship of the thirties. The extent to which the sexual field per se is identified with the foreign – as if German men lost the war through whoring with strange women – can be seen in the pairing of the American actress's Lulu with the foreign murderer Jack the Ripper. The male masochism of these films is that of a self-consciously disadvantaged Germany: Since the German male is no match for a Lulu, a foreigner is hired to assassinate her. As another does the dirty work, the German retains clean hands, disavowing his actions in line with the ideology that rendered *Faust* a congenial tract for the times. One does not see the evil one's double commits with his back turned. Indeed, one can pretend that the turned back does not belong to one's double at all but to another person, withholding something one desires, such as "a place in the sun." The turned back also belongs to the *Wunschbild* of the departing foreigner. To stare at another's back is to depersonalize him in order to render him interchangeable with everyone else. The obsession with the turned back thus legitimates *Gleichschaltung*: The person whose face one cannot see becomes all persons, a total and totalitarian image. The project of *Gleichschaltung* may even be seen to be present in embryo in the German grammar that so often defines woman as neuter in order to neutralize her (*das Mädchen, das Weib*). Neutralized, she becomes the excluded third. (Is this the source of Dietrich's androgyny?) The erasure of difference banishes the femininity men identify with compunction; it is part of the preparations for genocide.

*Lulu, Jack the Ripper, and the turned back*

Many backs are turned to us in *Pandora's Box*. They usually belong to burly, heavy-jowled men, each a *bête humaine*, a miser clutching his

---

* The femme fatale's allegiance to a foreign power is most patent in the myth of Mata Hari. Dietrich's X 27 in *Dishonored*.

hoard of selfhood and refusing us a glimpse. The recurrent shots of
turned backs in Pabst's film serve to enhance the realism, the Balzacian busyness of the world as a stock exchange of flesh, for which he
was famous. The figures seem to have been caught spontaneously
rather than posed for the camera. They stand for the indifference of the
world that turns its back on one, the indifference Lulu suffered in her
childhood spent in cabarets and cafés. Lulu's seductive arts have the
purpose of turning toward her men who would instinctively turn away
– men from a higher class. One does not marry such girls, Dr. Schoen
tells his son Alwa, and yet he himself does so, his death indicating
the price one pays for life with a femme fatale. Such girls are suitable
only for sowing wild oats. Schoen cannot see that Lulu's fatal arts are
simply an extension of the neglected child's importunity; whence her
innocence. When Alwa turns his face from Lulu after his father's death
and presents his back instead, she approaches him from behind and
coaxes him to turn round.

One of the main things the turned back hides is the image of death,
the unity of eros and thanatos. When Dr. Schoen is shot, we see only
the smoke rising from the pistol held between him and Lulu; we do
not see her pull the trigger, and the imperfect view we have – a sign of
the camera's deep investment in protecting her image – invites us to
give her the benefit of the doubt. Similarly, when Lulu herself is killed
by Jack the Ripper – who has earlier been shown from behind, hands
hidden from her as he drops the knife he holds in reserve for murder,
eschewing its use in her case because she has beckoned him in even
though she knows him to be penniless – we see only *his* back and the
death spasm of her hands. In each case Lulu faces the camera but another man occupies the place opposite her, into which the male spectator would like to insert himself. We are happy at the death of Dr.
Schoen, which unblocks the view to Lulu, removing the paternal principle that prohibits her image. Jack the Ripper is summoned by the
text to avenge Dr. Schoen's death, to reassert through his knife the
primitive male sexuality the femme fatale threatens. It takes a myth to
kill a myth: No ordinary bourgeois male could kill Lulu. In killing her
the Ripper enforces the bourgeois law of possession, ensuring that no
man will possess her after him. He embodies the violence bourgeois
patriarchy can no longer afford to sublimate. And if – as Thomas Elsaesser has argued* – he represents Alwa's double, he does so as his

* Elsaesser writes that Alwa disappears into the fog at the film's end "having found his
sexual salvation from ambivalence." The ambivalence surely persists, albeit repressed
through the splitting that separates Alwa from the Ripper. Moreover, it is surprising that
Elsaesser should refer to "salvation" without mentioning the Salvation Army band: In
following it, Alwa follows the girl who could offer the Ripper no more than mistletoe –
not the kiss that might wake him from his pathology. It is of course Lulu, the sexual
reiteration of the Salvation Army girl, who proffers the mirage of escape through free

active counterpart, the displaced executor of belated filial revenge: Laertes to Alwa's Hamlet. His escape is the sheathing of a dagger for possible reuse. It can be argued however that Dr. Schoen is a far better candidate for the Ripper's double: It is Schoen who fragments Lulu's body, as if chopping it up by his presence; we twice see her lying on a couch, once in her apartment, once backstage, bisected by his burly form – and on the second occasion the fragmentation is emphasized by Pabst's cuts between Lulu's heaving back and neck, and her kicking feet. It is of course Schoen who takes the revolver and presses her to kill herself. Nevertheless, Elsaesser's point has some validity. The London sequence, which begins transgressively with a close-up of *a character we do not know* walking toward the camera, is bounded by Jack's meeting with the Salvation Army band and Alwa trailing in its wake, as if the Ripper were his unconscious, followed into the mist. The Ripper may be read as a synthesis of father and son – the return within the son of the repressed father. Thus where Elsaesser talks of the unity within the Ripper of Alwa's tenderness and sadism, I would be more inclined to see a movement *from* tenderness *to* sadism in the murder sequence: From Alwa to the father, who returns in fantasy to restore to Lulu the death she misdirected to him. Schoen's brooding is the paralysis by imploding desires that finally *explodes*: He is the work's most clearly expressionist character. The shooting of the murder from behind the Ripper echoes the presentation of Schoen's death. This perspective – like that of all the other turned-back scenes – provokes speculation, compelling the viewer to employ the imagination: It is a device often used by Henry James, similarly intrigued by turned backs, to activate fantasy. (Thus James can be both knowingly Balzacian and a frustrated, speculative outsider.) It is this solicitation of fantasy that gives Pabst's work its haunting edge: Alongside the knowingness, there is always unknowing. In the end, that unknowing envelops the image: The smoke that arose from the revolver between Lulu and Schoen becomes the mist into which Alwa disconsolately disappears.

Lulu is stabbed in the back. The moment mirrors appear in the film, so does death, as Cocteau's *Orphée* would lead one to suspect. Lulu's death need not be read as an allegorical reference to the mode of German defeat in World War I, but rather indicates that the space behind one is dangerous, the realm of the unforeseen. Alwa is caught cheating at cards by a man standing behind him; Lulu is killed from behind; even Jack is a victim of the unseen, the *unconscious:* The knife with

love, without monetary or marital strings. In discarding his knife, Jack seeks to repress the self; it returns as the knife does, with magical fatalism. Profoundly pessimistic, the film shows the futility of the Ripper's effort to transcend a pathology that is part of the innermost weave of his being.[32]

which he kills Lulu is her accidentally glimpsed bread knife, not his habitual weapon. The unseen area behind one is dangerous because of the triangularity of Oedipal relationships: It is not enough to consider the person before one, for there is always another lurking behind – one's fate, the director with the camera. The mirror need not mean death, however; it can be used to see what lies behind one. A triangular relationship becomes safe when one steps in front of the mirror, which enables one to occupy two of the points of the triangle oneself, to monitor the approach from behind of the third party who has been redefined as a *second* party. Lulu is often shown in front of mirrors: After all she is Woman, a display object ever-mirrored in the camera eye – and so the turned backs of the men also indicate that Pabst's camera is not interested in *them*. In his other films of the twenties Pabst demonstrates a liking for mirrors that goes beyond their conventional uses for compositional balance. Instead, Pabst employs them to unsettle one's sense of space and reality, as at the beginning of *The Love of Jeanne Ney*. At the end of *Pandora's Box,* however, the London garret that is the final refuge of Lulu, Alwa, and Schigolch is so impoverished that it contains no full-length mirror, that appurtenance of a bourgeois world Lulu has now left behind. (In a sense no mirror is necessary because the new triangle is free of rivalry: Schigolch poses no threat to Alwa.) Lulu is thus unable to see Jack the Ripper reach behind her for the knife that is the sole reflecting (fetishized) object in the room. Loss of the mirror is the prelude to the death of "the feminine" – the camera loses interest in the woman who ceases to be a carefully maintained display object. And there is another reason why the disappearance of the mirror should herald Lulu's death: Her name itself, in its repetitiveness, is a structure of self-mirroring, an image of narcissism. And yet the Ripper is also her double, the murderous mirror-inversion of her benign eros. If there are no mirrors in the room in which the double appears, it is because he himself is the mirror, as described by Cocteau: the door through which death comes. Throughout the film, Lulu, with her free-floating and freely bestowed eros, is the third element that introduces movement and narrative into the stasis of binary relations, the disturbing excess on which narrative feeds. The substitution of Jack the Ripper for Lulu, rendered possible by the fact each is beyond the Law, reduces the triangle to a homogenized, all-male steady state, in which nothing novel – no family romance – can occur (cf. the triangle of males at the end of *Metropolis*). Fog obscures the object of desire, the female already eclipsed in the moment of Jack's frenzied gaze at the knife, which means more to him than Lulu. It becomes her glittering prize.

   In the introduction to this essay I suggested that Lulu may be read as an embodiment of the lure of America, which is both a place of wild open spaces ("nature," the Kansas from which Louise Brooks hailed) and city jungle ("culture"). The common denominator is the foreign: The femininity Freud termed a dark continent becomes another continent indeed. Lulu's lack of interiority in the film – often criticized and attributed to the silent cinema's inevitable shedding of Wedekind's all-important dialogue – is in fact part of an argument that the expressionist obsession with interior–exterior relations – with the obstacles to expression, the repression that causes its return as monstrosity – is a purely male pathology, which she blithely bypasses.* But if Louise Brooks's Lulu radiates innocence – her face at times very gamine – Wedekind's is far more ambiguous. It can be argued that in Pabst's film the aura of sexual ambiguity that hovers over Wedekind's Lulu is transferred to the cinematic apparatus itself, whose sexuality (as I argue below in relation to *The Blue Angel*, and as Elsaesser suggests) is of necessity fundamentally ambiguous, for its audience is unknown to it, unsexed. If Lulu is often described as childlike, her innocence is the infant's polymorphous perversity. The devastating impact of her slim waifishness embodies Pabst's critique of the nineteenth-century weakness for the child-bride, a motif alive and well in early cinema's melodrama. Both active and passive, her regressiveness fuses the sexes. In deriding Geschwitz's lesbianism as a failure of sexual definition, Lulu distances herself from her own inadequate double. Geschwitz's failure permits Wedekind to argue that she is his true tragic heroine. The argument is more than a means of fending off immorality charges by stressing the moralism of his play's documentation of lesbian despair, for it recognizes Geschwitz's status as more human than Lulu, whose pure narcissistic desire is beyond tragedy.

Deprived of Wedekind's dialogue, Brooks's Lulu is if anything even less readable, even more abstract, than her stage counterpart. She does indeed frustrate categorization in the manner of the Earth-Spirit that mocked Faust's inability to grasp it. ("Earth-Spirit" is itself a paradoxical term, conjoining the opposites of flesh and spirit.) Where Wedekind's reviewers had accused him of forging a heroine who was an abstraction, silent cinema was able to grant actual being to her while retaining her abstract quality: photography being both registration of, and abstraction from, reality. Spiritualization of flesh is the essence of black-and-white silent film: the body is doubly etherealized by monochrome and silence. Wedekind anticipates a cinematic Lulu by making her a dancer *who never sees the audience* when she performs. Born to enter the cinema, she further foreshadows the most mercurial of fe-

* Elsaesser: "*Pandora's Box* is ... a deconstruction of the pathos of repression/expression. A central complex of German Expressionism is inspected with serene indifference ... " (my ellipses).[33]

male stars – Monroe. The sexual molestation both Brooks and Monroe suffered in childhood (and which Monroe fulsomely mythologized) seems to have caused a radiant fusion of innocence and sexuality: Just as one's sight of old friends meeting may for an instant transport them in one's mind's eye to their ages when they first met, so an uncanny temporal double exposure presents Brooks and Monroe simultaneously as child and adult, in a spellbinding quicksilver shimmering of innocence and experience. Lulu's demand that Schwarz portray her with parted lips foreshadows Monroe's rhetoric of sensuality. Moreover, if one accepts Mailer's linkage of Marilyn's narcissism to institutionalization – in prison Lulu pounces delightedly on the dustpan that becomes an impromptu mirror – Pabst's subsequent *Diary of a Lost Girl* becomes as it were an apocryphal version of Lulu's adolescence. Pastless, the all-American is as enigmatic as it is fresh; Lulu sometimes terms Schigolch her father, but he denies this, and her background shifts as often as her name. If it is piquant to envisage a Lulu played by Monroe, one should remember that such a version would probably have unraveled in farce. In dreaming of an encounter with a sex maniac, Lulu fantasizes the early death that will set the seal on her stardom: The dream is a suicide received passively, as dreams always are, for the goddess is slaughtered by Fate, not herself. The Ripper's triumph is illusory, for his appearance was solicited by her desire. Brooks herself may be seen to have done likewise, self-destructiveness in life protecting her screen persona from visible decline. As Pabst once predicted, her life became a replay of Lulu's.

The turned backs that provide the leitmotif of *Pandora's Box* punctuate it with ciphers of something hidden, which is perhaps the mystery of Lulu herself: Like the box of Pandora, they are doors that ask to be opened. Indeed, each opening of a door in the film reiterates the opening of Pandora's box, revealing something deeply hurtful to the onlooker – usually a scene suggesting Lulu's treachery. It is apparent that the film's end is near when the urge to look behind doors is quenched as Alwa and Schigolch shut the door on Lulu and Jack. As they do so, the triangle – the film's fundamental model of relationship – dissolves. Only isolation remains.

Lulu's death is ambiguous: Her dream of death at the hands of a sex maniac allows males to justify her fate as less a comeuppance than what she in fact wanted – Casti-Piani's philosophy in Wedekind's *Death and the Devil*. It is surely significant that the Ripper's appearance should herald the end of another famous Weimar film, Paul Leni's *Waxworks* (*Das Wachsfigurenkabinett*). Leni's film shows a young writer who earns money from the owner of a collection of fairground waxworks by devising stories centered on the principal exhibits: Harun al-Rashid, Ivan the Terrible, and Jack the Ripper. The young man's stories also seek to woo the proprietor's daughter, who stands at his elbow throughout. As the film proceeds, the mood of the stories darkens. The first two concern tyrants who satisfy their desires surreptitiously: The Caliph dons a disguise to visit the baker's wife of whose beauty his vizier has informed him, while Ivan pays nocturnal visits to the palace cellars to savor the agonies of dying prisoners. The nearer we come to the present – to enunciation of the desire for the daughter animating the stories – the more disturbed the texture of the narration becomes. As this happens the female figures in the stories grow more closely akin to the desired daughter: Time runs backward from the safe, completed fantasy of the first story, which shows us a young woman already married, to the less complete fantasy of the middle one, depicting a wedding, to the end, when the unmarried daughter becomes available to the poet whose conscious work to win her has to be completed by dream work. (She has to prove herself the ideal both of the conscious and the unconscious minds.) Before this can happen, however, he must fall asleep, tired by his labors, after the second story.

Why does the film end with Jack the Ripper? The attempt to represent him explodes the narrative into a delirium of superimposition. His proximity to the present and uncertain identity are not the only elements sabotaging the effort to represent him. Unlike the protagonists of the two previous stories, he is not a tyrant figure, and so cannot be the object of Oedipal attack. The poet opposed to father figures is in fact the Ripper's double, and the Ripper his own disavowed self. In the first two stories the double had been the exclusive property of the father figure: A wax image in the Caliph's bed had preserved him from the baker's assassination attempt, while in the second story the bride's father was shot by conspirators who took him for the Czar who had exchanged clothes with him. The Ripper's appearance allows censored desire to speak; his pursuit throws the poet and the daughter into each other's arms. The contemporaneity of the Ripper's story causes it to flow into the poet's own. Period trappings are discarded, the previous stories' girls unmasked as substitutes for the daughter. This collapse of a reality overrun by desire had already been anticipated in the final madness of Ivan the Terrible, who believed he had been poisoned and sought to prolong his life by repeatedly inverting an hourglass to gain more time. Like *Caligari*, the film accelerates as its close approaches. The two wheels that appeared at the start of the film – the carousel and the Big Dipper – recur, interlocking cogs driving forward the mechanism of this film about drives. Such acceleration near the end is typical of stories that employ suspense, and is powered by an apocalyptic longing for revelation. This final episode is so short that it feels as if the half-hour duration that has been the norm for the stories up to this point has folded back upon itself to create a continual superimposition. The camouflage that has been a leitmotif of the first two stories begins to break down as the superimposition renders every image semitransparent. In *The Man without Qualities* Robert Musil was to speak of the sex murderer Moosbrugger as the collective dream of the epoch. In using the name "Moosbrugger" Musil shares the epoch's inability to speak directly the name of its desire; it can only do so – as it does in *Waxworks* – with the indirection of a dream. The true name of that desire – the desire of a patriarchal eros driven to crazed stabbing to reassert itself against the growth in feminine power symbolized by Lulu, an eros fearful of absorption by the female – was of course none other than Jack the Ripper.

## The cold heaven of the Blue Angel: Dietrich, masochism, and identification

*The Blue Angel* may be the name of the inn where Professor Immanuel Rath first catches sight of Lola Lola, but many of us – having heard the legend of Dietrich's seductive power, but not yet having seen the film – must once have imagined the blue angel to be Marlene herself. We may have recalled Rilke's interest in the blue-period Picasso and have parodied the opening lines of the "Duino Elegies": "every blue angel is terrible." The blue angel was the pop version of the melancholy Angelus Novus of Walter Benjamin. Like Benjamin's angel, it had a satanic majesty, thriving on ruin. One may have heard of blue devils, but who ever heard of a blue angel? Venus in furs, well-protected against the cold to which she will expose *you*, was clearly the devil as woman. If she appeared later as a *scarlet* empress, her ability to stand at both ends of the spectrum merely indicated her omnipresence as the devil who hath power to assume a pleasing – color-coded – shape.* There is however a more mundane reason why the blue angel is cold: The first time Dietrich's image appears, upon a wall-poster, a cleaning lady drenches it with a bucket of water. She is clearly trying to douse a flame while there is still time. Her envious attack on the image of the cabaret star is then echoed as Rath's landlady

---

* Of all actresses, Dietrich is surely the aptest candidate for incarnation of Hélène Cixous's "Medusa who laughs." But whereas the traditional Medusa surely laughed upon successful immobilization of her viewer, Marlene laughs as she freezes. The two moments' superimposition engenders *fascination:* the fascination of film's dual temporality, the irrevocable disjunction between the times of creation and exhibition. Thus Medusa laughs, as it were, because she need no longer squander her power upon a viewer forever alienated from the actual time and place of her being; the inherent distance of cinema preserves her from Perseus forever. The laughing Medusa is a Rapunzel safely ensconced in the tower whose possession symbolizes her expropriation of male sexuality: One will wait in vain for the helpful descent of her hair. (The androgynous beauty has cut it off.)

burns his dead canary – a songbird that will be reincarnated in his life as Lola Lola herself, feathers strategically decking her thighs in her postcard, the link with birds a delusive pointer to freedom. The opening of the film is highly compressed, for the caged bird also anticipates what Rath will become, a rooster crowing on cue as Lola betrays him – as surely singed by her flame as the canary was incinerated by the landlady.

The death of the canary is followed by the appearance of an egg on Rath's plate: the illogical sequence suggesting the imminence of something strange, as well as the reincarnation mentioned above. At this stage Rath may still be flanked by a globe, metaphorically on top of the world, but his larger globe is already rivaled by the smaller one of the egg from which the new songbird will emerge. Ruefully he remarks that his canary had not sung much of late. One can guess why: Song is now only to be found elsewhere, outside his bachelor haven, being heard again through a school window as a pupil peruses Lola's card. Although the singing is not Lola's, it is identified with her, for the card's confiscation is followed by the slamming shut of the window to keep the danger outside. The song in the streets will become the siren song to be heard at the Blue Angel tavern, and the film is surely punning when, as Rath walks through the foggy harbor streets toward the inn, it places on the sound track sirens anticipating the other siren in whose arms Rath will lose himself like a ship in the mist. Later, after Rath has spent his first night with Lola, we will see a caged bird singing, a reprise of the opening that marks the onset of Rath's decline. He too will sing, unconscious of the bars that surround him. The film is blatantly Freudian, in fact, in its use of repetitions to indicate compulsive behavior: Rath may crow with pleasure when Kiepert extracts eggs from his nose at the wedding feast, but eventually he will do so under duress as Mazeppa and Lola embrace in the wings. There are also repeated images of fog and veils, symbols of Rath's disorientation: He enters the inn through fog, encounters hanging gauze as he steps in – his old inhibitions hanging in shreds – and later makes his stage entry through a set of transparent drapes. The film presents repetition as something one vows not to do, but ends up doing all the same: Compulsive habits cannot be kicked. Rath swears he will never accompany the touring troupe to his old town, but Lola says he must. It is she, in fact, who is identified with the principle of repetition. After all, her name is itself based on repetition (a double repetition, for good measure, with two Ls in each name), as if flirting with the recognition that she is a reincarnation – to put it less politely, a ripoff – of Wedekind's Lulu. Early on in the film she states that all men come back to her. Just before Rath proposes to her, she tells him not to mourn her departure: She'll be back again. When she does return to Rath's home town, it is dressed in furs: No longer a bird but something more dangerous, she has become completely the woman at the heart of the masochist's fantasy. "Beware of blond women," she warns, knowing it is now too late for such an admonition to be heeded. It is fitting that some versions of the film should end with the repetition of "Ich bin von Kopf zu Fuss auf Liebe eingestellt." As she sings that she understands love "und sonst gar nichts" there is a bitter rasp to the "gar nichts." It is a sign of the nihilism that underlies love's reduction to sensuality, woman's transformation into a demonic sex doll that can be "eingestellt" (adjusted) to the eros whose other name is thanatos.

Of Emil Jannings, who plays the part of Rath, Von Sternberg was to assert in his preface to the script that "to be humiliated was for him ecstasy."[34] Irrespective of the biographical truth or falsity of the statement, it does seem to be true of the screen persona Jannings had developed in *Variety (Variété)*, *The Last Laugh (Der letze Mann)*, and *The Blue Angel*; it usefully gives the lie to the all-too-prevalent description of masochism as an essentially feminine trait. It is hardly surprising that a consideration of film should allow one to separate masochism from femininity, since the implicit spectator of film clearly exhibits a strong masochistic tendency, regardless of actual gender. Film, with its cuts, shocks, and interruptions of images upon which one would wish to dwell – for sexual, epistemological, or aesthetic reasons – always involves an element of frustration, with one acquiescent in the knowledge that this is the price to be paid for spectacle, the precondition of the experience of the Sublime. The cinematic experience attempts to accommodate the subject positions acquired through socialization by the two sexes – the passive/masochistic and the active/sadistic – in order to generate a total, ambisexual pleasure. (It is this fundamental ambisexuality that determines the modernism of the cinematic apparatus.) This totality of pleasure is bound in with film's totalitarian ambitions to assume everyone into its structures. Thus although the cut is inflicted upon one's eye and expectations, it also expresses one's impatient feeling that the world deserves to be disposed of – it has already been disposed of through one's departure from it into the darkened auditorium. This Mephistophelian form of sadism, which believes that everything that exists also merits destruction, is fundamental to film, providing a deep structure that underlies the more superficial male sadism of the look castigated by Laura Mulvey. The project of film is to fuse sadism and masochism, to derive pleasure from negativity. Its project is thus that of modernity itself, as exemplified in the poetry of Baudelaire. Just as Rath is also Unrat, the pleasure of identification in film is also *un*pleasure. This is true of *all* films, a taste for which is acquired through an initial surmounting of displeasure, like the taste for cigarettes. (Is this one reason why so many of the key cinematic stars have smoked?)*

For Laura Mulvey, the pleasure spectators derive from film is linked to voyeurism. *The Blue Angel*, however, warns against the fate of the voyeur. (The mainstream film depicts in lurid tones the consequences of attending the nonmainstream form of film known as pornography.) It is the fate of the voyeur (Rath) to be destroyed by the exhibitionist whose own pathology could not bloom fully without his complicity. The key scene in this argument is the one in which Rath glances up the spiral staircase after the departing Lola, and she drops her panties on his shoulder. Rath's fixation on the panties would be read by Freud as that of the fetishist who seeks to deny what their removal revealed. As Peter Baxter notes, utilizing Freud, the fetish aids disavowal of the female otherness the male usually reads as a threat to his own posses-sion of the phallus.[36] When Rath, mockingly rebaptized August – he is august no longer – has a bird conjured from under his hat – the impli-cation being that he does not know what is going on inside him, and that what he wanted to "keep under his hat" has become a public dis-grace – Kiepert comments that "his" August no longer has a bird. Bax-ter's linkage of this to the German double entendre of *vögeln*, which is virtually identical with the plural form of bird (*vögel*) and a vulgarism for intercourse,[37] is justified when a member of the audience, as if re-acting to the sexual undertones of Kiepert's remark, terms the incident a *Schweinerei* ("a swinish egg," to continue the pun). Note that the German for eggs, *Eier*, is also a term for the testicles.

*The Blue Angel* justifies stopping at the stage of fetishism by the necessity to avoid the dire fate of the voyeur. To show what Rath sees when he looks up the staircase would expose us to the petrifying mask of Medusa, identified with the female genitalia by Freud. The arrest of scopophilia is a preventive one that preserves the film from X-rating. The film lacks the tough-mindedness of pornography, a form for men who boast of their ability to confront fearlessly the final revelation of the striptease. Pornography can in fact be interpreted as part of a male repetition compulsion that provides training for viewing the terrifying sight of female genital otherness; it defines the female as immobile victim in order to dispel the male's fear of his inability to fill a hole

---

* Cf. T. W. Adorno on the film hero's violence as a transformation of violence he has suffered:

If all pleasure has, preserved within it, earlier pain, then here pain, as pride in bearing it, is raised directly, untransformed, as a stereotype, to pleasure: unlike wine, each glass of whisky, each inhalation of cigar smoke, still recalls the repugnance that it cost the organism to become attuned to such strong stimuli, and this alone is registered as plea-sure. He-men are thus, in their own constitution, what film-plots usually present them to be. masochists.[35]

that might otherwise become a gap at the center of the universe. It was doubtless a recognition of the dangers the exhibitionist poses to the voyeur that dictated the changes in the presentation of Dietrich that took place between *The Blue Angel* and Sternberg's Hollywood films. The dress cut away to reveal the famous radiant naked thighs and suggest the female lack of a penis virtually disappears. Dietrich is now less the exterminating angel of a near-blue movie than a fetish whose thighs are most often covered with male trousers or flounces. (The audacity of the trousers is pseudodaring, a dilution of the more dangerous *Blue Angel* image.)

The (female) exhibitionist destroys the (male) voyeur in this film by absorbing him. Indeed, Rath's identity is subject to dispersal from several sides. As he identifies with Lola Lola, the power of his position as male flows into her. The often-noted androgyny of the Dietrich image (although not present in this film) stems from her partial masculinization by the men she has consumed. "It took more than one man to change my name to Shanghai Lily" is not simply a marvelous piece of camp, but also an explanation of the genesis of Dietrich's persona in the Von Sternberg films. She has swallowed up many a man.

As Rath glances up the stairwell at Lola his look establishes her as both available and nonavailable; he can see all, but he cannot touch. In fact seeing precludes touching – this is very cinematic – for the observer is paralyzed by what he sees. Unable to see what Rath sees, we may envy him his scopophiliac privilege, and then be vengefully glad of his comeuppance. Rath's helplessness is reinforced by the collapse of the virgin–whore antithesis that is one of the keystones of his nineteenth-century ideology: The woman is above one, and yet one can see her genitalia; she is both idealized and degraded. Rath's obsession with "higher things" seduces him to look up, not realizing that in this case higher is lower, an overturning of height–depth relations that presages his own fall. It may be that the image Rath sees is unrepresentable because the unity of opposites causes them to cancel one another out.

Having left Lola's room, panties stuffed in his pockets by his students, the disavowed executors of his own infantile desires, Rath then has to return to retrieve his hat. Baxter notes that:

when Rath chooses a top hat to replace that slouch brim he had misplaced, he chooses a hat identical to Kiepert's. In this way he begins a process of encroachment on Kiepert's domain which ends in his own public humiliation at the Blue Angel, where the terrifying spectacle of castration is acted out.[38]

"Encroachment" is perhaps the wrong word here, since what occurs is a draining away of Rath's identity. The film argues that to identify with someone else is to surrender one's power to him: Kiepert becomes the Caligari to Rath's Cesare. Between them, Lola and Kiepert absorb Rath: If one half of one's identity belongs to a mother figure who can recall it at will, the other half is the property of a father who can do likewise. As Rath's power is transferred to them, he becomes his own negation, Unrat. Like Lola Lola he has two names but in his case the doubling does not reinforce identity but erode it. Whereas her second name reiterates her first one, Rath's inverts and replaces his. Rath becomes mere waste, the by-product of the process of his own disassembly. Although Baxter terms Rath "the figure of the father,"[39] the stress ought to be on the word "figure," for Rath is defined as the sham father – akin in this respect to Kiepert. Like his students, the film teases out the meaning of his bachelorhood, which is sexual inadequacy. (The marriage to Lola yields no children.) Rath's status as the actor of authority naturally impels him toward the stage. As he is drawn into the marginal world of the footloose strolling player, his decline strikingly resembles that of Gustav von Aschenbach in one of the best-known works of Heinrich Mann's brother Thomas. Rath can even be read as a parody of Aschenbach. Like Aschenbach, Rath is at home neither in art nor bourgeois normality; he is positioned between the prestidigitator Kiepert and the true authority of the headmaster. Hence although it is possible to see the film as Baxter does, as a network of images in "simultaneous relationship" to one another,[40] one ought not to overlook the changes effected by the temporal unfolding of the narration. For the film plots Rath's passage from a stable social position to a labile one, from the headmaster to Kiepert. The final loss of the former position is marked when the headmaster enters to restore order among the pupils mocking Rath, using to them words that had previously been Rath's own: "I'll speak to you later." Thereafter Rath's marginality will deepen. Caught between artistic and bourgeois orders, he will suffer the fate of the excluded third. The work may indict a society in which attempted departure from one's position in the hierarchy is rewarded with destruction, but it sees in that destruction appropriate vengeance.

The double exclusion Rath suffers is the quintessence of the masochistic fantasy. Here it becomes possible to read Dietrich's androgyny in her work with Sternberg in terms of the Freudian theory that discerns the figure of the father secreted within the domineering female form of the masochistic scenario – the suppression of the "true" referent representing a repression of homosexuality. Recently however Gilles Deleuze has objected to this Freudian theory, arguing that the oral mother in masochism is no mere substitute for the father but has primary status.* Neither Freud nor Deleuze considers the possibility

* Following Deleuze's threefold classification of the mother figures in Masoch's work

that Venus in furs constitutes a *fusion* of the paternal and maternal images, which has been placed under the aegis of the mother in order to avoid the uncanny image of bisexuality, and because in any case the maternal image was the first to be experienced by the infant. And yet this mingling of matriarchal and patriarchal principles is apparent in Dietrich's name(s): "Dietrich" had been her father's surname, which she had adopted despite her mother's remarriage. In identifying with the-Name-of-the-Father, nevertheless, Dietrich was not identifying with Law but with the polymorphous-perverse, the surname referring in German to a picklock, something used *to enter holes illegally*, rather as Marlene herself – the devil's passkey – picked the lock of Sternberg's marriage. There is a further ambiguity in "Marlene," a telescoping of her actual "Maria Magdalene" that streamlines it in accordance with the logic of exchange in modernity, repressing the past and the Biblical prototype. The taking of this name is a self-birthing that is also equivalent to a loss of virginity, since the part of the name she discards includes "Magd" – "maid" in German, in the double sense of maiden and serving girl: "Marlene" will thus be the insubordinate version of Maria Magdalene, humiliating men rather than herself. In *The Blue Angel* she clearly resembles the oral mother of Masoch's fantasies, cold, maternal, and severe. In terms of the fusion theory proposed above, the coldness and severity that goes against the grain of the maternal are internalized aspects of the father. The fusion is precipitated, I would argue, by the desire to resolve a contradiction. The infant, tormented by the question of which parent it belongs to, resolves the riddle by saying "both." Nevertheless, the torment the question occasioned lives on in the answer; both pain and pleasure (question and answer) coexist. The fantasy of reconciliation, of belonging everywhere, collapses, however, when the image of the sadist becomes separated from that of the oral mother, as Deleuze notes occurs at the end of Sacher-Masoch's *Venus in Furs*.

Deleuze's interpretation of masochism has been used by Gaylyn Studlar as the basis for a thoroughgoing revision of Laura Mulvey's influential proposal that the implicit spectator of film is male and sadistic. Mulvey's examples include the work of Von Sternberg. Studlar objects that Von Sternberg's work in fact delineates a masochistic aesthetic in which

(uterine, Oedipal, and hetaeric), Lola Lola appears most closely akin to the oral mother "who nurtures and brings death" and "has the last word" (Dietrich's song at the end). Nevertheless, she is also assimilable to the Oedipal mother "who becomes linked with the sadistic father as victim or accomplice" (though one may have doubts about the validity of a definition that can bracket victim and accomplice together, that very combination can testify to the ambiguity of Dietrich's persona, the repetitions within Lola Lola's name a sign of her multiple nature).[41]

the female ... is more than the passive object of the male's desire for possession. She is also a figure of identification, the mother of plenitude whose gaze
meets the infant's as it asserts her presence and power. Von Sternberg's
expression of the masochistic aesthetic in film offers a complex image of the
female in which she is the object of the look but also the holder of a "controlling" gaze that turns the male into an object of "to-be-looked-at-ness."*

Surprisingly, Studlar ignores the work that most fully examines the
question of masochism, *The Blue Angel*, an omission that is surely
symptomatic of the Americanocentrism of recent theory. Another shortcoming of Studlar's otherwise salutary attempt to correct what is now
a hegemonic theory in film studies (particularly among feminists) is
its failure to consider the relationship between "the masochistic aesthetic" and the positions of the characters within the films in question.
Is the masochist the male lead, Dietrich, Sternberg himself? Any spectator? All of these at all times, or only some of them some of the time?
No clear answer is offered, as Studlar situates her argument at a level
of generalization that allows little of interest to be said about the specifics of the text.

In *The Blue Angel* the masochist is, first and foremost, Rath himself; the positions of Von Sternberg and the implicit spectator are different, as I will seek to show at the end of this essay. Rath's entry into
relationships is blocked by the phantasm of the oral mother. As he is
absorbed by Lola and Kiepert, the by-product that is also garbage (Unrat) is the image of the clown. The clown is an insistent presence in
the early stages of the film, watching from without as the scenes between Rath and Lola are played out. Later on, he and Rath will coa-
lesce. The two are identified as the objects of Lola's look as she sings
in the white top hat that indicates her appropriation, and transposition into a different key, of Rath's authority. (An anchor at the top of
the image of the stage suggests that by now he is hooked.) As Lola
casts a glance at the clown, the camera then follows *his* look upward
toward the simpering Rath in the gallery. Rath, for his part, then looks
down at the statue of a naked woman in the bottom left-hand corner of
the screen. Intriguingly and enigmatically the moment hints at the imminent coalescence of Rath with the clown and imitates on the level of
camera movement the displacements that riddle the narrative. It seems
to dramatize Rath's delusion that his obsession with Lola is the disin-
terested concern for art of traditional aesthetics. Kiepert, however, will

---

* The awkward term "to-be-looked-at-ness" is derived from Laura Mulvey's famous "Visual Pleasure and Narrative Cinema," which is anthologized in the same volume as the
Studlar (pp. 303–15). Mulvey describes Von Sternberg's films as characterized by "fetishistic scopophilia" (p. 311) – a phrase whose application to *The Blue Angel* becomes
problematic if the reader accepts my argument that the film halts at the stage of fetishism so as to avert the dangers attendant upon scopophilia.[42]

deride his application of the term "Künstlerin" to her. In transforming the cabaret performer into a naked statue, he is both elevating her to the status of "art" and placing her beneath himself (cf. the confusion of questions of height and depth in his look up the staircase); it is profoundly ironic that he should disrobe her in his mind's eye as she is in fact destroying *him*. The camera movement underlines his mistaken belief that he can enter her sphere without losing his connection with "culture." At the same time it indicates that Lola and the statue are both pornographic images – the one "low," down on the stage, the other relatively "high," attached to the balcony. At this point in the film, Rath and the clown may still be separate – the former, occupying the higher position, is still the man who has nothing to fear from "die Obrigkeiten," even when he is down in the cellar – but by its end they will have fused. When Kiepert harangues Rath for his attack on Lola and Mazeppa, the scene's lighting lends prominence to the clown's collar.

The loss of status Rath undergoes was of course a widely documented fear among the newly created petite bourgeoisie of the late Weimar Republic – particularly among the *Angestellten* studied in their different ways by Kafka and Kracauer. All the same, one may wish to examine more closely how the Wilhelmine world of Heinrich Mann's novel relates to the late twenties, the period of the film's release. Could it be that the film's relentlessly archaic look functions as an alibi, enabling a current social pathology to be expounded on the assumption that it be disavowed through representation as a thing of the past? Is the projection of past into present, and vice versa, a device to demonstrate the stultifying changelessness of the bourgeois world? (With the consequence that the terms of Freudian analysis, derived from the treatment of the neuroses of the Viennese haute bourgeoisie, could be applied profitably to this particular film of the late twenties, made in Berlin and set in a harbor town and thus embracing the whole German-speaking area?) Is the mockery of Rath a celebration of the installation of modernity? And does the demonstration of changelessness – if this is what the text achieves – stabilize the present by broadening its temporal base, or undermine it by showing its continuity with the nightmares of the past?

Insofar as the film uses the contrasting acting styles of Jannings and Dietrich, and the contrasting meanings of the two main protagonists, to dramatize an encounter between the subject of nineteenth-century culture and the twentieth-century art form of film – together with the confusions generated by the application of the term "art" to film – it is about the masochism of a Germany that both fears to be outstripped by history and is terrified of a modernity it identifies with the principle of destruction. (There is a sense in which Marlene is the

Mephistopheles to Jannings's Faust.) If the reactions of the late Weimar audience can be ascertained, they must have fused delight that the fate feared for oneself had been deflected onto a substitute, self-congratulation at having adhered to the bourgeois path, Oedipal rejoicing in the abasement of the father figure, and the prurience that seeks a glimpse of what lies beyond the suffocatingly straight and narrow. The Jannings scenario of humiliation drew on the earlier structure of feeling of expressionism, employing the isolated exemplary sufferer of the *Stationendrama,* and on that of the emergent realist cinema of the late twenties. In both Murnau's *Last Laugh* and *The Blue Angel* Jannings embodies degraded authority. *The Last Laugh* shows that "Kleider machen Leute" and that without his uniform the hotel porter is merely a lamentable parody of Lear. Murnau's film, however, is closer in time and mood to the fissured aesthetic of the expressionist films, with their switchback movements between reality and fantasy – reflecting, perhaps, the German effort to wake up before "Deutschland erwache!" became the watchword of a false awakening.* But the film's romance ending is the sort of dénouement the porter himself might have dreamed; and so in the end, as it identifies with his point of view – an identification adumbrated in the drunken camera sequence – the film is compelled to submit to the ideology it had criticized up to this point. *The Blue Angel,* by way of contrast, offers no such fantasy relief. *Its* escape is one into the brittle glamour of Von Sternberg's American work, which begins as Dietrich sings at the end. Filmed several years after Murnau's work, it arises in a Germany where there is no longer any possibility of distinguishing between reality and fantasy, of aligning each with different stylistic registers between which it is possible to choose. Dreams and delusions are becoming realities. Thus *The Blue Angel* is both realistic and fantastic *throughout,* a consummate

---

* In *Deutschland erwache!* (1968), Erwin Leiser notes the ironically sleep-inducing characteristic of the slogan. A similarly lulling pseudoawakening marks the transition from expressionism to realism, begun by the *Neue Sachlickeit* and cemented by the coming of sound. *The Blue Angel* is a fantasy that masks its own fantastic nature (it will even claim to be part of the here-and-now, Lola's calendar telling us it is 1929). Awakening as in fact a fall into a deeper dream had occurred at the end of *Caligari:* Kracauer could have read the shift as an allegory of the movement of the era as a whole. The effect of pseudoawakening depends heavily on the use of music (think of how the final repetition of Lola's song coldly dismisses Rath's tragedy – a mockery set up as Sternberg permits tragedy to slide into the pathetic in the schoolroom death scene): The individual is absorbed into the collectivity. The musical was indeed to be a key Nazi genre, with Germans in Polish jails singing yearningly of the *Heimat,* or cockpitted Stuka pilots chorusing lustily. How far the Imaginary of the left overlapped with the sadistic one of the right is apparent in the contemporaneity of Brecht's play *Threepenny Opera (Die Dreigroschenoper)* and *The Blue Angel.* Brecht's lawsuit against Pabst over the *Dreigroschenoper* film disavows his own bad conscience (as does his film treatment of *Die Dreigroschenoper,* which tinkers frantically with the stage-hit's cynicism in an effort to redirect that work's uncontrollable, Golem-like progress).

example of the success of secondary revision. This is why so many of its "realistic" details do double duty as compressed signifiers of the traumas psychoanalysis takes as its object. The only mode of escape from this fantastic reality is departure from the land in which it has come to prevail: a land in which the schoolmaster's humiliation – as Kracauer noted[43] – is a dress rehearsal for that of the Jews, those other figures identified with learning. (Indeed, Rath's mannerisms in the film were derived from those of Von Sternberg's Hebrew teacher in Vienna.) In picking Rath out with a torch on his tragic return to his old schoolroom, the film itself identifies with the Lola who had first picked him out in the crowd in her search for "einen richtigen Mann." (A psychoanalysis of Heinrich Mann himself might discern here envy of, and revenge for, the limelight enjoyed by the *other* Mann, Thomas.)

And so Sternberg himself identifies with the *ressentiment* the crowd feels for the culture personified in the man whose egghead means he must be without *Eier* (testicles) elsewhere. Yet Von Sternberg's denigration of Rath is also a salutary mockery of German "Kultur" that facilitates his emigration to, and assimilation in, the United States. For if Von Sternberg himself was partly complicitous with a protofascist ideology, his Viennese *Schadenfreude* over the humiliation of the German furnished him with the ironic detachment that enabled him to leave the German-speaking area, relocating Dietrich in a series of fetishistic slide shows from which the tragic ghost of German masochism, represented by Jannings, and the diabolic mutuality of exhibitionist and voyeur, have been banished.

## Concluding unscientific postscript on expressionism and silence

Film is the lever of Archimedes, enabling one to dislodge the world and step outside it. Yet the step outside the space of the world is also devastating, akin to Razumov's birth into a silent world during the thunderstorm in Conrad's *Under Western Eyes*, when his eardrums are pierced by a member of the revolutionary cell he has infiltrated. (We are invited to anticipate this disaster by the title's reference to *eyes*, which will henceforth be Razumov's sole means of apprehension of the world.) The devastation the individual's world has suffered is registered in the form of silent film, its figures dumb and jerky, its colors drained. Only gradually did we forget the shock of our alienation from a world transformed into a ruin. Our hearing returned (sound film), grass and flowers sprouted amidst the rubble (color film). The silence of the silent film is thus salutary, reminding us that the modern world was born of catastrophe (of colonialism, industrialism, capitalism), and continues to be experienced as such, as – in that key motif of expressionist films – our machines transport us to realities of which we never dreamed. Such silence may provoke us to attempt to break it: The alternation of silence and scream in expressionism renders the experience of the victim, whose very taciturnity prompts ever more rigorous torture on the rack. Munch's scream is the one men call silence – Razumov's scream as he is precipitated into a world of mere image. That scream may however be the birth cry of the new man as he emerges on the far side of catastrophe. This is the fundamental hope of expressionism.

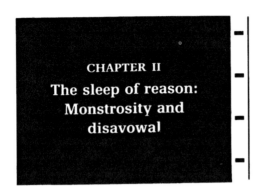

CHAPTER II

# The sleep of reason: Monstrosity and disavowal

## The German, the French, and the monster

Romanticism and expressionism dream of the unseating of a reason they identify with quantification, mechanization, and the tyrannous control of the father. When the reason of the Enlightenment sleeps, it dreams Romanticism; when it wakes, it deems monstrous the events that transpired during its abeyance. The valorization of the ugly and monstrous in Romanticism and expressionism embodies a split consciousness that partially identifies with the instrumental reason against which it is in revolt: These movements may bring into the light the repressed and oppressed of society, their features twisted by furious knowledge of their own marginalization, but inasmuch as the Romantics and expressionists depict such figures as deformed, they identify with the power they oppose, which also apprehends *them* thus. The classic instance is Mary Shelley's *Frankenstein*, split between revolt – the calls of sentiment link one, through pity, even to that which seems most monstrous – and conservatism – the oppressed return as a criminal class whose anonymous disaffection drives the revenge of the monster. Kracauer has discerned the same division within *The Student of Prague* (1913), where it leads naturally to the theme of doubling:

By separating Baldwin [sic] from his reflection and making both face each other, Wegener's film symbolizes a specific kind of split personality. Instead of being unaware of his own duality, the panic-stricken Baldwin realizes that he is in the grip of an antagonist who is nobody but himself. This was an old motif surrounded by a halo of meanings, but was it not also a dreamlike transcription of what the German middle class actually experienced in its relation to the feudal caste running Germany? The opposition of the bourgeoisie to the Imperial regime grew, at times, sufficiently acute to overshadow its hostility to the workers, who shared the general indignation over the semi-absolutist institutions in Prussia, the encroachments of the military set and the foolish doings of the Kaiser. The current phrase, "the two Germanys," applied in particular to the differences between the ruling set and the middle class – differences deeply resented by the latter. Yet notwithstanding this dualism the Imperial government stood for economic and political principles which even the liberals were not unwilling to accept. Face to face with their conscience they had to admit that they identified themselves with the very ruling class they opposed. They represented both Germanys.[1]

The German revolt against reason is in part a nationalistic one against principles identified with French culture: Lessing criticizes the prescriptive use of French neoclassical canons, and Kleist lionizes anti-Napoleonic warriors. When considering the genesis of the idea of the monstrous, it may thus be instructive to review its treatment in one of the most powerful works in the French language, Racine's *Phèdre*, which gives the lie to the stereotypical identification of "Frenchness" and reasonable clarity, and displays an exemplary foreknowledge of the doomed nature of the German quest for an alternative source of clarity in Winckelmann's mirage of classical Greece.

In *Phèdre* even the meter participates in the theme of self-division, each caesura corresponding to the mind's split between a desire that is half aspiration and half engulfment by the vengeful repressed. "Monster" is of course an obsessive keyword in the play: Virtually every character is designated thus at some point. It is shadowed by another word, "incest." If, as Empedokles notes, monsters are born of the attraction of like for like, then anyone who employs the word "monster" is almost compelled to speak of "incest" too. Phèdre terms herself incestuous so as not to have to term herself monstrous. Her self-accusation may seem excessive, for Hippolyte is only her stepson, but its rationale is obvious: It contains her effort to block her aspiration from becoming deed – to divide, as she says, black heart from innocent hands – by designating the deed in terms that ought to render it taboo. This self-splitting makes over the faculty of action to Oenone; thus in denouncing the nurse at the play's end, Phèdre is castigating the projection – the self-alienation into a project – of her darker side. "Monster" is a word that scythes polymorphously through the play, concluding in the deadly irony of the recounted scene in which Hippolyte stands his ground against the monster his father has summoned in order to prove himself the worthy son of that father. The greatest of all monsters, however, is time: Everyone is in the wrong place at the wrong time, pagans condemned for the accident of birth in a pre-Christian era, disguised Christians destroyed by their inability to live by Christ's exacting maxims. The rumors of Thesée's death prompt Phèdre's confession, and his return is equally untimely; Phèdre is on the verge of pleading with Thesée to mollify his wrath against his son when Hippolyte's overheard confession of his love for Aricie dashes her good intentions; and, in the most remarkable instance of this demonism of chronology – surely a reaction to the growing importance of the exact measurement of time in the seventeenth century – she fantasizes a revision of the story of the labyrinth, with Hippolyte replacing Thesée and she herself, Ariadne: She imagines herself as born too early to be paired with her young ideal lover. This premature birth is also a sign of her partial subjugation to the laws of a mythical era. Like her half-brother the Minotaur, Phèdre is bifurcated between the upper and the lower – Helios, from whom she was descended on the maternal side, and her father Minos, who is a judge in the under-world. If Phèdre is famously split between reason and passion, Hippolyte, the fruit of a later age, is all reason with nothing repressed about him; if this renders him a somewhat mechanical figure, it is also the source of his tragic inability to comprehend – to name, to speak of – the thing that horrifies him. Hippolyte's "forbidden love" doubles that of Phèdre ironically, for he can voice his, while hers remains unspeakable. Because he cannot name the horror he confronts – he cannot even hint that Phèdre is a monster, as Aricie does – he is overwhelmed by it on the beach: The father's words have the power of naming he lacks; the father's possession of this power, as it were, deprives him of it. The creature that emerges from the sea is Phèdre herself, doubly transformed: First into the Oenone who leaps into the waves, and then into the monster. No wonder instinct had once prompted Hippolyte to draw his sword in her presence. Ambiguously, the play often rhymes "silence" and "violence." To be silent is to be the cause of violence (Phèdre); to be silent is to be violence's object (Hippolyte). Phèdre's silence is all Oenone requires for successful denunciation of Hippolyte; while the queen's taciturnity is in fact a self-violation, as well as violence against Hippolyte, for it hands over the regal prerogative of action to the servant.

If twelve years of silence followed the writing of *Phèdre* in Racine's career, it is in part the expression of his horror at the collapse of a monarchy that has shown itself incapable of rule – a shocked anticipation of the French Revolution. Racine's play demonstrates that the formality that requires one to be "noble" forces other impulses into an unconscious in which they fester. Many reasons have been advanced for Racine's silence following this play: conversion; the coappointment to the post of Royal Historiographer; knowledge that any successor to *Phèdre* could only be anticlimactic; disillusion over the poor public reception of what he surely knew to be his masterpiece. At its deepest level, however, the silence is that of traumatic waiting for an echo or reply to a blasphemous challenge. *Phèdre* may be able to claim as an alibi that its image of life as an inferno is true only of the pre-Christian world, but its intensity shows it to be no mere academic demonstration that pagans are damned but a monstrous metaphor for Racine's own world. He places it in the ancient world for the self-same reason that Minos lodged his deformed offspring in the heart of the labyrinth. What Racine shows is not pre-Christian humanity but one bifurcated by Christian maximalism: Unable to adhere to the standards Christ propounds, it wars with itself to the point of exhaustion and collapse into suicidal depression. To confess to mortals, one of Racine's confessional sonnets tells us, is to fling one's soul hellward; language itself becomes the labyrinth of Hell. In this context Phèdre's death is Platonic liberation, as the light trapped in her carnal eyes travels back to the Sun, to the point of its ancestral emanation. As it does so, the dark flame of individual love is doused; the flame is no longer the dialectical generator of the darkness that necessitates its own kindling. As the monster of the body is slain, humanity steps out of its labyrinthine cage. Birth was simply entrapment; the monster – be it Phèdre, Frankenstein's creature, or the Job rendered horrible by his affliction – cries out that it would have been better never to have been born. As we, the onlookers, ascribe these words to the monster – as if they were merely the consequence of, or even retribution for, its deformity – we repress our sense of just how normal it is to feel that way.

### King Kong, on screen and off

For Adorno, King Kong is an image of the totalitarian state.[2] He adds: "People prepare themselves for its terrors by familiarizing themselves with gigantic images." Thus, one might conclude, the horror film becomes the essential form of cinema, monstrous content manifesting itself in the monstrous form of the gigantic screen. Upon recently viewing again the 1933 version (which, given the way Kong's breast beating is echoed by the gong that surmounts the gates leading to his domain, could equally well be called *King Gong*), what struck me most was the degree to which it is self-referential – despite the fact that Kong's bisyllabic name and year of release could indeed suggest parallels with Hitler. What matters here is less the plot mechanism that sends a moviemaker to the legendary Skull Island than the way the use of back projection in the scenes of Kong's monumental battles with prehistoric creatures engenders mismatches of perspective that trouble the aesthetic illusion and give us the impression that the characters are walking past *images of monsters* – a second cinema screen inserted into the screen of *King Kong* – rather than monsters themselves. I think one underestimates the sophistication of the thirties audience if one assumes this to be merely a modern critic's reaction to the fabled naïveté of the past. For the disparity between the syncopated stop motion of the animated monsters and the smoothness of the movements wherewith the humans skirt the monsters' battles only accentuates the sense that there is a screen within the screen.*

The consequence is that the film prompts a meditation on what it means to watch violence on a screen: Close up, like the minuscule characters at the screen's edge, who look on with bated breath as monsters' tails lash improbably near to them, and yet distant too – safely screened by the screen.†

The problem the film poses is of course the one of whether or not the screen events can be kept "out there," restricted to the domain of fantasy, or whether the reel can slip into the real.‡ The fantastic image of the great ape becomes real and verifiable through its transportation back to New York; and since, as a film rich in trick effects serves to demonstrate, seeing is not necessarily the same as believing, belief can only be sparked by the actual physical presence of the creature. The fantasy film is well aware of the camera's propensity to lie, for all its monsters are models moved into the separate positions the film joins up to foster the illusion of continuous motion. It thus encounters a problem of legitimation. How is its director (Carl Denham) to prove the real existence of the amazing prodigies that appear on screen? The only solution is to ship them back home in the flesh. And so one enters a realm of rich and polymorphous irony, as the film we are watching, entitled *King Kong*, whose credits have boasted that its cast includes "King Kong, the eighth wonder of the world," shows a crowd of people filing into a cinema in evening dress in order to watch the latest production of the famous filmmaker Carl Denham: a production that is *not* in fact a film but the exhibition of something billed as "King Kong, the eighth wonder of the world" – *in the flesh*.

The interesting thing to note is that throughout the film both we and the protagonists appear to be protected from the monster(s) by the use of projection. For example, when the first monster, apparently a stegosaurus, is shot by a sailor, its tail lashes out in a manner that would flatten him (as he congratulates himself on his aim) if the per-

---

* May not this screen-within-a-screen, a scene of jerky movement, be the *silent* screen so recently displaced by the talkies, of which *King Kong* was one of the first? The jerkiness of the stop motion thus reflecting the irregularity of movement in the silent cinema, as the cranking speed varied?

† If 3-D never caught on, it was surely because it abolished the screening function of the screen, which in this case extends uncannily into the auditorium. A viewer of *The Creature from the Black Lagoon* may feel as if the theater is in fact an aquarium. In 3-D the threat to the audience's powers of distanciation becomes so palpable as to prompt fearful rejection.

‡ It thus becomes possible to add another allegorical reading of the film to the multifarious ones that dot the history of its exegesis: If Kong is the totalitarian state, he is a *German* totalitarian state Americans fear may be coming to their shores.

spective were correctly aligned. The back projection establishes a spatial disparity between the characters' positions and those of the monsters, thereby enhancing the sense that the monsters cannot touch them. And we ourselves are protected by the projector behind us impersonally doubling the mechanisms of our own mental projection of our violent and "subhuman" qualities onto the screen. The screen screens us both from what it represents and from self-knowledge. But again and again the screen collapses: Kong steps out of the screen, out of the back projection that separates him from the helpless human observers, for only thus can his image become truth; he does so either to recapture a Fay Wray laid momentarily to one side, or to menace us, as he menaces the crowd whose disavowed power and childish fury he represents. In saying that the image cannot be tamed, the film also implies that violence cannot be reduced to an image. It will return, with the force of the repressed, overflowing the edge of the screen and inundating the thirties themselves. The frozen image will melt, rupturing the boundary of the frame in a manner that is often seen as the signifier of realism – an event read by Bazin, for instance, as the resurrection from rigor mortis of the posed expressionist actor: The life force it pins down will prove irreducible, much as the force of stylization in expressionism itself gave way to the realism of the *Neue Sachlichkeit* as interwar reality became a cataclysm defying representation.

Whenever this occurs, the film's own existence serves to demonstrate the dangers of physical presence: better by far, it says, to watch a film of King Kong than to see him in the flesh and risk trampling underfoot. (Are these the aesthetics of American isolationism?) Thus the film *King Kong* celebrates, among other things, the demise of the theater: Better the projected phantom menace that allows one the thrill of self-splitting and self-incarnation, in disavowed form, on a screen whose sheer size ministers to the monstrous capacity of one's appetite than the palpably threatening immediate physical presence of the naked ape who stands for the beast in man – as well as being, of course, a demonized image of the black and of the rage of a nature unable to make the evolutionary leap into privileged human status. Such splitting, in dividing the self, enables society to rule over it: The horror film is deeply conformist.

One of the most remarkable features of cinema is its capacity for allowing us to attend scenes of violence and yet ourselves receive no hurt. This characteristic is bound in with the general technological distancing and aestheticization of violence in the modern era. Opening doors to countries and classes we have never entered, cinema satisfies a fantasy of knowledge. And yet the photographic exactitude with which these worlds are rendered does not make them any less fantastic; the bars of melodrama (projection) separate the audience from an actuality of which it is granted only pseudoknowledge – the aesthetic equivalent of the pseudoparticipation offered by democracy.

In this context, the most interesting feature of cinema – and of the other image media of which it is the prototype – is the way it persuades us to think that violence is something "out there," that to represent it is to control it. In doing so, it panders to our wishful thinking, the fantasy of invulnerability through invisible omnipresence. The mere fact of the representation of violence leads us to think we can master it: either through contemplation of its image – often in analytic slow motion, as we step outside time, scientist-gods – or through staging it for the camera under controlled conditions. Our close-up studies of past violence render us strategists who plan for the unpredictable next war by going over the battles of the last one. So whenever we witness violence in our immediate vicinity, we are doubly paralyzed: On the one hand we respond to it as we habitually do to the media – for after all we view far more violence on screens than we ever experience directly – by adopting the position of helpless, irresponsible observer; while on the other we are stunned by the sheer shock of the event's brutality, which eludes the conventions of its mediated (media) representation. A frequent, widespread viewing of violent acts in the image media had seemed to establish them as these events' natural home. (Representation had been a magical means of ridding oneself of them.) Their renewed outbreak indicates that true violence defies representation, shattering the edge of the frame – as does King Kong – with trauma and shock. Violence is like a film image; it always catches one in the dark.

If the iconography of cinema is rich in monsters, this is of course in part an "innocent" consequence of the desire for spectacle, for that which will overwhelm the tedium of one's regimented twentieth-century life: A monster is, after all, something that is *shown* (*monstrum*). There are, however, less innocent aspects of the cinematic projection of monsters. The invisible men who comprise the crowd – shut out by the predetermined rhythms of the film – have become unseen by manifesting themselves elsewhere, transformed, on the screen. Their isolation in the dark has rendered them monstrous – not beasts *or* gods, as Aristotle speculated, but *both*. The role played by cinema in persuading us that the world lies beyond our control is far from neutral in its consequences. The screen itself is, in a sense, the monster that overwhelms us, with the eerie whiteness of the whale. In addition to institutionalizing the mechanisms of projection, the screen provides an alibi for the indulgence of desires under cover of darkness. The process is one of mystified self-knowledge, akin to the one Lady Macbeth invokes in order simultaneously to commit a deed and

have it undone – for it is too monstrous to be done, so steeped in negativity that it must be as it were nonexistent – scarfing Duncan's
murder from conscious awareness: "Come, thick night, / And pall thee
in the dunnest smoke of hell, / That my keen knife see not the wound
it makes."[3] In a marvelous pun, "dunnest" recalls the done/undone
theme. The alibi film provides for its audience is its own objective
form: It preexists, and continues to exist after, its screening. Hence the
monsters it displays appear to have no organic connection with the
audience, which disavows their relationship with its own ideology. Its
actors so much larger than ourselves, film argues that the world is so
much more powerful than we are as to resist all alteration. The form of
the world, like that of the film itself, is closed and predetermined.
Film's mystification involves the casting of a shadow in such a way
that it seems to be far larger – to be other – than the person casting it.
The screen displays a shadow self so magnified that we cannot but
capitulate to its promptings.

## The phallus and the sublime

Linda Williams has suggested "that the power and potency of the
monster body in many classic horror films ... should not be interpreted
as an eruption of the normally repressed animal sexuality of the civi-
lized male (the monster as double for the male viewer and characters
in the film), but as the feared power and potency of a different kind of
sexuality" (my ellipsis)[4] – the sexuality of the female. Williams speaks
of a monster whose difference renders it "remarkably like the woman
in the eyes of the traumatised male."* If this is to be more than feminist special pleading, a desperate effort to project a potential female
spectator into texts that reject and victimize the feminine, chapter and
verse have to be supplied and the working of particular filmic moments analyzed. Williams fails to do so. Only outside the mainstream
of horror films, in *Carrie,* do woman and monster fuse in the image of
the girl dripping with menstrual blood.[†] What that blood signifies
nevertheless has meaning only for a male spectator: the threat of castration. The assimilation of woman to the monster yields an image
both threatening and beguiling, the phallic woman. Classical Freudian

* When the woman catches sight of the monster she screams; and this of course allows
the implicit male viewer both to express and to disavow his own fear. But if Beauty and
Beast always go together, it is surely less because the woman is perceived as monstrous
(according to the stereotypes of classic film, she would be monstrous if she failed to
scream, for her independence would pose a "castrating" threat to the male) than because
the Beast is the mystified image of the Other with whom the hero competes for the trea-
sured girl.[5]
[†] This fusion has been analyzed by a student of mine, Jamine Ackert, in a paper entitled
"Bloody Repression" (unpublished), though without making mention of *Carrie.*

theory posits a male tendency to project the image of the phallic woman in order to assuage castration anxiety: If the woman has a phallus, then so do all human beings, and fears of its loss are unjustified. The image of the phallic woman is, however, far more dialectically charged than the theory allows. She can be seen as the very person who has appropriated (or become) the male's phallus – most blatantly so in the icon of Judith and Holofernes.

The woman with the knife is the most common image of this monster. Its appearance in two early Hitchcock films is worth noting, since to do so is to widen the notion of the horror film to encompass works often located outside its canon. The films in question are *Blackmail* and *A Woman Alone (Sabotage)*; in each case the meaning of the motif is blurred, for the murder of the male is defined as merely accidental. If the death of Stevie in *A Woman Alone* is far more savage than it is in Conrad's *Secret Agent,** this is partly to compensate for the work's muting of Winnie's vengeance upon Verloc – a muffling that is all the more surprising given the cinematic qualities of the scene in Conrad's text: As the ticking reveals itself to be dripping blood, it is easy to imagine a camera prowling the room remorselessly before arriving at the sound's true origin. The meaning of the murder is displaced onto the "Who Killed Cock Robin?" cartoon Winnie watches after Stevie's death: The killing of the cock as the theft of the phallus, perhaps that of Hitchcock himself (known to legend as "Hitch," the fat castrato whose partial loss of name corresponds to loss of the part of his anatomy designated by it). Not until *Psycho* does Hitchcock tackle the meaning of the motif head-on, and even then with a use of monochrome that takes out an insurance policy allowing him to maintain, in case of failure, the work's marginality to his oeuvre. The knife-wielding Norman is his own mother, denying his own sexuality while preserving the phallus by displacing autocastration onto the objects of desire. The knife that slices the girl is a sign both of the erection she has provoked and its impossibility. (Nor-man is no man, impotent.) Thus the image of the woman with a knife is profoundly ambiguous: *both* castrating mother *and* phallic woman, *both* problem *and* solution, the vicious circle generating obsession. The early Hitchcock glides over the image's contradictions by presenting a woman's knife murders as fortuitous: Winnie's killing of Verloc in *A Woman Alone* is as deliberately veiled as the stabbing of Nancy in *Sid and Nancy,* and is utterly devoid of the prolonged horror of the scene in Conrad's novel. The early work uses substitution to enable a sympathetic character to escape scot-free: It is the Bird-man who made the bomb that

---

* The novel (1907), not to be confused with Hitchcock's film, *The Secret Agent* (1936) or Hitchcock's version of the Conrad novel, *A Woman Alone (Sabotage,* 1937).

killed Cock Robin who dies, blowing up both himself and the evidence against Mrs. Verloc, her husband's dead body. In the more tough-minded later films, the chain of substitutions involves a dissolution of identity that places everyone, even the members of the audience, under threat, for the murderer's animus is always misdirected: Hence in *The Birds*, a film that can cause one to fear to step onto a beach, Norman Bates's mother has been generalized into the nature that employs sharp objects in a finally indiscriminate attack – even though it may have begun with beaks prodding Melanie under the remote control of the mother who fears to lose her son to her.*

Thus the fear of the monster evinced by both male and female protagonists involves fear both of repressed male potency and of potency's loss. If the female spectator can be located anywhere in the horror film, it is in the alarm at male violence: an alarm that may drive her out of the cinema, unless she can identify with the aggressor. "The civilizing process" has exacted a disavowal of the phallus (of "the lower" in general), which, metaphorically amputated, forgotten, resentful, be-

---

* The polar opposite of the psychopathology underlying Hitchcock's films is the "identification-unto-death" of extreme male masochism, the most extraordinary example known to me being Shimazu's *Okoto and Sasuke* (1935), based on a novel by Tanizaki. In it Okoto, a girl blinded at the age of nine, is served by the shy, adoring Sasuke, a mere apprentice in her father's house. Because of the class divide – and despite the rumors of carnal relations between the two, and her actual birth of a child – she refuses to marry him. Sasuke's identification with Okoto is adumbrated in the film's early intercutting of images of each playing the samisen. From the very outset Okoto is associated with problems of vision, even before we know of her blindness: Her first "appearance" is tantalizing, merely a hand at the left of the screen, then feet inserted into waiting sandals, before the camera eventually pulls back to take in her full stature. But even the full view tantalizes: Kinuyo Tanaka spends the whole film with her eyes closed. It is this that renders her beauty transcendent. There is also an edge of self-reflexivity here – for the star indeed cannot see us. (In her mother's dreams she opens her eyes, but we never see those dreams.) A dialectic of male powerlessness and power is implied: One's freedom to look does not allow one to touch. When Ritaro, Sasuke's lanky, rich, buffoonish rival, attempts to touch Okoto, he receives a head wound for his pains. Galled, he later burns her face at night, when he can approach her doubly unseen. The male image is split, for Ritaro's act is a diversion and disavowal of the violence Okoto's bullying could provoke in Sasuke (cf. the Alwa–Ripper relationship in *Pandora's Box*, discussed in Chapter I). Waiting for Okoto, shot behind bars, Sasuke resembles the caged larks that appear as of the middle of the film. Okoto fears that Sasuke will see her disfigurement when the bandages are removed, so he blinds himself before this can occur. The destruction of narcissism through identification is dramatized when he gazes at a hand mirror in which her bandaged image appears, followed by her earlier beauty, just before he blinds himself. Although Okoto approves, she cannot be blamed, for we have already seen a servant's needle exert an uncanny attraction upon him (and upon the camera, which dollies down to it) in the scene before her utterance of her vague wish. The moment the needle appears we suspect imminent self-blinding: We are beginning to divine Sasuke's thoughts as he divines Okoto's. Whereas the image of the woman with a knife is a worrying one for most males (as noted above), Sasuke takes the knife from her and applies it to himself, preserving the image of beauty from transience. The final titles note that "he leaped into eternity." It is almost as if such punishment is the just desert of spectators intrepid enough to look on a higher being unable to return the gaze. The viewless realm of the music Okoto has lived for then overwhelms the film.

gins to live a life of its own – that of the unforeseen or uncontrollable erection, the life of *lust*.* The lost phallus is, of course, also the organ the phallic woman surrendered during her unremembered castration. The woman is appalled at the sight of the monster-phallus, for her sublimated lover has shown no sign of possessing one, nor does she recall ever having owned one herself. The man, for his part, is shocked by the menacingly separate identity assumed by the repressed.

To talk of the sublimated lover is to touch on the link between sublimation and the Sublime, a process of exchange and anthropomorphizing projection whereby the male individual makes over aspects of himself – particularly the bodily component he fears may be alienable, the phallus – to nature. Horror deprives one of speech, transforming one into a helpless onlooker; one loses one's speech as one's words undergo translation into *images*. The process is like the dream work that takes "figures of speech" literally, objectifying – but also alienating – language into pictures. The advent of the Sublime often involves such a translation, a displaced phallicism. A good example is the emergence of the second, unseen hill from behind the first during the stolen boat episode in Book 1 of Wordsworth's *Prelude*. The unexpected growth of the second hill corresponds, among other things, to the transformation of the penis during erection; and so the young Wordsworth's futile rowing may stand for a frustrated masturbation, with the interdicting power being that of the monitory parental gaze emitted by what he describes as the "head" of the peak. This second peak is a projection of the superego, the introjected image of the parent animating nature even in the midst of apparent solitude. Similarly, at the end of Conrad's short story "The Secret Sharer" the steady growth in the size of the peak approached by the boat is a moment of the Sublime the captain is able to negotiate by splitting himself and associating his projection, the double Leggatt, with the realm of darkness ("Erebus"): Leggatt, the man hidden below deck like a secret weapon, is detached from the captain in the same way as the pallid hero of the horror film is dissociated from his own aggressive phallicism, from the shadow that alarmingly becomes substance and gets above itself, rising into the solid blackness of the peak. Nevertheless Leggatt, despite his murder of a man, is not seen as a monster: He too is split off from his shadow, in his case the peak, by the story. Thus Conrad's work effects a double repression, first separating the captain from Leggatt, and then Leggatt from the idea of the monstrous or Sublime embodied in the peak. Both Conrad's "Secret Sharer" and Wordsworth's stolen boat episode rationalize their repressions, overlaying

---

* For the relationship between the generalization of desire, mystification, and the growth of monsters, see Pynchon's *Gravity's Rainbow*.

them with an apparent realism that serves to divert attention from the fantastic nature of the events in question: a realism that is metaphorical, both expression and mask. It is the greater degree of compression and displacement in these works that renders them "high" culture – sublimations, the Sublime – whereas a *King Kong* is relegated to the sphere of "low" culture. For the deliberate charting of the space between these extremes, one has to turn to films like Murnau's *Nosferatu* or Dreyer's *Vampyr*, themselves monstrous paradoxes: high-art horror movies.

### Three faces of the Other in the horror film

There is no monster who does not tend to duplicate himself or to "marry" another monster, no double who does not yield a monstrous aspect on closer scrutiny.[6]

René Girard may not have had *Frankenstein* in mind when writing the words that form the epigraph to this section, but their applicability to Mary Shelley's work – and its appropriately deformed Hollywood progeny – is self-evident. In terms of genetics the affinity he posits between the monster and the double can easily be documented: Inbreeding – the excess of sameness found in the double – can result in monstrosity. In the cinema the monster and the double stand at opposite ends of the screen, the monochrome spectrum of the horror film. One can distinguish three shades on this scale:

1. films in which the principle of evil is visible and visibly nonhuman (monster films);
2. ones in which the alien creature is semihuman (*Frankenstein*) or only momentarily reveals his extraterritoriality to the human race (Dracula flashing his teeth); and
3. films in which the monster is visually identical with a human being (where only the mirror of art – *The Picture of Dorian Gray*, for instance – can disclose the truth about him).

Of these three categories 1 and 3 are the extreme cases, and hence more specialized than the middle one.

In the first type of film, the principle of evil has been successfully exteriorized and can easily be combated, usually with the help of high-powered and very tangible weapons. It goes without saying that this is the least sophisticated form of horror film; its capacity to evoke horror depends on its implicit address of a childlike or naive viewer, prone to associate deformity with evil – though *E.T.* may have modified this predisposition slightly. The monsters held at bay in this fashion can be deciphered as embodiments of class, sexual, or social fears; the class and sexual fears are usually linked, for the menace is of a lower class (or species) and is sexually potent. The third category – that in which the monster resembles ourselves – is the most uncanny and genuinely terrifying of the three, so much so that films of this type often employ religious antidotes, deeming mere reason insufficient to distinguish the human from the extrahuman. Here Lucifer comes clad as an angel of light – the devil being the (invisible, anti-)hero of these works. The world they project is appallingly problematic for film; since the evil that racks the world is invisible and resists easy externalization in a form corresponding to its monstrous nature – except in the damage wrought by the unseen spirit – they constitute a limit case of the filmic. Worst of all, the devil may appropriate one's identity – through possession – without one knowing it: The enemy can go to ground within one's own head. The position such films occupy at the border of the filmic renders the theme of possession congenial to directors engaged in testing the boundaries of the visible, such as Dreyer. The only apparent solution to the dilemma of possession is a suicide that would be very much to the taste of the great adversary: He would parachute out of the death-bound body at the last minute, abandoning it to its own fate. Film, with its dependence on the drawing of visible distinctions between the characters, exerts itself to entice evil to manifest itself in the light pouring from the projector, the rationalist light cutting through the darkness. It may see evil embodied in a prominent political figure, a person who is by definition highly "visible" – *The Omen,* for instance, gives the prehistory of the Antichrist's self-manifestation – or it may, as in *The Exorcist,* employ Christianity's images and ritualistic formulae to compel the demon to betray his presence. On glimpsing the cross, the face of the possessed contorts with pain. The religion commonly enlisted here is Catholicism: Both Rome and Hollywood worship images. As an imagistic religion for the huddled, originally unlettered masses, Roman Catholicism is more compatible with film than is Protestantism, with its emphasis on interiority and the word. It is perhaps also of relevance that the original sin that granted the demons a point of entry may be identified with the schism in the Church: The Protestant rebellion can resemble a replay of Lucifer's primal offense. Thus true authority resides with the Church Universal – and, after all, a moviemaker seeking international distribution will wish to appeal to the single most unified religious organization, which means the Catholic Church. In a world given over to demons, holy images are brandished as a last resort; the opportunism of the religious gesture is apparent in *Cat People,* where it is possible for an architect's T-square to serve as a cross.

But because Lucifer may be characterized as the primal actor, an interest in the idea of possession need not entail simpleminded scaremongering but can be a component in a complex self-referentiality. It is thus that it functions in the films of Jacques Rivette, which do not provoke horror in the conventional sense, though they do emanate an aura of tentacular evil. Rivette relates ideas of haunting and posses- sion to an interest in the status of actors and the modern actor's use of improvisation to dispel the danger of succumbing to the alien power of a preordained text (*L'Amour fou*). To live a text is to be possessed, caught up in a circular, endlessly repetitive time – the circling of Claire's tape recorder in *L'Amour fou* – like the denizens of the haunted house in *Celine and Julie Go Boating* (*Céline et Julie vont en bateau*). The ghosts in these haunted houses are never thrown out; rather, they unceremoniously eject unwanted visitors. The indestructi- bility of the haunted house is that of the world as text.

### Invasion of the Body Snatchers

Girard's thesis that the double and the monster are one is strikingly illustrated in one of the finest science fiction (SF) horror films of the fifties, Don Siegel's *Invasion of the Body Snatchers*. Near the begin- ning of his account of the body snatchers' invasion, the film's hero re- marks that at first everything in his home town had seemed the same when he returned to it from a medical convention. The ordinariness below whose surface horror is brewing is of course a standard trope of the science fiction or horror film, but the doctor's remark has another, more alarming meaning: It is not so much that the ordinary world is open to the incursions of evil as that it is already *indistinguishable* from it. The conventional everyday world loses its meaning when it is perceived as a world of doubles: the world of *film itself,* which dou- bles for a stolen or an alienated life. A subterranean self-referentiality thus pervades the film, which depicts the double as the most fearsome of monsters. The double's transformation into monster reflects one's fear of the threat it poses to one's "single state of man." It induces de- spair and the fear unto death, for the Other has already ingested one. To transform the double back into a monster is to retain a residual sense of oneself as *one* self. The film displays a paranoid fear of the unknowing symbolized by sleep – since it is while they sleep that the pods assume the features of the persons in whose vicinity they have been placed. Sleep is clearly a metaphor for the death that precedes transformation. The film's small-town fear of change generates a terror of the religious transformation of death and resurrection. It denounces the doubles born at our death as passionless imposters, not the future form of ideal selfhood. It is the coded revolt against religion that fears to speak its own name.[7]

It is ironically appropriate that a postmodern body culture has itself "snatched" Siegel's film through the pastiche of Phil Kaufman's remake. Kaufman presupposes a viewer with a fairly intimate knowledge both of Siegel's original and of SF in general. It differentiates itself from the 1956 version by its tendency to linger on moments of beauty, which yields a less compact and efficient narrative,* by its pessimism, and by its deliberate address of a self-conscious and increasingly intellectually sophisticated SF community. The things from outer space appear in the very first image in the rudimentary form of webs drifting languidly earthward; their sheer beauty implies a right to exist, which the film frantically countermands once they begin to invade the human body. The Other is tolerated, but only so long as it remains Other: The film is inconsistent, failing to realize that by the paranoid logic of extrapolation – well-known to SF fans – one small change in a system is sufficient to modify it entirely and so menace our position within it. The webs' beauty and seemingly vegetable nature hypnotize the viewer, who becomes easy meat for the carnivorous plant. The film identifies with the alien at first: An early shot through a doorway of a girl talking is clearly not aimed from any protagonist's point-of-view, and so comes to embody the alien within the camera, which then seeks to exorcise it. This shift prepares one for another modification: The female protagonist replaces the male one as the locus of our hopes for survival. Whereas Siegel's film begins with Dr. Miles Bennell running into the road to warn of the pods' spread, and ends with his warning being heeded, Kaufman presents the male protagonist as finally absorbed by the pod people. The possibility that an admonition might be heeded is rejected in the early scene in which Kevin McCarthy – who played Siegel's hero – is killed by a mob in the street. This is partly because the national hierarchy for crisis resolution has broken down: One cannot move from the small town to the higher instance of the state or big city, as does Siegel, for the pods' invasion begins in the city and, what is more, in a city whose denizens' reputation for weirdness (San Francisco) renders the pod people all the more undetectable. Kaufman's sole survivor is Nancy Bellichec, a doubly marginal figure, both woman and SF freak. At first the film defines her reaction to the invasion as female hysteria, at the same time offering the SF aficionado the opportunity to identify with her, since she is knowledgeable about Olaf Stapledon. She is the lone survivor, because an inoculation of SF has prepared her to live among aliens, but also – more disturbingly – because the SF fan is defined as already an alien. Why should the aliens expend effort on taking over someone who is already ''one of them''? The ambiguity of the consolation her survival

---

* The strategy of the remake's self-validation involves a bloating of the original – cf. the *King Kong* remake.

offers is surely deeply problematic to the traditionally *male* addressee of SF.

Kaufman's remake can also be read as the snatching of an SF film by the horror genre. (It can also be argued that only literary SF is able to fend off the possibility of horror of the Other, for the distanced nature of the signs it employs to evoke the aliens provides a protective shield.) Hence one has such elements of the horror vocabulary as the portentous dawdling of the camera, prompting unease about what will come next, or the menacing reverberations of single notes on the sound track. The slackness of the narrative in the film's midsection helps one understand why remakes have been so frequent in recent SF. Quite apart from fanzine nostalgia and a wish to color in the images of the past – either literally, by recasting monochrome in color, or by creating more overpowering and graphic special effects to demonstrate that the SF myth is still at the cutting edge of science – and quite apart from the allusionism of the would-be auteur, there is a perceived need for a strong narrative's support now that the bacilli of sixties art cinema have entered the body of commercial cinema too. Body horror and *Rambo* syndromes inflect the film also, the former generating the scenes in which the pods blubberingly assume the features of hapless nearby sleepers, and the latter prompting Donald Sutherland's single-handed incineration of the pod factory at the end. The horror conventions ultimately override the *Rambo* ones, for the pod distribution network is barely scathed; "Amazing Grace" plays with heavy irony as Sutherland's Matthew watches a ship receive a new consignment. The *Rambo* element in the film is far from being its only reactionary feature: Aesthetically and politically worse still is the transformation of Matthew's girlfriend Elizabeth. Once the pod people have claimed her, she rises up naked from the grass, a pornographic Lilith. The moment is fatally reminiscent of the technologically oriented misogyny of traditional SF, which perceives female sexuality as a predatory menace. Thus Matthew's torching of the pod-production line can be read less as an act of purgation than as a pathological diversion of desire's flame. Here the remake marks a clear regression from Siegel's version.

One way of describing what happens in *Invasion of the Body Snatchers* is to say that vegetables acquire human characteristics. To put the matter thus is to understand the role of projection and anthropomorphization in the creation of monsters; *Invasion of the Body Snatchers* is *King Kong* a step lower on the evolutionary scale. The two are in a sense fused in the lightweight campiness of *The Little Shop of Horrors*, where the plant with which the hero has identified "gets above itself." It becomes violent, with the human violence one has repressed to enter the realm of the vegetable in the first place; with the violence of the human entrapped in the nonhuman; and with the violence of the oppressed black. (The plant's voice belongs to Levi Stubbs of the Four Tops.) The myth of the black's exceptional potency indicates that what the hero Seymour has repressed is, first and foremost, his own sexuality. Designable as a weed, he has identified with the vegetable in order to escape the violence of unrequited desire, only to discover that violence persists, albeit transformed: The violence of self-splitting creates the monstrous double. The desire for Audrey – for whom the plant Audrey II is no adequate substitute – persists. The creation of an alternative Audrey – the process of doubling – diverts desire and renders it metaphorical, that is, *monstrous*. The destruction of the monster – the scapegoat – is one with the destruction/consumption of the film. If a short coda follows its destruction, this is merely a mechanism to repress the identity of the metaphor (work) and the monster. A monster is a metaphor that draws vampirical life from its begetter.

**From *Dracula* to *Nosferatu***

Of the three categories of horror film established earlier in this chapter (see section "Three faces of the other"), the most problematic is the intermediate one of the semihuman monster: the creature whose transformation from double to monster is arrested halfway. It has generated the more complex and abiding myths of horror, for the contradictory nature of the creatures on which it focuses credibly mirrors our own: The Minotaur is Phèdre's half-brother. The monster who yearns for the humanity he finds partly adumbrated in his own form embodies our own longing for self-transcendence. (Following the acceptance of evolutionary theory, he becomes the image of the missing link.) His distorted features could be those of the spastic child many women fear they may give birth to. Indeed, one of the most striking monsters was born in part of a woman's fear of the consequences of pregnancy: Frankenstein's anonymous creature is the offspring of Mary Shelley's anxieties. Mary Shelley's novel, however, offers him the possibility of a coup de grâce denied him by Hollywood, with its concern to maximize the utility of its properties. In so doing, Hollywood shows a shrewd awareness that a monster able to die can never be thoroughly monstrous, completely alienated into the other. (Frankenstein's mortality is surely one cause of Mary Shelley's sympathy for him, though it also reflects the ephemerality of the isolated literary work.) Immortality is the curse that renders one mythical – like the Sibyl who withered endlessly. The mortal who has purloined the gods' immortality is then punished with monstrosity. Thus if immortality is the essential characteristic of the monster, the primal monster of the modern age is surely Dracula, that witness of centuries of human crime and folly.

Bram Stoker's *Dracula* is a cautionary tale for an age tempted by materialism. One may seek, in the absence of the Christian afterlife, an afterlife of the body, but there will be a price to pay: enslavement to the evil that has granted transcendence of the bounds prescribed to mortals. The coffin brimful of Transylvanian soil borne about by Dracula is a tailor-made Hell. A seductive devotee of the flesh – it is hardly surprising that "to vamp" would mean to seduce – Dracula is a materialist. His search for an earthly afterlife entails the overreaching that convention deems the origin of all evil; it founds a world of disorder in which people and things refuse to remain in their places. Dracula is thus also a carrier of the Romantic revolt. The dead do not lie down as they ought to but walk again. Aiming to reestablish the habitual order, the horror work defines the earthly afterlife as a diabolic parody of the true Christian one, the fruit of the devil's activities as *simia dei*. This is, however, far from the only meaning of Stoker's figure, who lives a multiple, mythical life through multivalence. His story also draws on the nineteenth-century discovery, and terror, of catalepsy. The person buried alive rises again in our consciences to exact revenge for the agonies of death within the coffin. In a sense this resurrection expresses the dead's resentment of their forgetting upon earth. The criminality of the mind that wished another person dead, or, lured by modern mobility, abandoned the soil of ancestral interment and ceased to cherish its predecessors' memory, is then projected onto the corpse itself; it is animated by our projected energy (our blood). Its transgression of the bounds of mortality is in fact simply its desire to be remembered; labeling it "criminal" justifies the decision to pierce its heart with a stake. The sweetness of revenge lies in its escalating symmetry, the balance of terror: The vampire has punctured one's throat – a displacement into euphemism of the puncturing of the vagina – so one pierces its heart. The monstrosity of the risen dead is the monstrosity of our own forgetfulness. Their rising is also the return of the repressed sexuality that haunts the cellars of the nineteenth-century imagination. Particularly feared, in a period of growing female liberation, is the sexuality of the women Dracula empowers (his feminine name ending perhaps itself designating a cryptic feminism): As Franco Moretti notes, reading Stoker's work as an allegory of the threat posed to nineteenth-century liberal capitalism by nascent monopolism, Dracula is the future disguised as the past;[8] his future triumph, however, will not be merely economic, but will inaugurate a period of erotic liberation in which the common currency of the word "vamp" will stand as the sign of his victory.

In the myth of the vampire, the fantasy of the afterlife concludes in an afterdeath, the second death that dispels one's fear that the will to immortality in the flesh may doom one to rot in the grave, consciousness intact amid corporeal decay, rather as in the poetry of Emily Dickinson. The vampire myth thus encapsulates the fatal nineteenth-century mixture of idealism and materialism, allowing one to have one's cake and eat it too: to enjoy a bodily afterlife, but then return to the official fold, accepting cleansing death by the stake, one's soul floating finally free of the flesh.

Franco Moretti has argued that, when the image of the vampire enters mass culture, it undergoes a change of sex, becoming masculine rather than feminine (as it had been in the work of Poe or Baudelaire).[9] The change adds a layer of disguise to the original fantasy, in which the mother's vagina dentata bit the infant in revenge for its cannibalization of the breast. But other mechanisms cooperate in the generation of the changed image. Quite apart from the perverse logicality of the notion of the vagina dentata – if it has lips, then surely it ought also to have teeth, an image exploited in pornography – the male vampire whose name has a feminine ending (Dracula) is in fact more unsettling than the female one. Implicit bisexuality renders "him" "his own" double; his is indeed the sex that is not one, overpowering the viewer's mere singularity. This duality reflects the doubts concerning the nature of sexual identity rife in the fin-de-siècle, the period of Stoker's book. The aura of terror surrounding the vampire stems in part from the specter of the dissolution of male identity into a narcissistic primary bisexuality – and of becoming the object of molestation by the aristocrat whose foreignness and ambisexual desire symbolize the perversity of aristocracy in an increasingly democratic society.

Dracula is, of course, without a reflection; this is because he *is* one, the double of Harker. While Harker is staying in Transylvania, Dracula appears in his guest's clothes by night. His lack of a reflection also involves a deliberate rejection of the multiplication of his image that would dissipate its authority. The fact that Jonathan Harker owns a Kodak, with which he takes pictures of the estate whose purchase he is managing for Dracula, indicates the possibility of a different order than that of Dracula. Using his Kodak, with its casual and automatic doubling of reality, Harker de-demonizes the doubling process; similarly, his marriage to Mina Murray demonstrates that it is possible to become "one flesh" with another person without absorbing his identity. Mina then effects Dracula's defeat by seeming to accept him while in fact rejecting him: a double action that replicates, and so cancels, Dracula's own duplicity. As a mistress of shorthand, she has at her fingertips a secret script to match that of Dracula, to trump his ancient writing with writing impregnated with modernity. (The telegram, the phonograph, and the typewriter are all employed by the band of Drac-

ula's foes.) Thus if, as Moretti has argued, Dracula represents a form
of economic modernity, his opponents represent another: that of the
utopian forces of production, set against the evil traditional relations
of production. Harker's transmission of the photographs is part of the
shifting of places that enables Dracula to come to England. Another
name for this shifting is "exchange."

On one level of the book, as Moretti has noted, Dracula – with his
enviable knowledge of English law – is a type of the monopoly capitalist. His movement to England founds the multinational of the undead;
if heaps of gold lie unused around his castle, it is surely because it
has been superseded as a currency. The new universal currency is that
of the blood bank: as it were, the capital Dracula renders *liquid* in order to finance his trip to England, squeezing out the blood orange of
his gold.* Dracula is a harbinger of the breakdown of the sovereign
nation-state; knowing him to be their successor, the representatives of
that state demonize him. The mark with which he stamps each person's throat is as barely perceptible as the watermark in a banknote,
that abstract form of currency that replaces gold. Dracula confuses the
sense of identity by circulating blood, the fundamental carrier of human identity, drawing it all into his central clearinghouse. The fact
that blood can serve as currency indicates how deeply the principle of
exchange has penetrated society, for it runs in the individual's veins.

The vampire's appearance as double is a sign of a struggle *for the
same place* between two world orders. The party that triumphs cements its belief in the worthiness of its own victory by identifying
Dracula with the tomb and the past, thereby repressing his real identity, which is that of a future in which identity becomes infinitely ex-
changeable, where the force of identity will be sucked out by the
totalitarian leader. Dracula is apparently of the past, but really of the
future; and it is this ambiguity that gives him his irresistible power
over what Jameson has termed the political unconscious of our culture. Thus Stoker's work is as prophetic as it is ideological. The future
that comes disguised as the past is the totalitarian future of the first
half of this century, in which monopolism was linked to nationalism.
This linkage was perverse, but the delimitation of monopoly within a
single country (the totalitarian state) allowed that country to function
as an incubation chamber, a playpen, for multinationalism. When it
had grown up, it could proceed to create the multinational economy of
the present day. The fusion of monopolism and nationalism in the
first half of this century thus embodies a moment of transition between the liberal capitalism of the nineteenth-century nation-states

---

* In fact, the translation of money into liquid is a leitmotif of the book – as Seward et al.
repeatedly secure laborers' assistance by administering coins they convert into beer at
the nearest pub.

and the world economy. In this transitional stage, the foreign is nominally opposed but secretly embraced.* And so it becomes quite logical that *Dracula* should have been filmed in Germany under a different title, *Nosferatu:* The foreign text is appropriated while dependence is simultaneously denied. The politics of adaptation anticipate Nazi Germany's ingestion of the foreign. Nosferatu suffers defeat in Murnau's film because his time has not yet come in reality: Nina may stretch her arms toward him as she stands on the seashore and he rides across the waves, but she is also reaching out to Jonathan, whose return is intercut with Nosferatu's journey; although his disembarkation is followed by the plague-bringing rats' entry into Bremen, the relationship between his power and the plague is uncertain. Kracauer rightly asks, "Does he embody the pestilence, or is its image evoked to characterize him?"[11] And the two forms of power, that of eros, and that over nature, are disjoined from one another; he is not yet able – as Stoker's vampire was and Hitler was to be – to link the power of love with the power of mass domination. It is as if the vampire – like Hitler himself in the twenties – is still insufficiently strong to marshal a collectivity behind him: and so, whereas in Stoker's book a troop of upstanding stalwart men is required to defeat Dracula, in Murnau's film a single woman's sacrifice is sufficient. Dracula is an uncanny figure, but Nosferatu is poised between the uncanny and the monstrous; he cannot quite pass for a normal human. The rats may be seen as his emissaries, but they are also the aspect of monstrous (unnatural) nature he seeks to shed so as to enter Western civilization. His entry into the townhouse involves a passage out of the nature from which his Transylvanian castle has seemed to be an outcrop; the incompleteness of the passage is patent, however, for the point of entry is the virtually ruined house in which culture threatens to crumble into nature. The house is a form of entrapment, antedating even his ensnarement by Nina: His woeful, emaciated face at its barred window is that of a convict. This frustrated position at the window is that of nineteenth-century woman herself – one recalls Emma Bovary, or the paintings of Caspar David Friedrich – so his combination with Nina is a logical one: Each is marginal, each signifies uncanny sexuality –

---

* National Socialism absorbs elements of fascism and Soviet Marxism, and it is piquant to note the frequency with which foreign words were incorporated into the Nazi mode of speech, as does Victor Klemperer in his *LTI*. This may seem ironic in the light of (or may seem to refute) Adorno's contention that "German words of foreign derivation are the Jews of language." The contradiction indicates however that the Nazis used foreign words with the aim of inserting the German into the space occupied by the Jews, expropriating them. It is also symptomatic both of lack of self-knowledge and of unconscious identification with the Jews (Europe views Germans as Germans view Jews): Where the one nation rises up as smoke, the other is to be consumed by the conflagration of *Götterdämmerung.*[10]

think of how the cross-cutting during Harker's return suggests that she may long for the vampire – the threat of castration embodied in the woman being doubled in the vampire's ability to drain one's blood. Fused, they recall Marlowe's Helen, who sucks forth Faustus's soul. The final simultaneous elimination of both the uncanny body and the female shows that body to be an image of the female, and vice versa: The vamp is vampire (anticipating *Sunrise* in a sense, the female threat being particularly vivid for the homosexual director Murnau), whereas Nosferatu himself is the impotent (feminized, castrated) male, whose sexuality has been displaced from the genital to the oral zone. This final double exclusion, of the female and the uncanny body, anticipates the ending of *Metropolis* – thereby indicating the pervasiveness of the ideology in question.

The plague that accompanies Nosferatu may incarnate his power, but it is clear that to come armed with pestilence is to fail to win people over: Dracula's universal, polymorphous love is more efficacious. It seems almost as if Nosferatu is drawn to Bremen by suicidal infatuation with Nina – the *amour fou* the surrealists were to laud – instead of lust for world domination; as if he is Harker's dark double, bearer of a sexuality in which man and woman both drown.* But if Nosferatu seems to be no more than a tiny blot on the face of the nature whose images interleave the film, there are disturbing intimations that nature may prove unnatural: The shape of the polyp Van Helsing examines recalls Nosferatu's clawlike hands, and in the very last image – when the vampire has faded at cockcrow – Nina's raised hands echo his yearning gesture at the window of the abandoned building. Even as the narrative implies the vampire's cathartic dissolution, something of him seems to persist: the gesture that is the germ both of the vampirical and the horrified reaction to it.

Nosferatu's stereotypically "Semitic" nose, fabled wealth, and propensity for travel anticipate the repertoire of anti-Semitism; like the

---

* Remnant of a feudal order, Nosferatu enjoys a *jus primae noctis* to which the middle-class husband consents, for the baleful power of the virgin is diverted onto the monster. Harker is so skippingly boyish a figure (his hairdo eerily similar to Polanski's in his *The Fearless Vampire Killers*) that Nosferatu in comparison can seem to embody the power of sexuality. Harker himself seems rather to be a passive object of desire, with Nosferatu bending over him nibbling his throat. (His prone pose may recall that of the young Faust over whom Mephisto leans in Murnau's version of *Faust*.) Nosferatu's boardlike rise from his coffin below the deck of the *Demeter* is like the unfolding of a phallic switchblade. When Nina reaches out toward the sea we are shown intercut images of Nosferatu's ship breasting impressive waves and Harker crossing a mere ankle-high torrent. Nosferatu's surprising possession of a reflection as he makes love to Nina merely confirms his carnality. And so when Nina appears seated in a seaside graveyard with higgledy-piggledy crosses, our suspicion that she may be longing for Nosferatu is reinforced. The crosses will recur later, chalked on the doors of plague-ridden houses. There is a strange irony here: Had they been drawn there at the outset they might have sufficed to check the vampire's terrible reign.

1913 *Student of Prague,* however, the film contains potentially anti-Semitic elements to which history has not yet imparted their full future racist charge. The film is sympathetically fascinated by the character it defines as a monster. His contradictions bewitch; his attachment to the native soil he bears in his coffin belies his affinities with the deracinated Jew whose diaspora Alfred Rosenberg was to ascribe to a slothful preference for trade over tilling the Holy Land. Such inconsistency would have vanished had it been filmed in the thirties, which would have etched the lurid features of the bloodsucking Jew. Even so, his juxtaposition with rats provides a subliminal flash-forward to *The Eternal Jew (Der ewige Jude),* whose obsession with concealed identity renders it also a work of the uncanny: Rats become bearded Jews, who are then shorn, become assimilated, and climb the heights of the Berlin salons. *The Eternal Jew* exploits the real distinction between the *Ostjude* (the Eastern Jew – is Nosferatu's Transylvanian origin of relevance to this Imaginary?), whose identity is more apparent, and the assimilated Jew, in order to reinforce its ideological distinction between the master race and the subhuman. Eschewing possible appeal to the assimilated Jew's dislike of the *Ostjude,* it already anticipates the murder of all the Jews by incorporating the former into the latter, comparing both to vermin. Since Nosferatu is further marked as Other by his resemblance to Lombroso's "criminal personality," the film may be accused of conspiring with popular culture's belief that a monster is always recognizable as such. For if the Germans failed to resist Hitler, it was surely in part because his monstrosity was concealed; how could a man who resembled Chaplin seem dangerous? It is almost forgivable to ascribe demonism to the history that permitted such a resemblance, and the mistake made by those who deemed Hitler a clown becomes understandable.

*Postscript: Vamps, vampires, and the other world:* Sunrise

A possible genesis for the figure of Nosferatu is examined in *Sunrise:* When making love to the city girl, the man leans back beneath her, as if allowing her to feed upon his throat; and so later, when he stands up in the boat before his wife, murderously intent, hunched stiffly, hands clamped to sides, his posture's similarity to Nosferatu's – enhanced by the weights placed in George O'Brien's boots – suggests that he has been vampirized by the vamp. Furthermore, *Sunrise* suggests a link between the imagination of the city as "another world" and the otherworldliness of the phantom: The city is shown first as the spectral array of images unfolded above the man by the city girl, whose own form later hovers phantasmally around him, molded to his shape, below and behind – small below, as if flattering him by apparent insignificance, but enormous in the unseen space behind him – as he gazes at his wife in the doorway, contemplating murder. (The water in which he imagines drowning her is the unconscious in which he himself is submerged, like the protagonist dissolving into the bed in *Eraserhead*.) If the city girl is a strangely implausible presence – hardly surprising, for she is not part of the Sudermann story on which the film is based – treading high-heeled through the marshes, the implication is that she is a fata morgana, providing the scapegoat upon whom the man can blame (and then vent) his murderous urges, who can be banished at the film's end, the water having yielded up the wife reborn (and mercifully wigless), loosed hair betokening recovery of the sexuality ceded earlier to the dark city girl. Her very implausibility is a hint that the film knows she is to be categorized as a projection – and categorizes her as such in opposition to the solid reality of the wife: her continual disruption of meals at the film's start a sign that she feeds on air – or upon blood. If the film admits her implausibility, such self-consciousness can be linked to such features as the use of superimposition and back projection that suggests an occult self-referentiality; *Sunrise* would thus become less the simple allegory castigated by early critics than a deliberate investigation of the difficulties of sustaining the simple oppositions of fantasy (a theme I consider later in the section).

Dudley Andrew acutely notes that the film's self-definition as the song of *two* humans can only mean that the vamp "is non-human, inhuman" – whence her catlike perching on a branch near the film's end[12]: She is a phantom of desire. If the wife's image is etherealized also at one point, it is *naturally*, as the reflection in the doorway as she feeds the chickens. Later, man and wife will appear reflected together in the city photographer's window. (Here too the photograph is naturalized as a fixing of the reflection time would dissolve, and the photograph he actually takes is, significantly enough, a flash-forward to the final embrace.) If the shop window reflection is a common topos of late-twenties German cinema – in *The Threepenny Opera (Die Dreigroschenoper)* Mack's reflection beside a bridal gown shows that any girl foolish enough to wed him will find him as hard to hold as a phantom, and the shop-window reflection of the child murderer in *M (M, Mörder unter Uns)* famously embodies his unacknowledged desires – it is because it places the doppelgänger of expressionism under the aegis of the New Objectivity, postinflation alienation expressing itself in the inability to buy. The shop windows domesticate phantoms, bringing them down to earth. In a sense that is what the wife does also: The vamp may have invited the man to go to the city with her, but it is the wife who takes him there, the tracking movement of the tramcar flight replicating the panning exhilaration of the vamp's evocation of the intensities of city life. So although some critics have divided the film rigidly between several binary oppositions, the narrative in fact complicates such structural schemata by showing nature itself to be fundamentally ambiguous, containing within itself marsh, treacherous night, and the catwoman who is uncanny by virtue of her fusion with the animal world – the wife may be associated with animals, a sign of her nurturing power, but she is never fused with them. The opposition between wife and vamp is further complicated by the mutability of drives – the husband's desire to strangle the vamp being deflected by her into furious sexual embrace.

Superimposition pervades *Sunrise,* fulfilling several functions. Since it is readable as an expression of dissatisfaction with the image, the work's painterly references can be seen as efforts to anchor the image again by turning it into a painting, the object of a prolonged gaze, with the image's inevitable failure to become a painting generating the drama. Superimposition also corresponds to the excessiveness of the city, and can even manifest itself on the sound track during the couple's visit, its various tunes drifting across their romantic theme. Initially coded as erotic excess when presented by the vamp, the city the man and wife visit is reclassified as displaying the excess of *carnival.* It is utopian in its ability to accommodate peasants unmockingly; pig catching is a useful skill here, and peasant dances part of a city orchestra's repertoire. When the couple cross the street arm-in-arm, reconciled, betrothed anew in the manner of melodramatic lead figures, they walk with impunity through spectral, back-projected traffic, and the street momentarily becomes a forest; like ourselves, they go to heaven at the movies. The city's whirling, giddy chaos is benevolent, reconstructing them as a unity by forcing them to support one another. The demonic fun fair of expressionism loses its threat, tamed as it were by transportation to Hollywood. The lure of the Americanism the vamp embodies is salutary because temporary: the city becomes the fair, whose sole raison d'être is to furnish country folk with diversion.

Much has been made on occasion of the artificiality of the closing sunrise; this seems to me to be mistaken. Murnau wanted a real sunrise, but none of the naturally available ones fitted the bill; whence the studio dawn. Given Murnau's habit of mingling real locales with studio sets, however, it can be argued that it is ultimately irrelevant which of the two is employed at any one point; theoretically, either could have been employed. Thus the artificial sun iconically sums up the film's sense of the inextricability of "culture" and "nature" (for each term is a human construct). Art is sublimely justified by the recognition that to gaze at the real sun would blind us – as in a sense indeed happens: The sunrise marks the onset of darkness, as the film ends, city dreams expiring in day's blanching light. The vamp who leaves before dawn light, meanwhile, shows herself to be truly a vampire.

### Vampyr: From the house of the dead

The world of Carl Dreyer's *Vampyr* is subject to a disturbing intermittence. Narrative progression is punctuated by moments of startling, apparently "demonic" vision. The world is perpetually dissolving in the gray light of the exteriors, while the interiors too collapse and reform as the camera continually threads its fragile way from one person or object to another, tracking across the gaps between them, registering the intermediate space that apparently signifies absence because, to the eye *truly* able to see, this absence is presence: the presence of the other world of the dead. Death is interpolated into life in the form of the empty space the camera has to traverse in order to join up the isolated dots of the human beings, seeking to weave a net of society and solidarity: a net that is of course a way of assembling a series of *gaps* (holes) into a unity. The entire film is such a network, a tracery of lines upon nothingness. Its world is alternately present (the sharp interiors) and absent (the deliquescing image of the external world): while the interiors are part of the series of enclosures that stand as metaphors for the ultimate enclosure, the coffin.

The world is sown with gaps connoting otherness: ellipses in the narrative; paintings on the wall which (as in Poe's "Oval Portrait") stand for vampirism, though in this case it is not the artist's power vampirically to convert real flesh and blood into a two-dimensional phantasm, to turn life into death, but the power the dead wield over the living – the paintings all hang higher than the protagonists and dominate the scene; they belong to the same realm as Marguerite Chopin, the aged vampire who is terrorizing the village of Contempierre, and her accomplice the doctor, who draws the blood of the young – while the frosted and barred windows turn even the faces of the living into ghosts, showing how easy it is to traverse the borderline between life and death, and symbolizing the spectator's own exclusion from the logic of events. The portraits on the walls are like stills, the age of photography being one in which the curse of the painter's model, who has to imitate the stillness of the dead, is extended throughout society. As in "The Oval Portrait," vampirism and realistic portrayal are linked.

Repeatedly in *Vampyr* the camera focuses upon doors opening and closing, often of their own volition, with mysterious quietude. Doors are opened in response to the camera's will to link the disjunctive domains of the on-screen and the off-screen, following up the strange noises on the sound track, totalizing the film's fragments. At one point, just after Leone has displayed her vampirical teeth, Gisele asks,

"Didn't someone scream?" – though there is nothing on the sound track. At another, David hears the doctor conversing outside, though unable to see him. At first all we see is the image of David before the shuttered window. When Dreyer then cuts to the scene outside, we see only the doctor's *shadow*. Sight and sound are never synchronized, as the film occupies – and deliberately exploits – the uncanny moment of transition from silent cinema to sound.

As Dreyer stares hard at the faces of his actors and actresses, the intensity of the gaze transforms them into death masks. The gaze is justified by the fact that the apparently living are actually often the dead. Film, like Rilke's angels, cannot tell the difference between them. And so this film can only end when the face ceases to be the mask of death, when the confusion between life and death that has enabled the other world to tap the resources of this life is dispelled: As the stake is driven into the heart of Marguerite Chopin, it melts into a skull, and the coffin, which earlier on has held a living inhabitant (David Gray), is restored to its natural function, that of containing the remains of the dead. Death closes a sequence, rather as earlier in the film the camera traveled clockwise round a painting of figures standing at a deathbed, starting at the bottom of the picture, at the six o'clock position – in the midst of life, as it were – and then cut away on arrival at the bottom right of the picture, where a skeleton is seen. When the hidden comes to light, the revelation is one of death, the skull beneath the skin; however it takes time – the duration of the film, the time embodied in the initial rooftop image of the grim reaper – for the process of revelation to reach completion: When first laid in the coffin, the corpse barely differs from the living. Not until one is sure that this figure is indeed dead – a knowledge that does not arrive until the skull replaces the face, that mask of death – can the coffin actually be buried. When the hidden, the skeleton, has manifested itself, it can be hidden in the ground – like the doctor who, for all his apparent life, is an image of death, impersonally buried by the mill's flour as if by the sands of time.

*Vampyr* is dotted with irrational displacements, which may be a consequence of the imperfect state of the prints in circulation, but nevertheless conspire to enhance the aura of the uncanny. Perhaps the greatest art is that which – like Rilke's torso of Apollo – incorporates its own mutilation, growing in humanity through its own suffering. The book on vampirism quoted in the intertitles is at first intercut with images of David Gray reading it, only to give way – without any transition – to the manservant doing so. Meanwhile, as the servant is reading, David, whom one would have thought forewarned by the book, is giving blood, ostensibly for Leone, at the doctor's request. Of all the characters in the film, only David is shown in unequivocally modern dress: a surreal displacement that creates a sense that he is a modern man wandering in a nineteenth-century ghost house. His out-of-body experience, as his transparent form drifts away from his earthly shell seated on a bench, doubles the process whereby he – and we the spectators – entered the film's ghost realm in the first place. When he finds himself in a coffin with a small glass window, the face of Marguerite Chopin staring down at him, the appearance of the frame-within-the-frame (the coffin window) is part of the experience of death he shares with the audience – we too are locked immobile in the dark. As in the theories of Bazin, the appearance of the frame *within the frame* signifies death.

Again and again in Dreyer's work the status of the transcendent is both raised and begged. Religious themes lend weight and mystery to the works, and yet religion is also somehow bracketed by Dreyer's intense attachment to the flesh and blood of this world. In all these films the other world is felt to be a final cause, and yet is not represented. This may simply be because the invisible defies representation, but the nonrepresentation leaves a series of nagging, unanswered questions, some of which I will now mention. For instance, one wonders: Does Dreyer's Joan (in *The Passion of Joan of Arc* [*La Passion de Jeanne d'Arc*]) really see visions? Is Anne in *Day of Wrath* (*Vredens Dag*) really a witch, and if so, does she have a witch's power? Late in the film we are shown cross-cut images of her husband returning home while she tells his son, Martin, that she wishes his father were dead; as she does so, the wind gusts all the more strongly, and the husband is seen to clutch his heart and say that Death has passed nearby. Dreyer's mastery carries one over the moment, and yet, when considered objectively, it has some of the stiltedness of a woodenly moralistic silent film: Jutting up into this *sound* film, it acquires a strange, hypnotic stateliness. Is the cross-cutting simply a narrative convention, and the apparent efficacy of her wishes merely a coincidence, or is Anne truly in control of events? Similarly, one may wonder how and why the resurrection of Inger occurs in *Ordet* (*The Word*), and question the role of the camera here too, as the editing speeds up, its quickening seeming to cause the quickening of the dead. Another question: Is Joan of Arc a saint for Dreyer? And, in *Day of Wrath* again, what is the relationship between the cross of the church and the cross with two bars that is associated with the death of the witch? Can Anne be said to believe her own confession at the film's end, since she is clearly making it in order to commit suicide, affirming her commitment to this world by showing that her abandonment by Martin has left her with nothing to live for? Is Martin's fear of her simply pusillanimity, or does she really command occult powers? Dreyer's argument against the witch-hunt is not in fact the common post-

Enlightenment one that deems witchcraft mere superstition and its persecution the tormenting of deluded old ladies; *Day of Wrath* seems rather to suggest that witchcraft does indeed exist, and that the witch belongs to a natural and female order of love that is as much a part of reality as the male realm of tragically flawed law – for the men who persecute witches destroy the women they love and thus themselves.

The hypnotic rhythms of these three films seek to lull one into thinking that all that matters is the sequence of visible events. Yet in retrospect the gaps loom large, gaping most deeply perhaps in *Ordet*. Only in *Vampyr* is the other world these films occlude represented. The other world can be represented here because it is *demonic*; its representation is not taboo, for it has no sacred status. The other world is in a sense part of this world, present as *the shadow* – and the whiteness against which the shadow most clearly appears. It is not the invisible structuring absence that tantalizingly haunts the edges of the three other films. The other world can enter this world in *Vampyr*, of course, because materiality is open to the incursions of the demonic. But although Dreyer's decision not to represent the transcendent in the other films is a source of frustration, it also indicates his consummate artistic tact. There is none of the patent embarrassment generated by the public God-bothering of a Bergman. Instead, there is a pervasive unease it is extremely hard to localize. As Sartre remarks of Jaspers – whose Kierkegaardian existentialism is closely related to Dreyer's this-worldly metaphysics – the transcendent remains veiled and is apprehended only through its absence. One's unease is as hard to localize as is God Himself.*

### Horror and derision

At one point in the Books of Chronicles, the effect of God's anger against Judah is mentioned: "He made them repugnant, an object of horror and derision, as you see for yourselves" (New English Bible; 2 Chronicles 29:8). Why the linkage of "horror" and "derision"? It is surely not because of the frequency with which the horrid is also the absurd, be it laughably so – as in Hammer horror films – or more menacingly, as in *Texas Chainsaw Massacre*, with its air of frenzied cartoon. Horror and derision are in fact interconnected reactions to the

---

* The whiteness Gilles Deleuze sees as characteristic of Dreyer,[13] and which he contrasts with the expressionist concern with shadows, radiates a horror recalling Melville's "The Whiteness of the Whale." It is the horror of imagelessness: Empty Presbyterian church walls reject graven images and are inimical to cinema. Thus the dominant religion of Dreyer's own culture projects him into the space of the dead, the demonic and the feminine, which all converge in *Vampyr*. His position vis-à-vis Protestantism approximates very closely that of Emily Dickinson, with a similar dialectic of sensuality and asceticism.

sight of disaster, be it a catastrophic event or a person who can be termed "a disaster" (in the most extreme sense, a sideshow freak). The linkage of the two words ought to be as famous, and as frequently considered, as Aristotle's "pity and fear." Here horror results from the fear that such disaster might overtake oneself; derision, from the *Schadenfreude* that celebrates another's suffering in one's own stead, the suffering of the scapegoat. The order of the two words is not arbitrary: One's first reaction to catastrophe is horror, fear of engulfment; derision prevails when one realizes that the disaster is past and will not encompass oneself.

Todorov has noted that the fantastic as a genre is dependent upon a sense of linearity.* Since works of horror form a subset of the fantastic, it is clear that they too thrive on linearity. This linearity is a characteristic of the historical consciousness, from whose emergence the sense of horror follows: It is the unexpected and unforeseen that overwhelms one with horror through the lack of any prototype for the occurrence. The horrific event marks the end of mythical time, which is the time of repetition described by Mircea Eliade. Hence it is hardly surprising that the sense of horror should be widespread in Greek and Hebrew thought, which both posit a historical reality. Horror may oc-

---

* Todorov's definition of the fantastic as characterized by uncertainty resembles my own definition of the uncanny: "The fantastic is that hesitation experienced by a person who knows only the laws of nature, confronting an apparently supernatural event" (p. 25). He prefaces this statement by remarking that "once we choose one answer or the other, we leave the fantastic for a neighbouring genre, the uncanny or the marvellous" (ibid.) Todorov's distinction between "the laws of nature" and "the supernatural" is, however, of nineteenth-century provenance; prior to the enlightenment's assault upon religion, "the supernatural" was perceived to be part of "nature." This leaves Todorov unable to deal with pre-nineteenth-century texts, which lack this distinction (another one of whose forms is the opposition between "realism" and "fantasy"). His reference to an "apparently supernatural event" gives the game away by showing his implicit hero to be a positivist (i.e., a post-nineteenth-century figure), for whom all supernaturalism is merely illusory. Since "the fantastic" can be categorized as a variety of the supernatural, it is absurd to locate it outside ("confronting") it. Whereas the fantastic is dialectically dependent upon a corresponding notion of "the real," the uncanny – I would argue – emerges at the point of transition between them, at the moment of recognition of their interdependence. The uncanny is inherently indeterminate.[14]

If Todorov is right and the fantastic derives its effect (primarily an effect of surprise) from the linear nature of reading, there appears to be a profound affinity between film and the fantastic: Film too is always linear, forbidding one to skip forward to the story's end to resolve the suspense feeding the fantastic. This affinity should make it clear, however, that the fantastic of which Todorov writes is its modern form, which is the effect of the first reading: The second time around, prior acquaintance scotches uncertainty. The fantastic assumes this form in a world in which the authority of texts is very qualified: One does not return to them to savor their beauty or wisdom (the greatest living film critic, Pauline Kael, passionately advocates the one-night stand ... ), but undergoes them only once, as one does experience in general. They have lost what Benjamin termed their "aura" But, as Milan Kundera notes, when experience assumes the form of *einmal* (once) it becomes equivalent to *keinmal* (never): What happens only once might just as well never have happened at all. The linear world is nihilistic in its belief that nothing deserves repetition.

cur on two occasions in relation to mythical time: When the mythical order is first challenged, bystanders are shocked by the challenger's impiety, and his immediate punishment by the gods may deepen their horror (such is the case in Greek thought); in Hebrew thought, however, the horror is not exhausted in a single sequence of action and prompt reaction, challenge and punishment, for the penalty is likely to be deferred: When the Israelites fall away from God, He gives them ample opportunity, and frequent warnings, to repent. The penalty finally inflicted arouses all the more horror for having been unexpected by all parties: In Greek thought only God's challenger expects to emerge scot-free, while the chorus is appalled by his temerity; Biblical thought, by way of contrast, shows people becoming inured over time to a feeling of impunity, so that in the end no one expects retribution. The Bible depicts a world in which people entertain for a long time the delusion that they have eluded the mythical order, that is, God. Disaster befalls the miscreants as unexpectedly as the horror of the concentration camps broke upon a world priding itself on its progressiveness and enlightenment.

In Greek thought the offender's punishment is prolonged in perpetuity: Character is not conceived as mutable or capable of change. God is a tyrant crushing all opposition, not a father correcting His chosen people. Here the great Biblical counterexample to Greek thought is the Book of Job. Stricken by Satan, whom God has allowed to afflict his upright servant, Job becomes a monster in the sight of his family (19: 13–20). His comforters believe that only the evil suffer and that humanity is divided between the good and the evil; if Job suffers, he must consequently have offended. They fail to grasp that all humanity is evil in God's sight (Genesis 6:5–6, or Elihu's statement in Job 35:10–12 that no one calls on God) and that affliction is God's necessary instrument for bringing humanity to the repentance Job finally achieves, where he realizes that God alone is righteous. The book is thus far from being the protest against suffering many have found in it; suffering is shown to have a purpose and to be temporary: Job lives 140 years after his affliction, and is a changed man. He is turned into a monster, an object of horror, in order to become more fully a man.

## Conclusion

In the introduction to this book I argued that the uncanny is to be distinguished from the monstrous. The movement out of the self – the process of its disintegration – can end in one of two ways: with the precipitation of the monster or that of the double. The difference between the two outcomes seems to me to be one between the ideological

– with its deep-rooted investment in dualism and us–them mechanisms – and the possibly liberating and dialectical. This may be linked to the distinction between popular and high culture. The appearance of the double is usually abrupt, and although it may be preceded by a period of mental tension, this is not the tense anticipation that ends in the monster's emergence: Such anticipatory tension mobilizes the self's aggressive impulses against imminent threat; the accompanying feeling is that of the uncanny, as the self struggles with the passivity – it is passive because no enemy is visible as yet – that would render it an easy victim.

Whereas the confrontation with the double results from a two-part operation – from self to double – that with the monster is the terminus of a three-part process: from self to monster via the uncanny. Here the uncanny, the second stage, involves a repression of the appearance of the double: The latter is not, as Freud thought, a form of the uncanny, for it is rather the uncanny that swallows up the double. To see the double is to accept death: The mirroring of the self does not reinforce it, for the double's appearance indicates that the self has been discarded, as one becomes two and sees oneself as the Other sees one. Momentarily, one becomes God and pays the price for so doing: death. The generation of the monster out of the double's repression, however, betokens a refusal of death: One is going to do what one always does with a monster – that is, fight it. The difference is in a sense one between the murder that perpetuates the struggle for survival and the suicide that ends the world as one – the first person *singular* – knows it. The creation of the monster thus serves to mystify or disavow the suicidal recognition of the need to do away with the old self, for which death is a release. When the self's disintegration is resolved in the emergence of the monster, the self's own complicity in evil is repressed; when it brings forth the double, however, there is no clear resolution but rather a crisis within a self understood as part of a problem that may in fact never go away. There is nevertheless a blessing for recognizing that the problem lies in the self, for it does indeed dissolve: The double is death's ambassador. I offer this hypothesis as a more reliable means of distinguishing the "progressive" – read: human and useful – work of horror from the "reactionary" one than is proposed in Robin Wood's influential essay on horror film.[15] (Wood's stigmatization of the works of Cronenberg, for instance, appears to be purely capricious.) In the realm of fantasy it is the confrontation with the acknowledged double that can foster a self-transcendence that goes beyond self-repression; the repressed real returns without the mask of repression. The futility of the effort to kill the monster, meanwhile, is demonstrated in the myth of the hydra – Medusa in a hall of mirrors. One is compelled to strike at it again and again – the hydra is in a sense Medusa's *hair* – for the self that is its real origin remains unchallenged.

Striking again and again at the image of horror: This is the young Wordsworth's experience in the stolen boat episode, when his impotence stems from an inability to go beyond combating the image of horror – the peak as reflected in the lake, within reach of his oars – and wound its actuality. His sense of inability to escape is of the essence of horror. Perhaps the most powerful filmic embodiment of such incarceration in the moment is found in Eisenstein's "Odessa Steps" sequence in *Battleship Potemkin* (*Bronenosets Potemkin*) in which the single moment swells into an allegory of history as an unbroken administration of suffering, as the repeated salvoes of depersonalized soldiers mow down the civilian crowd. The film's discontinuous montage is a continual shattering of the walls of image cells: the graphic explosions, successive leaps out of imprisoning frames. The "Odessa Steps" sequence, however, denies the possibility of such escape. Since in actuality it would take little time to descend the 120 steps, and steps of their essence always *lead* somewhere, the bad eternity of slaughter becomes all the more oppressive. As Eisenstein himself notes, the movement of descent automatically leads to an ascent.[16] History's dialectic does not generate escape but eternal recurrence, as if descending water in a fountain had begun to rise. When the sequence *does* end, it is with a violent shock to the spectator, an image of loss of sight, as a cossack's sword puts out a woman's eye.* In the end, the only valid response to the vision of history's disasters is – as it were – to go blind, in an effort to shut out the horror. Even in the inner world, however, it may persist – with the persistence of "vision," uncanny, because an afterimage in the mind's eye.†

* Only for a surrealist – for the Buñuel of *An Andalusian Dog* (*Un Chien Andalou*), for instance – could such violence to the eye represent a new beginning, an initiation into the convulsive inner world of dreams. Eisenstein, by way of contrast, emphasizes that the person so afflicted has become more helpless still before the horror of history, which – even had it not blinded her – would have undermined psychosomatically the desire to continue to see. She is plunged into the realm of the darkness visible, where seeing only darkness only underlines one's inability to penetrate the inscrutability of events.
† At one point in Eisenstein's film, however, the transformation of horror into an image serves to avert real horror. When a tarpaulin is thrown over the mutinous sailors and their comrades are commanded to shoot them down (a moment at which Eisenstein diverges from actuality, in which the tarpaulin was placed below the sailors in order to protect the deck from bloodstains, the director's purpose being to stress the officers' knowledge that no crew will be able to shoot comrades they have to look in the eye), their transformation into a multilegged ghost may well be what saves them: There is no sense in firing at a phantom. The tarpaulin creates a collective subject, the unity the sailors require in their revolt.

Some of Kafka's words may be apposite here: "Es war eine Einheit, wie sie fast nur Lebloses bilden kann" ["It was a unity, such as almost only lifeless things can form"]. The unity of the sailors under the tarpaulin, however, is not the depersonalized alignment of men in serried military ranks, but the lifelessness that precedes resurrection.

The uncanny is by definition that which defies representation; to represent it would be to draw its sting. It is perhaps an image of the death that has become unimaginable following the collapse of the Christian iconography that once contained it in an image. Thus to call the concentration camps an earthly materialization of Hell – for instance – is to dispel the air of the uncanny that surrounds them – the uncanny question of just what it was that brought people to behave as the torturers did – by integrating them into an archaic system of representation. The suffering of the concentration camp victims was indeed deeply analogous to that traditionally symbolized in the image of Hell, but there is no simple equivalence between the imaginary locale and the reality that in a sense actualizes it; indeed, to suggest equivalence would amount to a justification of Nazi policy by implying that the Jews deserved this place in the scheme of things. That is why the procedure Von Trotta adopts in *Marianne and Juliane* (*Die bleierne Zeit*) is exemplary: In juxtaposing images of concentration camp corpses and Third World victims, it indicates that all are part of the same system, which persists precisely because it contains no Archimedean point from which it could dislodge itself. (Grünewald's Christ does not redeem the world, but is crushed by taking upon Himself the weight of its suffering.) All these things are related, but the nature of the relation is a mystery. Evil persists by hovering uncannily between signs, none of which can master it by naming it in full, for it always has more malevolence in reserve, beyond imagination.

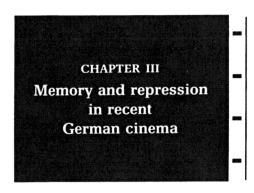

CHAPTER III
Memory and repression
in recent
German cinema

## On representation and repression

Representation is never neutral, for it is usually reserved for and by the strongest, who deem themselves the fittest to reproduce and be reproduced. And yet even when we are consciously aware of this we are still likely to concentrate so exclusively upon what the representation places before us that we fail to perceive what it omits. But if a society's prevailing modes of representation can therefore be experienced as uncanny, in league with evil, on the other hand omissions can be justified as the unavoidable corollary of the necessity of form: Structure is founded upon exclusion. In any case, is an event's omission always tantamount to its repression? This is one of the central questions the present chapter will address to a series of recent West German films.

### Thinking the unthinkable

It is often contended that certain things are best left unrepresented, and that their omission from the visual sphere is a matter of tact rather than repression. Foremost among these are intimate sexual encounter and death, linked by Elizabethan puns on "dying" and critiques that speak of a "pornography of horror." Refusal to contemplate images of sexual intimacy may nevertheless be bound in with repression: The repressed personality may be unable to view with equanimity the joy of others; it may be reminded of the incomprehensibility and apparent murderousness of the primal scene; whereas the wound of exclusion from the scene of affection may be compounded with alarm over the "reduction" of the human to the animal function. Yet the taboos placed on such images are surely necessary: If everything is preimagined for us by the text, the result may be a totalitarian world with no margin for individual interpretation or experience. Such totalitarianism is quite compatible with nominal democracy: The most blatant example of the predigested work, whose audience is built-in before delivery and hence rendered superfluous, is the sitcom with a laugh track. Unwillingness to contemplate images of death, on the other hand, may accompany a repression of knowledge of our own mortality, but the inability to countenance the sight of a corpse may also correspond to a utopian refusal to believe that this is all life finally amounts to. It may also render one less likely to tame the trauma of mortality, in a murderous version of Freud's "fort-da" game, by inflicting death upon another person.*

It is sometimes argued that the production of images of death panders to a pornography of horror. The phrase "pornography of horror" seems to me to be dubious, however. Pornographic experience involves the achievement of a sense of superiority over others – usually women, hence pornography may be connected to a male counterattack on feminism – through their dehumanization (people become images); even masochistic pornography is controlled by the contract between torturer and consenting victim. But when contemplating a corpse the victory is not one's own, but belongs to death, before which one can only feel horror and helplessness. Pornography implies the possibility of control, even if only of *images*; horror, its impossibility. Hitler's sadistic delectation of the footage of the Plötzensee executions depended on his ability to control images projected privately for him. Where Hitler was both their sender and their receiver, locked in a closed circle of narcissistic omnipotence, most of us are merely receivers.[†] Stiffly passive, or open and receptive to the inflow of images, but deprived of control in either case, one is condemned to view events in what Hayden White terms

the Metaphorical mode of construing the historical field, prefigured as a "Chaos of Being," [which] requires that the historian simply position himself before the field in a posture of waiting and of anticipating the riches that *it* will reveal to *him*, in the firm conviction that since every individual life is like every other, it is "like our own therefore."[1]

White's description of this Carlylean, post-Romantic theory of history-as-Sublime evokes the mood of the filmgoer "when the lights go down." Opposed to this is the finally triumphant-nineteenth century ideal of "objectivity" in historiography, in which order and Beauty subdue the chaos of the Sublime, instead of submitting to it, as to a film.

* At the same time, unfortunately, the physical distance from death that results from its transformation into an *image* reestablishes the *emotional* distance that made killing possible in the past, thereby restoring the ideological framework that enables us calmly to eliminate our fellow humans.
† Nevertheless, the possibilities of control furnished by the growing availability of the VCR may indeed promote an experience of horrific images that is inherently more pornographic than the experience of film.

But if the ideal of "objectivity" in the writing of history does indeed involve a repression of awareness of the terror of history – inevitably so, for it is, in general the victor who writes the history, reserving its terrors for the wordless vanquished – such repression is not an operation carried out once and for all, but an ongoing process: The order of Beauty defines itself as that which overcomes Chaos again and again. Indeed, it uses the storm clouds of the Sublime to accentuate its own light, vaunting itself on the difficulty of defeating a worthy adversary. Thus the logic of representation does not repress the Sublime entirely but grants it a token presence to recall the putative threat chaos once posed and may pose again. The preservation of the Sublime as a field demanding conquest preserves the ideology of conquest.* Nor should one simply valorize the Sublime, as many recent theorists – resurrectionists of Romanticism – febrilely do, since a glance at such traditional theorists of the Sublime as Burke and Schiller suffices to show that for them it allows the male mind to draw power from that which it contemplates: *Das Erhabene* renders the observer *erhaben* too. (In Carlylean terms, the historian becomes identical with the hero, whose conquest of chaos he reenacts.) If the beautiful is to be aligned with the feminine and the sublime with masculinity – as in the work of Wordsworth, for instance – then criticism of the former promotes a will-to-power that oppresses the feminine.

The preceding remarks have created a context, I hope, in which to consider briefly the representation of the most problematically representable of modern historical events: the Holocaust. The works in question are Claude Lanzmann's *Shoah* and Alain Resnais's *Night and Fog*. For Lanzmann, the past is not past at all: Anti-Semitism is alive and well – though sometimes hiding out in unlikely places – and the Holocaust could recur tomorrow. It is not the passage of time but rather our myopia regarding its continued present danger that has allowed us to achieve distance from it. Lanzmann's project has some dubious aspects, which I do not wish to consider at length here, having done so elsewhere[†] (see bibliography); it

* Cinema thus becomes a dialectical simultaneous submission to, and domestication of, extreme experience; and the less manageable the experience, the greater the triumph, even though it be a triumph of sensation over art – as in the IMAX system, which has not yet been yoked to artistic purposes.
† Lanzmann's endeavor might have been both more scrupulous and more effective had he treated the three-hundred-odd hours of interviews he garnered in a two-tier fashion. One tier, a book, would have contained transcriptions of almost all the material culled from all the individuals who gave Lanzmann their time and tears. This would have been an extremely important document in the oral history of the Holocaust. The second tier could have been a film that was not simply a selection from the three hundred hours, but also from the eight-hour version, whose length, repetitiveness, and frequently accusatory tone numb the viewer's awareness. Free of irritating reiterations (quotations relayed via interpreters and given twice, the omnipresent slow-clanking trains), this would have been a goad to conscience rather than a narcotic to the sensibility. Unfortunately, the printed version of *Shoah* merely duplicates the film's words. What right has Lanz-

is remarkable however in its resolution of the problem of historical perspective. We are not situated "here" looking at something that occurred "there": old traumas echo on into the present in infernal, eternal recurrence. If the past's specter is a revenant, nevertheless, it is partly due to the necromancy of Lanzmann himself, who will train his camera relentlessly upon anguished subjects, insisting that they continue talking despite their requests that he terminate the interview. If the phrase "the pornography of horror" often appears in discussions of the effects of the most appalling images of the Holocaust, Lanzmann's film paradoxically raises the possibility of another variety of pornography of suffering, despite its admirable refusal to utilize the horrific available footage of the concentration camps. *Shoah,* a film of the mideighties, may be read as the transference to an enormous canvas of Alain Resnais's thirty-one-minute documentary of 1955, *Night and Fog,* with which it shares an interest in the way in which time, nature, and perhaps forgetfulness have veiled the horror of the camps. *Shoah* may also be interpreted as a response to a characteristic of *Night and Fog's* commentary that may well irritate: As sentence after sentence in Jean Cayrol's script attributes a succession of appalling actions to the impersonal *on,* the apparent disinterest in individual agency can be worrying. (It surely worries Lanzmann, who may be accused in his turn of overzealousness in the effort to assign blame.) And since the muted modernism of Hanns Eisler's score suggests a dilution of the dissonances that embody suffering in a Schoenberg, the tone of the film may leave one queasy: It feels somehow distanced, even aestheticized. In addition to this, it is hard to dispel the suspicion that conventional existentialism has dictated the implied argument that nature conspires to conceal the pain of human history. It may feel as if the film is projecting onto nature its own incapacity to locate specific human agents of the disaster. Nevertheless, the question of agency is addressed with great force at the film's end and in a manner that far transcends Lanzmann's prosecuting enquiry: The voice-over notes the widespread disclaimers of responsibility, and asks just who is responsible. The insistence of the question is augmented by its positioning after a shocking series of some of the most haunting images of serried, skeletal corpses. And since the aesthetic of the atrocity footage shot by the Allies is perilously similar to that of the Nazis' own footage, the question becomes all the more urgent. The open ending compels the viewer to seek his or her own answer. Its fruitfulness is apparent in Von Trotta's *Marianne and Juliane (German Sisters / Die bleierne Zeit),* which may also have been prompted by Resnais's film, whose closing sequence it quotes. That response is, I think, a far more just and valid one than Lanzmann's.

mann to silence the testimonies he solicited? (For instance, that of Marek Edelman, excised because of Lanzmann's disagreement with him.) Many of the interviewees have a right to feel duped.

Our awareness of the subtlety of the relationship between representation and omission may be refined still further by reference to a widely noted feature of some of the films from the period a work like Von Trotta's seeks to assess. Thus it has been remarked that, whenever people die in the films of Weimar cinema, blood is never seen to flow – a feature that has also been observed in the films of the Nazi era.[2] This partial disavowal of death has been linked by Paul Monaco to the locations of the battlefields of World War I beyond the borders of Germany itself. In the case of Nazi cinema, however, the sight of blood may well be proscribed because its appearance would imply that the German public itself might yet see it flowing in its own, rather than exclusively foreign, streets. Its absence can also be correlated with a "German" aversion to mess, part of a general fear of chaos and the unpredictable: The blood's flow would stain the edges of the geometric sets upon which most Weimar films were shot. The derealization of the image of death also frees one from responsibility for it. No one has really been hurt; the man who has "fallen" is simply a stuntman. The absence of blood further serves to indicate the superiority of the German technology that can exact so patently "clean" a death. It illustrates the efficiency of a society striving toward the functionalization of the *Neue Sachlichkeit:* No time need be wasted on mopping-up operations. All this reflects the Weimar cinema's commitment to artifice, disavowal, and fetishism: "I know this is so, but . . . ," the fundamental formula of fetishism, is conjugated into "I know this man is dead, but . . . ." The spectator may congratulate himself on having recognized the illusory nature of the spectacle. Considered dialectically, however, the bloodless nondeath also reinforces paranoia. How can I be sure the enemy is dead if no blood flows after I've killed him? Prophetically, as it were, the cinematic nondeath anticipates the Nazi inability to destroy every potential enemy.

The above is clearly an example of omission as repression; with the economy of a symptom, it performs a number of functions – only some of which I have named – in the maintenance of a pathology. In postwar West Germany, the omission – the heart of the unrepresentable – has been the suffering inflicted upon Jews, Slavs, Gipsies, homosexuals, and many others in the concentration camps. Even where this horror is officially recalled, it seems to be repressed. A list of the concentration camps that stands outside the Wittenbergplatz U-Bahn station in West Berlin speaks of "Orte des Schreckens, die wir niemals vergessen dürfen" (places of terror we must never forget). The nature of the terror, who suffered it, and at whose hands is not stated. Is this because it goes without saying, and shame chokes one's speech, or does the sign itself pay lip service to remorse while at the same time pandering to a public desire not to continue to be bothered with the sordid details? In a series of West German films of the late seventies, however, the repressed past clearly returned, with directors such as Reitz, Syberberg, Fassbinder, and Von Trotta taking up the question of the meaning of *Vergangenheitsbewältigung*. Why did this development take place at this time? Was it simply a matter of the photogenic potential of "fascinating fascism" for a New German Cinema some of whose directors had run out of momentum, with Nazism an internationally bankable theme? Did the repressive state measures against left-wing terrorism prompt reflections that the hegemony of the SPD for much of the seventies was simply a freakish interlude in the postwar persistence of many National Socialist habits of mind? Was the German left no longer able to define itself in terms of desiderata, being forced instead to do so in terms of what it did not want – a recurrence of the past? And could it be that a left identified with terrorism by broad swaths of public opinion sought to legitimate itself by pointing to the sins of the fathers? I will be looking at works by Syberberg, Reitz, and Thomas Brasch in order to suggest answers to some of these questions. I will then consider, as an epilogue, films by Fassbinder, Szabó, and Wajda. First, however, another term needs to be added to *Vergangenheitsbewältigung*: that is, *Trauerarbeit*.

## The inability to mourn

*Trauerarbeit* – a term derived from Freudian psychoanalysis – was first brought into conjunction with postwar German reaction to the Nazi legacy in *The Inability to Mourn*, by Alexander and Margarethe Mitscherlich.[3] The Mitscherlichs interpreted West German attitudes as founded upon a derealization of the painful past, one of whose symptoms was a paralysis of the faculty of mourning. Who was it that the Germans were unable to mourn? For the Mitscherlichs the primary object of repressed mourning was Hitler himself, the powerful focus of national narcissism. It may nevertheless be more appropriate to speak here of the *impossibility* of mourning, proscribed by the occupying powers and frustrated by the confusion surrounding the nature of the Germans' relationships with the potential objects of mourning. To what extent could and should they identify with Hitler and the defeated Nazis, on the one hand, and the dead soldiers of the Wehrmacht on the other? The pressing urge to disown a Hitler who had himself disowned the Germans conflicted with memories of the profound emotional investment once made in – and satisfied by – his success. To repudiate Hitler completely would prevent one mourning one's own past and the loss of illusions bound up so closely with him. At what point had "things begun to go wrong," one might ask, seeking to preserve a scrap of one's past from the general devastation. With the establishment of the concentration camps? With the declaration of war? With the invasion of the Soviet Union? The mere posing of these questions was of course absurd; things has been wrong from the start. But when had that been? 1870? 1914? 1918? 1933? The question of responsibility for the murder of the Jews complicated matters still further. The very notion that the German could have identified with the Jews to the point of mourning those they had themselves put to death may seem absurd; and yet that is what true atonement would have required. The failure to mourn the Jews corresponded all too often to a secret conviction that one had nothing to atone for; after all, one had only been following orders. Memories of the Nazi past evoked as much shame as guilt among West Germans. So difficult was it to define one's relationship to the recent past that it was most politic to forget about it completely. Not only would the Jews not be mourned; the ethnic German dead would not be mourned adequately either. Not only did the Allied occupation preclude the establishment of German rituals for the mourning of the German dead – a fixation on the memory of the dead would to the Allies have been suspiciously reminiscent of the torch-lit funeral rites so beloved among the National Socialists – many Germans themselves identified with this refusal of proper burial. One instance will illustrate this. When the American artists Ed and Nancy Kienholz visited West Berlin in the early eighties they were surprised at the large numbers of photographs of Wehrmacht soldiers available in the city's flea markets and junk shops; they had not seen anything similar in France, England, or Italy. Clearly, the past had been discarded – a disavowal the Kienholzes themselves were to make good through their own *Trauerarbeit*, the 1983 installation entitled *Pawn Boys*, comprising fifty bricks, each bearing a photograph of a Wehrmacht soldier. The boys had been pawned doubly: exchanged as pawns of war and then again in the pawn shops. The Kienholzes were able to reclaim them when no German artist had been able to do so. In the light of their experience, one may wish to ask upon what terms a series of West German artists have appropriated the term *Trauerarbeit* to describe their own work – the most important of these being Syberberg (in *Our Hitler*) and Reitz (in *Heimat*). I will begin with *Our Hitler*.

**From the life of the marionettes: Approaches to Syberberg**

*An empire of signs*

Syberberg's *Our Hitler* (*Hitler. Ein Film aus Deutschland*) presents itself under the aegis of *Trauerarbeit*, a word the director explicitly uses. Syberberg's film may be underlaid with references to the ceremonial of Nazi funerals – particularly the pervasive quotations from the roll call for those who died in the attempted Munich putsch of

1923 – but it is clear that he is not mourning the Nazi dead. Near the film's beginning – in one of its many overtures – we are warned that it will not deal with the victims of the Nazi régime, but with "Hitler in us." The disclaimer is surprising, since one of the film's most powerful passages – and, like all the other recent efforts to deal with the Nazi past in the epic mode, *Our Hitler* has many dead spots – does in fact confront the extermination of the Jews. The success of the passage may well stem from its focus on Himmler rather than Hitler; it thus breaks free of the vicious circle that vitiates much of the remainder of the film, in which Hitler is alternately fetishized – as devil incarnate he is responsible for all modern evil – and miniaturized – he is merely a puppet animated by dreams that still persist within us. If the multiplication of the layers of signification in the film often smacks of arbitrariness (no system seems to govern the use made of the Nazi roll call, the excerpts from Hitler's speeches, the radio linkup, or the bursts of Wagner's music that make up the film's sound track), here every element counts and the meanings are clear – so much so, in fact, that the fine, taut first twenty minutes of the episode can then degenerate into a heavily signposted slow-motion drama à la Hochhuth in which top people take big decisions. Following sound-track excerpts from the anti-Hitler manifesto of the National Committee of the Freies Deutschland organization, we hear the voice of Hitler himself, speaking of the extermination of the Jews, and see a bespectacled, sweaty figure lying on a bed. It is Himmler, and he is undergoing a massage. As the masseur works on the prone body of Himmler, we see the phantom of an SS man approach the camera from the left-hand side of the screen, passing through Himmler's body. One after another SS men approach, declaiming about the eternal struggle between the human and the *Untermensch*, and the need to eliminate the eternal Jew who leads the hordes of *Untermenschen*. Himmler, lit with a sickly yellow, reflects on how the Germanic race had to dispose of the subhumans. As the SS phantoms continue to move forward one by one, we hear Harry Baer's voice reading Kurt Gerstein's description of the arrival of a Jewish transport at a concentration camp; a pretty Jewess who curses the murderers was whipped in the face. As one looked through the small window of the gas chamber – the voice continues its account – one could see how long the victims took to die. A mustachioed SS man talks of how the SS suffered more than their victims: members of a higher race, their nerves were more finely tuned, but they performed their terrible duty in the exemplary fashion required by Himmler, whose secret speech to the SS we hear on the sound track, exhorting the SS to remain honorable, not to take the victims' fur coats or cigarettes, and describing their role in the Holocaust as a glorious page in German history. Himmler imagines how a man's good deeds greet him as he leaves this life; "and what about the bad ones?" the masseur asks. The contrast between Himmler's meditations on the Buddhist respect for life and his own role in the Jews' destruction is drawn with cold, pointed irony, and is perhaps too protracted, but its simplicity is very effective in the context of the Baroque accumulation of the rest of the work.

Insofar as the rest of *Our Hitler* engages in *Trauerarbeit*, it is primarily mourning for German culture. Syberberg sees Hitler's rallies as the pastiches of Wagner's total artwork that prevented the proper realization of the dream of the arts' unification. In so doing they poisoned the sources of cinema. Yet Syberberg is also aware of the possibility that even in the case of Wagner the ideal was already tainted: Draped in a toga, Hitler rises from a grave marked *R.W.* And so, in the remarkable final sequence of the film, a flurry of allegorical images and tableaux organized around Syberberg's own daughter Amélie, the sound track carries Beethoven's orchestration of "An die Freude" from the Ninth Symphony. If Syberberg's tracking camera moves into a model of Edison's Black Maria out of a wish to return to the buried origins of cinema, the quotation from Beethoven corresponds to a return to the roots of the *Gesamtkunstwerk,* which Wagner had discerned in this very passage from Beethoven. The film concludes its obsessive attempt to begin to talk about Hitler – it is still talking of how to begin in the middle of its fourth and final section, about six hours from the moment the lights first went down – by shaking off the entire problematic, by replacing the effort to *talk* with a striking series of complex allegorical images: Their stunning quality retrospectively highlights the prolixity of the middle two sections in particular.

The problem that drives Syberberg's film ceaselessly to cancel itself and begin again is that of the representation of Hitler. How is one to do justice both to the banality and the evil? If one presents him purely realistically, the evil never becomes truly apparent: Complex chains of mediation are interposed between him and the worst consequences of his words. Syberberg's alternative strategy – to present Hitler as a puppet – is ingenious but problematic, and not merely because Hitler's miniaturization runs the risk of trivialization. If Hitler is simply a puppet manipulated by our age-old desires for Paradise and the earth's renewal (the Grail), Syberberg's argument needs to account for the specific ways in which Nazi Germany perverted those desires. Instead, he fulminates against the entertainment industry everywhere. Thalberg's destruction of Von Stroheim's grandiose dreams and the enforced recantations of Eisenstein arouse more passion in Syberberg than the construction of the image of the Jew that facilitated the Holocaust. Syberberg sees no difference between the perversion of dreams under Nazism, under capitalism, and in Hollywood. Any critic intrepid

enough to doubt the accuracy of the filmmaker's intemperate gener-
alizations is consigned to a specially built Hell, whose uncanny resemblance to the concentration camps – often described as the
transference to earth's surface of the Inferno – is something of which
Syberberg is blissfully unaware.

For Syberberg Hitler has destroyed representation; all the artist can
do is engage in a Brechtian presentation that is less the antiillusionist
mode of analysis Brecht himself advocated than a process of wandering through the ruins of the imaginary. In a futile quest for revenge
upon Hitler, Syberberg plays aggressively with the themes before
which art has had to capitulate, hoping perhaps to demonstrate that
the capitulation was a deliberate choice by an art that is sovereign vis-
à-vis the world. At one point in *Our Hitler* one of his puppeteers reflects
on the Nazi era: "They said it was the end of the world – and it was."
Syberberg gives us a guided tour of this dead world. Its death has reduced images of reality to mere images, projected on the screen
watched by an emcee, who sometimes pretends to be walking through
the imaginary space with which he is not aligned. The tour takes us
through a German unconscious where there is none of the ferment that
could generate an explosion of repressed material; the dust of desue-
tude lies everywhere. Facts lie around like lumber in an attic; this attic
is the part of the house beyond which there is nowhere to go, as if
history had been a process of building upward that suddenly stopped.
All one can do is look at the allegorical stars. Reality is merely a ru-
mor, like the sound of the sea in a seashell. Objects are lifted arbitrarily from the time capsule left by a distant era on a distant planet and
then inspected lackadaisically. Where criminals have become puppets,
everything is miniaturized, existing only in the form of a quotation.
History disintegrates in one's hands, all the particles becoming confused. And so Hitler can rise from Wagner's grave in a Roman toga
quoting *The Merchant of Venice.*

The arbitrariness of the combinations is that of an allegory in which
everything conspires to reveal (and conceal) the same thing: The apocalypse that has made the guided tour possible. For Syberberg reality is
now an apocryphal object, his film a Brecht play in the process of de-
composing toward Beckett (toward *Endgame,* for instance). Its mixed
aesthetic allegiances are the reason why most of its scenes fail. Syberberg shows a world the big lie has transformed into a stage in a theater that has closed down. Actors potter around it, recalling their past,
which was never a real past but only the pretense of life, playing with
roles. The emcee's voice drones on endlessly in a theater whose lack of
an audience is a guarantee of artistic purity. The only spectators are
the absent ones – we ourselves – who view the work in a time that is
separated forever from the time of its making. Thus the meaning of

cinema becomes the same as that of German history: It means disso-
ciation. A single frame – the face of Hitler – is endlessly frozen on the
mental screen, with no projecting agency present (no narrative or desire) to get the image to move on. Paradoxically, the sense of reality's
recession becomes a source of complacency: If reality has departed,
one need not attempt to comprehend it rationally. Hence Syberberg's
film contains no documentary analysis of the genesis of Hitler's Germany; it exists instead in an eternal present. Like Duchamp, the most
serene and complacent of the Dadaists, Syberberg draws handlebar
mustaches on the Mona Lisa – an activity that may seem somewhat
redundant in this case, in which the sacred monster already bears a
mustache. He inks it in by replaying Chaplin's parody of Hitler in *The
Great Dictator,* a film about how life (Hitler) imitates art (Chaplin,
who had already conquered the world), forcing art to imitate reality in
its turn in order to recover its own image. The fusion of parody and
pastiche in Syberberg's image ought to prompt a revision of the simple
theory of their difference that underlies Jameson's characterization of
postmodernism, of which Syberberg has often been deemed one of the
key representatives.[4]

The Baroque accumulation of detail in Syberberg's film renders it
less an example of *Trauerarbeit* than an updating for the twentieth
century of the seventeenth-century *Trauerspiel,* which, among other
things, chronicled the pettiness of the apparently great. The ruling
presence in seventeenth-century *Trauerspiel,* as in Syberberg's film, is
that of Dürer's *Melencolia,* the allegorical image of dispirited knowledge surrounded by its useless artifacts. For all its febrile inventive-
ness, the film knows its knowledge is futile: It is all of the past. To
use the terms of one of Freud's most important essays, it is a work of
melancholy rather than mourning. Where all is related to everything
else – for all his postmodernism, Syberberg is an Hegelian – any starting point is fatally arbitrary.

The film is thus an enormous kaleidoscope of images and texts
from the Nazi era, twisted casually by a viewer whose profound resistance to all he sees has reduced realities to endlessly variable signs so
as to dispel the danger of seduction by them. Except in rare cases
(e.g., when the snow that suggests Stalingrad, forgetting, and the
Black Maria begins to sift down on Hitler's droning valet) the combinations are not meaningful. They do not lock into deliberate constella-
tions of meaning but run sluggishly parallel to one another, as near-
automatically as if programmed according to a computer. To read
them as significant combinations – as Anton Kaes strives to do[5] – is, I
think, to misapprehend the nature of Syberberg's work. The offhand
bricolage leaves us to find our own way through the débris of knowledge. Syberberg is indeed Brechtian in requiring us to work on the ma-

terial, but he does not believe in the possibility of our arrival at enlightenment. His Brechtianism is shot through with the melancholy of the modern historian lost amid accumulated data; no ring or grail lies at the end of the film's endless search. Syberberg, unlike Brecht, does not precode the solution into the presentation. The only solution he envisages is the utopia of the closing allegorical sequence.

*Mourning and* Melencolia

Syberberg's use of the term *Trauerarbeit* justifies recourse to the works that first gave the term currency: studies by Freud, Alexander and Margarethe Mitscherlich, and G. H. Pollock. The particular aptness of Pollock's theory concerning the relationship between mourning and adaptation renders it a useful starting point. Mitscherlich summarizes it as follows:

He holds that productive work of mourning is possible only when the lost object, in addition to being introjected, can also be assimilated by the ego. In the case of the German people, that would mean their being able to assimilate even Hitler into themselves, i.e. progressively overcoming him.[6]

Here in a sense is the origin of the carnival barker's suggestion that we give the Hitler within us a chance. Nevertheless, since this opportunity is extended only within the confines of Syberberg's artwork, rather than within reality, that work cannot but reflect the real German inability to "progressively overcome" Hitler, and it does so by itself refusing to make any progress. All the film's scenes are arranged in a bewitched circle around an absent center. The escape from the circle is merely a dream: It occurs when, at the film's end, Amélie Syberberg *closes her eyes* and the choral finale of the Ninth Symphony wells up on the sound track. It is in darkened inner space – when the flow of cinematic images that represents Hitler's lifeblood has been stanched, along with the Wagnerian music of which the Hitler puppet had said that he would survive so long as it was played – that the escape occurs. But it is available only *for a child,* a person with no implication in the past, no burden of guilt to bear. The presence of the child and of pre-Wagnerian music doubly marks the utopian ending as dependent upon regression. Such regression can present itself as progress because the child really does represent the future: The dream can be sustained, though the work firmly underscores its quality of dream. For the final litany of quotations reminds us that we still inhabit the world posthumously ruled by Hitler's spirit, where to think of Germany is to weep in the night, where Hitler's children are the Baader-Meinhof group, and to think of the future is to imagine a black hole. The spirit of hope resides beyond the work's hermetic universe. The hermetic work can dream of something beyond its own confines, for although closed, it is, like the crystal ball (another source of considerations of the future), *transparent*. The snow of forgetting – reminiscent of the opening of "The Waste Land" – may indeed blanket the past, but it can be shaken up and the object cleared of its covering. At the same time, the work is fully aware of the elusiveness of dreams, and insists on their unattainability in an effort to forestall any further attempt to actualize them along the lines of the recent German past.

Since Syberberg invokes a notion of *Trauerarbeit* derived by the Mitscherlichs from a reading of Freud's "Mourning and Melancholia," and the *Melencolia* of Dürer is a presiding image in the film, it is appropriate to ask whether the mechanism of melancholia described by Freud is also the one driving *Our Hitler*. Freud defines melancholia as involving the defection of part of the ego to a position from which it then criticizes the ego's remnant. The violent reproaches addressed to the ego, however, are not aimed against the self but against an introjected love-object, which has been lost by or has failed the one railing against it.[7] One may extrapolate from Freud's remarks and liken the individual unable to withdraw libidinal energy from the lost object and transfer it to new ones to a mourner incapable of coming out of mourning; and one may speculate that the inability is due either to an absence of social rituals for the management of this form of grief, or to a rejection of the collectivity that imposes such rituals – as is the case with Hamlet, whom Freud cites as a classic instance of melancholy. There is thus a potential for endlessness, one richly taken up by Syberberg's work. The lost love-object in this case is the German culture that had to be abandoned when it engendered a Hitler. If Hamlet rejects the amnesiac rituals of the collectivity, the same may be said of Syberberg, with his reference to the Germans as *das Hitlervolk* and his protracted polemics with public opinion. Here the will to endlessness underlying melancholia is reinforced by the intensity of the artist's identification with his own words of reproach, which is a narcissistic identification with his own work. Indeed, Freud speculates that narcissism may have motivated the original choice of love-object:

As Otto Rank has aptly remarked, this contradiction seems to imply that the object-choice had been effected on a narcissistic basis, so that when obstacles arise in the way of the object-cathexis it can regress into narcissism. The narcissistic identification with the love-object then becomes a substitute for the erotic cathexis, the result of which is that in spite of the conflict with the loved person the love-relation need not be given up.[8]

In Syberberg's case there is surely a double love-relation: Syberberg's own love of German culture, which he does not expect his audience to share, and the narcissistic fixation upon Hitler he assumes is

present – if disavowed – in his public, so he can proffer it mockingly as the everyday German's point of entry into his film. Where the
actions or departure of the love-object occasioned pain to the melancholic, the latter counterattacks by bringing it into the self, incarcer-
ating it so as to abuse it in safety and at leisure. Introjection can thus
be a form of devouring, the first step in an elaborate revenge that is
entirely internal, a process of inserting pins into a wax doll representing the lost object (whence the film's use of puppets). If the melancholic smuggles the Other across the borders of the self so as to
berate it with impunity, he does so out of a fear of its continued real
presence – Hitler as unacknowledged legislator of the postwar world –
which requires one to camouflage one's attack by seeming to direct it
against oneself.* Revenge is exacted endlessly upon the other in a
shadow play of the mind.[†] But although the melancholic imports the
Other into the self, it is not the real Other: As Freud notes, it is the
*shadow* of the object that has fallen upon the ego. Turning Hitler into
a puppet is a form of vengeance upon him that simultaneously bla-
zons forth its own futility: It can only lay its hands on the shadow of
the object.[‡]

If Nietzsche was to criticize Wagner for his failure to recognize his
own true calling as a great miniaturist, it is both ironic and appropriate that Syberberg – apostrophized by Susan Sontag as the greatest
Wagnerian since Thomas Mann – can also be accused of working perversely against the grain of his own strength. For although it is his
stated aim to rescue the irrationalism of German Romanticism from its
misuse by National Socialism, he can also be seen as engaged in a
prodigious work of rationalization. For, alongside the Syberberg who
produces compelling surrealist allegories in images, arrays of props
and sequences, stands another who seeks continually to verbalize his
project in a manner that hovers between rationalization and metacri-
tique. It is as if Syberberg shares Thomas Mann's sense of the demonic nature of art and is striving to cocoon his powerfully irrational
surrealist images in a protective web of words. Conscious of the danger of seduction by the contents of the National Socialist cellar, Syberberg displays a probably unconsciously Kafkaesque reluctance to
relinquish the work he has made, surrounding it with a barrage of ap-

---

* This mechanism is fundamental to the novels of Kafka, the object in question being
the father.
[†] This is surely why Hamlet "delays" *his* revenge: He is too busy enforcing it continually
within his own mind to try, or need, to exteriorize it.
[‡] The mechanism of Syberberg's earlier *Ludwig – Requiem for a virgin king* (*Ludwig –
Requiem für einen jungfräulichen König*) is far cloudier: Ludwig himself is clearly not
responsible for his neutralization by the culture industry as a harmless "kitsch king";
consequently the film's search for a guilty party becomes so frustrated as finally to identify with the aggressor and engage in a Brechtian mockery of the virgin king.

parent propaganda whose hidden purpose is to quarantine it like a disease. It is as if his aversion therapy for the Germans – his avant-garde defamiliarization of "familiar" images – is also autotherapy, a brandishing of the shield of enlightenment against the blandishments of art. As Syberberg fragments Nazi iconography in order to drain it of its power, the spirit of the irrational – of the Surrealism whose birth coincided with that of National Socialism – migrates into new images whose bitter, dissonant quality preserves them from ever becoming the foundations of a new ideology. Turning Hitler into a puppet, and then into a toy dog representing a tamed past a child can play with, may strip the Hitler myth of its power, but it throws up at the same time the specter of a puppeteer. Only the Shadow – as the sound track excerpts remind us – knows the evil that lurks in men's hearts.* The puppeteer cannot be identified as the Devil: Syberberg may follow two of the Hitler puppet's speeches with "thus spake the devil," but the devil is then referred to as "the cynic" and "the moralist," allowing the film to oscillate between positive and negative figures (moralist/cynic) and religious and secular worldviews (the devil/Hitler). Thus the question of agency is suspended. If this is because the puppets are really animated by our own projected yearnings for the Grail, the dissolution of the religious framework in which the Grail dream properly belongs provides Syberberg with very few grounds for claiming the inappropriateness of an investment of transcendent hope in a (merely) human leader.

The question of agency summons up a famous phrase: "the banality of evil." Hannah Arendt's suggestive coupling of banality with evil fails, however, to analyze the process that conjoined two seemingly incompatible elements. If banality and evil meet, it is on the ground of shared meaninglessness, a destruction of individuality. The fact that the banal individual can become evil does not necessarily mean that evil and banality are one. Rather, banality is a sign of the hollowing out of personhood that creates the vacuum evil then fills.

Thus the evil force and the banal person only intersect intermittently: a duality that is reflected in the myth of Faust, which separates Faust from his demon instead of showing him possessed by him. In separating Faust from Mephistopheles, Goethe – and, later, Thomas Mann – recognizes their fundamental difference, but is blind to their possible conjunction in moments of possession. Here Goethe is clearly

---

* The Shadow was of course Orson Welles, who is conspicuously both present and absent in this film: Nothing is made, for instance, of the crystal ball in *Citizen Kane* as a parallel to Syberberg's own crystal ball snow-scene opening; and it seems almost as if Syberberg has displaced a lament for the butchering of Welles's career onto Von Stroheim, perhaps to hide his own debt to *Kane*, perhaps because Von Stroheim's German origins facilitate identification with him.

a son of the Enlightenment; and so, for all their fascination by "the demonic," are Thomas Mann and Syberberg. None of the three truly believes in possession, though Leverkühn's use of pastiche in Mann's *Doktor Faustus* does suggest that *Zeitblom* may be merely his persona, whereas Syberberg's use of puppets intimates the presence of larger forces animating the "demonic" individual. Syberberg's work can indeed be juxtaposed usefully with Mann's. For all its stated indebtedness to Brecht and Wagner – a coupling as provocative as Arendt's linkage of banality and evil – *Our Hitler* (cf. Mann's *Brother Hitler*) is perhaps best seen as a reworking of *Doktor Faustus,* which it implicitly accuses of lack of sympathy for – and hence true understanding of – the modern. Token borrowings from Adorno are not enough. Viewed thus, *Doktor Faustus* becomes an insertion of new wine into an old bottle, with Syberberg's collage form as the necessary new bottle. *Our Hitler* can be read as an Adornian treatment of material from Thomas Mann, an aleatory passage amid the ruined monuments of *Kultur.* Like *Doktor Faustus,* it has a dual attitude to the German musical tradition, which it defines as essentially ambiguous (Beethoven or Wagner?). It is focused in a statement placed in the mouth of Harry Baer: "Music over everything. Music overcomes everything." The first sentence is Adornian, dissonant, aware of the ideology concealed within the notion of music's supremacy, for the phrase is fatally reminiscent of "Deutschland über Alles." The latter seeks to escape the dialectical and ironic awareness of the former, and reasserts music's transcendent character.* The movement from "music over everything" to "music overcomes everything" is repeated, in another key, in the closing sequence, the quantum leap whereby the film seeks to move from the bad eternity of the Wagnerian to the untainted Beethovenian source of dreams. It is a step back from the Adornian suspicion that barbarism ("Deutschland über Alles") underlies even the most refined art, to the redemptive child ("and a little child shall lead them"). It is from this latter position that Syberberg's denunciation of postwar reality is launched: In the end, "Hitler in us" does not seem to mean "Hitler in me," for the artist himself is martyred by the same forces that animated Hitler. Amid universal guilt, the artist himself is ultimately *not* responsible, for his works are merely dreams of paradise – and dreams arrive independently of one's volition.

At one point in the film's first section Syberberg suggests that art's

---

* Something similar occurs near the film's end, when the Haydn Kaiserquartett that has been stained irrevocably by the imposition upon it of the words of the German national anthem is played in a restrained, classical style: It is a moment of intense mourning for an art the world has mutilated, rendered all the more poignant by the futility of the attempt to banish the memory of the "Deutschland über Alles" inevitably invoked by the melody.

mourning can be happy: "We live on the happiness of mourning, don't we? / Felix culpa. The happiness of guilt. A sadly beautiful business for art." The meaning of this remark – as of so much that emerges out of the work's reverie and rhapsody – is obscure, but demands consideration. If loss is the necessary precondition of art, art's gain is humanity's loss; Syberberg is here very close both to Sartre, who deems absence the necessary stimulus of the imagination, and to Thomas Mann, with his reflections on the inherent demonism of art. And when he asks, "Should we not live without this work?" he is also very close to the Adorno who suggested that art fall silent before the enormity of the concentration camps. If there is happiness for art in the post-Hitlerian world, it lies in the disappearance of the referent – the destruction of reality – that deprives speech of instrumentality, thereby rendering it innocent, childlike, as free of meaning as music. Nevertheless, since language can never lose its referents entirely, Syberberg's effort to transform language into music is the unfulfillable symbolist dream, the aspiration that pervades all Wagner's work, which cherishes its own heartbreak over unattainability. If Syberberg is entertaining the notion that Hitler has emptied speech of meaning, thus rendering the dream fulfillable – and I am by no means sure that he *is* – he is entertaining an obscenity.

Having arrived at *Our Hitler*'s point of greatest vulnerability, it is worth considering the most influential critical apologia for the work, the famous essay Susan Sontag published in *The New York Review of Books* and then reprinted in *Under the Sign of Saturn*. Sontag's essay typifies the widespread tendency for critics helplessly to adopt Syberberg's own tone of voice – the plethora of metacritical comments in the film leading them to see themselves as redundant, at which point they fall limp and become the dolls to his ventriloquism. Most fail to perceive that the presence of metacriticism within the work itself requires one to gauge the degree of its seriousness, of the threat self-doubt really posed to its generation. And although Sontag mentions Syberberg's lack of self-doubt,[9] she fails to see how it promotes a vatic and robotic tone that accords everything equal weight and removes the weight of the human. Sontag's elegant essay dissolves into hyperbole: Syberberg simply defies categories. Her shuffling of the names of the major twentieth-century artists and theses betokens an inability to pursue the analytic task of evaluating what Syberberg is doing; she defines him instead by negation. Proceeding associatively, she first claims Syberberg as a surrealist, then as a symbolist, and makes only one attempt to confront the reasons for, and nature of, the work's allegiance to both surrealism and symbolism:

In Syberberg's meditation on history in a sound studio, events are visualized (with the aid of Surrealist conventions) while remaining in a deeper sense invisible (the Symbolist ideal). But because it lacks the stylistic homogeneity that was typical of Symbolist works, *Hitler, a Film from Germany* has a vigor that Symbolists would forgo as vulgar. Its impurities rescue the film from what was most rarefied about Symbolism without making its reach any less indeterminate and comprehensive.[10]*

The tension between the visible and the invisible is indeed fundamental, and is a concomitant of Syberberg's allegorical style.† The allegorical image combines presence and absence: The presence of the sign defines itself as absence by drawing attention to the nonpresence of its referent. Whence Syberberg's Benjaminian passion for quotation. The scandalous coupling of Brecht and Wagner founds the work's nonidentity with itself, applying Brecht's notion of the quotable gesture to the *Gesamtkunstwerk* so as to block the possibility of the Wagnerian dream. This is retrospective magic: If the dream's fulfillment can be averted, perhaps the National Socialism that made such use of Wagner can be also. Paul de Man offers a definition of allegory that seeks to account for the split character that causes it frequently to be paired with irony (as in Hawthorne, Mann, or − in the case of De Man's essay − Baudelaire): "Allegory designates primarily a distance in relation to its own origin, and, renouncing the nostalgia and the desire to coincide, it establishes its language in the void of this temporal difference." Thus "it remains necessary, if there is to be allegory, that the allegorical sign refer to another that precedes it."[12] Allegory is therefore profoundly historical, even historicist, in nature. Its inability to enter into and identify with the past freezes the denizens of that prior era into statuary, puppets, or crumbling images of the human, deprived of human motion and variability of emotion. It can thus be argued that in the case of Benjamin the allegorical impulse conflicts with the urge to redemption of the past, a split that runs through Syberberg's work also. And so, to revert to the terms of Sontag's discussion, the eclipse of the symbolist sun by surrealism is the source of the deadlock in Syberberg's work. Surrealism is not a positive program for him, but a sign of the ruin of symbolism. Just as symbolism had decayed into surrealism by the time of the thirties, so the Wagnerian *Gesamtkunstwerk* had become *Triumph of the Will* (*Triumph des Wil-*

---

* Jean-Pierre Oudart nicely catches the film's equivocal relationship to surrealism, which had proclaimed the empire of dreams: He remarks that in effect Syberberg is saying "you are dreaming and you can take it or leave it" ["Tu rêves, et c'est à prendre ou à laisser"].[11] The dream alienates itself, suggesting an imminence of enlightenment, in line with Novalis's statement that when we dream that we dream we are near waking.
† In *Under the Sign of Saturn* Sontag anthologizes her Syberberg essay immediately after a similar meditation on Benjamin; hence her failure to carry over into the later work the Benjaminian categories of allegory and the Baroque (which similarly fuse surrealism with symbolism) is somewhat surprising, as if a desire to emphasize her idols' uniqueness had blinded her to the correspondences between them.

*lens*). Only the dream's removal from history – and henceforth from all possibility of realization – can forestall its perversion.

## Innocence regained

If Syberberg's film is a series of excerpts from the life of the marionettes, the role of the puppets is dual: Sarcastic images of the lack of personhood of the Nazi leaders, they derive a strange innocence from the fact of their direction by somebody else. Syberberg's use of them can recall Kleist's remarks at the end of "Ueber das Marionettentheater," alluded to by the Goebbels puppet:

Therefore, I said in some confusion, would we have to eat once more of the tree of knowledge in order to fall back into the state of innocence?
Certainly, he replied; that is the last chapter of the history of the world.[13]*

*Our Hitler* does not so much eat a second time of the tree of knowledge as chew the apple until it becomes tasteless: as if refusing to swallow it would undo the sin of biting it in the first place. It may then be possible to spit it out, reversing time in the magical manner of the film's very impressive final sequence, which withdraws from Wagner to Beethoven, to a moment before the emergence of a German nation-state, infinitesimally altering the past in order to change the future utterly, picking history's fabric loose to undo its evil. As Syberberg melts all myths – Germanic, Christian, and pop-cultural ones – into a single mass, he becomes a negative Jungian. Had George Lucas, rather than Coppola, been the American promoter of the film, the cat

---

* It may be instructive in the context of Syberberg's use of marionettes and dolls to represent the Nazi leadership to consider the representation of Hitler in the most famous of all Nazi propaganda films, *Triumph of the Will*. Despite the Olympian associations of the descent from the clouds, on landing Hitler is by no means presented as Superman. Indeed, it is the ordinary people in the crowd who are shot iconically: low-angle views of statuesquely jutting jaws. Hitler himself is shot side-on, or from a rear angle, but never iconically. He is the great man as defined by Dickens: He brings out the greatness in others. To adore him is not to be disenfranchised but elevated by the power flowing from him. A similar system of representation is applied in *Olympia*: Whenever Hitler looks concentratedly upon a German athlete, that athlete succeeds; athletes fail whenever the great man is distracted and does not dispense his full power to the gladiatorial mortal below.
  The idea of Hitler as "little man" does not demythologize him but extends his myth. This is why Friedländer is justified in discerning continuities between Nazi kitsch and the seventies "new discourse" about National Socialism – though he remains blind to the way Syberberg in particular employs alienation effects to indicate that kitsch is being *quoted* and subjected to analysis. Syberberg attempts to redeem myth from the kitsch into which it has degenerated. By dislocating kitsch he tries to prevent it from being apprehended unreflectively, as plenitude, or from being recuperated as "fun," as in camp. Instead, it is revealed as a fragment of something much larger, which it denies by representing it in part and passing off its own representation as a new whole: It is a fragment of myth.

would have been let out of the bag. In a sense, though, *Parsifal* can be seen to do just that.

Syberberg's career has been dotted with theoretical pronouncements concerning the importance of preserving myth as a repository of redemptive hope and the need to cleanse the degraded myths of German Romanticism. At times it has been unclear whether the degradation was inherent in the myths' faulty original formulation, or the consequence of their appropriation by later economies of desire, be they National Socialist propaganda or the emasculated cultural pornography of the Bundesrepublik. *Parsifal* is Syberberg's first concerted effort at such a redemption, an attempt that may indeed make this the "satyr play," the comic and optimistic postscript to the tragic inspection of the litter of the world's disintegration in the Hitler film.* Although this version of Wagner's opera is replete with interesting interpretive moves, two of them in particular aim to remove the pernicious features of the work's myth, attempting as it were to perform surgery upon it in order to excise the diseased organs that counteract the benevolent working of the whole system and then insert new ones. The two strands he seeks to remove from the work are its sexist polarity of male redeemer and female temptress and the notion that the female and the Jew (linked in Kundry, whom Wagner compared to the Eternal Jew) require redemption *from without*. A passage from Syberberg's notes on the film refers to both:

At the very start of the 'Parsifal' project it had struck me that Richard Wagner had coupled the problems of woman and of the Eternal Jew into a mutually intensifying form of seductive enticement and the eternal curse of evil, which – like so much else – has never been played. Why did Richard Wagner shudder so at the first thought of this 'Parsifal'? Inasmuch as in the second part Parsifal becomes a woman, the long tradition's problem – here evil woman, there redeeming man – is solved. What is involved however is a notion of redemption that can also occur, and occur directly, through a woman, through whom it must occur, for the sake of her better part. Applied to the Jewish problem, it is not the Jew – as bugbear and myth of the Christian curse – who needs a Saviour to cleanse him, for this development now takes place from within and up to the end of the world. And it is no longer a matter of racism but of spiritual development from within every one of us, if we are ready for it. These things are probably only apprehensible and representable for someone who has made a Hitler film, who has stared into abysses that are otherwise unimaginable in this reality.[14]

---

* It is perhaps symptomatic of the redemptive nature of the project that although the film juxtaposes Klingsor with a plaster half-phallus resting in part upon the heads of Nietzsche, Wagner, and Ludwig II, and in part upon those of Marx and Aeschylus – a reference perhaps to Marx's fascination by Prometheus – it makes no mention of Hitler's interest in the figure of Klingsor.

When Parsifal becomes a girl during Kundry's seduction attempt, the feminization can be seen as formalizing his resistance to seduction, which then becomes impossible. Jungian analysis might describe him as having saved himself through mobilization of the shadow self, the anima; a Freudian might read the feminization as expressive of a masochistic consent to the castration that then removes him from the realm of sexuality, a total identification with the aggressor that paradoxically permits one to overcome her, rather than – like Amfortas before him – fail after rejecting the attack as an assault on his identity as a male. One could argue that Parsifal thus avoids wounding by himself becoming the wound; and so, later, he can become the Saviour, the (menstrually) bleeding Host. Syberberg presents the splitting of the personality as utopian: Parsifal becomes two people, one bearing a sword, the other a cross, and the two meet again at the moment of the grail's disclosure, at the center of Wagner's split death mask. Syberberg's Grail is the reintegration of the personality that split in the moment of crisis, playing dead as it were in order to secrete the threatened (male) portion of the personality elsewhere, for later recovery.

In the case of Kundry, the splitting of voice and appearance (she is played by Edith Clever, but sung by Yvonne Minton) can be read as simply a sign of the exigencies of a *film* version of an *opera*: Both eye and ear must be pleased. Cinema thereby gives the lie to the spell of the *Gesamtkunstwerk:* It admits that no single person can satisfy both demands, that the only individuality capable of so doing is the utopian construction of a superindividuality (Nietzsche's *Uebermensch?*).* Thus when the boyish girl sings with a man's voice the result is not the uncanny, as would be the case in a horror film, but a utopian moment that explicitly declares its own fictive nature and rejects any claims that it has been achieved in actuality. Nevertheless, the undertone of deathliness that runs through the latter part of Act III may suggest that the uncanny still persists, albeit displaced. It is as if the worms secreted beneath Wagner's death mask are emerging, in a version of *Parsifal* filmed by the Nietzsche who identified Christianity with death and denial. Yet in allowing so deathlike a tonality to pervade the second half of the utopian final act, Syberberg is simply responding to elements of dissonance and despair present in Wagner's own music, which does not so much present utopia as a goal achieved but rather as a way station amid wandering, like the musical leitmotif: Thus although the knights' ceremony at the end of Act I did not con-

* Wagner himself seems to have viewed the original singer of the role, Wilhelmine Schröder-Devrient, as just such a superwoman: And Syberberg feels that the combination of Edith Clever's acting with the singing of Yvonne Minton has permitted the recovery of the aura Wagner ascribed to that singer.[15]

stitute anything like a resolution of the work's narrative, it *felt* like a resolution – the individual voice losing and finding itself in the warmth of the choral collectivity. Hence, contra Nietzsche contra Wagner, it is possible to assert that Wagner was aware of the difficulties of utopia, which is continually threatened, glimpsed, and then lost sight of. If the other side of utopia is death, then Wagner's own work shares Syberberg's awareness of the tantalizing, ambiguous quality of the mythical promise. Wagner becomes redeemable through his work's transformation of its own redemption motif into a fata morgana.

## The uncanny homeland: *Heimat* and *Welcome to Germany*

Freud's essay on the uncanny contains a remark by Gutzkow stating the ultimate identity of the *heimlich* (the comfortable, the snug) and the *unheimlich* (the uncanny).[16] Gutzkow's remark is itself uncanny, though it chimes with Freud's own comments elsewhere on the ambiguity of primal words, and would have been endorsed by Bergson, who described the negation as preserving within itself the negated object. Given Bergson's interest in the possibility of an analogy between the workings of the camera and those of human consciousness, it may not be inappropriate to gloss "the negative that preserves the positive" as a description of the film *negative*. And thus Bergson would be the theorist of the status of negation in his own historical moment. In *Heimat* Reitz, like Bergson, draws analogies between the human eye and the sights of machines – the camera and the gun. One-eyed Hänschen is described as a born sharpshooter, for he has no need to close one eye to take aim, and his monocular perspective is that of the camera also. The link between the camera's shots and those of a gun is made twice in the film: once, when Hänschen shoots off the telegraph poles' insulators as Eduard is posing and snapping a lady watering flowers; and, in a more somber vein, when Anton films the machine-gunning of Russian hostages in the woods.

The uncanny is linked to film in another sense too. As the color repeatedly drains out of the image and then unpredictably bleeds back in, the film itself becomes potentially uncanny. Color can always become monochrome, and black-and-white could equally well be color – an alternation that may correspond to Reitz's knowledge of the imminent introduction of color film stock in the thirties; after watching the film, one may even find oneself remembering black-and-white scenes in color, and vice versa, a feature of the work that may well highlight memory's unreliability. Ultimately, and paradoxically, however, the effect partakes less of the uncanny than of self-congratulation: the potentially "uncanny" shifts simply indicate the filmmaker's sovereign freedom vis-à-vis the past, and *both* the monochrome (the conventional signifier of "pastness" in a film) and the color (the sign of presence) are reassuring. In permitting himself these shifts, Reitz seeks to have things both ways. Monochrome allows us the pleasure of nostalgia, the narcissistic cherishing of the sense of loss; color meanwhile generates pleasure in seeing the past "come alive" through the miracle of film. It is as if one need only twist the color control knob on one's set to bring the past into the present – to discover in the largely depoliticized world of Hunsrück a utopia in which the past is no longer compromising but rather inviting. Moreover, the analogies between the human eye and that of the machine serve overwhelmingly to *humanize* technology, rather than to suggest a relationship between identification with technology (libidinal investment in the machine, à la *Metropolis*) and dehumanization. The camera that inverts images becomes a child standing on its head. The color shifts are novelties to spice up the material, not components in a radical project of defamiliarization. And if *Heimat*'s absorption in the past precludes its interrogation, it is hardly surprising that it should seem *unheimlich* to those who recall just what that past involved.

Like Syberberg, Edgar Reitz employs the term *Trauerarbeit* in interviews about his fifteen-and-a-half-hour family saga. The term bestows on his work some of the cachet derived from its use in the Mitscherlichs' book, even though it is redefined in terms incompatible with their project. Reitz defines *Trauerarbeit* as the recovery by the Germans of the ability to tell stories about the past.[17] The stories to be told, however, are as evasive as the one told by Reitz himself, whose film adroitly sidesteps potentially compromising material. Conceived as an anti-*Holocaust*, a recovery of "our" past from the dollar-dirtied hands of the Hollywood invaders, it allows one of its characters to remark incidentally that times are hard for the Jews and exonerates the little people on the basis of their understandable willingness to leave politics to the bigwigs in Berlin. Reitz may speak of how his film made it possible for many Germans to recover the memory of the past, but the stories it released were those of people who were peripheral to the administration of evil. The stories of the most guilty remain untold. Perhaps mercifully so: The war crimes trial transcripts suggest that such stories would have seesawed between self-pitying self-justification and frightening self-satisfaction. Pauline may overhear Wilfried – the mayor's son who has joined the SS – speak in an undertone of the Jews "going up the chimney," but she does not ask further or relay what she has heard to anyone else. The film's habit of leaving events open – the murderer of the naked woman in the woods is never found – allows it to drop inconvenient details very casually, without any repression seeming to be present. At the same time, the film's wealth of detail makes it seem unlikely that anything of importance could

have been omitted. And yet it has, as a consideration of a comparable
work reveals. The work is Wendelgad von Staden's memoir *Nacht über
dem Tal* (*Night over the Valley*), which documents her mother's efforts
to discover, and then counter in some way, the concentration camp
hidden in a nearby valley. The book is set in an area very close to the
Hunsrück region that is the site of Reitz's film. In *Heimat*, however, no
one asks any questions. Eduard may be shown reading the newspaper
out loud in the first sequence, when his brother Paul Simon returns
shell-shocked from World War I, but there is no mention of any reaction to newspaper items from the thirties. With almost everyone in the
village related to everyone else, the community is turned in on itself. It
may be unusual to criticize a film for what it fails to do, but Reitz's
work is complicitous with a nationalist desire to ignore certain things.
Reitz's admirable eschewal of the melodramatic form of *Holocaust* extends to a far less admirable censorship of its content. It is because
Reitz mostly concentrates upon what he does well – with the exception
of two cliché-ridden sections, "The American" and "The Feast of the
Living and the Dead," which, interestingly enough, are the only ones
to depart radically from the screenplay jointly written by Reitz and Peter Steinbach – that the film is so often so convincing. Particularly fine
are the three longer sections: the first one, showing Paul's return
home, his vague disaffection with village life, and his inexplicable departure; "Soldiers' Loves," with the powerful Maria–Otto love affair
during World War II; and "Hermännchen." The last of these three is
particularly interesting, for it gives clear reasons why a young man
should want to leave the stifling, censorious narrowness of his native
village, and so contrasts usefully with the enigma of Paul Simon's departure. Since one of these episodes is set in the twenties ("Fernweh")
and another in the fifties ("Hermännchen") one can guess that each
profits from the absence of the careful evasions that surround the Nazi
period* (the camera *glides past* groups discussing sensitive topics).

Insofar as Reitz's film incorporates potentially defamiliarizing devices (the color shifts, the gaps), they have a dual effect. Intended on
the one hand to forestall the work's recuperation by a television audience, they signify Reitz's allegiance to "higher things" (in other words,
*Kultur*): The occasional strangeness of the *discours* indicating that, although the *histoire*, the recounted story, might resemble a soap opera,
it is far-removed from the sphere of TV melodrama. At the same time
the devices achieve an effect perhaps undesired by Reitz: They render

---

* The series might best have ended with "Hermännchen," since it loses its way in the
hysterical flailings of the last two episodes, which entrap the characters in all-too-evident
makeup. The extraordinary poignancy of the brief flashbacks attributed to Ernst and
Herrmann in the very last episode derives in part from a sense that their perspective is
also the director's, and embodies the series' nostalgia for itself.

more palatable the idea of living in (and with) Hunsrück. Since all the characters who leave Hunsrück are subsequently compromised – think of Paul or Hermann, who return as caricatures; whereas even though Eduard makes only a brief excursion to Berlin, he brings back the grasping Lucie, the whore of ambition, rather than venereal disease – the only way to remain untainted is never to leave home. Those who stay, however, are unable to scotch all stirrings of an urge to escape. The film's identification with the marginalized position of women and children is incomplete. Moreover, considered closely, the women themselves are far from content in their marginalization. The shifts back and forth between black-and-white and color fidget and dream of escape as ineffectually as does Maria when watching *La Habañera*.* The insubstantiality of her yearnings is underscored when she merely draws Spanish curls on her mirror image – the sense of the moment's meaning created by the image's presentation in color is cancelled by Reitz's general refusal to use color for such a purpose – whereas her friend Pauline had actually altered her hairstyle and mimicked Zarah Leander for her husband. So long as technology is a toy, it is harmless. But it can only be so for the duration of childhood. Anton's optical works is a partial exception to this rule, but it too is identified with the past: New farming methods are introducing impurities into the air, thoughtless technology threatening the artisanal craft of lens making. To carry over an interest in it into adulthood is to condemn onself to the position of awkward, overgrown child: Eduard, with his unappreciated photography, his sympathy with Hänschen, and his impotently childish riposte to Wilfried Wiegand's doubts over the purity of the Simons' ancestry. (Wiegand – doesn't that sound French?)

The West German public may have used Reitz's film rather as Lucie used Eduard, but this was only possible because Reitz himself – beaten down by the commercial failure of *Der Schneider von Ulm,* as Michael Geisler has noted in a fine article that performs its own "work of mourning" for the shortcomings of the debate that materialized around the film[18] – was insufficiently rigorous in the dissection of complicity. The self-reflection in his film primarily concerns the technology of the apparatus, not its own institutional and ideological positioning. Not that a radical alienation is needed: The subtle one that pervades Von Trotta's *Marianne and Juliane* would have sufficed. The edge of the formal alienation devices is blunted by nonalienating content. The irony of *Heimat's* praise of the margins is that the dynamics of reception have marginalized Reitz himself within his own film.

In retrospect, *Heimat* appears to mark the beginning of the end of

---

* Interestingly enough this was Sirk's last German film before his departure to the United States; would Reitz view the American Sirk as witheringly as he does Paul Simon?

the wave of reckonings with the past that surfaced in the German consciousness in the late seventies. Even Syberberg and Von Trotta – authors of the most serious exercises in *Vergangenheitsbewältigung* – hailed Reitz's achievement. Four years later, however, a film by Thomas Brasch, the official West German entry at Cannes, marked a venture into an area that had been taboo to West German narrative filmmakers: the representation of the Jewish experience of the Holocaust. Brasch's film is clearly an extension of his work as a playwright; not representation of the events of the past, but their Brechtian presentation, as the film thematizes the problem of their representability by questioning the director-hero's efforts to turn his own experiences into a film. In his combination of a Brechtian distaste for illusionism with a willingness to probe the legacy of the Nazi years, Brasch is perhaps closer to Syberberg than anyone else. The fact that both men came to West Germany following an education in the GDR suggests that the East German may be better equipped to speak of these things than his Western counterpart: The East German state ideology that deems the Bundesrepublik the prime refuge of fascism having given him from birth the sense of the past's distance and difference that renders it representable, whereas his own experience of East German rule facilitates identification with the victims of an earlier German totalitarian régime.

*Welcome to Germany* reads the subtitle of Brasch's film about a Jewish film director who returns from Hollywood to the country where he once suffered in a concentration camp. Even before the story begins, however, title and subtitle ought to have intimated the ambiguity of the welcome. The title, *The Passenger* (*Der Passagier*), was also that of the last, unfinished film of the great Polish director Andrzej Munk, set in a concentration camp, whereas a welcome to "Germany" was an uncanny invitation to a place that did not then exist. Despite the half-lazy, half-compensatory German usage that pretended otherwise, there had been no "Germany" for more than forty years when Brasch's film was released. The Germany that exists in this film is a trauma in the director's mind. He is returning to its geographical location in the hope of divesting himself of its vampirical mental weight.

In theory, then, Brasch's film is welcome, and not just in Germany: The ironic subtitle offers an appropriate rejoinder to the self-righteousness of the "Made in Germany" logo of *Heimat,* itself an intended riposte to *Holocaust*'s Hollywoodization of German experience. And yet Brasch's film does not work. What goes wrong?

Tony Curtis is Janko, a famous Hollywood director who has returned to Berlin (West) to exorcise his experiences in Nazi Germany. He is received ambivalently: The German technicians he will work with savor the whiff of Hollywood he brings, but no one is really very keen to dig up matters that are best left forgotten and were in any case the responsibility of a previous generation. For Janko the matter in question is the death of his friend Baruch, shot while trying to escape from the film studio where the two of them were among a group of Jews given a brief stay of execution by the director, who selected them from Auschwitz to play bit parts in an anti-Semitic *Heimatfilm*. Janko's restaging of the past expresses the amorphous guilt that besets the survivor. He, Janko Cornfeld, plays the part of Körner, the Nazi director who had pulled Baruch, himself, and a motley group of other Jews from the huddled ranks at Auschwitz. He casts himself in an ambiguous position, between the alternatives of Körner and a Jewish rabbi who is himself singled out in a multiplying regress of "director" figures to select fellow camp inmates for roles in Körner's film. But the survivor cannot dispel his sense of guilt over his refusal to try to escape together with his friend. The reenactment of his trauma simply cements its hold over him, and at the film's end he sits in the Berlin airport lounge, his flight having already departed, trapped in the ungovernable past.

The scenario has a troubling and moving ring. Brasch, however, turns what could have been a felt drama into a Pirandellian thriller about the director's past and identity, complete with such false clues as the resemblance between the names of the Jewish and Nazi directors (is Cornfeld "really" Körner?), which suggests a different and more substantial source of guilt, or the way the sound is artificially drowned when members of the director's entourage discuss, or his wife enquires after, his true identity. The regress of plays-within-plays only conspires to alienate us from a protagonist who may be victim or villain. Either/or and neither/nor, in the end the director – with his dark glasses – becomes a blank cipher.

Janko's reenactment of Baruch's abortive escape attempt is given twice in the film: once, at the very beginning – when he takes us from the dressing room, alongside the studio buildings and past a clump of watching actors to the gate over which Baruch slumped when he had been shot – and once near the end. The first presentation has an air of authority subverted on the second occasion by the makeup girl Sofie, who loved Baruch and appears now, a cross-eyed Fate in a wheelchair, to denounce Janko. Her choice of scapegoats is very canny (it matches that of Reitz): In the often anti-American climate of modern West Germany, who better to blame than a successful Hollywood director? Sofie accuses him of passing off as real experience the fruits of imagination; he remained in the dressing room as his friend went to his death. And yet her own statement that "the eyes are two liars" ought to warn against placing too much credence in the eyewitness. Even so, strangely, the film lends plausibility to her reproach by giving her the last word. The éclat of her revelation – clearly inserted as a dramatic climax – implies a certainty the remainder of the film is careful to question. Sofie is not the only figure to argue that Janko is guilty because he tries to imagine what he never saw. (Thus Janko's guilt becomes in a sense a projection of Brasch's own self-reproach over his own lack of experience of the camps.) The rabbi's quotation of the Old Testament proscription of the fashioning of graven images suggests that filmmaking is inherently a guilt-ridden activity. Here Brasch's Brechtian indictment of Hollywood illusionism confuses still further the question of the reality of Janko's guilt. Since filmic representation is guilt-ridden, the playwright can in theory resort to theatrical *presentation* and so get himself off the hook on which he leaves Janko dangling. And yet the rabbi himself, when selecting Janko for his bit part, had told him to come back as a victor. The Germans on his set do indeed see him as such, the incarnation of capitalist bad taste. If Brasch's film shows them to be wrong, it simultaneously exudes a vague resentment of Cornfeld, suggesting that they embody Brasch's own disavowed attitude regarding the Hollywood success Tony Curtis personifies. Imprisoning him behind dark glasses can be an indirect form of revenge.

During the screen test, when casting the role of the rabbi, Cornfeld judges the actors by their ability to tell a Jewish joke. The man he chooses simply recites Heine's lyric about the girl who loves a boy who loves a different girl, though he leaves us to fill in the ending: "Es ist eine alte Geschichte," yes, but it still breaks the heart. The film itself shows an old story perennially renewed by the repetition compulsion that seeks to master trauma, to lose it in a hall of mirrors. Perhaps this is why it cannot be told properly: It can only echo endlessly, rather as the Heine lyric is cruelly echoed by a puppet play of a German girl who marries the rich Jew to cover her father's debts, and that in turn is reiterated in the plot of the *Heimatfilm* in which Janko and Baruch were acting. Yet Brasch's retelling of Janko's untold story has little of the devastating irony and poignancy of the Heine lyric it takes as its motto. The regress of director figures does not explicitly encompass Brasch himself, for whom Cornfeld's is a merely hypothetical dilemma. The characters who cannot find their author are wanderers in the trap of a maze maker himself lost in admiration of his own elaborate, self-baffling contrivance.

## Late Fassbinder and popular culture:
## À propos *Lili Marleen*

When Willie, the singer star of *Lili Marleen,* is criticized by Robert, her boyfriend in the Jewish Resistance, for consorting with Nazi high-ups, she retorts that all she is is a singer – and "Lili Marleen" is only a song. Reproached by viewers with making a work that exploits to the hilt the spectacular fascination of fascism, Rainer Werner Fassbinder could give a similar answer: It's only a film. He could add that his melodramatic film is attuned to popular desires, to the longings of the rank-and-file soldiers who can only express resistance to the régime by singing a favorite banned song. Their longing for a little bit of glamour is coded opposition. But although fighting may stop for the duration of the song – bombs raining soil the moment it stops, as flowers rain on the singer – the readiness with which the soldiers return to their warlike pursuits may cause one to wonder about the depth of their opposition, and that of Fassbinder himself. At this point Fassbinder could switch to a second alibi. Accused of presenting Jews as a ghoulish bunch of financiers well able to buy a way out of any trouble the Nazis might provide, Fassbinder can then point to his own part as the man who hands Willie a roll of film to be used during her Polish tour to document concentration camp atrocities. Like Willie, Fassbinder himself is a whore with a heart of gold. Fassbinder thus has two stand-ins in this film: one the innocent Aryan Willie, who only sings and who is shut out at the film's end (classical culture returns, displacing popular culture and the sexual license of wartime); and the other a man whose death is mentioned casually near the film's end by the rich Jews who have survived. (The dictatorial director disguises himself as a victim to avoid his comeuppance?) It may be argued that Fassbinder's film achieves the status of ideological critique through its parody of melodrama – though the parody is most evident at the level of the score, which underlines certain key moments with overblown exaggeration. It may also be argued – somewhat more ambiguously – that even if it is (in Jameson's terms) less a parody of melodrama than a pastiche, it fulfills a critical function by demonstrating through its own success that there is still a market for fascist spectacle. (Fassbinder as agent provocateur, luring the petite bourgeoisie to the cinema – where they can then be executed?)

Fassbinder's enterprise is of course anything but unambiguous, though the mode of presentation of Hanna Schygulla as Willie may help one define where the film's bias ultimately lies. Its intimation of the futility of Robert's – somewhat unmotivated – desire to discover "which side Willie is on" is surely part of a tactic to discredit any efforts to discover its own allegiances. Willie has been apostrophized breathlessly by Thomas Elsaesser:

By resisting all constructions of herself in terms of binary oppositions, she achieves a particular kind of freedom. She becomes a sign without a unique referent. Instead, *several* referents – notably her star image and the phonograph record – are simultaneously attached to her, allowing her desire to exist outside either possession or fulfillment. Neither her show-business "personal-ity" nor the song she records and sells represents or expresses her desire, ex-cept in the way they permit her to constitute herself outside fascism and outside the family. Spectacle becomes a form of escape. Whereas her lover for-cibly unifies himself in a discourse of repression, she lives desire as pure dis-placement and difference without fetish or object.[19]

Despite Elsaesser's words, which have something of the giddy tone of a poststructuralist panegyric to alienation, Willie's attachment to Robert can indeed be read as fetishistic – a fetish being of course an allegorical signifier of something perennially absent. Rather like the heroine of *The Marriage of Maria Braun* (*Die Ehe der Maria Braun*), also played by Schygulla – the casting is surely intertextual – Willie is bound almost throughout the film to a man situated at a romantic dis-tance – a variety of love in which modern popular culture has invested deeply, be it in the form of the screen idol or a song like "Lili Marleen" itself. *

The question of "which side Willie is really on" is a displacement of the one that actually perturbs Robert: Does she want me or her career? It arises because of the film's operation of several incompatible melo-dramas, superimposed like shifting stencils in a now-you-see-it-now-you-don't procedure. In one melodrama, a fascist narrative which one hopes is not the film's master narrative, youthful love and the true-hearted German blond are victimized by the Jews; in another, "demo-cratic" one, the "good German" works clandestinely for the Resistance. One melodrama presents Willie as victim, exploited by the Nazis, the Jews, and the history that has granted her the unwanted success that prevents her obtaining the real object of her desires – Robert. Yet an-other shows her as the artiste tragically compelled to sacrifice per-sonal wishes to the necessity that the show (or the cause) go on. Mingled in with this is an expressionist father–son conflict given a fas-cist twist: It's the Jewish father who oppresses his son; loath to dilute the concentration of his financial and cultural capital, he prevents the German–Jewish alliance that would provide an allegorical resolution of racial tensions. Needless to say, the upshot of this congeries of su-perimposed narrative lines is incoherence.

Fassbinder's presentation of Willie is profoundly ambiguous, for he both sympathizes with her starry disorientation and stresses that she has no voice and her accompanist no talent. On the level of popular cultural critique, the implication is that any old rubbish is good enough for the masses: Fassbinder in no way disagrees with the hard-boiled wisdom of the moguls. Willie's technical incompetence is

* The title is surely fetishistic also, seeking to obviate the nagging German loss of the real Marlene and Lola Lola: Dietrich.

surely the reason why Elsaesser can describe her as "escaping possession," for her song does not "express" her and could as easily have
been sung by another: The culture industry recruits her exactly as a
soldier is conscripted into the army: whence the rhyme between her
alienation from Nazi Germany and that of the Wehrmacht soldiers, all
displaced persons, an ideal cinema audience. Shifted from one uncontrollable situation to another, they virtually embody the principle of exchange itself. Although one may imagine that Fassbinder sees himself
as a more self-possessed, populist Von Sternberg to Schygulla's Dietrich, he can also be read as setting his lead actress up: She really is
devoid of singing and dancing talent, and it is hard to know whether
her pact with Fassbinder is a Warholian folie à deux, deliberate parody, or even masochistic submission to his effort to turn her into the
glitter queen whose mindlessly excessive femininity is so ludicrous as
to reinforce the misogyny of the gay. At the same time, any attempt to
set Schygulla up – assuming that one is indeed underway – founders
on her trancelike equanimity, which renders her impervious to mockery. (Hence when Willie's torrid telephone conversation with Robert
goes out over the PA system, the fact that she does not seem to be
mortified arrests one's incipient compassion for her.) The false populism that says anyone can be a star leaves one unenlightened over why
particular people (and works) should become successful at particular
moments. Fortune is simply a matter of fortuity, the coincidences
Fassbinder remorselessly accumulates. The speed he imparts to the
melodramatic merry-go-round is surely sadistic, intended to leave us
dizzy and sick. Hence, for all its historical trappings, the film is ahis-
torical: It melts into one homogenized mass such widely divergent moments in the history of popular culture as 1942 and 1982. Marlene
becomes Lili becomes Hanna: Regal succession in the culture industry. The directorial machine of the eighties may whip up more spectacular suds than most forties melodramas could boast, but the basic
material is still soap.

Nevertheless, occasional hints of depth unexpectedly corrugate the
film. Perhaps its most sobering moment occurs when the Nazi super-
vising the exchange of Jewish prisoners for the Auschwitz film wonders if it is indeed a fair trade, for although a film can be copied,
people cannot. The potential significance of this chilling remark is enhanced by the late Fassbinder's preoccupation with mirrors and doubles (though I would argue that the appearance of these doubles
mystifies and short-circuits the autobiographical impulse that nour-
ishes Fassbinder's best work; more on this later in this section). And
yet nothing follows from it. Similarly, the subsequent dynamiting of
the bridge between the two parties by Robert's brother, who opposes
such "dirty deals," is undercut by the absurdity of the character. In-

deed, the film finally undercuts itself completely near its end when it drifts into the wood of Mieze's murder in *Berlin Alexanderplatz,* which it plugs with knowing allusions: The one-man culture industry directs us to another product from the same firm. When the little heroine eventually vanishes into the night, a brave German thrust out by clannish Jews, our sympathy with her desolation stems from a projection of our own sense of emptiness on leaving this self-congratulatory, cynically sentimental film, which has substituted knowingness for knowledge and, by placing us in the know, has left us out in the cold.

For all its apparent delectation of Nazism as camp spectacle, Fassbinder is disdainful of camp's empty-headedness. Sadistically cramming an excess of candy-floss into a digestive system addicted to junk food, he is kind to be cruel. His contempt for camp, however, is not dictated by his occupation of the higher ground of analysis. There is no more illumination of the sociopsychological mechanisms of Nazism in this film than in the mordantly self-regarding, pretentious and sexist *Despair (Eine Reise ins Licht)*; indeed, far more understanding of the National Socialist mentality is to be garnered from Fassbinder's early films, which focused on xenophobia and persecution. By trading in melodramatic clichés, the later films flatter the audience into the delusion that knowingness concerning the generic conventions of the past is equivalent to an understanding of the real historical moments at which they appeared. Peer Raben's music – melted-down Weill – performs a similar function, which is less one of camp than of kitsch: As Eco puts it, a quotation unable to generate a new context.[20] If one accepts Hermann Broch's definition of kitsch as the product of a desire to work "beautifully" rather than well,[21] then *Despair* – with its pyrotechnic camera – may be deemed kitsch.* If *Lili Marleen* is more interesting, it is because it institutes a dialectic between kitsch (the fruit of a failed aspiration to art) and entertainment (which is blithely indifferent to art). Whence the film's double-bind, its inability either to transcend or become entertainment. The problem is painfully inescapable, as the work's self-referential touches raise unfulfilled expecta-

* The following remarks by Milan Kundera indicate the relevance of Broch's theory to Fassbinder's work:

Today, fifty years later, Broch's remark is becoming truer still. Given the imperative necessity to please and thereby to gain the attention of the greatest number, the aesthetic of the mass media is inevitably that of kitsch; and as the mass media come to embrace and to infiltrate more and more of our life, kitsch becomes our everyday aesthetic and moral code. Up until recent times, modernism meant a nonconformist revolt against received ideas and kitsch. Today, modernity is fused with the enormous vitality of the mass media, and to be modern means a strenuous effort to be up-to-date, to conform, to conform even more thoroughly than the most conformist of all. Modernity has put on kitsch's clothing.[22]

The widely current name for the modernism that decks itself in kitsch's clothing is of course postmodernism.

tions of seriousness, even as entertainment's insertion into the Nazi context precludes naive enjoyment. Indeed, the title song's repetitiousness can become a source of torture, as it is for Robert in his surrealistic cell: The film's most acerbic metaphor for the workings of mass culture identifies the song's "catchiness" with the automatic irritation of a record stuck in its groove. The gusto with which Robert is tormented may be Fassbinder's imaginary revenge upon the backer who imposed Giancarlo Giannini as the price of the deal. The film tantalizes us – as it does Robert – with the fata morgana of a denied pleasure. The ostentatious tracking shots past scenes of rancid glamour exude masochistic exclusion from them.

Fassbinder's pseudo-Brechtian devices seek on the one hand to derive sadistic satisfaction from the *Publikumsbeschimpfung* that was so common in the late sixties, even as on the other his mimicry of melodrama solicits the obedient tears of the masses. If Sirk is a key figure for Fassbinder, it is because the auteurist orthodoxy concerning his work suggests that he succeeded in resolving the contradiction between art and entertainment – unlovable authenticity on the one hand, mass popularity on the other – that so tormented the younger director. In actuality, Sirk solved his problem opportunistically, by reducing the imperative of art to the small matter of retaining a tasteful tone, while explicating his supposed true intentions in interviews dispensed after the fact to eager auteurists. Attempts to derive pleasure from the films by identifying with the power position of Fassbinder himself founder on his self-divisions and self-hatred. Nevertheless, the early films, particularly *The Merchant of the Four Seasons* (*Der Händler der vier Jahreszeiten*) and *Fear Eats the Soul* (*Angst essen Seele auf*), have a certain low-key, grubby authenticity as evocations of petit-bourgeois self-hatred and the squirming of the pimply, outcast adolescent. The later films, however, are fatally compromised by pretension: Their empty, mannered virtuosity glazes the low-ceilinged power games of the early films with a distancing sheen of allegory. As we watch little people going about their pursuits as would-be world-historical events issue from the radio or television, a double disillusion sets in: The indifference to "great events" of ordinary folk bespeaks no Brechtian peasant wisdom, only unquenchable triviality. If media messages fail to penetrate their world, providing only aural or visual wallpaper, it is partly the fault of provincialism and partly indicative of the hollowness of the public sphere. Since art's entry into that sphere entails its prostitution, there is no point in being anything other than opportunistic in one's art.

Fassbinder identifies his own self-alienation with the self-alienation of the Germans. Intended as essays on German history, the later films do not probe the past, however, but surround it with decorative ricochets of reflections. Fassbinder's work definitively demonstrates that the presence of mirrors in a work is no guarantee of self-knowledge. *Berlin Alexanderplatz* is typical: Fassbinder's omission from the early scenes of Döblin's reference to a cinema is symptomatic of his own blindness to his own work's place in film history. (For all its shortcomings, *Heimat* does at least show an excerpt from the Zarah Leander film that is its namesake.) The melancholia of Günter Lamprecht's Biberkopf is understandable, for he is oppressed and partly erased by the directorial interpositions of monotonously flashing neon lights, Peer Raaben's floating pastiches of Weimar cabaret tunes, and an indifferently circling distant camera. Not until Barbara Sukowa's astonishing Mieze ruptures the synthetic stylization does the film come to life. For the rest, however, Fassbinder is a depressive Godfather, dragging around his limp puppets. The world-weary director has conquered the public and is still unsatisfied. He fails to grasp that his dissatisfaction stems from his perversion of the director's seat into a throne from which to dispense favors to those who grovel most adeptly. Fassbinder did indeed achieve his ambition of becoming a one-man Hollywood. He recreated the studio system in all its meretriciousness and oppressiveness.

Up to this point, the tone and content of this essay have come close to a thoroughgoing denunciation of the works of Fassbinder's final years. The balance can be corrected slightly however by consideration of the one late work that seems to me to be of value. It is not a work of the Fassbinder whose assertion that "love is the most effective form of social repression" indicates how his own desire to be loved motivated self-betrayal and caused him to enter into a devil's pact with the imagery and modes of production of popular culture, but rather that of the Fassbinder who was able resolutely to confront the image of his own unloveliness: *In a Year with Thirteen Moons* (*In einem Jahr mit dreizehn Monden*). Pure lunar caustic, it is a work whose unremitting dissonances beat out a threnody for the monster in the mirror. The only comparable passages in late Fassbinder are his autobiographical contributions to the *Germany in Autumn* (*Deutschland im Herbst*) omnibus film.

The creature categorized as a monster is marginal to society, subsisting in the interstices between its categories. It is demonized, attacked, and destroyed by those who understand it to be seeking a place at the center, rather than in the borderland where it "belongs." In its onslaught upon the monster, society conveniently forgets its own role in first bringing it into the limelight, whose mockery of love maddened it into truly monstrous frustration and deeds: One recognizes the scenario of *King Kong*. Although it yearns for a place in the light (though it shuns the limelight it knows to be too harsh, too revealing), society will only grant it this place as part of a freak show. One may think of that enormously cultivated man, John Merrick, and of David

Lynch's plangent, exemplary act of mourning for him, *The Elephant Man*. One may think also of *In a Year with Thirteen Moons*, the only one of Fassbinder's late films to escape the effect of a cynical ringmaster's play with an empty glamour. It does so following the salutary shock of Fassbinder's bereavement by the death of his ex-lover, Arnim Maier. In this film Fassbinder is the reverse of a ringmaster: If he places a freak before us, the crepuscular lighting veils the gaze to allow the all-too-human monster a place of retreat. The film mourns the monster who cannot have any progeny because in him/her the sexes cancel one another out.

The protagonist of *In a Year with Thirteen Moons* has assumed a name that is unspeakable: Is he to be called "Erwin," "Erwin/Elvira," or "Elvira"? The person in question – the person whose being has undergone fundamental questioning, in this case as the result of a sex-change operation – can be designated by the pronoun "s/he." This is, of course, the preferred pronoun of a feminism that has failed to think through its own position. "S/he," being unpronounceable, is writing that can never enter the everyday world: A merely utopian gesture, it privileges alienation in the blind manner of a Derrida. "S/he," the divided word, designates a subject whose consciousness is contradictory and self-destructive: Fassbinder would surely describe it as the exemplarily damaged consciousness of late capitalist society. The new pronoun, like the sex-change operation, solves everything in theory and nothing in practice – for to fetishize a pronoun and deem a text "sexist" on the basis of its pronouns is to ignore the really important issue of attitudes; it is a simple and draconian measure for simple minds.

*In a Year with Thirteen Moons* can be read as the history of "s/he." It is the story of a superfluity. A note at the film's beginning informs us that a year with thirteen moons is a period of disturbance; the one in question is 1978. Given the traditional identification – a beautiful, but also a sexist one – of woman with the moon, the year of lunar superfluity is one of a superfluous woman, a woman who should have never been. That woman's self-creation – Erwin's sex-change operation – proves the beginning of his/her end. The discarded lover discards "herself": Erwin has undergone the operation because Anton, with whom he is infatuated, once said, "It's a pity you're not a woman." In a sense, the film is about Fassbinder's lover Armin Maier, a response to Maier's suicide after his abandonment by Fassbinder on the latter's birthday. The satellite was secondary and could always be discarded: Fassbinder was a planet with a steady entourage of at least thirteen mooning actors and actresses. "S/he" is, however, also Fassbinder himself, as the posthumous film *A Man Like Eva* – with Eva Mattes in the role of Fassbinder himself – was to emphasize. Thus the film is autobiographical in two senses, one obvious, the other cryptic.

*In a Year with Thirteen Moons* traces the thirteenth moon's eclipse. "S/he" wanders the cold city of Frankfurt, suffers repeated rejection and humiliation, and finally commits suicide. There are lights in this world, but they are not placed for the characters to see or be seen by. The lighting partakes of impersonal process, and so there is no difference between the light of the public and that of the private sphere: The interior lighting Fassbinder controlled is as alienating as the garish strip lighting of the amusement arcades. The figures are perpetually on the verge of vanishing into the darkness. Silence too always threatens to engulf them. The theme of the inability to speak recurs: Goethe's remark in *Torquato Tasso* that "When the man fell silent in his torment / a God gave me to utter what I suffer," is itself virtually inaudible, mocked by its falsetto delivery by Erwin as the camera tracks remorselessly past slaughterhouse carcasses. Later on we see pinned to the wall a note from Elvira/Erwin, expressing her/his fear of completing a sentence, for the consequences are incalculable. (Consequences truly are incalculable in this film: "s/he" gives an interview about his old friend, the magnate Anton Saitz, which causes his wife to fear Saitz's reprisals – but nothing ensues.) The slaughterhouse scene is clearly intended to be provocative, but is far from gratuitous: Armin Maier had in fact worked in one. What is more, a thematic linkage of butchery and betrayal runs through Fassbinder's work (cf. *Bolwieser*): Elvira/Erwin's lover calls her/him meat just before he leaves. The lover who sees the partner's body as merely flesh is about to betray it. Images of butchery do double duty in Fassbinder's work, providing a working-class equivalent of the violence of everyday fascism, which is by no means simply a bourgeois preserve, and invoking fears of castration of one's animal potency (though Erwin has in a sense castrated himself to become better beefcake).

Fassbinder's film is excruciating, though it is unbearable through the pain rather than – as in *Despair* – the embarrassment it evokes. The camera, wielded throughout by Fassbinder himself, is not placed so as to render the characters visible. A door may take up the foregrounded left-hand side of the screen as dialogue takes place among characters coming and going at the far end of a corridor on the right. The insistence of objects has a radically different meaning from similar images in Ozu. Fassbinder is anguished by the human marginality that Ozu simply, impassively records. Here, as in general, Fassbinder's work becomes most compelling, and most disturbing, when it is most overtly autobiographical.*

---

* The exception here is the slack final forty-minute section, which concentrates upon Anton Saitz: As it demystifies power on one level, showing Saitz to be far from the threat he was feared to be, it remystifies it on another, for his power is associated with a lukewarmly surrealist perversity, nothing at all to do with the everyday world.

Hence although films like *Despair* and *Querelle* contain autobiographical elements, they are etiolated by a refusal of explicit autobiography that corresponds to their short-circuiting of their own patterns of doubling. In each case, Fassbinder casts as the lead actor's double a person physically unlike him. (Genet's Querelle resembles his brother Robert; Fassbinder's is utterly dissimilar.) The obscuring of the theme of the double refuses self-knowledge, and the knowledge of death the double represents, rendering these films far more alienated in essence than the superficially more rebarbative *Year with Thirteen Moons*.

As the film nears its end, the eclipse approaches completion. If Elvira/Erwin is still present, it is as a voice only, on the verge of total disembodiment, consummation of the self-alienation of the body begun with the sex change. Neither "s/he" nor the film is able to contemplate her/his mutilated body: Friends and relatives try to break into her/his apartment, fearful of the worst, as her/his voice runs on in interview on the sound track, haunting it like a ghost. The total disjunction between an image of Elvira/Erwin's absence and a sound track upon which "s/he" is overwhelmingly present marks the film's end. For Fassbinder (like Welles, like Conrad when writing of Kurtz in *Heart of Darkness*, and unlike Derrida) the voice is a sign of absence, not presence: absence, for the voice in the dark is disembodied from the person even before it is disembodied still further by its mechanical reproduction. It is like a soul banished from its body – beyond the thirteenth moon.

### The view from abroad: East Europeans and the German past

In recent years two of the greatest of East European directors – Andrzej Wajda and István Szabó – have made films in West Germany, two of which – *A Love in Germany* and *Mephisto* – have sought to confront the National Socialist era. These have been more than mere nostalgia pieces;[23] the East European origins of their makers have generated a radicalism and directness of indictment of the German past generally unavailable to native German directors working under the ambiguous rubric of *Vergangenheitsbewältigung* (a word whose retention of the notion of mastery – *bewältigen* – Primo Levi acidly emphasized). In this respect they may be contrasted favorably with such films as *Heimat* or *Despair*. Nevertheless, it can be argued that they too have blind spots, shortcomings that are particularly glaring in the case of Wajda's film. The following essay attempts to map both their achievements and their limitations.

*The white devil: Mephisto*

An air of the academic often hangs over the historical film. In a modern era that has developed a polarity between the historical and the historic, only the latter overcomes the curse of universal overdocumentation and lays strong claims on remembrance. If a film, meanwhile, is to be more than a display of fetishized period trappings, it must penetrate past ideologies analytically to reveal their kinship with those of the present. An exemplary film in this respect is Bertolucci's *Conformist* (*Il conformista*), where the politics of socialization under the aegis of Oedipal configurations furnish the common denominator between the thirties and the present. Given the general East European skepticism of psychoanalysis (a humanist skepticism reinforced by a Marxist one), it is, however, hardly surprising that István Szabó's *Mephisto* adopts a different method for dispelling the specter of academicism. It allegorizes the past by despecifying it at certain points. This can be done with historical periods that are sufficiently well-known to allow the audience to fill in the missing details or – as in the case of a cartoon – identify the referent on the basis of a sketched image; thus in *Mephisto* no mention of Hitler follows the "Heil" salute. Such allegorization both outwits the Hungarian censor and renders the film more easily marketable in the West, more generalized. Given the degree to which oppositional work has been permitted in Hungarian cinema (*Another Way, Angi Vera*) one may feel nevertheless that Szabó's work is overdiscreet, excessively symbolic and camouflaged. The allegory can seem instead to be a method for achieving the false universalism of the self-serving aura of art.

A common method for the universalization of history employs a personalizing that seeks in the need to focus a work – a focus usually achieved through a single individual – an alibi for the excision of context. Szabó's Hendrick Höfgen is a riddle the film insists it has solved, and yet it is unsettled by its semirepressed awareness of the inadequacy of its pat rationalizations of its actor-hero's psychology. Höfgen is surrounded by contradictory signals. Is his acting genuinely good, or simply the duplicity of the careerist? What does it mean to be "good" at playing the devil? Is there such a thing as "the authentic" in the realm of the mask (which is of course also the totalitarian world that compels everyone to wear a mask; one notes that the film's most famous image is a close-up of Höfgen in his Mephisto makeup)? Does Szabó see all actors as potential careerists, the fabled soullessness of the actor? And if so, what happens to the intended indictment of Höfgen's collaboration with the allegorized Third Reich? Like Bertolucci, Szabó suggests a link between fascism, repressed homosexuality, and acting: The repressed homosexual who hides his true face from self and society enjoys the mystified spectacle of his own performance in the actor's mirror; he invests his libido in the image of another man who is himself.*

Narcissism thus becomes a form of repressed homosexuality. Szabó may have disposed of the explicitly homosexual allusions of Klaus Mann's novel – and may have done so in order to 'universalize' the text – but hints of perverse sexuality surround Höfgen (the whip cracking in the scene with his black mistress); the homosexuality is displaced onto his wife, who exchanges knowing glances with her best friend, secreting hints of lesbianism. In a glittering, baffling vicious circle of a thesis, both opposition and conformity to the Third Reich are associated with sexual perversion. If this then renders it impossible to "identify" with any of the characters, that impossibility becomes a signifier both of "pastness" and of allegory: In signifying "pastness," it implies that issues are no longer so immediate as to exert a compulsion to take a stand, thereby perversely vindicating Höfgen's conformism, since as allegory it renders Höfgen's a universal dilemma.

Höfgen may no longer be coded as homosexual in Szabó's film, but there is a clear feminization of the image of the actor. It is most patent in the way the mise-en-scène of the ending echoes that of the beginning: At the start, in a staging of Millöcker's operetta *Dubarry*, an actress appears at the top of a flight of stairs and walks down, spotlighted; and at the film's end Höfgen is instructed by his patron, the General, to run down the Olympic Stadium's steps, at whose bottom a spotlight transfixes him. Is Szabó implying that Höfgen's betrayal includes a betrayal of his own sexuality, leading to his unsexing? (An ironic implication, given Szabó's own doctoring of Klaus Mann's homosexual allusions.) Höfgen's spotlit face dissolves into white. The transfixing is symbolic rape (and may recall Nixon's rape by Uncle Sam at the end of Robert Coover's *Public Burning*): Höfgen becomes the passive homosexual partner of the General, his repressed homosexuality brought out into the open (an open-air auditorium, not a closed one – in this respect the ending is the necessary opposite of the beginning). Such revelation ruptures Szabó's textual system, causing it to close at this point. "What do they want with me, I'm only an actor," Höfgen wails, realizing his loss of control. Too late he grasps that there are plays not scripted in advance, in one of which he is acting: the improvised drama of history.

The German word for spotlight is *Scheinwerfer:* literally, something that casts a light that is illusory – the double sense of the word *Schein*. If the white face that appears in the blanching spotlight is typ-

* If the scopic drive is initially narcissistic, as Freud suggests, it can only be satisfied through the presentation of *the whole* of one's own body, through its alienation in the mirror of another male body.

ical of the actor in Szabó's film, the question is whether it is his or has been imposed upon him. Höfgen wears a white mask when playing Goethe's Mephistopheles, a part he designates ambiguously as "the role of my life": The actor himself carefully applies the white to his face. The whiteness imposed by the spotlight at the end merely reinforces the actor's preexistent pallor. It becomes apparent that in Nazi Germany, where politics are aestheticized, there is no offstage, nowhere where one is permitted to breach the prescribed bounds of one's role. The eye of the State keeps one always in place, dazzling one just before it destroys one with the blinding revelation of where one truly stands.[24] The totalitarian inferno is comprised of stages within stages. Although Höfgen has moved from dominating the stage to running an entire theater, the ending underlines his theater's subordinate position in society's Chinese box of stages: The enormous theater of the Olympic stadium is reserved for the Nazi hierarchy itself, and Höfgen is not allowed to feel at home in it. The General is warning his protégé to stay in his place, not rock the boat by interceding for his friend's life.

If our culture tends to associate virtue with whiteness and evil with dark, Szabó's film – flawed though it is in so many ways – executes an exemplary critique of that identification. As in Thomas Pynchon's hallucinatory analysis of Nazism, *Gravity's Rainbow*, whiteness is identified with death, the mask of Mephistopheles. Höfgen is clearly morally inferior to his black mistress. Even if at the film's beginning Szabó exploits the demagogic association of blackness with sexuality and perversion, Höfgen is damned when he severs ties with her to facilitate upward mobility. The devil here is the white one who treats blacks as the embodiment of sexuality, and renounces them as he invests more and more libido in his own white image.

As Mephisto, Höfgen is a confusing mixture of devil and Faust. As devil, he is a tempter – luring the audience, for instance, into identification with the devil's unpredictable energy, thereby training them for submission to the irrational leaps of Hitler's discourse; but as Faust he is tempted by the General, who understands Mephisto so profoundly because on the stage of history Mephistopheles' is really *his* role. This duplicity is at the heart of the lament Goethe places in the mouth of his Faust: "Zwei Seelen wohnen, ach, in meiner Brust" ["Two souls, alas, inhabit my breast"]. If Faust does have two souls, then one of them is called Mephistopheles; Goethe's last-minute rescue of Faust thus becomes profoundly dubious, since in theory he ought not to be separable from his shadow self. (Goethe is seeking to revoke the duality of drama and restore the monism of the lyric.) Höfgen's moment of transcendence, however, follows a passage down the steps that featured so prominently in Weimar cinema (as images of society as a scalable hierarchy – everything fixed in place, on the one hand, but with endless possibilities of upward mobility on the other): The spotlight the General wields burns Höfgen out as an actor, eliminating his legendary changeability and replacing it with a rigid light. The face becomes a blank screen on which the demonism of history can project whatever it likes. The face blanks out as it loses the mask that has protected it up to this point. As the General appropriates Mephisto's mercurial unpredictability, Höfgen is suddenly vulnerable. Left with only his face, whose weakness he has sought throughout to hide, he is lost. This ending is a triumph for two directors: the General and István Szabó. Höfgen is burned out by them as if by laser beam. But if the General resembles Szabó, is Szabó himself aware of the likeness? Does it not compromise his indictment of Höfgen's tergiversations, which appears in retrospect as a clever act of framing? Is not *Mephisto* fatally vitiated by its failure to criticize the play's writer, as well as its actor? Could it be that Höfgen is the fall guy for the really powerful off-screen, whose power resides in their secrecy, their useful lack of the glamour that would invite exposure? And is it not the excessive size of the final theater that causes the overexposure of Höfgen's face – a face that is unlike Hitler's for it cannot withstand the glare of a whole nation's attention? Was the artist's success the fruit of his corruption, or did the State corrupt him? *Mephisto* raises more questions than it can answer.

Szabó's film gains in cogency, however, if one considers it as a meditation on the nature of film acting and film's effect upon acting in general. The film actor is unable to step out of the role he has assumed; the cinema melts the barriers separating the stage from the offstage, turning life itself into theater. Outside the theater Hendrick Höfgen (his name self-doctored – castrated? – for showbiz appeal) is termed "My Mephisto" by the General who cultivates him. He defines the secret of Höfgen's acting as the unexpectedness of life itself. Not only does the mercurial Mephisto slip through others' hands; his actions slip through his own fingers too. Two of the film's sequences present him in a rapid montage of roles: donning and discarding theatrical costumes, and striking poses as director of the National Theater. The repetition of the device illustrates how life itself has become theater in the age of film, acting itself truly demonic, for the actor is never able to shed a mask that becomes more expressive than his own face. The degree to which the typecast actor "plays himself" in film may prompt one to correlate the emergence of role-performance sociology with the influence of cinema on the behavioral patterns of this century. Höfgen ruminates on whether to accept the directorship of the Berlin theater; will it be just another role? Wandering the streets of Paris while visiting his exiled Negress mistress he stares at the signs, asking, "Why do I need freedom?" Why indeed, when one's life is lived in the cage of a role.

Höfgen can in fact elude even the harshest oppression through inward flight into a role. He can do so because his face is a blank. Its masklike quality leads one to expect that it conceals something other than a void. Again and again one expects him to drop the mask, and even suspects that he might already have done so. On leaving the General's study after his plea for a friend's release has been declined brusquely, he gazes for a moment in the General's direction in a manner that is almost sardonic but finally blank: His face is a sentence cast in the form of a question, but without a question mark at the end. Similarly, at his wedding, immediately before his delivery of a welcome speech to the General, we are shown a series of close-ups of his impassive face and almost expect him to pronounce a derisive oration. When the General instructs him to inscribe his commendation of a "Blut und Boden" statue in a visitors' book, he lingers so long over it that one suspects him of having written something subversive. This sense of a negation held constantly in reserve – marvelously embodied in Klaus Maria Brandauer's performance – turns Höfgen into a man who lives his life in quotation marks. The continually hovering possibility of self-assertion only underlines his inability to achieve it. And if none of the explanations of his behavior suggested by the film ring true, it is because the existential confusion of art and life engendered by film undercuts all explanation. If he remains in Germany when others flee, it is not *simply* because, as an actor, he needs access to a German public, because his replacement would be worse, because he wishes to use his influence to shield friends, or because he is a coward or careerist: The possible explanations are so multifarious as to render his actions fundamentally mysterious, with the mystery perhaps of the *allegorical* image, dislocated from any single historical context. (That dislocation is of course a characteristic of the devil himself.)

The blankness of Höfgen's face lays it open to various interpretations that conclude in reverie. The reverie includes the flawed narcissism of Höfgen's own reflections on his own mercurial essence as he sits before his actor's mirror, talking to himself. This self-communing overrides relationships with others. In one scene with his wife Barbara, she is seen only as reflected in a mirror; and as he asks Nicoletta's advice over whether or not to accept the Berlin theater directorship, the camera begins with a close-up of his face before slowly drawing back to reveal her listening presence: His discourse thus fuses "soliloquy" with "dialogue." Julietta, his black mistress, remarks that he loves only himself, and that not enough. The sentence is surely the universal key to his character. At one point he recounts how in his youth he had sung loud and, he thought, angelically in a choir, when in fact he was an octave too high and was told to shut up. His choice of a black lover is bound in with his nagging suspicion that he is forever beyond the pale.

Everyone and no one, Höfgen is half a figure in a political allegory, half an example of a private pathology. He can slip in and out of Nazi ideology because – like the Nazis himself – he never defines it clearly. Nor does the film ever specify the extent of his knowledge of others' fates under the Third Reich. The occasional violence in Szabó's slightly candied film is presented too elegantly to arouse horror; the spectator is placed too much in the position of Höfgen himself, frustrating any effort to resolve the issues raised. The camera often shoots into naked lights that bedazzle us as the spotlight and footlights do Höfgen himself. Only at one point is Höfgen's confusion over ideology clearly apparent, when his "Bolshevik" idea of a spectacle that abolishes the distinction between auditorium and stage finds its fulfillment in the "total theater" of the Olympic Stadium. The fundamental thesis of the Klaus Mann novel Szabó adapts may seem tendentious: to identify the actor as soulless is to beat the worn drum of an old cliché. But the mere act of filming it strips the story of its tendentiousness: It brings into focus the possibility that it is acting in film – or acting in the age of film – that is demonic, not acting per se. For it is film that turns one's reflection into a two-dimensional man, the specter of the haunted screen.

*The ideology of Polishness:* A Love in Germany

Questions of fidelity bedevil discussions of film adaptations of literary texts. A widespread Western Platonism often deems the primal form superior to its secondary material incarnation – and all the more so when that incarnation is further degraded by the need to pay its way on the mass market. Fidelity ought however to be a nonissue. The task of the adapter is not so much slavishly to transpose every detail – usually an impossible undertaking given the difference in the degrees of abstraction of language and image – as to prevent the prototype depreciating during the process of transformation. Although film, the less prestigious medium, is often castigated for audacious divergence from the original, it is only through independent use that the primary text's spirit is liberated to pass into a new form: The laws of artistic Karma forbid the next life from repeating the form borne in this one. And so the exemplary adaptations are the divergent ones: Tarkovsky's *Solaris* (*Solyaris*), Bertolucci's *Conformist*, or Kurosawa's *Throne of Blood* (*Kumonosu-jo*).

The case of Wajda's *A Love in Germany* (*Ein Liebe in Deutschland*) is, however, somewhat more complex. Rolf Hochhuth's German text was both a novel and a documentary reconstruction of an event from World War II in two German towns near the Swiss border: The 1941 hanging of a Polish forced laborer condemned to death under the Nazi laws forbidding intercourse between members of the *Herrenrasse* and those of supposedly lower races. It was – to use an ugly but appropriate term – a work of provocation *faction* – a mode Wajda himself had employed in *Man of Iron* (*Człowiek z żelaza.*) Adaptation has long been a staple source of work for Polish directors unable to obtain state backing for cherished projects, and Wajda's adaptations have generally been very "faithful" – exercises in mise-en-scène. *A Love in Germany* – for all the period minutiae that led viewers to exclaim over the meticulousness of its re-creation of the past – is something else again.* This would be of little significance if Hochhuth's text were not as much a work of historical investigation as a novel. Hochhuth probes an appalling incident in an often-repressed German past; at one point he describes the exemplary air of sincerity one of his interlocutors is able to wear precisely when he is lying through his teeth. Wajda shows less inclination to question appearances, and in fact obscures Hochhuth's documentary work by altering certain key details in the book. He does so on the basis of a Polish ideology almost as self-serving as the German ideology Hochhuth unmasks.

Since Hochhuth's work documents an actual case, and Wajda's own organizing device – the visit to the scene of past outrage – stresses the importance of uncovering obstinately concealed truths, the film's divergences from the book are alarming. Hochhuth speaks of Zasada's claim that his mother in Łódź came of German stock; Wajda has him staunchly resisting any attempt to save his skin through Germanization. The real Zasada was blond, an important point in his favor as far as the Nazi authorities were concerned; Piotr Łysak, who plays the part in the film, is swarthy. Hochhuth describes Zasada's hospitalization as due to septic tonsils; Wajda heightens the air of passion and presents him as having been trampled by a horse – horses being a leitmotif of Polish Romantic art, and also of Wajda's other films. Whereas in reality Pauline had two children, a son and a daughter, Wajda reduces this to one son, a simplification that may sharpen the contours of the drama – the son travels back in time in search of the mother, replaying the Oedipal quest – but troubles the film's veracity. The sexual practices of Pauline and Stasiek are cleaned up (I will discuss why later on): The forms of intercourse born of endangered lovers' fear of pregnancy all disappear. Nor does Wajda make it clear that

---

* Moreover, the accuracy of at least one of the details is dubious: The widely reproduced image of Pauline's child licking a lollipop with a swastika pattern may be an anachronism, since a law "for the protection of national symbols" had been introduced in the early thirties expressly to prevent such "abuses."

under the Byzantine Nazi race laws Zasada was not hanged for sexual intercourse with a member of the master race but for engaging in this practice after having been warned (together with all the other local Polish workers) that this was a capital offense. In fact, under a law introduced in mid-1941, those who committed this offense without prior warning became eligible for Germanization; Wajda presents an unwarned Stasiek. If Stasiek's is one of the great love stories, however, it is because he was aware of the possible penalties and was prepared to risk dying for his love.

It can be argued that the changes Wajda makes indicate that he was the wrong director for this material. In the hands of an Oshima, for instance, the combination of *amour fou* and bureaucratic farce would have linked the strengths of *Death by Hanging* and *In the Realm of the Senses*, fusing deadpan irony and passion. (The sexual practices of the lovers would not have been adulterated.) Wajda's farce, however, is ponderous, and scene after scene is overlong or repetitious. When Pauline's malicious neighbor makes love to her pilot husband during his leave, she strips with ecstatic theatricality at the thought of his becoming an officer. The slack direction culminates in the poor staging of what should be one of the film's key moments: As the assembled Polish laborers are ordered to about-face and view the gallows from which Stasiek Zasada's body is hanging – a monitory image – the timing deprives the scene of its latent terror and irony and renders it merely perfunctory.

Wajda's decision to cast one character as an investigative prober of the past is a mechanical overspill from *Man of Marble* (*Człowiek z marmuru*) – a decorative addition, little more than a key he uses to wind up the narration and then more or less forgets about. Wajda fails to capitalize on the possibilities he himself creates by replacing Hochhuth with Herbert, Pauline's son. If Hochhuth speaks of Herbert's resentment of the Pole who came between him and his mother, Wajda ignores the possible ambivalence in Herbert's reaction to what he encounters in his hometown, forty years later. (How is he to reconcile his sympathy with the persecuted Pole with his past resentment of his intrusiveness?) Even though the film filters its narrative through Herbert and his return to Brombach, we are not shown any compelling reason for his return, nor do we learn how much mother, friends, or acquaintances may have told him about the past, all of which should be crucial. Because Herbert already knows the main outline of events – except for the matter of who actually denounced his mother – the only candidate for initiation into its secrets is his son; thus the possible intensity of a focus upon Herbert is dissipated between father and son. No interest is generated by the question of who denounced Pauline and Stasiek, partly because the film rapidly becomes caught up in the corrida of their romance, but also because Pauline's recklessness rendered the affair an open secret. The film mystifies events by implying that it could have been anyone. Hochhuth's work is free of such mystery mongering, for it identifies the guilty party as Josef Zinnruber, former Brombach mayor and local Nazi leader, who informed the Gestapo. (Though Elsbeth Schnittgens, Pauline Krop's bookkeeper, handed over the letters, which Pauline had given her to pass on to Stani, to the Gestapo member sent to follow up the denunciation.)

If Wajda was indeed the wrong director for this material, it may well have been better suited to Fassbinder. As one reads Hochhuth's account of the interesting linguistic interplay between Pauline and Stani – Pauline's alemannic dialect being poorly understood by Stani, she generally had to switch to High German when speaking to him, so that, in a sense, both lovers were meeting on the common ground of a foreign language – one may be reminded of Fassbinder's *Fear Eats the Soul* (*Angst Essen Seele Auf*), its ungrammatical German title reflecting the Turkish lover's alienation from German society. And Hanna Schygulla is of course a perennial presence in Fassbinder's films. One may feel here that she is too beguilingly opaque to project the despair she must feel as she watches the truck bear Stani away to his death: Her built-in alienation device – a feature of many of the greatest female stars, being perhaps the characteristic that allows them to float from film to film and a reason why Fassbinder employed Schygulla so often – introduces a nice cooling element into Wajda's habitually overheated atmosphere, but by lowering the temperature it dispels the desperation of *amour fou*. Drastically different as Wajda and Fassbinder are in so many respects, a tendency to allegory, misogyny, and a frenetic rate of production are common to them both. The key difference lies in Wajda's concern for the actor and for tense imagistic tableaux, which lend his works an energy Fassbinder's lack.

As one wonders why Wajda took on this project, several reasons suggest themselves. One – always of relevance in the case of so prolific a director – is simply the desire to have work in hand, blotting out the usual intervals between films, those times of possible self-doubt. Just how devastating self-doubt could become in Wajda's case is shown by his fascinating *Everything for Sale* (*Wszystko na sprzedaz*), one of the key films of his career. Another evident motive was a wish to produce a statement on German–Polish relations to coincide with the fortieth anniversary of the end of World War II, an anniversary of which much was made in the propaganda of the East European media – one of the few ways in which Soviet power could legitimate itself being to point to the liberating role its army played in 1945. It may even have crossed Wajda's mind that such a work might also help him regain the support of the Polish authorities, at a low ebb after his oppositional films of the late seventies.*

Wajda may have envisaged having the best of both worlds: delivering an ecumenical message on Polish–German relations, while at the same time pleasing a Polish government eager to raise the specter of West German revanchism. One can clearly separate these two strands in the story. On the one hand, love equalizes the races; on the other, such moments as the one set in the present, in which the daughter of Pauline's assistant angrily berates Herbert for seeking to rake up a best-forgotten incident, clearly pander to the Polish ideology regarding West Germany.

There are, however, other levels of calculation in the film. It is of course possible that Wajda himself shares the Polish fear of "the German threat," so assiduously touted once by Gomułka and revived to coincide with the access to power in the Bundesrepublik of the CDU–CSU. The chauvinist belief that no Pole could even consider renouncing his country in order to save his own skin is nevertheless also part of Solidarity ideology, and Wajda may have felt a compulsion to portray Zasada as a superpatriot lest the Polish audience withhold its sympathy from him. The logic of character has to be ruptured to yield a martyr, in line with the Polish tendency to think exclusively in black-and-white terms (terms that forestall comprehension of the true complexity of the choices a Wajda, and even a Jaruzelski, has to make). The traduction of the logic of character and history may come all the easier to Wajda, since – as many critics have noted – characterization is not his strongest suit. His protagonists tend to be demiurges or dervishes animated by the force of history, which magnifies their twitchings into grand gestures. But the failure of characterization becomes glaring in the light of what is essentially a chamber drama. Cleaning up the sexuality of Hochhuth's two protagonists increases the work's appeal to Polish audiences warned against libertinism by both church and state.

As well as amending the details of Hochhuth's narrative, Wajda abandons its form. Hochhuth's mixture of historical essay and narrative, which would in the cinema have yielded a more-or-less Brechtian form, is reduced to mere narrative. If Hochhuth is far from being an aesthetic radical, Wajda is even more conservative. Again there are sound crowd-pleasing motives for this: The film has to be sold both in Poland (where experimental work is marginalized and banished to the theater) and in the West (the mainstream cinemagoer drawn by the

---

* I realize that this is an uncharitable imputation, and offer it only as a possibility, one that may simply betray both my own deviousness and that of the Polish intellectual scene in general.

prospect of a love story with the eminently bankable Schygulla). The result is a deeply ideological film. Its multiple levels of calculation represent Wajda's devious return to the allegorical mode he once threw off so decisively in *Man of Marble*. Here Wajda parts company with the younger generation of Polish directors, who drew inspiration from *Man of Marble:* Zanussi, Agnieszka Holland, Kieślowski, or Bugajski. He may well feel too old to change his workaholic habits and opt for austere silence rather than garbled, compromised speech. The result however is the empty production for production's sake that is the bane of Polish cinema.

CHAPTER IV
# Expressionism
# in America

It is often claimed that there are two tendencies in film history: on the one hand, realism, transparent reproduction of the world's appearances; and on the other the stylization and distortion associated with expressionism. The assumption – subscribed to, for instance, by Kracauer – is that realism is the more virtuous of the two. (In Bazin's terms, mise-en-scène and deep focus are to be preferred to montage.) It would however be too large a generalization to subsume expressionism under stylization; if this were the case, then Von Sternberg would be an expressionist. Expressionism's legacy is in fact the use of stylization to indicate the state of the mind viewing the world. A vindication of expressionism might argue that it does so in order to counteract the reifying behaviorism of the camera – the result being a fusion of the objective and the subjective that allows one to view both a figure moving through the world *and* the way that figure perceives the world. Expressionism in film thus becomes profoundly dialectical, and is far from a simple negation of realism – a term that is itself far more multivalent and problematic than its proponents like to admit. The fundamental premise of expressionism can nevertheless be said to be that reality is permeated – and sometimes utterly enveloped – by fantasy: Magical images and mental projections may occupy the same plane of apparent objectivity as "real" people (*The Student of Prague*) – a leveling facilitated by film's habit of detaching a person's image from his or her presence. Alternatively, all "real" people may be no more than the pegs on which fantasy hangs its afterimages of the shadowy, now inaccessible figures (usually parental) who once determined one's past: such works, in which "real people" are simultaneously "unreal," will often use flashbacks and framing devices to enable us to perceive the difference, the fact of doubling (e.g., *The Cabinet of Dr. Caligari* or *Invasion of the Body Snatchers*). If narrative can be described as a process of mediation between opposites, then expressionism's focus upon the isolated individual may seem to render it antinarrative, apparently antidialectical. (Since the result is often

**156**

the marking time of the *Stationendrama*, expressionism is most power-ful in its painting, which presents the anguish of paralyzed narrative, nightmarishly frozen to the spot.) In expressionist narrative however – that seemingly oxymoronic object – narrative is preserved through the hostility between self and autonomous part-self, or between self and double. An expressionist-influenced work such as *Citizen Kane* will pro-pose a dual existence for its hero, "communist" in the eyes of some and "fascist" to others, "Hearst" to some and "Welles" to others, and so on. *Caligari*, meanwhile, presents a series of part-selves in a hall of mirrors in which the originary self disappears. It complicates this with a tension between a sober self and a world so hallucinatory that its existence is surely only mental – as it proves to be at the end, when the narrative is closed down by the insinuation that the narrative self is not sober at all, but infected with madness; nevertheless, since it has been demonstrated that a two-way street links madness and san-ity, there is no consolation available through identification with the Caligari who then proposes to "cure" Francis. The asylum's décor ex-udes insanity, and the film's failure to mention wherein the cure might consist leads one to doubt its feasibility. *Caligari* is thus exemplary of the strategies the expressionist artwork employs in allowing us both to partake of delusions and to step outside them: On the one hand we see what the central protagonist is seeing, but on the other we see the protagonist himself as potentially unreliable. The individual who stands at the work's center is simultaneously decentered by the projec-tions issuing from him. The result is a powerful, disorienting oscilla-tion between subjective and objective viewpoints, an alternating current in which opposites seem to fuse in the sense of Rimbaud's "je est un autre."

The expressionist legacy left Germany along with the directors dri-ven abroad by National Socialism. Their sense of internal exile, of a world out of joint, became real exile. But if a continuity between expressionism and *film noir* can be clearly documented through the careers of certain key directors and cameramen, later flowerings of the expressionist impulse have owed more to elective affinity than direct transmission.* That is why the following chapter concludes by consid-ering a film which has no link with *film noir,* but nevertheless perpetu-ates the expressionist legacy: Kieślowski's *A Short Film about Killing.* It is evident from this film that so long as horror can burst the protec-tive bounds of generic fantasy and invade reality, expressionism will be undead.

---

* Perhaps the most remarkable film influenced by expressionism in the sixties is Anto-nioni's *Red Desert* (*Deserto rosso*), which becomes the more disturbing through the way it superimposes dislocations of sound, color, and focus upon a realistic narrative, leav-ing one perennially in doubt regarding their origin, subjective or objective.

**"Ended before it began...": Citizen K. and *Citizen Kane***

Given the fact that the letter K. adorns the entrance to Citizen Kane's Xanadu, it was perhaps inevitable that Orson Welles would eventually become interested in Kafka. The strained monotony of his version of *The Trial* may make it seem as if this interest was misplaced. Yet as one contemplates Welles's career and his passion for the imagination of power and powerlessness one may also feel that the obituaries of *The Trial* were too eager to pronounce Welles incompatible with Kafka. *Citizen Kane* itself, for all its air of mountebank Gothic, has a nightmarish claustrophobia that has its equivalents in Kafka: "Rosebud" is the message despatched by the Chinese Emperor, never to arrive. If one can understand why Welles's *Trial* was almost universally deplored – his broad and arbitrary theatrical strokes seen as vulgarizations of Kafka's inscrutable suggestivity – there are several filaments linking the two men, from the letter K, which in *Kane* was to become Welles's self-imposed fate, to the fascination by Chinese themes (*The Lady from Shanghai*) and the construction of works as Chinese boxes, and the reworking of expressionism. Those who aligned Welles's blustering rhetoric with power and Kafka's masochism with powerlessness failed to perceive the dialectic whereby Welles's men of power are also impotent.* They are men too small for their robes (*Macbeth*), whose term of power has expired (*The Stranger*), and who even employ others to pierce the secrecy that has been the basis of their power (*Mr. Arkadin* [*Confidential Report*]). It is as if self-destruction is the only way for the genius to become a good American democrat.

*The door one cannot go through*

"Ended before it began...": the words are Emily Dickinson's, but they denote a feature common to the works of both Welles and Kafka. In the case of Welles, they may remind one of how *Citizen Kane* opens with its protagonist's death (he even dies metaphorically before his actual death, as the light in the window gutters before the camera enters it), or how *Touch of Evil* starts with an astonishingly modulated tracking shot concluding in an explosion. If beginnings are associated with death, so is disorientation: Almost all Welles's films begin with sequences that pose riddles. If this is true even of a potboiler like *The Stranger*, it is hardly surprising that Welles should have prefaced his *Trial* with the riddling "Before the Law," a parable that appears very

---

* A position Welles himself may be thought to have maneuvered himself into vis-à-vis the film industry, perhaps so as never to have to face the question of what possible follow-up there could be to a début as stunning as *Kane*.

near the *end* of Kafka's novel, so its placement here clearly links beginning and ending. Kafka meanwhile speaks, in a passage deleted from *The Trial*, of the danger of beginnings:

Jemand sagte mir – ich kann mich nicht mehr erinnern, wer es gewesen ist –, dass es doch wunderbar sei, dass man, wenn man früh aufwacht, wenigstens im allgemeinen alles unverrückt an der gleichen Stelle findet, wie es am Abend gewesen ist. Man ist doch im Schlaf und im Traum wenigstens scheinbar in einem vom Wachen wesentlich verschiedenen Zustand gewesen, und es gehört, wie jener Mann ganz richtig sagte, eine unendliche Geistesgegenwart oder besser Schlagfertigkeit dazu, um mit dem Augeöffnen alles, was da ist, gewissermassen an der gleichen Stelle zu fassen, an der man es am Abend losgelassen hat. Darum sei auch der Augenblick des Erwachens der riskanteste Augenblick im Tag; sei er einmal überstanden, ohne dass man irgendwohin von seinem Platze fortgezogen wurde, so könne man den ganzen Tag über getrost sein.

[Someone said to me – I can no longer remember who it was – that it is after all remarkable that on waking up early it is at least generally the case that one finds everything in the same place it had occupied in the evening. In one's sleep and dreams, after all, one has been at least apparently in a state that differs essentially from waking, and – as that man rightly said – an infinite presence of mind, or rather quick-wittedness, is required to grasp, as one opens one's eyes, all the things that are there in more or less the same places where one had left them the previous evening. That is why the moment of waking is the most risky of the entire day; if one can only overcome it, without being dragged away somewhere from one's position, one can rest assured the whole day long.][1]

Kafka's omission of this passage from the early pages of *The Trial* may well have been prompted by an unwillingness to leave any hints of an explanation of his method, except very near the end of the novel, where they can be found in the commentary given on "Before the Law." He may also have omitted the reference to dreams in order to forestall the reader's attempt to read the novel – as so many Kafka readers have done – as simply a dream's transcript: one recalls the double insistence near the start of *The Metamorphosis* that "es war kein Traum" [it was no dream]. The passage itself exemplifies the very danger of which it speaks: first, by posing a danger to the early stages of the novel from which it was excised; and second because it too is threatened at the outset by an interpolation. (There is in Welles also an association of montage – the shifting of the scene – with threat.) Sentences containing interpolations are quite often found near the beginnings of Kafka's works (e.g., *The Metamorphosis*), chapters or paragraphs. They embody on the level of form the theme of "Before the Law," *Metamorphosis,* and many of the other works: that of the door one cannot go through, that has turned into a window (a cinema screen?), whose space beckons but cannot be entered. (It is hardly surprising that Joseph K. is often shown looking out of windows.) The interpolation is a countersentence invading the sentence Kafka has just begun to write. Its appearance reflects his difficulties over committing himself, even to paper ("the impossibility of writing"). Early in its development the text is still uncertain, exposed to attack by possible alternative beginnings. But the alternative beginning is also – to recall one of Kafka's aphorisms – the true opponent from whom boundless energy flows. In other words, sentence and countersentence cooperate to generate the energy of the text; this dialectic is deeply characteristic of Kafka, whose writing combines subjective and objective viewpoints to create a sense of double exclusion. Thus he allows one to see only what Gregor Samsa sees, but not from his viewpoint; replaces the "I"s of *The Castle* with "he"s; forces one to share Joseph K.'s disorientation without permitting one to identify with him. This duality is the source of the text's endlessness: The incorporation of Other into self turns all threats to writing's interiority into extensions of interiority – rather as the courts are disavowed extensions of Joseph K. Since the primary external threat to one's writing is the holy text that condemns it as profane or even demonic, the writing absorbs the holy text. Here Kafka's tactic is very similar to that of Freud. At a time when the holy texts of traditional religion have lost their authority, the locus of authority shifts to dreams: The stories revealed to one by dreams have more authority over one than any other story one is told in one's waking life. That is why Kafka and Freud can transfer to dreams the procedures of Talmudic exegesis.

By 1962, when Welles came to film *The Trial*, it was probably already too late to do so: The "prophetic" elements in the novel had already found horrible fulfillment. Welles's images of housing wastelands and Auschwitz prisoners show some of the fulfillments, dissipating Kafka's enigmatic aura. But if Welles's version is a failure, it is also because it seeks to undermine the work on which it is based – most explicitly so in K.'s hysterical and indignant rejection of the absurdist reading of the world. The scene in question, expressing K.'s reaction to the law, is both jarring and fascinating: It gives Welles's vulgar critique of the vulgar existentialist misreading of Kafka. And, in a weird paradox, Kafka's own text comprehends Welles's reaction to it: Welles may cast himself as the advocate and present "Before the Law" as a slide show, but his attitude to Kafka's work reproduces Joseph K.'s view of the courts. The show of virtuoso mastery of the original merely indicates the degree to which that original cannot be mastered. To attempt to do so is to indulge in the grandiose self-destruction that was the leitmotif of Welles's career: Failure becomes triumph.

*Power and graffiti*

In the introductory volume of his *History of Sexuality,* the late Michel Foucault criticized a certain widely prevalent view of power as the force that represses desire – a motif of the libertarian left's critique of power in general, and of Deleuze and Guattari in particular, though Foucault – in what one suspects is itself a power strategy – loftily declines to name names:

Underlying both the general theme that power represses sex and the idea that law constitutes desire, one encounters the same putative mechanics of power. It is defined in a strangely restrictive way, in that, to begin with, this power is poor in resources, sparing of its methods, monotonous in the tactics it uses, incapable of invention, and seemingly doomed always to repeat itself. Further, it is a power that only has the force of the negative on its side, a power to say no; in no condition to produce, capable only of posting limits, it is basically anti-energy. This is the paradox of its effectiveness: it is incapable of doing anything, except to render what it dominates incapable of doing anything either, except for what this power allows it to do.[2]

Foucault emphasizes the limitation of this notion of power as pure negativity and sterile taboo, implying that the poverty ascribed to power by its critics is in fact a feature of their own imaginations, which fail to grasp its complex concatenations. Foucault's strictures are in a sense rebukes against the late sixties, uttered by a voice of the late seventies: the voice of an intellectual member of the opposition who has himself become a power and has identified with its array of seductions. They can be applied also to *Citizen Kane,* a sixtiesish text inasmuch as it too is a work of youth revolt. The fundamental emptiness the film ascribes to Kane is that of its beholder, who is excluded from the exercise of power and incapable of imagining its rich interiority except through cliché; and this beholder is as powerless as the spectator subjected to the unilateral caprice of cinema. The lives of the rich are emotionally impoverished, runs the reassuring populist banality, assuaging one'e envy and soaking up the discontent that might otherwise foster a will to alter the distribution of property. It is possible, however, that Foucault's strictures are misplaced inasmuch as they display a failure to comprehend the relationship between privation (which includes the incarceration of the self in the privacy of its own individuality) and imagination. To imagine something is to attempt to render an absence present – an impossible, even utopian, undertaking. The conjured something remains absent even as it is present to the imagination. It thus remains essentially unknown: like Kane himself. And so the image of the powerful presented by Welles in *Citizen Kane* projects onto Kane the actual helplessness of his beholder. One repeatedly sees Kane not as the master of events but framed, relegated to the background by the deep focus, as foreground characters determine his fate: As in Egyptian bas-reliefs, their greater size indicates their superior, godlike status. Such is the case when we see the young Kane snowballing outside, framed by the window, while his parents within agree to his exile for education. Similarly, he appears reflected in a window in the background during the celebrations of his acquisition of the best journalists of *The Chronicle*, the rival newspaper, with Leland and Bernstein in the foreground. Leland remarks that the bought journalists may well end up changing the tone of Kane's own paper, rendering apparent success hollow. This is the message of the insistent deep focus: The ostensible hero is in fact banished to the edge of the visible. If real power lies elsewhere, in the hands of the invisible director, and that director is Welles himself, is the powerlessness of the on-screen image a sham, since even as he twitches impotently and blusteringly in the lead role his own hands are pulling the strings off-screen?

And yet, and yet . . . that sense of partial powerlessness subtly saps the power of the director too. For *Kane* is very different from the prismatic works of investigative reporting it has inspired, such as *The Mattei Affair* or *Man of Marble:* It is not a political film, intent on effecting changes in our false consciousness of real events, but a handlebar mustache drawn on the Mona Lisa, the image of the sacred monster. It is less akin to satire than to graffiti. And in this respect it suffers from the depoliticization that has dogged American culture, as the fixed nature of the Constitution has frustrated the ability to imagine alternatives, the sheer size of the country has made it impossible to focus opposition on any one key point, its ethnic diversity has rendered it a patchwork of ghettoes, and the violence of its founding revolt has generated a corresponding subsequent desire for a counterbalancing period of conformism and tranquillity. It is perhaps because graffiti are inherently anonymous that Welles has been so obsessed with the establishment of his status as sole author – a status usually impossible in cinema, except at its avant-garde outer limits. The symbiosis of film and graffiti is paradoxical but profound: Projected onto blank walls, they are the artforms of the anonymous; they deface surfaces whose depths they cannot reach. Is not the writer of graffiti fatally akin to the impotent directorial god of the auteurists, secreting semivisible clues to his identity in the margins of the Hollywood product? It is this anonymity that Welles seeks to destroy by rendering himself visible as lead actor and creating a stylistic tour de force that renders the director's presence all-too-palpable. The necessity of collaboration clearly weighed heavily upon Welles, who must have experienced the M's of Mankiewicz and the Mercury Theatre as frustrating inversions of his own W. He must surely have known that the mogul similarly unable to leave his true imprint on the world was his own double.*

*To the distant observer*

If the individual often feels powerless in modern society, Kafka's fables "Before the Law" and "A Message from the Emperor" can help explain why. In the former a countryman is unable to reach the law through the door that has been created for him alone; in the latter the most physically powerful man in the Chinese empire proves incapable of traversing the various palace courtyards to deliver the message to you, its intended recipient; and even had he succeeded there, he would have got no further: The effect of watching him in one's mind's eye is like that of fixing one's gaze on a person as the camera continues to draw back from him. In each case two separate points are made aware of one another but fail to establish physical contact. In a sense this is because the existence of physical contact is precluded by the rival, mental contact of the imagination, which depends upon absence. It is this that makes Kafka the poet of media-society frustration: What ought to be a medium proves also to be a blocking agency. Whereas in earlier ages people were tied to their localities and were only intermittently made aware of the existence of larger hierarchies – on Sunday, for instance – the inhabitant of technologially advanced twentieth-century societies is almost continually conscious of the totality of the world beyond him or her: Electronic media render the world uninterruptedly present and untouchable; the best the viewer can do is make it disappear – practicing for apocalypse *now* – by pressing the off-switch, whose designation "power" mocks his or her impotence. The awareness of the existence of the totality renders local action so limited by its local nature as to seem pointless. (The deterritorialized utopia of Deleuze and Guattari is thus hardly a solution.) The demoralized individual ceases to act at all, and it becomes all the easier for the centralizing, totalitarian forces in modern society to keep him/her in place. As the body atrophies, only the eye (the mind's eye) remains active. Everyone becomes a double of Citizen K.

---

* In retrospect it seems possible to analyze "Kane" in terms derived from Derrida: The film moves from the spoken seen (the lips pronouncing "Rosebud") to the written unseen ("Rosebud" written on the sled). The trajectory of the narrative links writing with death – a second death, in fact. A chill of the Sublime accompanies this ending. The impossible, unspeakable word becomes in a sense utopian, but also death dealing.

## INXS: *Touch of Evil*

To draw up a list of films to be classified as "excessive" would be a Trivial Pursuit to rival the attempted definition of film noir. Yet if "excess" is characteristic of expressionism, the American film most deserving of the INXS label – and hence the most expressionist – is surely *Touch of Evil*. It is studded with grotesque and striking images arrayed around Quinlan/Welles, from the moment he pops out of the constricting body of his car like a fat pea from a pod to his spastic demise in oily water under the epitaph "he was some kind of man." The excess in *Touch of Evil* is associated with sexuality and has been theorized at enormous – and fascinating – length by Stephen Heath.[3] Nevertheless, the appearance of exhaustiveness evoked by the sheer length of his article is misleading, for his chronicle of the transformations the narrative functions undergo is limited by a blind spot: Heath's Barthesian aversion to the notion of the author, which causes him to denigrate Welles's style as mere gaudy packaging and prevents him from perceiving that the transformations are not restricted to the female body but extend into the overblown figure of Quinlan/Welles, rendered grotesque by its effort to contain within itself the initial explosion, and akin to the Rabelaisian body as described by Bakhtin.

Although the film's obsession with borders is fueled by a determination to erase the boundary between art and trash (in a sense art and fairground), Heath's description of it as a classic realist text whose parti pris is "obvious"[4] tendentiously strives to redraw those borders in the reconceived form of the distinction between Hollywood and the avant garde. Heath – the finest of the *Screen* writers – ought to have known better. The subtlety of the notion of the "obliquely political" devised by him to described work by Oshima had transcended the simple binarism of the opposition between commercial and progressive film. His *Touch of Evil* analysis, however, was vitiated by a schizophrenic alternation between theoretical passages declaring the film an arbitrarily selected example of traditional narrative, and brilliant critical insight into a work of whose vertiginous complexity Barthes would surely have approved. It was nevertheless perversely fitting that Heath should be attracted to the perverse film he condemns as conventional. His analysis thus aquires some of the imperious tortuousness of Welles's own work. It is obvious why he takes Welles's film as an example of traditional narrative: Really conventional works – as Bordwell, Thompson, and Staiger have shown in their book on classic Hollywood – are simply too boring to sustain the extended analysis Heath wishes to pursue. In this respect he replicates the gesture his mentor makes in "S/Z": He selects a work by a great author, surely aware that it will probably repay lengthy analysis, while at the same time being careful to choose one from the margins of that author's career, so its dismissal will command near-automatic assent. Indebted to "S/Z" as Heath is, one can only laud his self-restraint in not mentioning it in connection with the interplay of the names "*Suzy*" and "*Zita*" – or is this a case of the anxiety of influence?

Early on in his essay Heath provides a breakdown of the opening sequence arranged under such headings as "narrative," "character," "partitions," "exchange," "repercussions," "light," "music," and "author." Given Heath's Barthesian premises, "author" is clearly a problem heading. Of the two cursory remarks given under this heading, one is extremely symptomatic:

> Quinlan's arrival exceeds the diegetic space; it is prepared as "a great moment of cinema," a star turn – the colossal entry of Quinlan-Welles. Doubled with effects of style (shot angles, distortions, framing), by the signature, it marks a circulation and a division: actor-director; of interest if it signifies in the system as a problem of position.[5]

Heath nowhere says whether or not he thinks this moment does have the significance it would require to be of interest. Nevertheless it does: Questions of positioning and borders pervade this film, the ultimate border being the one between Welles as visible star and unseen director, which runs along the bottom of the screen. Heath shelves this question in order to lose it in the labyrinth of further speculation. And because – as his commentary momentarily recognizes – Quinlan is fused with Welles, the repression of the question of the status of the author saps the analysis of Quinlan's functioning within the textual system.

Heath's probings into the multiple repercussions of the explosive kiss with which the film opens are reduced in scope by his blinkered view of the psychology of Quinlan/Welles. His lack of interest in the grotesque double body the film posits blinds him to the significance of the film's wide-angle style. Heath derides the style as simply the decorative inscription of Welles' presence, a commodified trademark; the old form–content distinction is reinstated as style is dismissed – as one might expect a Cambridge Puritan to do – in favor of what's *really* important – the story! But if one can talk of "systems and partial systems" in the work, as Heath does, why not consider the whole film as a partial system within the larger system of works bearing the Welles signature? Heath's decision to remain within the confines of this work is, in his own terms, arbitrary. His lack of interest in the Quinlan/Welles pairing prematurely amputates the mapping of the chain of transformations. He cannot see, for instance, that Zita and Welles are part of the same chain: If Zita can die instead of Vargas – the acid thrown at him burning up her poster, the pathological repetition of her

earlier actual killing serving to indicate her continued *life* in the realm
of the imaginary – and if multiple overlaps link Suzy, Zita, and Tanya
(Su/zi/tan/ya), as Heath notes, then in the end the overlaps and repetitions reach a point at which Suzy comes to stand for Quinlan's dead
wife, who can herself be seen to have died instead of a Quinlan whose
own place has dissolved, dispersing his identity (*exploding* it, in fact)
throughout the whole work. Heath's early closure of the film's substitutions blinds him to the fundamental mechanism of the narrative system he proposes to analyze: a mechanism founded upon the magical
retrospective rewriting of events. Retrospective redefinition is characteristic both of Quinlan – whose career has been built upon the framing of suspects – and of the narrative. A filmmaker is of course also
someone who "frames" people. Perhaps the most striking instance involves the molestation of Suzy at the motel. When the leather-jacketed,
sub-Brando motorcycle boys close in on her at the motel, someone
shouts out "hold her legs" and the door closes on the scene; the style
and syntax of the images clearly tell us that a rape is occurring. Later,
however, we will be told that Suzy remained miraculously intact. "The
magic of film" rewrites the scene: Welles himself acts as a "good" version of Quinlan.

A similar urge to rewrite underlies Quinlan's repetition compulsion.
Framing suspects is – among other things – his attempt to make good
his failure to establish the guilt of the man he knew killed his wife.
The killing of Uncle Joe Grandi retrospectively negates the murder of
Quinlan's wife, the rhyme completing it to erase it and render it a non-
event. The flashing lights in the room mark an alternation between
the illumination of reason and the darkness of the unconscious. Inter-
mittent light had already been identified with sexual pathology – and
impotence – in the scene in which Pablo, separated from Suzy's hotel
room by the intervening street, flashed a light at her as she defied his
would-be voyeuristic gaze by removing a light bulb and hurling it at
him – an image of castration. His lack of access to her is underlined
by Vargas's subsequent entry into the room. Sexuality and intermittence are also linked in the bobbing movements of the oil pumps. (A
connection also present, incidentally, in *Written on the Wind*, which
had the same producer.) The dreamlike, noirish state evoked by the in-
termittent light acts like hypnosis, precipitating Quinlan into psychosis. In strangling Grandi – murdering him in the manner of his
own wife's death – Quinlan rewrites the scenario of the earlier event: It
was not the woman who was murdered but the man; cords are used
only to tie Susan, not to strangle her; and as she wakes up, the murder
becomes merely her bad dream (since "she" overlaps with everyone
else in the film, the bad dream is a shared nightmare). The murder of
Grandi is clearly "excessive," overspilling the purpose of framing Su-

san; it would have been obvious that Susan lacked the strength to kill him. The murder itself is thus as telltale as the cane Quinlan leaves on the scene with unconscious deliberation: Leaving the cane behind redefines the murder of his wife as an event whose perpetrator is easily identifiable, since concrete evidence was found on the scene. In the film's final retrospective redefinition, we are told that Quinlan was right about Sanchez, who confessed to the murder for which he had been framed. Similarly, on one level of the text Quinlan himself is guilty of the murder of his own wife – betraying her, as it were, with the Marlene Dietrich figure? – for which he frames himself in a hallucination.

At this point it may be worth thinking about Quinlan's cane, and not merely because it establishes an echo of *Citizen Kane*,[6] implying a crippling at the very start of Welles's career. Quinlan's limp, when coupled with the film's concern with borders, may recall Cocteau's remarks on Oedipus: He limps because he has one foot in life and one in death.[7] In other words, he walks the borderline – between light and darkness, like film itself – and not only film in general, but this film in particular, as it zigzags along the line between art and trash. For Quinlan the home of trash is Mexico, the other side of the border, the explosive political unconscious. If the bomb – and hence death – comes from there, Quinlan brings murder back home by killing Grandi on the Mexican side of the border. To cross the border is to risk destruction, loss of one's (American) identity, something already lost by Charlton Heston: Linneker is blown to bits by the explosive sexuality he imports from Mexico, by Zita as "sex bomb" (no wonder she feels a ticking in her head). Only the badge of Law enables one to cross and recross the border with relative impunity, though even here there is no complete safety: It is as if Quinlan is the survivor of an explosion – the perverse explosion of desire in the murder of his wife – though at the cost of damage to his leg. His possession of some of the dynamite that explodes when the car crosses the border indicates his partial mastery of the danger of such transgression. (Framing suspects has subordinated transgression to the demands of law enforcement.) The film of course is also able to go back and forth across the border: As the smooth virtuoso tracking shot at the beginning shows, it – like Vargas – would like to think of the border as open. An open border, however, is also a place along which identity dissolves: The murder room, with its flashing light, in which the daylight of the U.S. side of the border is spliced with the darkness associated with the Mexican side – Mexico as the Other for U.S. consciousness. The open border that is the utopia of Vargas is a nightmare for Quinlan. Quinlan's utopia would be a place beyond the double-bind relationship between Mexico and the United States. Here he is clearly at one with Welles.

This is where Tanya's bar and the image of Dietrich come into play: It is in a sense the world of expressionist (European) filmmaking, toward which Welles can only yearn, condemned as he is to remain within the confines of the American filmmaking that is destroying him. Dietrich's heavy German accent here is just one of several features that work to create an alternative world in her bar. (These features include the bull's head, a reference to Spain and an earlier stage in Welles's life.) Like an embassy, Tanya's bar is another country: the land of regression and death. Her cigars identify her as the phallic mother, the fetishist's ideal, who once gave life and has now come to take it away; hence Quinlan's consumption of his candy bars seeks a substitute for maternal milk and accompanies the dwindling of life and phallus.[8] The disappearance of the penis, the culmination of Quinlan's loss of touch with self and sexuality, precedes the disappearance of Quinlan himself, the phallic law grown impotent. The pianola playing itself is in fact played by the ghost Quinlan becomes when he approaches Tanya. Its automatic playing is an image of the automatic nature of the narrative, the story that brushes Quinlan aside, and from which Welles himself stands apart. At Tanya's bar, on the other side of the border between life and death, Quinlan is like Linneker, annihilated. His wife is still alive as the imago of Dietrich, the fantasy lover of cinema, at the place at which he is dead.

When the border opens, separate identities dissolve: The consequences of this initial cataclysm reverberate throughout the film. In the utopian dimension, it means that Mexican and American can marry, and the Mexican can occupy the position of the law. (Indeed, the Mexican is already American, being embodied in Charlton Heston; his promotion is the utopia of an America apparently ceding what it really retains.) In the dystopian dimension, meanwhile, Quinlan can lose his identity to the Mexican element he defines as criminal, becoming submerged in the criminal side of his personality (the oil-fouled water). Having lost his identity in the murder scene, he then forfeits that most Wellesian of his properties, his potent voice, appropriated by the mike. "Mike" is, of course, the American form of "Miguel."[9] The displaced Oedipal motifs floating through the film (Quinlan's limp, the references to blindness in Vargas's dark glasses as he crosses the border and the blind woman next to the telephone as he rings Susan at the motel) show his victory over Quinlan to be the son's defeat of the archaic father. In Welles's film the body of the father has become grotesque. It is indeed, as Tanya notes, "a mess." The grotesque body, as defined by Bakhtin, is a double body: It is, furthermore, the assembly of all the characters contained within Quinlan/Welles.

One of the fundamental tendencies of the grotesque image of the body is to show two bodies in one. ( ... ) In contrast to modern canons, the age of the body is most frequently represented in immediate proximity to birth or death, to infancy or old age, to the womb or the grave, to the bosom that gives life or swallows it up. But at their extreme limit the two bodies unite to form one. The individual is shown at the stage when it is recast into a new mould. It is dying and as yet unfinished: the body stands on the threshold of the grave and the crib. No longer is there one body, nor are there as yet two. Two heartbeats are heard; one is the mother's, which is slowed down.[10]

Bakhtin's words allow one to correlate Quinlan's infantilism with his agedness, and with the key theme of Welles's work: the idea of that which ends before it has begun. The double body is that of Welles/Quinlan, on the one hand, and the American fused with the Mexican.* To identify with what one has defined as the Other, as Quinlan does in the murder scene, is to destroy oneself. His murder of Grandi undoes his wife's killing, and also rhymes with – and revenges – the murder of Linneker. In destroying himself Quinlan frees the image of the American woman – as represented in the past by his wife, and in the present by Susan. The death of the crippled lawman is the utopian demise of the crime upon which he – Welles as Falstaffian Lord of Misrule – once fed, and with which in the end he becomes consubstantial, his body bloated with the accumulation of humanity's sins, redemptively rejected. However, in terms of the film history connecting film noir with German cinema, Quinlan's double body results from the fusion of the bodies of Lohman and Becker – the childish child-murderer – in Lang's *M*: the cigar-puffing image of the former seen in grotesque low-angle at his office desk fused with the jellylike infantilism of the latter.[†] In the end, perhaps, the double body is one

---

* This double body is present from the very outset of Welles's career, prompting split reactions in reviewers. When Pauline Kael terms *Citizen Kane* "a shallow masterpiece,"[11] the oxymoronic formulation straddles the split. In *Kane* the body's duality lies in the conjunction of Mankiewicz and Welles; and although it might be tempting to Welles's apologists to attribute the shallowness to Mankiewicz and the masterpiece theater to Welles, shallowness is essential to Welles's talent also: He can be termed a Baroque artist because, like the Counter-Reformation painters who brought back the lost faithful with dazzling aesthetic devices, he uses virtuosity to compel assent to a work one nevertheless continues to distrust in a corner of one's mind (or, in the mind, as the eye is seduced). In Welles's case the seduction is worked through a magical maximalization of contrast, which creates a euphoric, discarnate dynamism – be it through extreme contrasts in linear time, as in the juxtaposition of contrasting genres at the start of *Kane* (horror film–avant-garde film–documentary), or in space, through chiaroscuro or the wide-angle lens that strengthens the contrast between background and foreground and lends a preternatural, vertiginous rapidity to movements between the two. The double body in *Kane* is present before the camera, as Welles–Hearst, and also behind it, as Welles–Mankiewicz.
† There are other piquant intertextual links also: the final scene of *M* recalls Kafka's *Trial* – particularly in its serried faces and the absurdity with which the defense lawyer

that is both German and American. Welles's Germanized Americanism meets the Americanism of the German Lang, whose first sound feature is as it were the sound bridge leading him to American cinema (and to the acoustic sphere in which Welles will excel) – thereby closing the circle of the film noir–expressionist link. And the mother whose slow heartbeat – the cause of her drawl – is also heard as the infant god dies? It is deeply appropriate that Quinlan's demise should be witnessed by that other American German, Marlene Dietrich. If Professor Immanuel Rath became grotesquely double by merging with his own negation, Unrat, Quinlan follows the same path. His death in the mud is a masochistic self-abasement before the haunting phantom of the femme fatale, the Devil who is a Woman and has come to collect his soul.

## The big sleep and the little dreamer: The political unconscious of film noir

Of all the terms employed to denote the genres whereby classic Hollywood films atomized the social totality into a series of parts forbidden to join up and reveal the falsity of the whole, film noir is the least easily defined. This is partly because the term was forged by critics extrapolating from the "série noir," the hard-boiled novel of the thirties, rather than by the industry itself. The apparent debility of the term is, however, a strength, as it cuts across genres, linking such diverse forms as the detective story, the gangster film, and melodrama (e.g., there are strong noir elements in *Mildred Pierce*), leaving a trail of clues one may connect to piece together the ideological totality. The most obvious element that floats between these genres, leaving deposits upon each as it disintegrates in passage, like thistledown, is that of style: The rooms crosshatched with light and shadow by blinds, the flashing neon, indicative of a preoccupation with light effects and the elusiveness of reality in a treacherous world. This preoccupation is one with the vulnerability and intermittence of the individual and of one kind of individual in particular: the foreigner.

The style is often described as having been imported into American film by émigré Germans schooled under expressionism. It was also found in the work of other European émigrés, such as Jacques Tourneur, whose *Cat People* presents an image of an America that is determined to demonize the foreign so as to feel justified in extruding it: Its heroine, played by Simone Simon, may be seen as someone lured by the utopian image of the second home, only to discover the delusive-

appointed pro forma by the kangaroo court actually begins to *defend* his client – and thus draws one on to Welles's *Trial.*

ness of her dream. But if the noir style was also adopted by native American directors, it was because they too felt themselves to be exiles in their own country, the American trailblazer here being, of course, the Welles of *Citizen Kane.* Hence the expressionism of these films is no merely decorative foreign veneer spread over American themes, but serves as their medium. Thus the preoccupation with father–son relationships and repressed homosexuality – isolated as constants of Weimar cinema by Kracauer – pervades film noir also. The tough guy is in a sense the son pretending to be the father; whence the slightly ludicrous and even campy excessiveness of his toughness. These themes can be read as constituents of the political unconscious of the film noir period, the forties; they embody a revolt that cannot speak its name (the fate of so many revolts in American culture) and that displaces and diverts itself from substance into style. The politics of film noir, repressed by film noir itself, only become overt thirty years later, when noir scenarios and style are adopted by young directors for whom the rejected father is the country that sends its sons to slaughter in Vietnam, and who find in the noir detective a fetish to brandish against militant feminism. I mean, of course, such directors as Coppola, Penn, and Scorsese. The most telling and self-conscious of the latter-day resurrections of film noir is not to be found in American cinema, however, but in the Europe from which the noir aesthetic originated. The film in question is Bertolucci's *The Conformist,* to which I will return at the end of this essay. My remarks on the anterior and afterlife of a film form are intended as a contribution to the theory and practice of periodization and to the debate on the usefulness of stylishness to the radical will.

*Fathers and sons*

In the world of film noir, crimes are notoriously difficult to track to their origin. Their source among the rich is veiled by the numerous smokescreens – "buffers," in the language of *The Godfather* – that they can afford to put up. The smoking gun is only ever held by a disposable hired hand. The consequent ease with which evidence disappears forces Marlowe continually to have resort to guesswork, hypotheses that are themselves eminently disposable. This is the key difference between *noir* and the gangster movies that characterized the early thirties: The criminal is no longer an outsider seeking to break in (what else can a po' boy do?) but a safely shrouded insider. (If De Palma's *Scarface* fails, it is surely – incidentally – because it pours film noir moods into the gangster film's bottle.) American society is no longer the open jungle in which one can hack out one's own clearing, as it had been for the gangster: Money is now always old money, a situation rendered all the more ironic by its documentation in Chandler's California, where one could expect novelty still to remain. Once California has closed, however, there is nowhere left to go. Whence the sense of despair in noir. No longer translatable into actuality, the American dream festers. It is characteristic that the two archetypal heroes of noir – the detective and the lover – are defined as poor. The detective never makes his fortune: A mere private *eye*, he is permitted – like the audience – to observe the rich but not to touch. Marlowe may be offered fat fees, but he never accepts them; if he did, his newfound riches would render him an impossible object for audience identification. (Marlowe is of course something of a figure in a pipe dream; how on earth does he manage to live between assignments?) His power of knowledge is also impotence. To use it to blackmail the rich, as everyone else does, would not only compromise the knight of the mean streets; it would also endanger him. The other archetypical noir hero, the lover, may kill the rich father in an effort to supplant him, but he is never able to collect the anticipated spoils: In the sharply divided world of noir, sons are by definition unable to become fathers. The patriarchal law hunts down the offending lover, arguing that the corrupt father who seemed so richly to deserve his despatch is merely a local blot on the copybook – even though the films derive their power from the strong suspicion that he does indeed stand for the whole. If he is hunted down by the cops rather than the detective, this is simply another indication of the hidden identity of the two figures: He is as it were a detective who is no longer merely content to observe the sins of the rich, seeing them instead as a warrant for the overthrow of their power. Thus if the style of noir is expressionist-influenced, so is its content: In expressionism the sons revolted against tyrannical father figures; and in noir, as in expressionism, this revolt coincides with a world war. The sons sent into battle see through the corruption of the fathers who sent them – the old men left behind will steal their girls in their absence.

Both the detective and the lover-murderer have an alibi in their ostensibly democratic motivation: They bring the high down low. Their animus – which is also the films' animus – is also directed against "high" art, which is identified as un-American and aristocratic. As Benjamin notes, the mission of photography and film is to dispel the aura of the art object. Thus the man who frames the hero of *The Dark Corner* is an art dealer; a statue witnesses the perverse scenes in Geiger's house in *The Big Sleep*; the Maltese falcon brings death to its would-be handler; and – in a later version of noir – South American art treasures lie at the murky heart of Penn's *Night Moves*.

The most interesting of these examples is clearly the statue in *The Big Sleep*. It is in fact hollow and contains a camera: Aristocratic art hypocritically masks its dependence upon the mass art of photography.* Art's pretensions to uniqueness are in fact hollow. If the camera represents the realistic substratum of art – to which the film reduces it – it is also art's conscience. The statue may stare unblinkingly at horrible events, but the camera *does* blink, registering its shock in the flash of lightning wherewith it draws attention to the offender's misdeeds. It also draws Marlowe to the scene: The camera as the natural ally of the detective. Once the camera's flash has attracted his attention, however, its by-products – the photographs of Carmen – must be eliminated. All signs of the evil sexuality the film replaces with monogamy must be repressed. Perversity must be absorbed into normality as the sexual glamour that brings Marlowe and Vivian together. It is absorbed by the narrative as photographs are by a film.

*Repression in* The Big Sleep

If the objects of mass culture are society's dreams, in which it self-obliviously reveals the truth about itself, this truth is nevertheless difficult to decipher. Condensation and displacement turn it into a code. The illusions of coherence wrought by rhyming plots and secondary revision conceal the ferment of contradictions below: The lava may have hardened at the top, but underneath it still glows with life. An inspection of the literary and film versions of *The Big Sleep* can help establish an archaeology of the layers within the lava. The film version has of course been subjected to a far more thoroughgoing process of repression than the literary one. Drugs and nudity are out, and the union of Vivian and Marlowe takes the place of Marlowe's illusionless retreat into the night. The film whitewashes Carmen, pins everything on Eddie Mars, and delegates to his own boys the dirty work of disposing of him. Vivian is not "Mrs. Regan" but Mrs. Rutledge. Since in the novel Regan's ambiguous status as possibly alive or dead removes Vivian from the sphere of the legally desirable, the film's redefinition of her marital status – and of Regan's role – allows her to be written into scene after scene from which she is absent in Chandler's version. If her star rises as Regan's sets, this may well indicate a complementarity or rivalry between the two in the original material.

Whereas the film severs the links between the detective tough guy and repressed homosexuality, the book is perturbed by the problem of how to reject women without seeming to be homosexual. The film can clearly incorporate woman into its spectacle – when Marlowe invites Vivian to scratch herself, she scratches the side of her leg the audi-

* If film noir is less trustful of the will to style than is expressionism, it is because – as in this image – it sees stylization as mendacious, opposed to the truth-telling of photographic realism.

ence can see – and so finds the homosexual subworld less of a temptation and looming abyss. Like Chandler's later books, *The Big Sleep* defines woman as trouble, and is beset by a narcissism of style and content that is only a step away from homosexuality. (After all, Narcissus was in love with another male, and the Narcissus myth may be read as an embodiment of repressed homosexuality.) The possibilities of homosexual affiliation are partly banished by dispensing with the male companionship generally enjoyed by the late-nineteenth-century detective. This omission is also a sign of the individual's diminished ability to control and decipher society, whose workings are now more opaque: Marlowe's lame guesses cannot rival the glittering trains of deduction wherewith Holmes or Dupin edify and enthrall their admiring companions. Chandler may accentuate the detective's narcissism rather than his potential homosexuality, but he is unable to dispel the specter of homoeroticism entirely. This is less a matter of Marlowe's congenital lack of a weapon, which can be coded as effeminacy – the only one he ever sports is Carmen's small gun, as if the dick remains private through fear of revelation of the actual smallness of his own bodily hardware – than of the obsessive quasi-identification with Regan. The search for Regan is pursued largely on Marlowe's own initiative: It is not ordered by Sternwood, who seeks in fact to countermand it, and so it can seem "excessive." It is interesting that a photograph of Regan should be available even though none can be found of Eddie Mars's wife, with whom he is rumored to have absconded. "That's funny," Gregory remarks; it is symptomatic of the text's greater interest in men. Marlowe identifies himself with Regan's Irishness by terming himself "Doghouse Reilly" before Carmen, and exposes himself to the self-same fate Regan suffered at her hands. The second time around, however, the tragedy is played as farce: Carmen's attempt to kill him is frustrated by the blanks he has inserted in her gun. The insertion of blanks into the gun undermines its phallicism, while also indicating that the phallic woman is a mirage. The empty gun rhymes suggestively with the empty camera in Geiger's house: The camera's flash is like a gunshot with a blank.

If the film shows us a Marlowe concerned primarily to clear Vivian, the book shows one whose main interest is in tracking down Regan. Would it be going too far to see in the quest for Regan an attempt by the twentieth-century detective to revert to the nineteenth century, when he enjoyed a soul mate and a double (a quest whose inevitable failure removes the other male to the safety of an ideal whose loss one can bemoan with crocodile tears)? In an American culture beginning to succumb to corporatism and obsessed with the difficulties of male self-assertion, Proust – perhaps the greatest of all homosexual writers – can only be invoked as a connoisseur in moral degenerates. The individualism and vulgar Freudianism of forties America deny the detective his male companion: For if individualism separates all people from one another, Freudianism divides man from man in particular, fostering a climate in which the constant male companion is read and reviled as a lover.

Paradoxically, in repressing many of the features of Chandler's original Hawks's film moves away from repression. Chandler's private eye could indeed be pigeonholed by Adorno's analysis of the tough guy:

He-men are thus, in their own constitution, what film-plots usually present them to be, masochists. At the root of their sadism is a lie, and only as liars do they truly become sadists, agents of repression. This lie, however, is nothing other than repressed homosexuality presenting itself as the only approved form of heterosexuality.[12]

Bogart imparts charm to Marlowe; this occurs through the introduction of a heterosexuality that suggests the actor's amusement by his own tough-guy role. The film swarms with a bevy of no-nonsense Hawksian girls, including the girl in the bookstore (who is no longer Chandler's Jewish intellectual), the taxi driver, and even Vivian herself, who is not content to let her maid do her living for her but helps Marlowe convey the stupored Carmen into the house herself. The Bogart Marlowe is no longer the lone knight who walks the mean streets, the liberator of the naked girl in the Sternwood family emblem the film omits. He is a more congenially utopian figure – both tender and tough – than Chandler's detective, one less neurotically intent upon defining himself as a law outside the law, since he readily cooperates with the police; he is thus far more of a conformist. It may seem paradoxical to state that the book is more deeply irrational than the film: Books allow one the breathing spaces films forbid, while their foregrounding of language would suggest a greater devotion to rationality (to the Symbolic rather than the Imaginary?). And yet Chandler's verbal construct is far more irrational, for it need not be measured against the obduracy of real people – strange though it may seem to ascribe reality to actors, particularly those of Hollywood. Chandler's isolated detective is the solitary reader, caught up in a paranoid effort to document the semiology of everyday life; he resembles Pynchon's Oedipa Maas. The film's greater rationality can be seen in its legendary struggle to sew up such loose ends as the question of who killed Carmen's chauffeur. Where Chandler leaves this open – the book derives its coherence less from a narrative structure than from the inescapability and bittersweet seduction of the narrator's voice – the film strongly suggests that the guilt is Eddie Mars's. The film can be seen as a therapeutic reworking of the Chandler material, society's taming of the isolated detective: Where id was, ego has entered. The film is driven to integrate the individualistic detective into society by its awareness of the collaborative nature of its own mode of production, which renders it skeptical of the existence of Chandler's solitary quester. Its assertion of the feasibility of integration, however, makes it far less modern than Chandler's text; indeed, figures analogous to the hard-boiled dick of thirties fiction were not to appear on screen before *Dirty Harry*. It is surely no coincidence that Harry too materializes on the West Coast, at the point where society crumbles away and the boundaries between legality and private justice grow friable. But that is another story, the story of the detective's long good-bye, which I do not intend to tell here. Instead, I would like to end by considering how the political unconscious of film noir is analyzed in Bernardo Bertolucci's *The Conformist*: an analysis far more telling than the recuperation of Chandler the Hawks film carries out.

## Postscript

If film noir has a political unconscious, it is dredged into consciousness thirty years later, in one of the greatest films of the seventies: Bertolucci's *Conformist* (*Il conformista*). Bertolucci's work is not, as Fredric Jameson implies,[13] an example of postmodern pastiche, a meretricious exhibit in the gallery of nostalgia film; rather, it rethinks and reexperiences the past in order to unmask the contradictions of an id that betrays itself through its compact with the superego, through the nonconformist's febrile urge to conform. The film is a palimpsest that superimposes the father–son question upon the question of repressed homosexuality: The gunshot Marcello Clerici fired at the chauffeur who sought to seduce him in his childhood is a displaced parricide that deprives him of the courage and will for the true parricide that would enable him to become himself. A film noir ambience is present from the very first scene, in which Clerici, the would-be fascist, sits on his bed, about to descend to the chauffeured car taking him to the murder of his spiritual father, an antifascist professor living in exile in France. As he sits on his bed, a neon light flashes on and off outside. The conjunction of the man on the bed and the flashing light is a classic noir motif, a sign of repression, the tough guy's fear of sleep and dreams. As he fights the sleep that would make him vulnerable, the noir hero twitches in and out of wakefulness with the clicking light that is also the film's flickering passage through the projector's gate. (It is hardly surprising that the film should later allude to the relationship between the idea of cinema and the troubled flamelight of Plato's cave.)

The struggle against sleep in noir is an existentialist motif, the ease with which the self can slip into unconsciousness and become an adjunct of the administered world causing the strenuousness of the effort to monitor the project of one's life. Where film noir is deeply indebted to the existentialism that accorded hard-boiled fiction the dignity of a *Weltanschauung, The Conformist* parodies the existentialist belief that character is precipitated solely of action, with no admixture of inheritance. Marcello Clerici's attempt to re-create himself is in fact a mystified struggle with the heritage of his father's madness, which is also that of the fascist state on whose behalf the father had tortured. (It is his memory of his father that causes him to wince when the antifascist professor's wife reads him a letter about torture in Mussolini's Italy.) And yet, for all his striving to escape the past, he walks in its footsteps: His step in front of the chauffeured car in 1938 triggers a flashback to his similar action as a child; he makes love to his wife when he hears of how an old man seduced her. The existential belief that one's deeds define one's nature is most devastatingly undermined by the aftermath of the childhood shot at the chauffeur. Ever since that day Marcello has defined himself as a murderer required to conform so as to cleanse his life; and yet at the film's end we discover the chauffeur to be still alive. Here, as in *The Big Sleep,* the phallic gun is loaded with blanks. Marcello's entire project has been founded upon delusion; his insight is blindness. Bertolucci's film, by placing the film noir hero in a social and ideological context and subjecting him to psychoanalysis, reveals the absurdity of his heroic pose. The American hero's transposition to thirties Italy further implies an Adornian diagnosis of the totalitarian nature of modernity on both sides of the Atlantic. The life of the film noir hero becomes the tragedy of a ridiculous man, seated on a bed he cannot use for either lovemaking or slumber, only for reading Chandler and dreaming a waking dream of parricide and of the big sleep.

### *Vertigo,* visual pleasure, and the end of film noir

It is an odd thing, but everyone who disappears is said to have been seen at San Francisco. It must be a delightful city, and possess all the attractions of the next world. (Lord Henry to Dorian Gray, *The Picture of Dorian Gray,* Chapter XIX.)

Although *Touch of Evil* is conventionally deemed to be the epitaph of film noir, a far better candidate is another film from the same year: Hitchcock's *Vertigo. Touch of Evil* lacks the essential noir element, the femme fatale who inhabits the center of Hitchcock's film. Whereas most films noirs – as I have argued above – separate the detective from the lover and develop different scenarios for each (works focused upon the detective end optimistically, those centered upon the lover darkly), *Vertigo* dissolves the noir system by uniting the two, identifying the mystery to be solved with a married woman to be appropriated. It thus transcends both the noir genre and the series of other genres it transsects: ghost or horror film, thriller, love story. Such corrosion of categories has prompted several critical attempts to "put it back in its place." The most virulent of these is surely the short analysis of the work contained in Laura Mulvey's influential "Visual Pleasure and Narrative Cinema."[14] Recently, however, some feminists – notably Tania Modleski[15] – have directed attention to some of the flaws in Mulvey's argument (of which more later in this section). Modleski herself, however, fails to perceive some of the text's complexities. Thus she notes parenthetically that "critics tend to slight all those parodic elements of the film which work against the seriousness of the 'love theme' and in this they reveal themselves to be like Scottie, who rejects Midge's demystificatory act of painting her own face into the Carlotta portrait as 'not funny'."[16] The implication is that such objections are merely quaint (one can praise Modleski for her abstention from terming them "sexist"); no consideration is accorded the question of the justifiability of such reactions – even though the parodic elements can be read as defense mechanisms Hitchcock employs to protect himself against the deadly seriousness of the material, to recover the safe detachment of the entertainer. (The use of monochrome in *Psycho,* Hitchcock's next film, would be a similar defense mechanism.) Moreover, although Modleski's discussion of *Vertigo* argues that the pain the film causes the viewer stems from the bisexual position it constructs for him/her, her analysis is not free of moments of Mulveyesque sexual dualism. Remarking that the film alternates "between a hypnotic and masochistic fascination with woman's desire and a sadistic attempt to gain control over her," she concludes, "Of course sadism wins the day."[17] Why "of course"? Is the knowingness of the tone attributable to our knowledge of what happens – we certainly have no such knowledge during a first viewing, and the film's development is highly unpredictable – or because sadism "of course" pervades the male psyche? The latter implication may not have been intended, but it is present nevertheless. Modleski's final verdict is that "the man desperately tries to necessitate a sense of himself that necessitates the end of woman."[18] One wonders why "the end of woman." The final scene is far too complex for this sort of summary, whose loose phrasing adds a tinge of complexity to a Mulveyesque position. For Scottie's intentions are unclear throughout. Even if his aim *is* to precipitate Judy from the tower (and this is far from certain), it is not the generic "woman" he opposes but *this woman,* who has duped him. Indeed, "woman" survives the film (even if Scottie then jumps) in the form of the nun. Since even an analysis critical of Mulvey's simplicities cannot fully extricate itself from a nostalgia for them, it is surely imperative that Mulvey's analysis be subjected to the close critique that will reveal the sheer extent of its flaws. Thus the following essay will take sentences from the Mulvey analysis as the point of departure for a dissenting view. (The reasons for my dissent from the theoretical framework that makes possible so flagrant a misreading can be found expounded at greater length in my *Blue Angel* analysis [Chapter I], and in Appendix I.)

"Visual Pleasure and Narrative Cinema" has been perhaps the most influential theoretical text of the past fifteen years. Arguing that mainstream film sexes the gaze as male and constitutes the female as victimized object of that gaze, it finds in the dissemination of unpleasure the remedy for a dispensation that grants textual pleasure exclusively to males. Mulvey's position is clearly vulnerable to criticism, particularly for its omission of the space between "Hollywood" and the avant garde – a space occupied by the best works of a Bergman, an Antonioni, and even a Von Trotta. The mainstream is cut so broad that everything except the feminist avant garde crumbles into it. Mulvey herself has amended her original position statement. Nevertheless, it is that original text that continues to be widely reprinted and whose critical preferences have become canonic in a self-styled anticanon. Mulvey's comments on *Vertigo* seek to cement the overall dualism of her thesis by assimilating even Hitchcock's finest work to mainstream Hollywood. It will be my contention that in so doing she perpetrates a caricature of the film that relies on loose thinking, loaded terminology, prejudice, and confusion over narrative temporality and detail. Implicit in my argument is the further contention that the influence such a text exerts shows that the belief that no text is innocent can lead all too easily to a deliberate embrace of guilt, in the name of "conviction politics": Like Welles's Hank Quinlan, the critic is merely framing someone who was guilty anyway. I will follow the shifts and slides of Mulvey's analysis sentence by sentence.

In *Vertigo*, subjective camera predominates. Apart from one flash-back from Judy's point of view, the narrative is woven around what Scottie sees or fails to see.[19]

At first sight these two sentences seem unexceptionable. The first is hardly objectionable, though the loose acceptance of the notion of "subjective camera" is problematic. More problematic however is Mulvey's inability to recognize that the flashback from Judy's point of view is not a momentary aberration in a narrative that reverts to type following its insertion, but in fact radically revises the narrative perspective. From this point on – the revelation of the real circumstances of "Madeleine" 's death – the focus is as much on Judy as it is upon Scottie. And although it is clearly Kim Novak playing the roles both of

Judy and of Madeleine, only the flashback reveals that she is meant to be the same person in the textual system of this film.*

From this point onward we focus on Judy's motives for submitting to Scottie's remolding of her image: Indeed, Scottie's own motives are so opaque that she becomes the main agent of our identification with the film. When she asks him what purpose the makeover is meant to have, she is nevertheless in a sense also asking herself, and his "I don't know" could be her reply to herself. (I will return to the question of Judy's motivation later in this section.)

The audience follows the growth of his erotic obsession and subsequent despair precisely from his point of view.

As we have seen, because the flashback alters the rules of the game, it is false to assert that the audience follows events precisely from Scottie's point of view throughout the film. The matter of vocabulary is worth noting here, however: firstly, "erotic obsession" degrades Scottie's love and serves to frame the suspect; secondly, the "precisely" is a recurrent tic of *Screen* articles, deployed to create an air of pseudo-scientific exactitude whenever something far from clear is being relayed.

Scottie's voyeurism is blatant: he falls in love with a woman he follows and spies on without speaking to. Its sadistic side is equally blatant: he has chosen (and freely chosen, for he had been a successful lawyer) to be a policeman, with all the attendant possibilities of pursuit and investigation. As a result he follows, watches and falls in love with a perfect image of female mystery and beauty.

Voyeurism is indeed an element in Scottie's constitution, but the insistence on just looking is also part of refusal to touch; one of the reasons for his status as bachelor is a lack of the usual male aggression (termed "sadism" here) that would reach out to touch. (Although Scottie does indeed touch the perfect image – undressing "Madeleine" following her leap into the Bay – we are not shown this, and hence are not invited to identify with it; the suggestion is also that it was something Scottie himself would rather put out of his mind.) Here one may compare Scottie with Strether, another unmarried man, in James's *The Ambassadors*. I am reluctant to concede even this much to Mulvey, however, for if Scottie follows "Madeleine," it is first and foremost because he has been commissioned to do so by her husband, despite his own reservations. Mulvey's moral strictures against Scottie might bet-

---

* After all, there are films in which the same actress plays different characters – e.g., *The Conformist* – and even ones in which different actresses play the same character – e.g., *That Obscure Object of Desire*. The mere fact that the same actress plays both parts does not in itself determine whether Scottie is "right" or "wrong" to fail at first to recognize her as "Madeleine."

ter be applied to the murderer who sets him up as perfect witness to the flawless crime. Scottie's choice of career is rendered doubly diabolical by Mulvey's insistent and unwarranted "freely chosen": The factors underlying Scottie's choice of career are never given, so one cannot say whether the choice was "free" or "unfree." Mulvey's ritualistic denunciation of the police could equally well be turned against her: After all, has not she freely chosen to be a critic, "with all the attendant possibilities of pursuit and investigation"? If there is a sadistic element in Scottie, it is only brought to the surface by the appalling events he suffers: As it changes mood and mode, flirting with chamber drama, horror, and detective thriller, the film itself embodies its theme of instability and wandering, and shows how a man who is not sadistic can become so, as occurs in the final tower scene, in which Scottie seeks to make Judy suffer as he himself has done. If Hitchcock's film is harrowing it is because it shows how the innocent can become guilty – how Scottie can become like Elster: It is in a sense Hitchcock's own coded confession of how he came to enter the state of mind in which a *Psycho* can be made. "There but for the grace of God go I" is not an emotion Mulvey entertains; doubtless femininity insulates her from sadism. She therefore ignores the degree to which the perfect image of female mystery has been *constructed* as such by Elster so as to entice and entrap Scottie. (Ironically, she overlooks the self-referentiality that allows the film to attack our culture's constructions of the female image with a virulence comparable only to her own.)

The essential element in the construction of perfect mystery is, of course, the fusion of opposites. One example, mentioned by Spoto, is the ambiguity surrounding the colors red and green. "The reiteration and transference of these colors link the two characters, and suggest the up–down, stop–go polarity which is itself vertiginous."[20] When Scottie first sees "Madeleine" at Ernie's it is profiled, facing right against a red background. The moment is profoundly ambiguous: The left-to-right movement she is engaged in is coded positively in our culture, but the same culture also identifies red with interdiction. This scene sets the narrative in motion paradoxically ("stop" means "go"), as Hitchcock cuts immediately to Scottie in his car: The potential for irony residing in the speed with which his objections to the new assignment have been quashed is swallowed up in the mystery, whose onset is marked by the introduction of the drifting musical theme. Red provokes and attracts, but also halts. One notes that the door to Scottie's apartment is red – the same ambiguity. It recurs when Judy later appears silhouetted against the green neon of her hotel room, this time facing left, which has negative, regressive connotations. (It is thus hardly surprising that Bernard Herrmann's score should here become most intensely reminiscent of the "Liebestod" theme from *Tristan und*

*Isolde,* as the regressiveness of love points to death.) The image rhymes with, and negates, the earlier one at Ernie's. As Scottie follows "Madeleine" in his car, repeatedly turning, spiraling downward, he seems to enjoy a dreamlike "freedom and power" (to use Elster's words) but is really being drawn by an invisible thread, haunted. Quasi-magically, San Francisco seems to have lost its traffic lights.

Once he actually confronts her, his erotic drive is to break her down and force her to tell by persistent cross-questioning. Then, in the second part of the film, he re-enacts his obsessive involvement with the image he loved to watch secretly.

Here Mulvey may be confused, or it may be that she uses uncertainty concerning the narrative's temporal order to insinuate points by legerdemain. "Once he actually confronts her" – one wonders at which point in the film this occurs. It is only at the very end of the film, as Scottie thrusts Judy up the tower, that he breaks her down "by persistent cross-questioning." Yet Mulvey's reference cannot be to that scene (whose memory commands our provisional assent to her initial statement), for her next sentence talks of "the second part of the film." One's conclusion is that Mulvey is either (a) referring to something that never happened or – and this is more likely – (b) collapsing all the film's complex stages of development into the final stage, which she then claims to find (like the Hegelian Absolute) present from the very start. One notes again the denigration of Scottie: Eros and obsession are the bases of his actions; love clearly plays no part.

He reconstructs Judy as Madeleine, forces her to conform in every detail to the actual physical appearance of his fetish. Her exhibitionism, her masochism, make her an ideal passive counterpart to Scottie's active sadistic voyeurism.

"He reconstructs" is only apparently true; it is also true that Judy allows herself to be reconstructed, as the second sentence implicitly concedes. And here the role played by *her* desire – all but ignored by Mulvey, who types it as exhibitionism – becomes paramount in the film. It is piquant to note that a piece first published in *Screen,* a magazine programmatically interested in fusing Marx with Freud, fails to notice that *class position* provides a primary basis for her desire. It is clear that Judy allows herself to be reconstructed as Madeleine for more than one reason. The reasons include a sense of guilt vis-à-vis Scottie, a wish to recover the love *she* lost when the plot to which she had been a party stripped her of the role of Madeleine, and a recognition that to consent to become Madeleine again – returning from the dead like the Madeleine of Poe's "Fall of the House of Usher" – is to enter the "other world" that is redolent of mystery, languor, idle wandering, the past and – above all else – *money* in this film (the noir topos of the origin of mystery among the rich). It is more for these reasons than because of exhibitionism or masochism that she submits to, and so participates in, the fantasy. Such meretricious emotions as exhibitionism and masochism (as well as sheer greed) may well have prompted her initial compliance with Elster's plan, though the withholding of these scenes makes past motivation a matter of guesswork. One thing, however, is certain: She is like Scottie – and, ironically, both she and Scottie are like Elster – in wanting "a second chance." Mulvey's notion that Scottie is guilty of "active sadistic voyeurism" is peculiar, and may be a form of quasi-psychoanalytic bombast: Voyeurism depends upon a readiness merely to look, and so is not active or sadistic. Anyone wishing to pin a rap on Scottie might indeed call him voyeuristic in the first half of the film, but it is only at its end that he becomes a sadist (and the end explains how and why he has become one).

She knows her part is to perform, and only by playing it through and then replaying it can she keep Scottie's erotic interest. But in the repetition he does break her down and succeeds in exposing her guilt. His curiosity wins through and she is punished.

If Judy is a performer, her performing talent is exhibited primarily during the first half of the film, when she enacts the text written by Elster. In the second half she has no text and plays her role by ear, dangerously, existentially. The interest she solicits from Scottie is that of love, not mere eros. (The tendency to conflate the two, sponsored by aficionados of the avowedly sadistic Georges Bataille, should be resisted.) The subsequent sentence resembles the earlier "once he actually confronts her" in its confusion over time. It is not clear who is doing the repeating here. The previous sentence has associated the idea of repetition with Judy – she is "replaying" her role as Madeleine – but the form of the sentence implies a repetition of the old scenario by Scottie with the specific aim of breaking her down and exposing her: "His curiosity wins through and she is punished." Again one wants to ask, "When?" The moment she allows Scottie into her hotel room, Judy begins punishing herself for her guilty secret, long before he can be said to have exposed it. Her guilt only becomes patent to him when he sees her don the necklace, after he has been "remaking her," for motives obscure even to himself, for quite some time. The sight of the necklace snaps him out of his unfocused somnambulism. What is Judy's "punishment"? Her death? If so, is it desired by Scottie? Probably not, since he kisses her immediately before her fall. That fall, of course, is occasioned by the strange, floating entry of the nun (of which more below). On one level the nun is Judy's better self; on another, she is Scottie's disavowed self – the chaste self of the bachelor.

for whom it is now "too late" to change ("too late" is an insistent re-
frain in the final scene), the self he would like to leave behind (the
self identified with law), but which follows him now like a shadow. It
is not Judy alone who is punished, however. Scottie is the victim
throughout the film, and nowhere more so than at its end, when the
price for overcoming vertigo proves to be loss of his love. Eros, the
ability to scale the tower, triumphs at the expense of love, so the final
loss infinitely exceeds the gain. Since Scottie's dream had closed with
his fall onto the roof of the Mission Dolores, Judy's death is equivalent
to his own. Devastating though this ending is, I have known it to provoke laughter, perhaps as a hysterical defense against its horror. It
may justify itself by pointing to a failure of timing in the nun's appearance and Judy's leap, or by remarking that the close is "too bad to be
true."*

In a sense the nun appears at this point as dea ex machina. For if
*Vertigo* ends film noir by bringing the detective and the lover together,
positing woman as mystery to be solved, her duality the signifier of
duplicity, in this final scene Scottie oscillates violently between the
two figures conjoined within him, confronting Judy with the damning
evidence in the manner of a detective one moment, and kissing her the
next. The nun's appearance resolves the resultant aporia, saving both
Scottie and the narrative from the necessity of choosing either love,
and the attendant criminality of ignoring Judy's offense, or dutiful service of the law. It is interesting that she should emerge through a trap-
door that can be taken to symbolize the simultaneous separation and
connection of levels within the mind, for at this moment the discourse
of art opens up onto that of religion, with the Catholicism that had
been implicit throughout the film in the adoration of a single perfect
woman becoming explicit. (And hence separate from the woman hith-
erto deemed perfect; that separation is the death of her.) The religious
can supersede the aesthetic because the bachelor without hope of marriage can be reclassified as a monk, the unattainability of the ideal
woman having transformed her into the Madonna. The moment this
happens, however, the film has to end. When the artistic system generates out of itself an element incompatible with it, it has to conclude,
even at the risk of leaving loose ends dangling. (Scottie may or may
not jump; Hitchcock mercifully deleted a draft ending in which Scottie
and Midge hear a radio report of Elster's capture in Europe.) It cannot
show the workings of the higher system – incomprehensible within the

---

* Judy clearly thinks she has seen a ghost (given the time and place of the manifestation, it must be Madeleine's). The horror genre, present at the film's outset and then
supplanted by the detective mystery, returns, a return of the repressed, enlightenment
crumbling into myth. The ghost story itself gets the second chance all the protagonists
pursue.

terms of this one – that might render the nun's final "God have mercy" something other than the appalling irony we feel it to be.

In *Vertigo,* erotic involvement with the look is disorientating: the spectator's fascination is turned against him as the narrative carries him through and entwines him with the processes that he is himself exercising. The Hitchcock hero is firmly placed within the symbolic order, in narrative terms. He has all the attributes of the patriarchal superego.

Again one begins with the telltale, framing "erotic." Mulvey's description of how the spectator's fascination is turned against him is tantalizing, as it approaches – and then fails to achieve – an awareness of the work's self-referentiality. One may wonder also whether "he" is a generalizing reference to all spectators, in the prefeminist manner, or designates the male viewer exclusively. If the latter is the case, then it ignores the extent to which the female spectator is offered a clear mode of entry into the text through identification with Judy's quest for a second chance – together with the possibility that the female viewer may also experience disorientation. The purpose of the film, however, is less to link Scottie to the patriarchal superego – he is in a sense the victim of a patriarchal id, the amoral Elster – than to demonstrate how the typical Hitchcock male comes to be constituted. Insofar as this is its project, *Vertigo* transcends all Hitchcock's other works, becoming their metatext, and explaining how the desire to inflict pain – mild, in the form of suspense, violent, as in *Psycho* or *The Birds* – is generated by the pain one has experienced oneself. In becoming akin to Elster in the final scene, Scottie becomes like the Hitchcock of *The Birds*.

Hence the spectator, lulled into a false sense of security by the apparent legality of his surrogate, sees through his look and finds himself exposed as complicit, caught in the moral ambiguity of looking. Far from being simply an aside on the perversion of the police, *Vertigo* focuses on the implications of the active/looking, passive/looked-at split in terms of sexual differences and the power of the male symbolic encapsulated in the hero.

Somewhat against the grain of her earlier disparagement of Scottie's choice of career, Mulvey here acknowledges that *Vertigo* is "far from being simply an aside on the perversion of the police" (an interpretation of the film that she alone has advanced). She fails to see, however, that the passive and active qualities are not distributed symmetrically between Scottie and Judy; rather, the distinction is destabilized by Scottie's double identity as active quester and passive victim of a plot, by Judy's deliberate complicity in two makeovers – the second an attempt to undo the first – and by the awkward fact that if the male symbolic in *Vertigo* is to be defined in terms of "power," it should rather be identified with the Elster who pulls the strings than the Scottie whose life is devastated. One person's death may guarantee another's happiness in Elster's case, but for Scottie the equation does not work: Judy's death is tantamount to his own. The complex self-knowledge the film unfolds renders it Hitchcock's greatest work, and one of the greatest works of all cinema. To pretend otherwise, as Mulvey does, is to establish oneself as a bad cop with bent methods. Her analysis does not help found an alternative to mainstream cinema but in fact creates an obstacle to the achievement of that goal, for it subordinates to a stereotypical notion of Hollywood one of the few films to have transcended Hollywood from within.

## Anatomies of murder

### Strangers on a Train *and the demonic fairground*

A recurrent motif in Hitchcock's films is the relationship between a blackout and a substitution. One finds it in *The Lady Vanishes* (she does so during the heroine's faint, when she is replaced by a similarly dressed impersonator of Mrs. Fray), in *Vertigo* (the bodies are switched in the tower as Scottie's vertigo disables him), and in *Strangers on a Train* (Bruno loses consciousness as the sight of Ann Morton's sister Barbara recalls Miriam, whom he has strangled as part of his "bargain" with Guy Haines).* This third instance is the most complex in the series and suggests the occult meaning of the motif: It links orgasm, loss of consciousness, and murder – and shows Hitchcock to stand surprisingly close to Oshima, fascinated by strangulation as a means both of murder and sexual stimulation. Interpreted allegorically, the moment suggests a connection between Hitchcock's position of directorial power and his murderous sexual fantasies: Underlying them may well be a wish to replace his wife with another woman, the star he is able to cast in her place and victimize at leisure to obtain revenge upon the world that has withheld the dream woman from him.

Bruno's mock strangulation of a guest at the Mortons' party changes from "fun" to earnest as he catches sight of Barbara's glasses, which remind him of Miriam. His use of the word "fun" indicates a closeness to Hitchcock himself, who notoriously termed *Psycho* "a fun picture"; and, of course, Hitchcock himself liked to play at strangulation. (Does the common abbreviation of his name to "Hitch" indicate an identification with rope, which can be hitched?) The glasses constitute a problem–object in the film. Guy is handed them by Bruno, but is not

---

* Scottie's blackouts in *Vertigo* can also be read as repetitions of the faint following castration – his inability to climb the phallic tower the sign of his emasculation.

shown disposing of them; one's lack of knowledge of their location generates unease. In fact one never finds out. The glasses are the unconscious of the film, its "blind spot" – the look of the camera itself, with its desire to remain unseen. They are explicitly identified with the camera during the murder, which we see reflected in them "expressionistically." (The event is "distorted," as are all events when reflected in art, but the *excess* of art here itself reflects a bad conscience in the voyeuristic onlooker.) As one lens is broken, the glasses literally become a camera, a *monocular* optical instrument: The voyeur, who for Freud is always dependent upon the exhibitionist, flirts exhibitionistically with the self-exposure of filmic self-reference. In the blind kingdom of the darkened auditorium, Hitchcock himself has the position of power of the one-eyed man who can see.*

*Strangers on a Train* is concerned throughout to reduce the double to the singular. It is about how to dispose of the character who is defined as unnecessary – that is, a double, a superfluous duplication of the already existent. Thus one has to dispense with Miriam, who is unnecessary because she has already been displaced in Guy's affections by Anne Morton, and with Bruno, the embarrassing Mephistophelian double. The film deals with divorce, in various senses, and particularly that of disavowal, the fictional mechanism of projection that allows one to separate oneself from one's deed just as Guy dissociates himself from Bruno. (And perhaps in doing so from his own name: "Guy" is anonymous.) Hence the work begins with a reference to Guy's prospective game of doubles, though the climactic game it shows is one of singles. It may be that Hitchcock plants the initial reference to a game of doubles on the sound track – itself so often the disavowed portion of a film, helping it to achieve its ends but then suffering consignment to oblivion – in order to allow us to deduce that Bruno is Guy's double: a subliminal suggestion that grants the work a "depth" on the level of the sound track that never disturbs the imagistic surface – a tactic in Hitchcock's simultaneous bid for the dual position of entertainment mogul and artist.†

The word "doubles" embedded in the term "doubles match" is closely followed by Bruno's suggestion of a "crisscross" murder. The words fuse to yield the sense of "double cross": Miriam's double-crossing of Guy, by refusing to grant him a divorce, which leads to *his* double-crossing (in a sense – the sense of the film's fundamental

---

* It is interesting to note, given Guy's status as a tennis player, that the electric eye now employed in championship tennis is known colloquially as "Cyclops."
† This is art misconceived as artfulness, of course: Thus one has the hypocrisy of *Rope*, for instance, which seeks the shocking frisson of "murder as a fine art" and yet wishes to be considered virtuous. Similarly, the James Stewart character dissociates himself from his two apt pupils, even though his Nietzschean talk of the rights of "superior" beings has provided a rationale for their deed.

equivocation) of Bruno by refusing to carry out "his part of the bargain" and despatch Bruno's father.

*Strangers on a Train* – like much of Hitchcock's work – is clearly influenced by the stylistics of expressionism: The murder reflected in the glasses, the unnatural angles, the demonic fairground – all are of expressionist provenance. And since the leitmotif of expressionism was the suffering involved in the individual's splitting into an ego and the projections out of that ego,* its stylistic parti pris is of patent relevance to the theme of the double. The expressionist touches – a mainstream American film could never be thoroughgoing in its expressionism – lend plausibility to the undertone of suggestion, which the viewer is programmed to congratulate himself on perceiving, that Bruno is Guy's "double." The order of the initials in their names has the same effect: one set is BA, two letters in the wrong order, indicative of Bruno's derangement – and of his getting ahead of himself, his precipitous performance of execution before he can be sure Guy will carry out his part of the supposed bargain – and GH, letters in the *right* order, indicating the appropriateness of our identification with Guy. When the balance achieved through doubling collapses, so does the film: Like the merry-go-round, it has been flung off its axis. It concludes when the two lines with which it began converge as one line (Guy's) absorbs the other: Parallel lines *do* meet in this story of doubles, like railway lines meeting in the distance. As they do so, the two-wheeled train of narrative falls off the track.

*We still kill the old way:* A Short Film about Killing

I have stated above that a mainstream American film could never be thoroughgoing in its expressionism; yet thoroughgoing expressionism has been extremely rare in European narrative cinema too, even that of the period following the Nouvelle Vague's radicalization of traditional storytelling norms. This may be due in part to the same period's deification of the director, who becomes consequently less willing to cede authority to his cameraman (or, as in the case of the progenitor of all expressionist cinema, *The Cabinet of Dr. Caligari,* to his set-designers): Most of the great expressionist-influenced films owe almost as much to their cinematographers as their directors. *Citizen Kane* is unthinkable without Toland, *The Conformist* unimaginable without Storaro. And, as Krzysztof Kieślowski readily admits,[21] the same is true of *A Short Film about Killing,* whose green lenses were suggested by cameraman Sławomir Idziak. If *Strangers on a Train* bestows a sexual

---

* In Munch's *The Scream,* the whole landscape is an extension of the individual, rocking with the sound waves of the scream he may have emitted or simply heard, while expression's departure from him leaves him as it were dead, skull-like.

aura on strangulation, Kieślowski's film – perhaps in part because it shows one man strangling another, not a male killing a female, though also, of course, because Kieślowski is less inclined than Hitchcock to succumb to the seductions of inhumanity – is without this ambiguous sexuality. The atmosphere is rather one of unrelieved horror.

A Short Film about Killing is a work of visionary irony. The ironies set in with the very first images, as the titles roll: a dead rat in a puddle and a hanged cat dangling against the background of oppressively serried apartment blocks. Varsovians will instantly recognize the irony that juxtaposes the dead animals, emblems of an urban inferno, with blocks that in fact contain the apartments of many of Poland's best-known TV and film stars, who have been lured there by the complex's proximity to the old town and town center. The title itself secretes a deadly irony: The short film about killing (it is only ninety minutes long) shows how lengthy and arduous is the process of doing a man to death – approximately eight minutes of screen time. The time it takes to complete the first stage will be marked excruciatingly by the slow passage of a bicycle along the yellow-lit horizon.

Kieślowski's ironies, however, are not signs of sovereign authorial superiority, but the dissonances of tragedy, and they strike in particular at a young lawyer whose celebration of graduation to the bar is pierced by a sudden premonition that his future will not be as straightforward as he hopes. The murderer he will be called on to defend is already drinking in the same café. It is in the scenes in which the young murderer wanders around Warsaw, the deed still undone, his own future still open, that the film is most remarkable. The boy walks through a world turned to slime by the green filters (it resembles the drained aquarium street of Conrad's Secret Agent), with color appearing only at the center of each image. This partial desaturation of the image echoes the effect of the tinted band across the top of the window in the taxi whose owner the boy will kill. With its realistic equivalent – and perhaps even origin – Kieślowski's device is never ornamental; instead it suggests, quasi-expressionistically, the closing down of the world of the murderer, whose name – Jacek – we will not learn until after the killing. (As if the deed gives him a name by attaching him to a fate.) At the center of these muddied images virtually only one color is present: red. It is worn by a series of girls, and here there is a double irony: Girls are unattainable for Jacek, one of whose possible motives for the killing was to acquire a car to take a girl to the mountains; the film's parade of girls in red leads naturally to the blossoming of another red, the blood that stains the taxi driver's head. (Jacek covers the bloodied head with a brown checked blanket that, as it were, completes the desaturation of the world's colors by removing even red from it.) The only girl with whom Jacek is associated in the scenes preceding the murder is a crumpled photograph of a young girl in a communion dress; the film's end reveals her to be his dead younger sister. She wears white, not the red that signifies life, and even before the end we suspect that she is dead: Jacek asks the shop assistant he wants to enlarge it whether it's true that one can tell from a photograph if someone is no longer alive.

Ironies proliferate across the film. The taxi driver wants Beata to go with him, and it is Jacek who invites her for a drive in the dead man's car; the taxi driver savors the outlaw qualities of a stray dog, unaware that a human outlaw will kill him; (Jacek's frantic efforts during the murder to halt the nightmarishly prolonged blast of the car's horn are ironized when only a horse in a field looks round and when, the moment the horn has fallen silent, a passing train picks up its note (implying that Jacek's activity has been futile – since the sound would have been drowned anyway – and that the murder will repeat itself like a nightmare of eternal recurrence in the mind of the man who committed it); the taxi driver is congratulated on his good luck by a man selling lottery tickets; Jacek meanwhile refuses to let a Gypsy read his fortune as he enters the café in which Piotr Balicki, the young lawyer, is having *his* palm read by his girlfriend. This world of diabolic coincidence[22] is clearly one of the circles of hell.

Jacek's murder of the taxi driver may seem to be motiveless, its apparent inevitability simply the result of Kieślowski's expressionist style and the remorseless accumulation of such details as the severed head that is the taxi driver's good-luck charm, which presages his strangulation, and the dead cat. With his fluffy punk hair and jean jacket Jacek stalks Warsaw's streets like an edgy existential angel of doom. Yet it is not just the stylistic tour de force that persuades us to accept the experience of the appallingly protracted murder. Kieślowski in fact offers several possible explanations: the need to obtain a car (the actual motive in the real case on which the film draws); the search, by means of a murder for which one knows one will be hanged, for a mode of suicide that will not preclude one's burial in consecrated ground alongside one's beloved sister (the suicide motif being first suggested by the boy's visit to a cinema in which *Wetherby* is playing); the country boy's need to assert himself in the city; and – that very expressionist theme – youth's revenge upon age (the sense of the material deprivation of the young that has been a constant in Polish cinema since Skolimowski). If Kieślowski privileges none of these explanations, it is partly because he wishes to allow also for the essential mysteriousness of human action. Equally important, however, is his somber insistence on its typicality in a contemporary Poland in the process of becoming Hell. The consequences of Poland's economic decline are seen to include a slide toward gratuitous violence in human relations. Whether it be the taxi driver deliberately leaving his would-be clients standing or Jacek telling people at the taxi stand that his destination is the opposite of theirs, hostility is pervasive. Jacek's deed simply reveals its implicit murderousness.

The only alternatives to this are children and the idealistic young lawyer, who is modeled in part on Kieślowski's script consultant on legal matters, Krzysztof Piesiewicz. When Jacek flicks coffee dregs at the café window through which two young girls are watching him, they smile and he smiles back: Their reaction transforms his violence into play; and in retrospect it will seem almost as if he has been flinging mud at the image of his sister, and then smiling at her untouchability, the invulnerability of the dead. Piotr's exuberance as he weaves his way in and out of traffic on his scooter is virtually the sole other relief in the stalking darkness of the film. His defense of Jacek is useless, and its hopelessness is daringly embodied in the cut wherewith Kieślowski excises everything between the moment of Beata's recognition of the taxi driver's car and the judge's statement that the trial is closed. Piotr's speech against the death penalty may be among the best the judge has ever heard, but we are not shown it. This is partly because Piotr's role as secular priest, hearing Jacek's last words in prison, is more important to Kieślowski. But it is also because the director has his own argument against capital punishment, framed purely filmically. Individual and state-sanctioned murder are placed on a single plane by their parallel gruesomeness: As militiamen bundle Jacek into the death chamber, knocking down the curtain, and the man tightening the noose shrieks instructions to his assistant, the frantic hysteria echoes Jacek's realization of the difficulty of killing a man. It is as if the law that has violence at its heart is itself partly responsible for the murder Jacek has committed. This is the final – the most deadly – irony of Kieślowski's film.

With its polemic against the death penalty and its probing of the context of the *acte gratuit, A Short Film about Killing* is clearly reminiscent of a novel by Camus, an author the director holds dear: *L'Étranger*. The resemblance extends both to the two-part structure and the relative merits of the parts. In each work the first part is the more stylistically radical and successful. Kieślowski's film does not descend into the tendentiousness of much of the latter part of *L'Étranger*, though it does have one very shaky moment when Jacek tells Piotr of Marysia's death. Its manner – run over by a tractor driven by a drunken peasant – is absurd in the preexistentialist sense, resembling a piece of gallows humor about the life of the Polish peasantry, while the angelic music that accompanies it suggests a nobility in Jacek that clearly contradicts Kieślowski's stated intention of rendering both murderer and victim equally unsympathetic. The dissonance stands out because the rest of the film has raised one's expectations so high.

# CHAPTER V

# Elective affinities and family resemblances: For Margarethe von Trotta

## Introduction

In this final chapter, the separate preoccupations of this book converge, filings congregating around a single work: Margarethe von Trotta's *Marianne and Juliane (Die bleierne Zeit)*. Here the horror pervasive in expressionism is sparked by a return of the historical repressed, the resurgence of the German past, as the fearsome images of concentration camps or Grünewald's painting of the crucifixion spawn further images of tortured bodies, the fruit of the terrorist's futile attempt to end terror through further terror. Von Trotta's film, a reworking of the story of Gudrun and Christiane Ensslin, invites comparison with two other films in particular: Bergman's *Persona,* whose terrifying images (a burning monk, the Warsaw Ghetto photograph) harrow the mind like Grünewald's painting, and which resembles Von Trotta's work in its concern with doubling, splitting, and dead and victimized children; and Straub's *Not Reconciled (Nicht versöhnt)*, a film version of Böll's *Billiards at Half-Past Nine,* which also considers terrorism as a cry in the echo chamber of the Nazi past, and reflects on how that past is to find a future – that is, children. Where Bergman's Elisabet Vogler is silenced by the world's violence, Von Trotta's Juliane strives to articulate horror. If horror can only enter speech through a paradoxical dialectic – as when Elisabet says the word "nothing" – Juliane's story proposes the possibility of a paradox that is more than deadlock or double-bind: The silence that follows the film, and the child's demand that she begin her story, may indicate its unspeakable quality, or may be simply the pause during a Proustian rewinding of the reels, the ending taking us back to the beginning, allowing us to draw breath before starting again. (Here the story's repetition would tame trauma – the shocks flesh and film are heir to – for we now know *beforehand* what will be said.)

Earlier in this book, writing of *Phèdre,* I noted Racine's use of "silence" as a rhyme for "violence." If that which is passed over in silence, buried in the labyrinth's depths, is the monster, such an epithet could well be applied to Marianne: the "monstrous" mother who abandons her child. To use this word of the terrorist, however, is to construct terrorism as an incomprehensible Other, and to fail to grasp that it may in fact also be read as the logical fruit of a democracy simultaneously loud in praise of its own ability to involve citizens in social decisions, and reductive of participation to a token, quadrennial vote. Terrorist violence is in a sense born of the fear that sanctioned speech is really silence, and only action truly speaks. *Marianne and Juliane* seeks to dissolve the monstrous Other into a double: Juliane's identification with Marianne gives a voice to silence, to the dead, and provides a "mise-en-abîme" image of Von Trotta's own response to the media-born specter of "the terrorist." And if the two sisters can be described (in Adorno's terms) as the two halves that do not add up to a whole – the one an activist, hag-ridden by appalling images; the other a writer, capable of rationalization – they meet in Von Trotta herself (united on a plane ontologically discontinuous with that of the story, and thus utopian from the perspective of those entrapped within it, the prisoners of German history), an image-maker who also writes (the script to *Marianne and Juliane* [*The German Sisters*] is her own). *Marianne and Juliane* eschews the terrorizing violence of Elisabet Vogler. Refusing to identify with the aggressor, it both deals with and enacts an effort to break the silence – to speak the word that will end German history's curse.

### Bergman, Rymkiewicz, and Von Trotta: Women and children as doubles

Throughout Bergman's work the lot of the artist is humiliation. In the following essay I would like to examine two of the interdependent forms this humiliation takes: The male artist's status may be reduced either through feminization, or through his diminution to childhood. The interdependence of these alternatives becomes apparent in *The Silence* (*Tystnaden*) and *Persona*. *Persona* experiences feminization as claustrophobia, pure pain; the famous burning out of the film provides a hole through which the director as it were crawls out to become the figure of the male child observing events from which he is separated as absolutely as the dead from the living. If there is a point beyond the film's dialectic of negativity – a negativity it identifies with the feminine – it is the child. The child, however, is only an illusory image of a point beyond suffering, for it is doubled by – and thus sucked back into – the narrative: as Elisabet's child, whose photograph is torn up, and as the dead child in the Warsaw Ghetto photograph Elisabet confronts. After considering the antinomies in Bergman's work that culminate in *Persona*, and the related use of the same Warsaw Ghetto photograph (as double) in Jarosław Rymkiewicz's *Umschlagplatz*, I will proceed to a film that clearly summons up the specter of *Persona*, while seeking simultaneously to transcend its terms of reference: Margarethe Von Trotta's *Marianne and Juliane* (*Die bleierne Zeit*). In von Trotta's film the child is woven into the narrative, not placed ambiguously as a possible point beyond its aporias.* On my way to a consideration of the relationship between Bergman and Von Trotta I will describe how the antinomies embodied in Elisabet and Alma derive from more general oppositions between theater and film, speech and silence, reality and dream, and masculine and feminine in Bergman's earlier works.

## Toward *Persona*

Ingmar Bergman's films are curiously fractured, veering back and forth between sequences of great intensity – these are often symbolic or dream sequences, sometimes shot overexposed, as in *Sawdust and Tinsel* [*Gycklarnas afton*], *Wild Strawberries* [*Sumtronstället*], or *Hour of the Wolf* [*Vargtimmen*] – and rather prosaic ones. *Sawdust and Tinsel*, for instance, begins with a nightmarish sequence on a beach where a clown and his naked wife are degraded before a group of soldiers, to the accompaniment of dissonant music and the derisive interjection of phallic images of cannons. The whole sequence – an astonishing beginning – visualizes a narrative related by the driver of one of the circus carts to his companion on the driver's seat; and when the film shifts into the far less memorable gear of scenes of the circus caravan drawing to a halt, its members emerging and stumbling through the mud, the drop in tension seems only appropriate, for one is still recovering from the fearsome overture. (This has given compressed advance notice of the theme of the sexual and artistic degradation of the troupe that will run through the film, and much of the remainder of Bergman's work.) *Wild Strawberries* evinces the same structure: The elderly professor's dream of his own death is shorter and less impressive than the opening of *Sawdust and Tinsel*, but is still the finest section of the film – the brief sequence in which a hearse's wheels are caught on a lamppost and are yanked repeatedly by the horses, until the wheel is wrenched off and rolls away being particularly striking. The rest of the film will be a somewhat labored and unconvincing depiction of the abrasive professor's conversion into

---

* Though there is a utopian element to the child's presence in the film: Through him Juliane acquires a child without needing to have one. The question of how to have children without the usual transactions with males is raised by much feminist work, one of the best examples being *Celine and Julie Go Boating* (*Céline et Julie vont en bateau*).

amiable old codger. One reacts to this transformation rather as his housekeeper does: She wonders if there's anything wrong with him, and says that their relationship was quite fine as it was on its old footing. (She thus explodes the banality of the film's domestication of the sacred monster.)

Both these films can be said to insert compressed, intense, and imagistically very impressive *cinematic* scenes into a fundamentally theatrical context.* Thus the oscillation of Bergman's career – between stage direction and filmmaking – is built into the films themselves. It is played out between sequences of dislocated experience that are usually silent and "excessive" in relation to the narrative, and theatrical overall structures that strive to recuperate these moments of shock, to name them in language. The relationship between these two components resembles that between the artist and the psychoanalyst: the latter tries to transform the autonomous artwork into a dream, and hence a symptom, part of "the *talking* cure." If *Persona* seems to be his finest film, it is because it thematizes this split and so generates a position *between* the cinematic and the theatrical. Its dialectic, however, is a negative one: Unable to arrive at a point of synthesis, it is compelled finally to repeat itself and then tail off. Yet the capacity for self-knowledge the film demonstrates is unique in Bergman, who here transcends his habitual self-obsession, achieving self-awareness.†

In *Persona* the actress Elisabet Vogler falls silent in the middle of a performance. Her overpowering presence embodies the force of the silence of God – that which so disturbs Pastor Thomas (and Bergman himself) in *Winter Light* (*Nattvardsgästerna*). In a sense her silence also echoes that of her namesake, the title character of *The Magician* (*Ansiktet*). In both cases the artist's silence represents the final form of his/her radical challenge to society. In *Persona* this silence acquires additional significance as a female provocation of the male, defying him – the child at the start of the film? – to interpret it. Eros charges *Persona* with infinitely greater power than *The Magician,* which affects one as a convoluted piece of special pleading, largely because the depth of Vogler's humiliation by the municipal authorities prompts one to doubt the authenticity of his magic: It is simply a matter of legerdemain. Bergman identifies too profoundly with him to ascribe to him the uncanny power of the genuinely Other, which he reserves for

---

* I am well aware of the dubiousness of the attempt to assign an inviolable specificity to each of these media. In Bergman's case, however, I feel that the distinction is potentially fruitful, for he has worked in both forms – one assumes because he senses possibilities in the one medium not available in the other.

† I will return later to the question of whether nevertheless this self-awareness is also mystified, since the film's main protagonists are women, and their relationship with the watching child is unclear.

women. And so, in *Persona,* he is also his own Other: identified with a woman from whom he is split off, as is Alma, the nurse in that film.

Throughout Bergman's work a split runs between a series of men, identified with the super ego, and women assimilated to the id. It can be seen in films as different as *Summer with Monika (Sommaren med Monika)* and *Winter Light.* In the earlier work the beleaguered shop assistant Harry is of a higher class than Monika and – after they have returned from their summer interlude – resists immediate gratification, in the best bourgeois way, in order to better himself. Monika, meanwhile, ignores the baby she has borne (her own orality is shown by her constant chewing), complains of the lack of the ready cash invested in Harry's studies, spends the rent money on a new dress, and finally leaves him with the child. Monika is the child of summer, and Harry's idyll with her is almost unbearably poignant. The rapid dissolves of the summer sequences embody the fleetingness of the idyll; their near-languagelessness shows that the young couple has reached a level of gratification that antedates speech. In a surprising and interesting convergence with the early Fellini, Bergman presents Monika as a junk-culture addict: She weeps profusely at *The Song of Love,* and consoles herself over the inevitable return to the city by noting that at least she will now have the opportunity to see films again. Monika represents an idyll that resists narrative, the stories of progress whereby the world's inhabitants define their own identities. The film, however, shows the escape from narrative and law to be all too brief: Reality returns – the couple sailing to the city, drums on the sound track suggesting future obstacles – with the inevitability with which winter follows summer. The mechanical nature of the seasons' succession provides Bergman's alibi for abandoning the idyll.

By the time he makes *Winter Light,* Bergman has rejected the popular culture Monika loves and sees the theater as the site of the self-humiliating rite of the artist's self-purgation; hence a self-serving masochism will vitiate this film. Yet if the contrast between *Summer with Monika* and *Winter Light* is almost programmatically absolute, one element is constant: the identification of the female with the libido. Märta, the provincial schoolteacher in love with Pastor Thomas, remarks in a letter to him that she grew up amid warmth and tenderness in an un-Christian family, and castigates his religiosity as primitive neurosis. The Bergman woman denies God because He is her rival. (In *Cries and Whispers* [*Vishningar och rop*], Woman will become an alternative Trinity.) As she seduces man to adore her in God's place, she undermines his belief; behind the mask of her face, she may either be Other or Adversary. She torments the Protestant pastor, who is permitted to marry but not to bow down before the image of Woman, as a Catholic priest might worship the Virgin: One can only idolize that which one cannot touch, as it were, possessing the flesh only at the price of nonpossession of the image. Thus if Bergman's relationship with the pastor is so convoluted – he both does and does not identify with him – it is because of the attraction image exerts upon filmmaker. Like the pastor, the film is forbidden to bring the image of the loved woman into the present: That image is lodged irrevocably in the past: The wife has been dead for five years. There are no flashbacks. "When my wife died, I died," Thomas states. Her death meant the coming of winter, the film's restriction to an eternal present that knows neither nostalgia nor hope. That is why *Winter Light* is so much less satisfying than *Summer with Monika,* or that other evocation of a lost idyll, *Summer Interlude (Sommarlek).* Its matter-of-factness is austere self-mortification, with an eye on the transcendent Viewer rather than the earthly one.

*Persona* resembles *Winter Light* inasmuch as it too is a film about self-defilement aspiring to a purity it knows to be unattainable, but it has an intensity lacking in the earlier, more monotonous film; it gains it by bringing the dilemmas of winter into summer, and by a radical self-splitting that reformulates the problem by distributing elements of the male minister between the woman who identifies with the silence of God and her nurse. Perhaps the best candidate for precursor of *Persona* among Bergman's earlier films, however, is *The Silence.* The initial camera movement from the boy to the two sisters in the train rehearses *Persona*'s opening; and here too one has the image of woman bifurcated, between the ailing intellectual Ester and the more carnal younger sister Anna. (The duality also anticipates *Cries and Whispers,* though in that film the process of splitting has been repeated yet again, yielding four women rather than two.) Much of *The Silence* is about looking at a world as alien and forbidding as that of Elisabet Vogler's apparent madness. One may strive to enter it by identification, as Anna identifies in fantasy with the lovers she sees in the back seats at the Variété, subsequently acting out her fantasy with the man from the bar; she had once identified in like manner with Ester, before realizing her sister's dislike for her. (If *Persona* is superior to *The Silence,* it is partly because it turns the screw on the question of identification by showing how the desire *to be liked* by another encompasses one *to look like* that other.) The film is, however, too cryptic at the beginning and too explicitly "existential" at the end, swinging from imagistic secrecy to exhibitionistic verbalization. The turning point is the moment at which Anna remarks to her one-night stand, "How nice that we don't understand each other": Nonunderstanding is clearly a relief from the deadly familial intimacy, the hostile comprehension, of Ester. But Bergman needlessly spells things out by having her add, "I wish Ester were dead." Ester's "There's no need to discuss loneliness; it's a waste of time" may indicate Bergman's awareness of the danger of dissipating tension through a welter of words, but the recognition of temptation does not necessarily entail the ability to resist it. Rather as in *Cries and Whispers*, the luxuriant pacing renders the pain stately, anaesthetized. If the theme of looking – and belittling through the look, whence the presence of the dwarfs – links *The Silence* to *Persona*, the latter film treats it far more incisively – without the decorative symbolic paraphernalia of dwarfs, a foreign country, and a nonexistent language. The self-referentiality of *Persona* permits of a far more serious interrogation of the relationship between the protagonists' pain and the atrocities of an outside world, which appear as both real (the monk's immolation, the child in the Warsaw Ghetto) and mediated (via photographs or television). *Persona* replaces the metaphorical window with the TV set. "He talks a funny language because he's afraid," Johan says of his Punch when addressing Ester; the same may be said of Bergman here too, as he shows us Punch and Judy and a tank in the street as Anna makes love. (The montage is like a half-hearted, dislocated parody of Eisenstein.) For all the famed explicitness of some of its scenes, *The Silence* mystifies the love–hate relations *Persona* will examine more directly.

*Dissolving the space of art:* Persona

*Persona* is about the self-hatred of an art whose own very presence stains the purity of the silence to which it aspires. All it feels it can do is chatter: It may seek to go beyond relationships, beyond the world, but if it did, it would cross the boundary of art – or mark the end of the representational, interpersonal cinema Bergman himself practices. In occasional spurts of disconnected images, it enters this other space, only to retreat of necessity to its own sphere. The film is shot through with a profoundly Manichean sense that matter, the source of words and images, is evil, and exudes the feeling of humiliation experienced when one surrenders one's identity to a hostile other – when, in effect, one consents to one's own rape. The relationship between the two women duplicates that between the silently intense, and the theatrical, scenes in Bergman's earlier films. Virtually every sequence is poised on a knife-edge between fantasy and realism, symbol and language.

Writing of Bergman's practice of art as ritual, Paisley Livingston very acutely notes a tendency in the films' presentations of the artist:

It is one thing when a clown stands forth and invites an audience to laugh at his role; it is another thing when the audience is a mob forcibly making a spectacle of someone. In one case the mockery and violence are only represented, but in the other the violence is painfully real and unrestrained. In Bergman's episodes the difference becomes blurred; performances where

violence is only mimicked become bloody spectacles and often regress to violence. Bergman's performers balance precariously at the edge of this difference.[1]

This threatened dissolution of the space of art also embraces its
history – Elisabet Vogler falls silent during a performance of *Electra* –
as art reverts to the level of the ritual out of which it once emerged,
and then defies even ritual's formalization of violence: The sublimated
violence of artistic spectacle passes through the symbolic violence of
ritual, finally arriving at the real violence it cannot contain. Similarly,
Elisabet's mind cannot contain the shock of her reaction to the Warsaw Ghetto photograph; it swells to occupy the whole screen. This
confusion of the different historical spaces of art is, I think, the cause
of the messiness and unsatisfactoriness of much of Bergman's work,
which seeks to melt art into ritual with the ugly motive of enhancing
the artist's power over the audience. (This becomes very explicit in
*The Ritual [Riten]*.) In *Persona*, however, Bergman follows the process
to its necessary conclusion, passing through ritual to address the
question of how to represent chaos – the pouring forth of abrupt, disconnected images. In doing so he is responding to cinema's capacity
to dissolve distinctions between "art" and "life" and overwhelm audiences in a manner that triggers a resurgence of experiences normally
associated with myth and relegated to an archaic past. The messiness
of *Persona*, unlike that of the other films, is not self-aggrandizing but
is the defining quality – the "specificity," to revert for a moment to a
cardinal preoccupation of early film theory – of cinema in general. In
*Persona* art's dissolution into the "raw material" out of which it arose
initially robs the artist of his or her role and space, causing the silence of Elisabet Vogler, and brings about the humiliation he or she
feels when no longer able to "sublimate" emotions in art: the emotions
have become too immediately powerful – even though his death is mediated by a television screen, the monk is burning *now*, in the present
of the TV world, not the preterit of art – or too confusing, for that. This
collapse or regression in the form of art ends in the formlessness that is
culturally coded as representing "the feminine." If the shame that is a
recurrent motif in Bergman – so much so that it provides the title of one
of his finest films – is primarily a social emotion (as opposed to guilt,
with its sense of interiority – a distinction allowing one to clarify the difference between Bergman and Dreyer), this may help explain why the
protagonist of *Persona* is an actress: It is woman who is generally
defined through her continual visibility to others.* Thus *Persona* also

* Apart from its meaning of mask, "persona" thereby becomes "person" with a feminine
ending – Bergman himself perhaps, masked by the appearance of the feminine. If the
eyes in a mask are uncanny, it is because they hint at the presence of life behind apparent death: One has a double body that is inherently uncanny, both living and dead.

has a protofeminist subtext – and is perhaps unique in this respect among Bergman's works – in which Elisabet is in revolt against the perpetual display that defines her as a woman in the terms of modern Western society. (Von Trotta's interest in this film thus becomes more comprehensible.) Bergman may tend to view the artist as a male who has been "feminized" in the sense of being placed on display, humiliated, and rendered helpless either by the demons that beset or the society that victimizes him, but he himself perpetuates the pattern of patriarchal dominance through the use to which he puts his actresses. He may, of course, be seen as simply engaged in transmission of what Canetti has termed "the sting" of dominance. If *Persona* is superior to the rest of his work, it is surely because its failure to resolve itself corresponds nevertheless to a hope for equality between its protagonists; because, in utopian fashion, it finally refuses anyone the dominant position.

The images of *Persona* are ascetic – figures against white walls – and reflect the insistence of the impossible search for purity – a search that, as we will see, involves the renunciation of children. The sadomasochistic, Strindbergian struggle between Elisabet and Alma – with its actual reminiscences of Strindberg's *The Stronger* – is full of the retrospective self-disgust of the person who has confessed (a very Protestant self-disgust) – as Alma has confessed her love on the beach to Elisabet, and as Elisabet (like Bergman?) has exposed her anguish to a public, allowing life to overwhelm her art – and has thereby placed him/herself in the power of the attendant Other. If the deadlock between Elisabet and Alma is irresoluble, the failure is Adornian, quite deliberate: a negative dialectic. In *Persona,* Bergman's art reaches its peak in the articulation of its own self-division. The film is not, like so many of Bergman's other works, an academic replay of Strindberg, for it incorporates the logic of the surrealists' dream plays. Unlike surrealism, however, *Persona* is aware that the dream extracted from its natural habitat is born dead. (The waking consciousness's distinction between dream and reality facilitates the artwork's dismissal as only a dream, or the dreamwork's pallid imitation.) The surrealists – colonists of the unconscious – sought in the unpredictability of dreams a remedy to the rationalization of the world; they failed to perceive the suicidal irrationality that pervades reason itself, the lining of myth secreted within enlightenment and known as rationalization. Bergman, however, is well aware of this: The nurse represents a science that seeks to carry a torch into the darkness of madness, only to discover madness within itself. Unable to heal either her patient or herself, Alma abandons the relationship – and perhaps flees all relationship. Like Alma, Bergman himself was clearly frightened by what he had discovered. For him – as has often been the case for other directors – the self-reflexive work marked a crisis and watershed in his career. The whole of the rest of that career can be read as a flight from, and repression of, *Persona*, whose exemplary clarity he would never again recover – toward the self-delusive self-absolution of *Fanny and Alexander*.

## The image of the dead child

*Persona* is a process of action and reaction in which personalities fuse and harrow one another. The moment of fusion is also one of fission, an explosion in the psyches of the two women. This moment occurs as Alma recounts how Elisabet came to want a child and then to wish it dead. As she says this, the film transforms her into Elisabet's mouthpiece (Aaron to her Moses), the soul sister (Alma) who allows the actress to speak while denying that she is doing so. There is clearly a sense in which Elisabet's repressed words have possessed Alma, who had laid herself open to such possession by envying Elisabet and wishing to be like her. Suddenly, however, as the desired identification threatens to expunge the last traces of Alma's own personality, those vestiges regroup to expel the invader. As she talks of Elisabet's wish that her child die, she is perhaps reminded – as the viewer cannot help but be – that in this crucial respect she is *unlike* the actress: Whereas Elisabet, according to Alma, wished for a dead child but gave birth to a living one, Alma wanted to keep her own child but was persuaded to abort it. She is perhaps disavowing her own complicity in this action by projecting it onto Elisabet. In any case, she now feels that the decision she made jointly with her lover violated her nature; with him, as with Elisabet, she first succumbs and then rebels, belatedly and desperately. As Alma pronounces these words, one notices that the left-hand side of her face is shadowed; as the left side of Elisabet's face emerges there, she becomes Alma's shadow self. (For the child watching the dream screen, the dark side of the moon becomes visible.) At this point Alma cries out, "No, I'm not like you, I don't feel as you do," seeking to reverse the process of identification that had led her to call herself cold in one scene and apply the same adjective to Elisabet in another, and had allowed Elisabet to use her hand to caress the face of her own husband. She will no longer be the servant who does Elisabet's living for her. She says, "I am Sister Alma," and to emphasize this appears in uniform in the next scene. Because the separation is willed, the pattern is then repeated as her speech devolves into an incoherence that may be seen as mirroring Elisabet's madness; but as she says "us-we-no-I," the "no" again revokes the fusion implied in "we." When Alma then clenches her fist so hard that the blood flows, it is a reprise of the nail being driven into the hand in the first scene of the film: Christ's Passion is displaced into the Passion of

Alma. Yet again the pattern is one of the establishment and then rejection of an identification: Alma allows Elisabet to suck the blood from her hand (the link between doubling and vampirism becoming explicit) but then desperately slaps her. This series of fusions and divisions is terminated when Alma – in fantasy perhaps – derives a solution to Elisabet's dilemma. She goes up to her, comforts her, and says, "Say after me: nothing." Thus speech and silence are reconciled. Elisabet is brought to speak but she says, "Nothing."* The "cure" is not the talking cure but is achieved through a single word, a sophism that allows Alma to maintain the illusion of communication while dropping Elisabet back in her madness. The "reconciliation" is thus no reconciliation at all, but a dissonance. We then see Alma cleaning up and preparing to go; when she stands in front of a mirror and strokes her hair, the momentary imposition of an earlier image of Elisabet doing the same functions as a reprise, a memory of a distant experience, not a resurgence of the fusion pattern. The liberation is one into sterility. Alma has replicated Elisabet's earlier gesture of renunciation of relationships. Hence for the child at the end the mother is only an image, not a reality. She is the mother he does not have, either because he was never born (Alma's child) or because his photograph has been ripped in two by the mother who wished him born dead (Elisabet's child). Elisabet can in fact identify only with the dead child, the Jewish child in the photograph from the Warsaw Ghetto. It does not make the demands a living child would – though its existence as the embodiment of demand is reflected in the blow-up of its image to fill the whole screen. This Jewish child is simply an image one can play with – the impulse to play with the image a transformation of the maternal play with the infant? – and that is what Elisabet and the film do, as the camera jumps around within the photograph, shifting focus between the German soldiers, the boy himself, and the bystanders, almost as if a film were about to emerge from it. But of course no film can emerge from it: There is only the single image, and whatever film there might have been is born dead, ripped from the womb of its context, trapped in the *nature morte* of the photograph.

*Persona* is often described as a work of fiction so illusive as to render futile any effort to construct a referential narrative out of the material Bergman places before us. Since the film's fascination stems from its provocative suspension between fantasy and realism, self-referentiality and representation, to consign it to the former category alone is, however, grossly to distort it. The film's formal procedures do not issue in formalism, but feed into its dominant theme, which may

---

* This is also, incidentally, what Bergman himself does in *Persona*. His saying "nothing" renders his work akin to Elisabet's letter, which is not a true letter; if it were, it would be sealed, and the fact that it is not precludes its delivery.

be described as that of exclusion or abandonment. The theme is rehearsed in the discontinuous pour of images in the precredit sequence, which alludes to positions occupied by earlier Bergman films (e.g., the spider God of *Through a Glass Darkly* [*Såsom i en spegel*], the child of *The Silence*), and then excludes them formally from the subsequent film, from which the credits separate them. The persistence of these images as an element repressed by the subsequent film – but in fact running underground in parallel to it – becomes apparent when some of them reappear when the film "burns out," seemingly in response to Elisabet's pain after treading on the broken glass. It is hardly surprising that this initial sequence should end with the image of a child who may be dead, or may never have lived (and never lives in the narrative that follows): The work as it were aborts the sequence itself. The boy's inability to enter the story – and the difficulty we ourselves will encounter when we seek to do so – is emphasized when he dons spectacles, and the female face on the wall *still* remains out of focus.*

If *Persona* finally abandons its own narrative, it is perhaps as a sign of the final victory of the repressed, underlying film, which returns to "close the frame." This is not a matter of self-celebratory formalism, however, but a self-abandonment betokening the child's identification with those who declared it an abortion. For abandonment does indeed pervade the film: Children are abandoned, faces are laid aside like masks, and both the name of and the aspiration to God – so prevalent in Bergman's previous works – disappear. It is as if behind the desire to be unlike oneself – the film's desire to be unlike its precredit sequence, Alma's will to be Elisabet, the actress's institutionalized self-abandonment – there lies Job's "Why died I not from the womb?" The precredit sequence stands, as it were, for the dream the artwork can never become.

## Umschlagplatz, *the double, and the child*

*Persona* presents us with a child who reaches out toward the dream screen of his mother's face: He is the double of the children of Elisabet and Alma, of the Warsaw Ghetto child, and of Bergman himself, who describes the fades to red in *Cries and Whispers* as memories of the womb. It is a startling coincidence that another artist should also have perceived in the Warsaw Ghetto child a double of a photograph

---

* The face's continual dissolution echoes the film's theme of dissolving identity, as well as furthering its self-referential, self-interrogating effort to recover the starting point of cinema – an effort apparent also in the silent slapstick film insert, the direct addresses to the camera, and the camera's shifts within the Warsaw Ghetto photograph, sequence becoming imminent and immanent within fixity, as in the photographs in *Blow-Up* or Chris Marker's *La Jetée*.

of himself. Toward the end of Jarosław Rymkiewicz's *Umschlagplatz* we read:

A photograph everyone knows: a little boy in a peaked cap and knee-stockings and his hands up. It is not known when the photograph was taken. During the large-scale liquidation in July or August 1942? During the uprising in the Ghetto, April 1943? Or perhaps at some other time? The second liquidation – in February 1943 – has to be ruled out, for it is clear from the photograph that it was taken in spring, summer, or autumn, but certainly not during the winter. The boy is standing in a courtyard or in the street in front of a gate. This cannot be determined, since we can only see the dark interior of the gateway and one of its corners. One can deduce from the appearance of the corner – its detached flakes of plaster – that the tenement house from which the boy had been led out was old and crumbling. And so we are somewhere on Miła, Gęsia, or Wołyńska street. Or perhaps somewhere else again. Behind the boy with raised hands runs a ditch with something in it: something white. It's probably rubbish, so this is a garbage ditch, and we are dealing with a court-yard rather than a street. On the right-hand side – on the right as we look at it, that is – are four Germans. One in the gateway, three right next to it, next to the damaged corner and the cast-iron gutter-pipe. Two of the faces – in good reproductions, as many as three – are clearly visible. I have looked at this photograph for so long and on so many occasions that were I now – after 45 years – to meet one of these three Germans on the street I would certainly rec-ognize him instantly. One of the Germans has an automatic pistol under his arm: The pistol is, as it were, aimed at the back of the boy in the cap and stockings. The Germans are helmeted, and the one with the pistol has a mo-torcyclist's goggles on his helmet. On the left-hand side of the photograph we can see several women, a few men, and several – probably three – children. All have their hands up. The men are wearing caps. On the far left stands a little girl five or six years old – she's smaller than the boy in socks – wearing a headscarf. She too has her hands up, but because it is the edge of the photo-graph we can only see one hand above the head with the scarf. I have worked out that on this photograph twenty-three people are visible, though I may be mistaken, for the figures on the left are bunched up: nineteen Jews and Jew-esses, and four Germans. I draw the attention of those who are going to look at this photograph to the extremely beautiful face of the woman on the left, doubtless the mother of the girl in the headscarf. Hair combed to one side, she has pronounced cheekbones, big eyes, and a large mouth. One may guess that the extremely pale cheeks are flushed. A white armband on the raised arm. One cannot see the Star of David. After forty-five years I would also recognize this woman on the street – though it's obvious I'll never meet her.

The boy standing in the center of the picture is wearing a brief coat that stops short of his knees. Underneath the coat he is probably wearing a sweater, though that is not certain, for the coat is buttoned up. The cap – slightly askew, or rather pushed to one side – appears to be too big for him. Perhaps it is his father's? Or his elder brother's? The boy's personal details are recorded: Artur Siemiątek, son of Leon and Sara née Dąb, born in Łowicz. Artur is my contemporary: We were both born in 1935. We stand next to one another, he in the photograph taken in the Warsaw Ghetto, and I in the picture taken on the high platform in Otwock. One may assume that the photographs were taken in the same month – mine merely a few, a dozen or so, days earlier. Even our caps seem to be somewhat similar. Mine – slightly the lighter – seems to be too big for me. He in his knee-stockings, I in my white socks. Standing on the platform in Otwock I smile prettily. Nothing can be determined from his face, which was photographed by some SS sergeant.

You're tired, I say to Artur. – After all, it must be very uncomfortable to stand with one's hands up. Let's do as follows: I'll raise my hands, and you lower yours. Perhaps they won't notice. Or, you know what, we'll do it differently: We'll both stand with our hands up.[2]

*Umschlagplatz* is a remarkable work: an act of expiation for what the Polish author (born in 1935) sees as his countrymen's inability to mourn the death of the Jews. It is thus salutary to consider it in this book, particularly in conjunction with the works of Brasch, Syberberg, and Reitz. Rymkiewicz's book moves on three intersecting planes: an attempted reconstruction of the layout of the Umschlagplatz, the final gathering point of the Warsaw Ghetto's Jews before their despatch to the concentration camps; a meditation – part tortured and tortuous, part whimsical – on Polish–Jewish relations; and the imagined memories of a fictitious Yiddish Nobel laureate, Icyk Mandelbaum, whose sense of guilt at having survived the Holocaust and efforts to retrieve the past double those of the author himself. It is significant that the Warsaw Ghetto child should appear as the author's double in the last pages of his book: Death has traditionally manifested himself in the guise of the double, whose appearance indicates that one's body has been discarded already. The photographed child is a double who is always already dead, the image taking a death mask even before his physical demise. As he imagines his own abortion from history in the same manner as the child, Rymkiewicz strives to assuage the guilt of the Poles who survived and looked on. The gesture may, perhaps, have too much of the fanciful to be completely effective, but it is welcome all the same; and the very whimsicality of the tone displays a salutary awareness of the imagination's impotence really to change anything.

## Bergman and Von Trotta

*Persona* may be a very great work, but it has limitations which are probably more apparent to women than anyone else, who have a particular right to object to the secularized theology of Bergman's view of the female as Other. To juxtapose *Persona* with Margarethe von Trotta's *Marianne and Juliane* (*The German Sisters / Die bleierne Zeit*) is to realize that the later film includes both homage to and implicit critique of the former. The debt and critique are most apparent in the scene that superimposes the reflection of Juliane's face upon Marianne's in the glass of the prison where Marianne is being held for terrorism. What one sees is not Bergman's technical trick, which fuses two half-faces into a single monstrous one with the sovereignty with which men have always manipulated the images of women, but simply the sliding of one reflected face onto the image of another one separated from it. As Juliane identifies with her sister, it is as if her shadowy being as reflection feeds upon the substantiality of the other's opposition, enabling her to recover the radicalism of her own adolescence. It is as if that radicalism has been transferred to Marianne, and upon her death will revert to the sister from whom it originally stemmed.* In Von Trotta's film the superimposition is a natural part of the motif of self-discovery through self-loss begun by the sisters' identification with the filmed bodies of concentration camp and Third World famine victims. The identification *mobilizes*. And although it is Marianne who is about to die, the imminence of her demise seems to involve an intensification of being that renders her sister's all but insubstantial. (Marianne's substantiality here also underpins the argument that it was not through suicide that she met her death.) Juliane's visage hovers over Marianne's, for she does not contest her younger sister's right to primacy; as it floats over the place of her sister's image, content to be merely a reflection, it has the ghostliness that will fit her to enter the place vacated by Marianne's death and so become her afterlife. Marianne's face is seen left of screen, through the prison glass, with Juliane's reflection to the right. As Juliane worries about the sudden unclarity of her sister's image – as if she were fading away – an uncanny silence descends as the microphone between them also breaks down, a harbinger of death.

Bergman's image, by way of contrast, is one of nightmarish confusion. On viewing this scene it is reported that neither Bibi Andersson nor Liv Ullmann recognized themselves in it; in this respect, each is like Alma, who protests at this point, "I am not Elisabet Vogler." (Their failure of recognition may well indicate that Alma is far less pathological than Bergman would have us believe.) Their rejection of the image is a rejection of the violence inflicted upon them by a film-

---

* The doubling of Marianne by Juliane has been examined insightfully by Ann Kaplan, who proceeds to read the fusion and overlapping of their faces at this moment as follows: "The wordless, purely visual linking suggests a mystical bonding transcending the patriarchal Symbolic now seen as inadequate for embodying the sisters' new way of relating."[3] This seems to me to be far too positive – and constrained by Lacanian terminology: the moment is indeed suggestive, but is as painful as it is positive. And there is unconscious irony in speaking of "a new way of relating" when the sisters are more firmly separated, by the interposed glass, than ever before. A mystical bonding may indeed grow more intense as distance increases, but such union is achieved through a *via negativa* whose *painfulness* is always before us.

maker who divides the image of woman in order to rule it, counteracting his inability to control it in reality. Bergman's image radiates a horror from which his actresses retreat as surely as Elisabet Vogler backs into a corner when confronted with the televised image of the burning Buddhist monk. Her retreat is surely a model of the reaction Bergman would like to elicit from his audience; this is also the significance of the moment at which the film immolates itself like the monk, imitating its own conflagration in the projector. Bergman's images of horror are distant, depoliticized: newsreel from the Far East, a photograph from the Warsaw Ghetto. Von Trotta's, however, is far more immediate, a personal and political intervention into recent German historiography. The judicial system may think it can silence Marianne, but it has not reckoned with the power of the sisters' bonding, which allows the silenced woman to be replaced by the articulate one who tells her story, who is also an image of Von Trotta herself in her relationship with Christiane Ensslin. Juliane will tell the story again and again – first to an unresponsive newspaper editor, who deems it stale news, and then to Marianne's son – circling around it just as the end of the film circles back to its own beginning, telling it again and again until a sympathetic audience is found or the traumas it embodies disperse.

If *Persona* had a subtitle, it could well be "the inability to mourn" – that postwar German pathology that furnishes the title of the Mitscherlichs' influential book. Is it significant that Elisabet breaks down while playing Electra, who has to mourn her lost brother Orestes and her dead father? Neither Alma nor Elisabet know how to mourn their dead children: the social rituals – perhaps even the sense of the existence of society in general – that might have shown them how to do so have withered away, collapsing with the demise of Christianity. And yet loss is still felt, hysterically, even when consciousness denies it. For Von Trotta, unlike Bergman, Christianity need not simply be discarded; its traditions can be reworked so that the Grünewald crucifixion, with its image of Mary and John confronted with Christ's agony, provides a model of solidarity in the face of appalling suffering. The pastor father may be a fiery image in the pulpit in the sisters' memory, but it is also he who shows them *Nuit et brouillard*. The alienation from modern German society apparent in Juliane's ability to mourn is adumbrated by the father's willingness to confront his German daughters with a foreign view of the atrocities of the war; and in this context alienation is a sign of health. When juxtaposed with *Persona*, *Marianne and Juliane* further suggests that the inability to mourn gives birth to the vampire – note the bloodsucking images in Bergman's film – which takes revenge upon society for the oblivion visited upon him or her. The vampire becomes the destructive representative of the dead whose burial and mourning is prevented by the self's refusal to admit the fact of death: a denial with which both the petering out of and the extreme modernity of look of Bergman's film are complicit. Only identification with death can ever free one from it. And if Marianne's death then threatens to engulf her child also, who is attacked while playing in the woods, there is a sense in which Juliane's identification with her dead sister serves to protect him. (As well as preserving the memory of her sister as child, it upholds the possibility of a new start.)

Throughout Von Trotta's film the images of the dead are mutually reflecting. The central one is perhaps that of the body of Christ, which represents a particular concentration camp or famine victim, singled out for consideration, individualized by identification. The terror of history is manifest both in the generalized image of Christ's suffering on behalf of humankind, and in the particular suffering of the Jews under Hitler's rule. These images are dialectical: The image of Christ is abstract in its simultaneous relation to all history, but concrete in its tormented singularity, while the corpses of the Jews are the product of one concrete historical moment, even as their horrible accumulation renders them abstract. The mutual mirroring of these images – in the mind of Marianne, who is terrorized into terrorism by the horror they embody, and in Von Trotta's own exemplary film – is an antidote to all anti-Semitism; it also indicates the complexity of the process whereby images are received, for the sight of Jewish bodies is one of the forces that propels Marianne into a pro-Arab position. In Von Trotta's film the Jews are not the people who killed Christ, but partake of his death themselves, are themselves crucified; and the juxtaposition reminds one of Christ's own Jewishness. In *Marianne and Juliane* – unlike, say, Syberberg's *Our Hitler* – the traumatic images do not gather dust in a museum of the collective unconscious but haunt the awareness of the sisters, compelling each to identify with the victims: the one to the point of adding further links to the chain of historical suffering, while the other attempts to understand from an appalled distance – the distance of *art*, fed and dissolved by identification. When she says she will tell Marianne's son all she knows, though her knowledge is imperfect, there is a genuine dawning of the possibility of catharsis, of expiation.

*Marianne and Juliane* concludes with a dissonant synthesis of personalities that is a more successful version of the one that ends Von Trotta's previous film, *Sisters or the Balance of Happiness (Schwestern – oder die Balance des Glücks)*. The previous film had closed with the elder sister, Maria, resolving to fuse with the personality of her dead sister, Anna; similarly, at the end of *Marianne and Juliane,* Juliane remains herself and yet identifies with Marianne – as mother, by adopting Jan, as prisoner (for the barlike window frame of the opening, from which the whole of the rest of the film has been a sort of flashback, suggests a prison, a suggestion reinforced by the somber colors and bleakly fluting music), and ultimately as corpse. The earlier film had fused the personalities with Gothic means reminiscent of *Persona*, producing a composite image of Anna and Maria in a mirror; in *Marianne and Juliane* the fusion is less spectacular and finally more telling, being internal. Juliane's own rebellious impulses have, as it were, migrated back to her from their temporary lodging place in the body of her sister. She ends in an alienation that is all but total: opposed like Marianne to the existing social order, but lacking even the alternative minisociety of the terrorist group – or the transferred nationalism of Palestinian sympathies – to assuage isolation. Yet there is a hint of hope in her mind's movement away from the past and childhood with Marianne to the future of Marianne's child. There is certainly a hint of the utopian in her acquisition of a child (though in dreams the child can symbolize illness as well as hope): Childbearing had been tainted in her eyes previously by the premium placed upon female fertility by the National Socialists. (In the early scenes she researches Nazi family policy for the feminist paper at which she works, and is seen participating in a rally against abortion restrictions.) Thus Marianne's decision to bear a child may even have been a subliminal reason why Juliane accused her of being a potential member of the Bund der deutschen Mädel. Yet Jan's appearance suggests the possibility of a child free of links with the Nazi past, even though he bears its scars upon his body: With his dark hair and sallow complexion, is it too fanciful to see him as perhaps a *Jewish* German child?

## Magarethe and Julia

*Persona* is threatened by a collapse into a chaotic *prima materia* that can be defined as "the abject": that which art normally utters and thereby purifies, as Julia Kristeva remarks in her book *Powers of Horror.*[4] It is also possible to interpret Von Trotta's film as concerned with the management of the phobias Kristeva described as constitutive of the experience of abjection. The following passage from her essay on abjection can be read as a series of variations on scenes from *Marianne and Juliane*, including such elements as the skin on the sisters' coffee, which triggers a childhood memory; the sisters' retreat to the lavatory to vomit on viewing concentration camp footage; and Juliane's encounter with Marianne's dead body, and subsequent collapse. In each case, horror envelops the body before it can be screened by the mind.*

* Elsaesser writes: "A flashback in *The German Sisters,* for example shows the two girls sitting through a screening of *Night and Fog* at school, one of them vomiting afterwards in the lavatory, her body rejecting what her mind cannot grasp."[5]

Kristeva's passage, quoted in full, runs as follows:

Food loathing is perhaps the most elementary and most archaic form of abjection. When the eyes see or the lips touch that skin on the surface of milk – harmless, thin as a sheet of cigarette paper, pitiful as a nail paring – I experience a gagging sensation and, still farther down, spasms in the stomach, the belly; and all the organs shrivel up the body, provoke tears and bile, increase heartbeat, cause forehead and hands to perspire. Along with sight-clouding dizziness, *nausea* makes me balk at that milk cream, separates me from the mother and father who proffer it. "I" want none of that element, sign of their desire; "I" do not want to listen, "I" do not assimilate it, "I" expel it. But since the food is not an "other" for "me," who am only in their desire, I expel *myself*, I spit *myself* out, I abject *myself* within the same motion through which "I" claim to establish *myself*. That detail, perhaps an insignificant one, but one that they ferret out, emphasize, evaluate, that trifle turns me inside out, guts sprawling; it is thus that *they* see that "I" am in the process of becoming an other at the expense of my own death. During that course in which "I" become, I give birth to myself amid the violence of sobs, of vomit. Mute protest of the symptom, shattering violence of a convulsion that, to be sure, is inscribed in a symbolic system, but in which, without either wanting or being able to become integrated in order to answer to it, it reacts, it abreacts. It abjects.

The corpse (or cadaver: *cadere*, to fall), that which has irremediably come a cropper, is cesspool, and death; it upsets even more violently the one who confronts it as fragile and fallacious chance. A wound with blood and pus, or the sickly, acrid smell of sweat, of decay, does not *signify* death. In the presence of signified death – a flat encephalograph, for instance – I would understand, react or accept. No, as in true theater, without makeup or masks, refuses and corpses *show me* what I permanently thrust aside in order to live. These body fluids, this defilement, this shit are what life withstands, hardly and with difficulty, on the part of death. There, I am at the border of my condition as a living being. My body extricates itself, as being alive, from that border. Such wastes drop so that I might live, until, from loss to loss, nothing remains in me and my entire body falls beyond the limit – *cadere*, cadaver. If dung signifies the other side of the border, the place where I am not and which permits me to be, the corpse, the most sickening of wastes, is a border that has encroached upon everything. It is no longer I who expel, "I" is expelled. The border has become an object. How can I be without border? That elsewhere that I imagine beyond the present, or that I hallucinate so that I might, in a present time, speak to you, conceive of you – it is now here, jetted, abjected, into "my" world. Deprived of world, therefore, I *fall in a faint*. In that compelling, raw, insolent thing in the morgue's full sunlight, in that thing that no longer matches and therefore no longer signifies anything, I behold the breaking down of a world that has erased its borders: fainting away. The corpse, seen without God and outside of science, is the utmost of abjection. It is death infecting life. Abject. It is something rejected from which one does not part, from which one does not protect oneself as from an object. Imaginary uncanniness and real threat, it beckons to us and ends up engulfing us.

It is thus not lack of cleanliness or health that causes abjection but what disturbs identity, system, order. What does not respect borders, positions, rules.

The in-between, the ambiguous, the composite. The traitor, the liar, the criminal with a good conscience, the shameless rapist, the killer who claims he is a savior... Any crime, because it draws attention to the fragility of the law, is abject, but premeditated crime, cunning murder, hypocritical revenge are even more so because they heighten the display of such fragility. He who denies morality is not abject; there can be grandeur in amorality and even in crime that flaunts its disrespect for the law – rebellious, liberating and suicidal crime. Abjection, on the other hand, is immoral, sinister, scheming and shady: a terror that dissembles, a hatred that smiles, a passion that uses the body for barter instead of inflaming it, a debtor who sells you up, a friend who stabs you....

In the dark halls of the museum that is now what remains of Auschwitz, I see a heap of children's shoes, or something like that, something I have already seen elsewhere, under a Christmas tree, for instance, dolls I believe. The abjection of Nazi crime reaches its apex when death, which, in any case, kills me, interferes with what, in my living universe, is supposed to save me from death: childhood, science, among other things.[6]

The near-simultaneous conception of *Marianne and Juliane* and *Powers of Horror* indicates that Von Trotta's classicism is far from removing her from the forefront of feminist thought.[7] Indeed, it can be seen as introducing a necessary order into a sphere Kristeva confuses as well as illuminates, as her prose slides in negative rhapsody between forms of abjection. Von Trotta's use of *narrative* enables her to separate the elements of the experience Kristeva crumples into a single mass (to *plot* them, as it were). Moreover, Von Trotta's use of identification mechanisms permits, among other things, an identification with the Jewish fate that preserves her from Kristeva's irresponsible submission, later in her book, to the fascination of Céline's anti-Semitic diatribes (valorized as "delirium"). She is free of the inconsistency that allows Kristeva to call a corpse "a thing" and then claim that she does not protect herself from it "as from an object," or to sketch questionable distinctions between the ambiguously amoral and the ambiguously immoral. Nevertheless, there is an intriguing multiplicity of points of intersection. The idea of the corpse as *that which falls* has a many-layered resonance in Von Trotta's film, in which Juliane crouches fetally, herself unable to fall any further, watching the fall of the doll she has made in replica of Marianne (cf. Kristeva's last paragraph) in order to test whether her sister really did hang herself. "Deprived of world, I *fall in a faint*": Is this not Juliane's reaction to the sight of Marianne's actual body, the death that invades *her* life? Like Kristeva, Von Trotta is concerned with the disjunction between a signified death that is manageable and a real one that is not; but she goes beyond Kristeva in considering the death that is both signified *and* real by virtue of identification with the person – real or represented – who has suffered it. This transgression of the order of selfhood is momentarily evoked in the breakdown of grammaticality in Kristeva's " 'I' is expelled," but this is no more than a flicker of awareness in the prose passage. Von Trotta realizes that one can be, without a border, when one identifies with another. If abjection is "what does not respect borders, positions, rules," the identification that occurs between the sisters and what they see, and between Marianne and Juliane themselves, is part of their rebellion: rebellion against a world in which individuation precludes solidarity. If vomiting means "I give birth to myself," is it not significant that it is Marianne, who later bears a child, who vomits on watching the concentration camp footage?* "The killer who claims to be a savior": is this not Marianne herself (the word "savior" recalling also the Grünewald crucifixion)? Kristeva may claim later that "abjection is elaborated through a failure to recognize its kin,"[8] but the definition is undermined by her earlier reflections, which show its experience to involve recognition of affinity with a person or thing one would rather reject – or would indeed reject if the conscious mind had time to have a say. "Something rejected from which one does not part": Could that not be an epigraph both for *Persona* – "as in true theater, without makeup or masks"? – and *Marianne and Juliane*?

### Father, son, and daughter: Böll, Straub, and Von Trotta

This final section constructs an imaginary intellectual family based on a shared concern with the issues that bred terrorism – and a terrified state clampdown – in the West Germany of the seventies. The family is utopian, an antifamily: not one whose offspring inevitably inherit a parental legacy of guilt, but one constituted through elective affinity – as it were, through the *adoption* that closes Böll's *Billiards at Half-Past Nine*. Both the films and filmmakers under consideration can be described as inspired by Böll, for all their final divergence from him – a divergence that is more marked in Straub's case than Von Trotta's, perhaps because his decision to film a Böll novel required him to radicalize it lest his own position seem merely an otiose duplication of the intellectual father's. *Not Reconciled* (*Nicht versöhnt*) is, of course, derived from Böll's *Billiards at Half-Past Nine*; Von Trotta, for her part, had worked with her husband Volker Schlöndorff on the filming of Böll's *Lost Honor of Katherina Blum* (*Die verlorene Ehre der Katherina Blum*), and *Marianne and Juliane* can be read as a modern-dress re-

---

* Child-as-waste is a very Freudian equation, embracing both sisters: both Marianne, who expels the child in the sense of abandoning it as well as thrusting it out into the world, and Juliane, who does not want to have children or clear up Marianne's *mess*, embodied in Jan.

working of the play upon which the Böll/Schlöndorff contribution to
*Germany in Autumn* is based, the *Antigone* of Sophocles. All three
works – the two films and the book – probe the origins of violence and
the relationship between terrorism and the desire to destroy the legacy
of National Socialism.

*Literature, film, representation, and distance*

For an event to be representable, it must be distanced in some way,
either by metaphor or other aesthetic devices, or by time. The first
reckonings with the Third Reich appear in literature and are the work
of figures literally removed from it by exile: figures such as Hermann
Broch or Thomas Mann. Later still Celan will write in Paris, and Grass
will deal with the geographical edge of the German empire; each will
employ balladic or nursery rhyme forms that are particularly appropriate because of the absolute quality of the experience, which rendered
one as helpless as a child. Literature can clearly distance events more
readily than film: partly because the metaphor is obviously nonidenti-
cal with the event to which it refers,* but also because individual writers could come to terms with themselves and their culture to a degree
that was far harder for the collective subject to attain – be it the German people as a whole (a subject that in fact no longer existed after
the country's division) or the microcosm engaged in the making of a
film. Moreover, the outlay filmmaking requires would have necessitated a public forum for self-investigation, a place far harder to find
than the movable site of a book's consumption. Those German directors who had departed in the thirties remained in Hollywood, with a
new set of preoccupations that had the additional attraction of being
easier to manage: a dereliction that lends plausibility to Kracauer's indictment of Weimar cinema. Thus National Socialism was not to be
represented on any large scale in the German cinema until almost
forty years after the beginning of World War II, when the generation of
filmmakers born in the forties began to come into its own. (There had
been a certain amount of East German analysis of the Nazi legacy, but
it had mainly involved accusation of the inheritors in the West.) It is
interesting to note, however, that even these directors – with the signal
exception of Straub – did not begin their careers with an act of reckoning with the past, as had Grass and Celan, but arrived at the National
Socialist theme only after they had established a reputation that would
protect them against the odium of raking up a best-forgotten past. In
some cases the turn to the thirties was contaminated by the nostalgia

---

* Whereas in literature the absent events are allegorically *present* behind the metaphor,
in film metaphor involves a cutting away from the stream of events, as in Eisensteinian
montage, where the flock of sheep may be intercut with the crowd.

film cult and the ambiguous, sadomasochistic fascination of fascism (e.g., the films of Fassbinder). The very use of the term "fascism," however useful as a generalization stressing the continuities between forms of repression and between past and present, may itself have entailed a muting of the specifics of memory. The simultaneous operation of these – and other – motives renders the collective act of remembrance enacted in German cinema in the late seventies an extremely complex event.

*Böll and Straub:* Not Reconciled

The first attempt at filmic reckoning, however, had been far more clear-cut. *Not Reconciled,* Jean-Marie Straub's film of Böll's *Billiards at Half-Past Nine,* is a radically provocative work seemingly formulated under the aegis of Adorno's dictum deeming the resumption of poetry after Auschwitz a form of barbarism. If Straub's film is considerably more fractured than Böll's novel – and markedly less comprehensible – this can be read as indicative of the greater degree of difficulty Germans have addressing their past in the more public medium of film. Straub himself does not share this difficulty, but mordantly presents a film whose reception is already jammed by the defense mechanisms of its anticipated receivers. The film broadcasts itself as unreceived – as the sign of a blockage, impregnated with its audience's psychosis. Straub deliberately fractures the novel, eliminating its whimsical and anecdotal features, for they embody a spirit of *Versöhnung* (reconciliation) with a public he sees as still guilty, unrepentant, and hence undeserving of forgiveness. The realist novel's assumption that truth discloses itself through the surface of the world is for Straub part of the problem; alongside Straub's film Böll's novel appears old-fashioned, its post-Faulknerian play with time and perspective merely academic. Straub is surely mindful – pathologically mindful, many a viewer may think – of Adorno's thesis that any representation of negative experience secretes within itself, through the mere fact of its own existence, an element of affirmation the official culture can employ to neutralize it. His aim is to reduce the affirmative element to a degree zero by alienating the audience far more comprehensively than ever Brecht would have dared. The title *Not Reconciled,* although drawn from the book, encapsulates the film's mode of composition, which juxtaposes elements with an austere *harte Fügung* (harsh articulation): There is no trace of what film theorists have defined as the system of the suture. And even though Böll bestowed the rights to film upon Straub gratis, the film is clearly not reconciled with Böll's aesthetic. But it has the paradoxical effect of sending one back to the novel, functioning virtually as a trailer for it. (The avant-

garde and the marketing agency – those extreme opposites – here
*meet.*) It differs from all other "filmed literature" in its refusal to assume the place of the book, to which one has to return in order to decipher the events it shows as pure, incomprehensible surface.

What are the events one discovers upon reversion to the book? *Billiards at Half-Past Nine* examines the interrelations of three genera-
tions of an architect's family, focusing on a single day in 1958. It is the
eightieth birthday of family patriarch Heinrich Fähmel, whose reputation was established among the town architects when he, the new gun,
won a prestigious contract to build a local abbey. During the closing
days of World War II his son Robert dynamited it, acting under the orders of an insane general. Robert however was not reluctant to level the
building, viewing the destruction as a commemoration of the martyrs
of the anti-Nazi adolescent group, the lambs. It is he who provides the
novel's title, for he plays billiards for ninety minutes daily in the Hotel
Prinz Heinrich, accompanied by Hugo, a young porter in whom he sees
some of the character of the lambs, and whom he finally adopts. Only
under one circumstance is the hotel management to permit an intru-
sion while he plays: in the case of a visit by Schrella, another lamb,
who now lives in exile. (He is almost arrested on his return, for the arrest warrant for his part in an abortive anti-Nazi bomb attempt is still
in force.) Where Robert admits the problematic nature of father–son relationships in Germany by adopting Hugo, Schrella does so by refusing to marry, fearing lest potential children turn against him. The
characters muse in interior monologue on the continuity of German
militarism and on the cycles of destruction and reconstruction – about
to be prolonged in the rebuilding of the abbey by Robert's son. Robert's
father had been unable to identify with the Wilhelmine ethos, though
only his wife had been able to express his opposition by terming the
Kaiser a fool; she was subsequently declared insane, and toward the
novel's end attempts to assassinate a nameless minister associated
with the reestablishment of the old order. Robert's attempts to defend
the lambs had caused him to flee to Rotterdam during the early Nazi
years, before family prestige negotiated his return. Reflecting the title of
Straub's version – based on a key passage from Robert's interior monologue – the main characters have been unable to reconcile themselves
to German militarism, and have refused to eat of what Böll terms "The
sacrament of the buffalo" – subsisting instead in a half-light of irony
and withdrawal, sustained and protected by the cocoon of eccentricity
they spin around themselves.

It can be argued that Straub's film involves an identification with
Robert Fähmel: his destruction of Böll's narrative parallels Robert's
demolition of his father's church, an act that provides an antimonu-
ment to the lambs, those marginal martyrs to no political cause. So

marginal are they that the sole monument to their memory exists in Robert's head – like the novel we are reading. But whereas the interiority of the characters is extremely important to Böll – all are isolated with their thoughts, this being part of the sense in which they are "unpolitical," which for Böll means internal exiles – he demonstrates that even though father and son are "not reconciled" on one plane, they *are* of one spirit in their synchronized, mutually obscured opposition to the German militarist tradition, in Straub's film interiority undergoes an externalization that amounts to reification. For although the characters recite to one another many of the thoughts that simply echo within their heads in Böll's work, this does not engender any atmosphere of intimacy or understanding between them: The rapid-fire, Brechtian monotone of their delivery renders it extremely difficult to keep pace with them, and replicates the "he who has ears to hear, let him hear" of Straub's own clipped mode of address. Straub stresses instead the opacity of the characters – the opacity Robert assumes in the eyes of his American interrogator, who cannot fathom his motives for following the orders of a mad general and destroying a church that was a cultural monument. We are given no time to make the connections between the brusquely presented narrative elements.

Straub's film is shaped very differently from Böll's work. As the credits run over an image of the Cologne monument to five victims of the Gestapo, the question of the German past becomes primary, the family drama secondary. As Robert Fähmel's voice then asks Hugo what story he should tell, the process of narration – of memory and repression – is foregrounded also. At once the film presents the incident in which Robert hit the ball out of the ground in order to shield Schrella from victimization; ending with Heinrich Fähmel imagining how the look of astonishment will never leave the face of the politician his wife has shot – the satisfaction this prospective persistence generates being expressed in the sublime leftward pan of the camera, out of the window, to the music of Bach's Suite No. 2 in B Minor. In plunging into the game at the very beginning, Straub indicates that his primary focus will be on the determining force of the past. The juxtaposition of Fähmel's billiard game with the game in which he once broke his bat succinctly shows the choice that has led to internal exile: away from the sadism of outdoor sport as collective ritual of discipline and punishment, toward a contemplation that is free of competition, balls rebounding from one another like the thoughts in Robert's head, the thoughts as firmly enclosed within the period with Hugo as the balls are within the billiard table.

The externality of Straub's film brings out the behavioristic tendencies of filmic registration; in so doing it banishes psychiatry even more effectively than does Böll's novel, which fears the danger the individualism of psychoanalysis poses to the different individualism of the novel. Like the existentialists, Straub believes that to speak of the unconscious is to disclaim responsibility. Hence both he and Böll privilege the characters' conscious explanations of their deeds: Robert's aim in destroying the abbey was to punish the church that failed to feed its sheep and to subvert the nationalistic obsession with monuments. (Heinrich Fähmel states that any monument to himself would deserve only to be spat upon. Hence the only permissible monument in the book – the image of reconciliation – is one that is *built to be destroyed*: the birthday cake replica of the abbey at the end.) If Böll dismisses the possible unconscious motives Freudian analysis proposes, it is because the abbey's destruction is the work of history, not the expression of Oedipal enmity. When Heinrich lops off the tower of the cake, and hands it to Robert, one wonders if Böll is mocking the analyst who would see this as a symbolic resignation to impotence, autocastration. He may well be ironically handing his own work to psychoanalysis on a plate. Böll employs a variety of novel that privileges psychological analysis, and yet at the same time declares parts of the plot no-go areas to it. The resultant inconsistency generates such weaknesses as the figure of Hugo, who is presented as a contemporary version of the spirit of the lambs but who – unlike them – stands for nothing in particular; he is an allegorical cipher and not really a character at all. If his face carries the same glow as that of Edith, Robert's dead wife, its meaning is problematic and may even be the product of Robert's projection, of the urge to recover the dead. The degenerate afterlife of the lamblike spirit in the knitting circle can be read as the novel's unconsciously self-satiric comment on its own effort to establish a continuity of the tradition in Hugo. Straub solves the problems created by Böll's mixture of psychology and allegory by the simple expedient of dispensing with psychology. The voice that says "nicht versöhnt" thus ceases to belong to one of the story's characters and becomes that of Straub himself. His deliberate affront to the audience identifies with the terrorism Böll himself tries to soft-pedal: It is hardly surprising that his film should bear as its subtitle a quotation from Brecht, "Es hilft nur Gewalt, wo Gewalt herrscht" (only violence helps where violence rules [*St. Joan of the Stockyards*]). Böll himself is less assured of the virtues of violence. His heroes either destroy property rather than people (Robert) or mercifully fail in their assassination attempts (the bomb that explodes at the feet of the oppressive Nazi schoolteacher, the shot that leaves a shocked expression on the face of the complacent politician, but does not kill him). But what if the teacher or the politician had died? Would it have been so easy for Böll to present his children (the bomb throwers) or women (Fähmel's antimilitarist wife) as simply victims?

Böll's image of terrorism can thus be accused of excessive coziness; in essence he does what Thomas Elsaesser (see below, "Vergangenheitsbewältigung and the German context") accuses Von Trotta of doing – renders familiar the radically Other. When a son dynamites his father's church, no repressed psychic violence is involved. Robert may say he is "not reconciled," and be unable to speak to his father, but the latter has guessed the identity of his abbey's destroyer and approved his action – he feels that any monument to himself would deserve only to be desecrated – so there is a species of *Versöhnung* here. The internal monologue that pervades the book may correspond to internal exile, but such endless internalization is not enough. Women and children are allowed, or have the courage, to say directly what their menfolk are forbidden to utter: "Johanna sprach aus, was ich dachte" (Johanna expressed what I was thinking),[9] the older Fähmel thinks of his wife. But the actions of the women and children are not taken seriously: The authorities deem them essentially irresponsible, and even Böll can be viewed as minimizing the seriousness of their deeds, for he intervenes – a benevolent providence – to prevent their violence from having the desired murderous effect. In protecting them, Godlike, from the sin of murder Böll condescends to them. He surely shares Fähmel's belief that irony is not enough, yet the alternatives to it are manifestly ineffectual. Only anarchist gestures are authentic – the worthlessness of political parties is shown by their indistinguishability at the hotel convention – but the actions of "the subversive Madonna" change nothing.

Böll presents a world in which nothing one does is ever right (he would not say that "Gewalt hilft") – and in this sense is paradoxically closer to Adorno than Straub, whose intransigently modernist aesthetic might seem far more Adornian. Straub feels there is a right way of acting – simple provocation; Böll implicitly recognizes that matters are more complex and could well assent to Adorno's statement that there is no possibility of acting correctly where life as a whole is false. Whereas Straub denies all channels of audience identification, Böll proposes a dialectic of compassion and unmoved steadfastness, the double movement of the Hölderlin line he quotes: "Mitleidend bleibt das ewige Herz doch fest" ["Compassionate, the eternal heart yet stands fast"]: *mitleiden* and *fest,* with their opposed connotations, stand appropriately at opposite ends of the line. *Mitleiden* seems to be identified by Böll with the feminine: Erika's and Ferdi's mother wept her soul away out of pity for the youngsters who looked on as she fried fish, which she gave away rather than sell them. Opposed to this is a male *Festigkeit* – that which builds, creates solid objects. Böll may identify with the feminine, but he cannot become it – which may be why Hugo, who in a sense reconciles the two impulses, is so unreal a figure. The novel does not seriously believe in their fusion. *Versöhn-ung*, for Böll, is not reconciliation but *Ver-söhnung*: the son's inevitable departure from the way of the father. The only way to stop the billiard ball rolling is Schrella's: not to have any children at all.

*Identification with the dead:* Marianne and Juliane

Any consideration of the thematics of self-division, ghostliness, and the uncanny in works of German cinema and horror must also ask whether the fear associated with terrifying images can be managed without repression. This is in part the project of Bergman's *Persona*, a deliberate effort at self-transcendence, at placing in a clinical context the often fatally Gothic bugbears of his other works. If Bergman's film fails to advance into enlightenment, it is surely in part because of its Strindbergian conviction of the impossibility of individuals ever dispelling the power of their personal demons in the dawn of mutuality. The vision of the dead generates horror in the expressionist, who believes that "they" have come to recruit him to "their" ranks. If his scream of horror truly is, as Freud would argue, among other things the expression of a fear of castration, then perhaps women are better placed to devise strategies for assimilating the image of the dead. Lacking "the phallus," they stand outside the administration of death.

In *Marianne and Juliane* "the dead" does not mean simply Juliane's dead sister, but also the concentration camp and famine victims who enter her world as phantoms, as film – which is thus peculiarly privileged in the task of mourning. Her sister is merely one more member of the traumatic series of specters twentieth-century history – and the history of Germany in particular – has brought before her. Observation of film from the death camps, for instance, has shown that it is humans' maltreatment of their fellow humans that turns the latter into shuffling phantoms and then reproachful corpses. Identification with the dead allows one to alleviate the specter's clamorous importunity by showing that one is already with it in spirit, one's alienation from the world that mutilated one being so profound as to render one virtually a spirit oneself. One can preserve oneself from appropriation by the dead by agreeing to feed their project with one's life's blood. Selflessness defuses the envy the dead feel for the living. Here, as always, survival is best achieved by playing dead, playing at being the dead – participating in a mystery play that stages their resurrection in the body of our life, which is in any case an extension of theirs through the remixing of their genes. To go beyond the terror of the dead is to escape the confines of paranoia, with its obsessive will to visualize a tantalizingly – hauntingly – invisible threat. One no longer projects oneself into the world, losing the self and rediscovering it everywhere and nowhere, but uses projections to animate that which now lies out-side the world: the dead, the necessity of whose resurrection one antic-ipates by resurrecting them within one's own flesh. Already dead – dead to this world – one can dispel paranoia, with its constant fear of imminent demise.

## Marianne and Juliane *and the uncanny*

From its very outset *Marianne and Juliane* unfolds under the aegis of the uncanny. Ann Kaplan notes:

The date of the film's present, and of the time-span of the main flashback, is established in the opening shot when the camera moves from Juliane's point-of-view shot (looking out of the window) to pan her bookshelves with files dated from 1968 to 1980. In its unrealistic, dark lighting and non-realist use of sound – echoing footsteps and the atonal music used throughout the film – the scene sets up an uncanny space – a space of difficulty, of questioning rather than harmony.[10]

This space is uncanny in Freud's sense also: Juliane is determined to restore to the light – of public attention, of justice – the buried body of her sister. Von Trotta's film can be read as her separate female con-tribution to *Germany in Autumn (Deutschland in Herbst)*, the omni-bus film the leading *male* representatives of the New German Cinema made in meditation on the hysterical West German response to the ac-tivities of the Baader-Meinhof group, which culminated in the arrest and mysterious death in Stammheim prison of three of its members. One of the three – Gudrun Ensslin – was of course the main prototype for Von Trotta's Marianne. *Germany in Autumn* begins and ends with funerals: the state funeral of Hanns-Martin Schleyer, one of the terror-ists' victims, and the more modest interment, under heavy police sur-veillance, of the three terrorists. Collaborating with Heinrich Böll, Von Trotta's husband, Volker Schlöndorff, had contributed a sketch in which a meeting of TV executives decided against screening a perfor-mance of Sophocles' *Antigone*: Such themes as denied burial and indi-vidual opposition to a police state might prove touchy in the early chill of this autumn. *Marianne and Juliane* can be read as Von Trotta's *Antigone,* reworked in a feminist vein that replaces the dead brother Polyneices with a dead sister and compresses the two brothers and two sisters into simply two sisters, thereby achieving a stark dramatic economy that is congruent with the Sophoclean identification of the feminine with the powers of earth and underworld. (It is interesting that one German reviewer should have described Juliane's transforma-tion after Marianne's death as "Ismene becomes Antigone.")[11] From a feminist perspective such films as *Persona* and *Vampyr* may be criticized as demonizing the woman who refuses to be put away prematurely.* In Bergman's film in particular the banishment of the female to the living death of speechlessness can be seen as a cauterizing of the compassionate/artistic component of the male mind, an element often designated "female." The originally intended title of Von Trotta's film was *Der Tausch* (The Exchange): It is *Trauerarbeit* as a blood transfusion, mourning that is also work (*Arbeit*) on behalf of the dead.

## Vergangenheitsbewätigung *and the German context*

Of all the German films to take up the question of *Vergangenheitsbewältigung* in the late seventies, perhaps only Von Trotta's work was able adequately to focus the forms of persistence of the National Socialist past. It eschewed the overgeneralized and self-indulgent mannerism of Syberberg's *Our Hitler,* which deemed Hitler omnipresent in the whole range of postwar excrescences, from terrorism to kitsch; and it answered those who have sought to defend *Heimat* against selective memory by doubting "the representability of Auschwitz in narrative form."[12] And, as we will see, it overcame the conventional antinomy – reproduced at virtually all levels of film criticism, even in the highly sophisticated Puritanical modernism of *Screen* – between "documentary truth" and "narrative falsity," an antinomy that can abet the overvaluation of Lanzmann's extremely problematic *Shoah.*[13] Von Trotta's film scrupulously traces the mediations linking the facts of terror (the concentration camps) to images of terror (newsreel of the camps, Third World disasters, and the tortured body of Christ in the Grünewald crucifixion)† and the birth of terrorist projects among people attempting to respond to the near-impossible demands these images make on our sympathies and comprehension. Perhaps only Von Trotta's film draws conclusions from the West German reception of *Holocaust,* which prevented the curtailment of the period of validity of war-crimes statutes. *Holocaust's* reception had shown that unless mechanisms of identification are present, a work will be unable to address anyone outside the already-concerned intellectual élite.‡ *Mari-*

---

* The vampire may be, among other things, an image of the woman with whom the man has become one flesh, but whom he would like to divorce for a younger one: He might then project onto the mate his own desire for "fresh blood."
† An image situated (significantly?) beyond the edge of the German consciousness, *across the border* in the Colmar Museum (as part of the Isenheim altarpiece).
‡ Those mechanisms, of course, require simultaneous problemization, a feat Von Trotta achieves with great adroitness.
   One obvious way to assay the subversion of public expectation is simultaneously to draw on and to critique existing genres – the most spectacular attempt being *Heimat,* Reitz's anti-*Holocaust,* which is both *Heimatfilm* and *Antiheimatfilm.* The audience however is adept at focusing on the familiar elements, viewing the element of critique as distracting "noise" – what John Fiske and John Hartley have termed "mainstreaming."[14]

*anne and Juliane* marks a step forward from *The Lost Honor of Katherina Blum,* the Böll novel about the tabloid demonization of terrorists jointly filmed by Von Trotta and Schlöndorff. Where the earlier film offers all-too-immediate a view of the media and mediation, the latter meditates pregnantly on the mediation of images. It thus connects spheres of experience all-too-often divorced in the sub-Brechtian polarization of (bad) representation and (good) presentation – transcending Brechtian orthodoxy with a pragmatism equally characteristic of Brecht himself.

The primary strategy in this achievement is the incorporation both of documentary images of the camps *and* of a documentary employing those images (Alain Resnais's *Nuit et brouillard*), whose effects are then documented. *Marianne and Juliane* fuses documentary and fiction: Based on the story of the Ensslin sisters, and dedicated to Christiane (the elder of the two, whom Von Trotta met while working on part of *Germany in Autumn*), it is also profoundly autobiographical. Von Trotta felt no compulsion to be constrained by all the details of the Ensslins' lives, and the image of the fifties as "a leaden time" is intimately grounded in her own experience. This fusion has caused much confusion among critics prone to mistake the image for the prototype – something Von Trotta's concern with mediation warns us against – and then to lacerate the director for putative sensationalism, opportunism, or infidelity. One can indeed argue that Von Trotta is more honest than filmmakers who claim that resemblances between their characters and living persons are accidental. (A grain of reality is almost always the nucleus around which works of art build up the pearls of their characters.) Thus Reitz could add the customary disclaimer to *Heimat,* despite conceding elsewhere that he and Peter Steinbach had specific people in mind when writing the screenplay. The female solidarity that mixes Von Trotta's own experience with Christiane Ensslin's may be *Heller Wahn* (*Sheer Madness* – to borrow the title of the director's far weaker subsequent film), but it is tremendously productive artistically and politically. There are even hints within the film itself that Juliane's prototype is dual, not single: the disparity most viewers discern between Ina Robinski (Juliane as a teenager) and Jutta Lampe (the adult Juliane) has a disorienting effect that recalls the use of two actresses for a single role in Buñuel's *That Obscure Object of Desire.* This effect is not so much "Brechtian" as an intimation of the mystery of the connection between a person's appearance and his or her inner life: As Von Trotta has noted, of the teenagers screen-tested for the role of the younger Juliane, Ina Robin-

It thus seems advisable to avoid drawing on established genres, lest the dead weight of tradition accumulated within them smother one's intended protest against it.

ski resembled Jutta Lampe the least but possessed the largest portion of Juliane's rebellious spirit.* That spirit was, of course, that of Von Trotta herself, who was also reprimanded for wearing black jeans to school. Indeed, given Von Trotta's interest in the theme of doubling, it is hardly surprising that if anything Robinski resembles the director herself more than Jutta Lampe – a similarity most apparent in the photograph of the cast found in the film's printed screenplay.[16]

Generally speaking, non-German criticism of Von Trotta's work has been too respectful of the tendentious reproaches of some of the younger German feminists and filmmakers. Deferring to the Germans' right to speak in their own internal affairs, Ann Kaplan quotes younger filmmakers' criticisms of the successful older woman, not mentioning the extent to which such remarks are the mask of envy,[†] while Thomas Elsaesser describes the film as tainted by its lack of the radicalism of other feminists, a shortcoming that renders it – in the worst of all reproaches – petit bourgeois.[‡] This may indeed be true of much of Von Trotta's other work, but even if *Marianne and Juliane is* petit bourgeois in the sense of being recounted from the point of view of the nonactivist Juliane – though films generally *are* told by on-lookers rather than participants – it simultaneously reveals that per-spective's limitations. Not that Von Trotta is a practitioner of Jamesian irony; her approach is, rather, a *dialectical* one. Elsaesser has apparently forgotten that Marxism defines the position of all intel-lectuals – in a sense, all onlookers – as petit bourgeois. His critique of Von Trotta is thus blindly devoid of the capacity for self-criticism she displays.[¶]

---

* "Bei der Wahl der jüngeren Juliane hatte ich zehn Mädchen, die alle noch keinen Film gemacht hatten und die alle nur nach Ähnlichkeit ausgesucht worden waren. Und da war Ina Robinski, die ich jetzt genommen habe, die, im Vergleich zu allen anderen, Jutta Lampe am unähnlichsten sah. Ich habe mit allen eine Probeaufnahme gemacht und alle anderen waren entsetzlich. Sie war die einzigste, die Momente spontaner Rebellion so ganz beiläufig rüberbrachte."[15]
† "Somewhat older than the current generation of explicitly feminist German women filmmakers, von Trotta (like many first generation female feature-film makers) cannot avoid being marked as a woman who has made it because of her relations with an es-tablished successful male director – her husband, Volker Schlöndorff." Kaplan's uncriti-cal use of "marked" and of the verb "made it" (no quotation marks in original) is either careless or distasteful.[17]
‡ Very cannily, the reproach is placed in the mouth of an imaginary Roland Barthes, enabling Elsaesser to have his cake and eat it: "Roland Barthes would call Von Trotta's approach part of a specifically petit-bourgeois attitude to the world, where knowledge is bounded by what can be recognised in the other as part of the self, by identification, by placing oneself in the position of other." The petit-bourgeois approach is astonishingly productive: Thoroughly applied, it would solve most of our political problems.[18]
¶ Elsaesser seems somewhat to have modified his original view, for the criticism is toned down in his subsequent book, *New German Cinema*:: "Von Trotta's films, 'classical' and even conformist when viewed in terms of an antinarrative avant-garde, nonetheless have a political dimension both within and outside feminist positions, in their intense preoc-

The trend-setting article in the denigration of Von Trotta's film has been Charlotte Delorme's review in the influential feminist journal, *Frauen und Film*. Ellen Seiter begins her conspectus of the film's reception with one of Delorme's most questionable assertions, which she nevertheless fails to question: "If *Die bleierne Zeit* were really what it claims to be it would not have gotten any support, distribution or exhibition."[19] Delorme's comment is doubly tendentious, for it both ignores the very real funding problems Von Trotta encountered* and employs the us–them rhetoric the film strives to undermine. Delorme states that Von Trotta's view of Marianne is identical with the Springer Press's opinion of her prototype, Gudrun Ensslin. She overlooks the film's profound empathy with Marianne, which exists in symbiosis with rejection in the mind of Juliane; such empathy and understanding are singularly absent from the Springer Press, which would have denounced Von Trotta as a *Sympathisant*. Delorme's argument recalls the Stalinist propensity to deem any internal criticism of the Party line "objectively fascist." (One cannot help but wonder if Delorme approves of terrorism.) Denunciation from both left and right is the fate of the dialectician, particularly that of the negative dialectician. (I use the term in Adorno's sense.) The near-universal West German discontent with Von Trotta's film is a sign of the accuracy with which it probes a wounded consciousness.

In its brevity, Von Trotta's film admirably breaks with the German ideology that deems it impossible to say anything of significance in a work less than four hours long. It becomes far easier for it to find a forum, free of the compulsion to automarginalization that can stand as the badge of one's purity. Thus if the film has been marginalized, it is clearly because it touches the nerve centers of German ideology: Neither WDR nor ZDF would help with its financing, which took a year to arrange, while the television transmission was strangely delayed. Since West German filmmakers' dependence on public subsidy has prompted a general avoidance of such sensitive topics as terrorism or the *Berufsverbot* – with many directors retreating into depoliticized existentialism (Wenders) or neo-Romanticism (Herzog) and a Fassbinder courting scandal so as to enjoy the status of enfant terrible and taste the delights of exhibitionist provocation – both the theme of Von Trotta's work and the seriousness of its treatment become all the more admirable. The suspicion with which the left has viewed it becomes all

cupation with identity, doubling, splitting, and the transference between self and other" (p. 237).
* The problems are documented, for instance, in the *Filmfaust* interview, p. 33: After rejection by the WDR, with which Von Trotta had made her previous films, and the ZDF, it was accepted by the SFB, though the two young editors who supported it encountered strong resistance. The SFB financing was inadequate, however, and funds had to be assembled from three other sources.

the more disturbing. Its dialectic of familiarity and Otherness, which discovers Otherness in the family rather than at the distance that permits its safe idealization, destabilizes the dichotomies that enable one to establish satisfaction with one's own position. In an article that antedates the analysis in her "Women and Film," Ann Kaplan seems to hold against Von Trotta the degree to which "her text leaves itself open to various, contradictory readings," noting "the danger that the positions of her narrator, Juliane, will be taken as the positions of the film."[20] Lest it seem that Kaplan underestimates the sophistication of the viewer, one should remember that it is precisely this danger to which the *Frauen und Film* reviewer succumbed – as do all viewers who simply identify Marianne as Gudrun Ensslin. Von Trotta's film clearly problematizes the realist worldview of such critics through its own unsettled relationship with its own prototypes. It is not a documentary window on current West German reality, but a fiction whose occlusion of the reality of the Ensslins' lives allows it to illuminate those lives through the creation of *typological* characters, rather like those of Proust – whose great work is also about memory, repression, and reconstruction – and rather as advocated in Lukács's theory of the typical character. Von Trotta's uncanny world is one in which the exact import of surfaces is unclear. When the father shows his daughters such images of suffering as the Grünewald crucifixion or the concentration camp footage in *Nuit et brouillard*, is he seeking to persuade them that pain is all that awaits woman in this world, to imbue them with masochism, or is he seeking to enlighten them? If the film is full of echoes – presenting in a sense the suffering body in a hall of mirrors – are the echoes familiar or alienating? The film's reality is fundamentally ambiguous.

## Black and white in color

The ambiguities of *Marianne and Juliane* extend into its look, which is black and white in color. It is perhaps an anticolor film. Black and white are the colors of the sweaters Marianne exchange during one of the prison visits: a swap that also shows neither side here can be black or white. Black and white are also the colors of "Schwarze Milch der Frühe" ["Black milk of dawn"], the first words of Paul Celan's shattering poem about the concentration camps, "Todesfuge," to which both sisters obliquely refer.* Black milk is the color of their *Frühe* also, their youth. The film's colors are heavy, drained. Daniel Cohn-Bendit suggests in his review that the flashback sequences could have

---

* Within Von Trotta's film Celan fulfills a function analogous to that of Hölderlin in Böll's novel. The appeal of "Todesfuge" for Von Trotta surely derives in specific part from its recurrent "dein goldenes Haar Margarethe."

been done in monochrome[21] – an option in fact weighed and rejected by Von Trotta and her cameraman, Franz Rath.[22] Like the leveling of different times in Straub's *Not Reconciled*, the persistence of muted colors shows the fifties and the late seventies to be cross sections through the same leaden time. History's changelessness is numbing. As she packs some makeup for her imprisoned sister, Juliane remarks that Marianne needs more color in her life; yet she herself is so attuned to her sister as to be hardly able to provide it: Marianne will tell Juliane to wear something more colorful when visiting her. The only color to rupture the greens, blues, and browns is the red that issues from Hell on earth: red of the flames dancing on Jan's back as he runs from the forest den set on fire by someone aware of his mother's true identity; red of the pulpited father perceived in the glow of hellfire-preaching by his daughters. In eschewing the monochrome associated with nostalgia in recent films, *Marianne and Juliane* shows it feels no longing for the past. Nor does it hover between monochrome and color in the unsystematic fashion *A Mirror* or *Heimat* employ to lend mystery to the past.* For Von Trotta, the past is no mystery, but cut from the same gray cloth as the present. It has never gone away.

It is intriguing to place *Heimat* alongside *Marianne and Juliane* for another reason also. Whereas *Heimat* prefaces each of its episodes with a narrator figure – Glasisch-Karl, who shuffles photographs that seem mostly to have originated in Eduard's collection, presorting the past, perhaps in order to omit the unexpected or the traumatic – it is not until the end of *Marianne and Juliane* that a narrator figure emerges. Although retrospectively the whole film can be seen to have been filtered through the consciousness of Juliane, who is about to begin telling Marianne's story to Jan (her narration will be a response to Jan's *tearing up* of his mother's photograph, rather than to a whole photograph, as in the case of Glasisch-Karl), the postponement of the revelation of a narrator until the film's end allows us to experience its events without the sense of a protective presence interposed between them and ourselves. The "unmediated" quality of classic cinema is exploited to expose us directly to the horror of events. With the designation of one of the characters as a narrator figure, we become aware that the story can be told differently – and that it is our task to do so. In *Heimat* this awareness is suppressed by the (very traditional – think of the many novels "introduced" by editor figures who have found a bundle of letters in the attic) movement away from Glasisch-Karl and into the heart of the narrative. Its postponement until the end

---

* Reitz's film does finally develop a sort of system for the regulation of the shifts, which are often associated with moments of violence or epiphany, and very often with flame, but in the early sections the alternation is deliberately random, as it is in Tarkovsky's great film.

of *Marianne and Juliane* leaves it at the forefront of our minds. It is significant that we are placed in Juliane's position as we leave the cinema, for after doing so we will in all likelihood have to tell the film's story to somebody else. The moment at which the narrator's presence is unveiled is the sting in the tail of the film. Von Trotta thus compels us to share Juliane's burden, to measure our own seriousness against that of the surviving German sister.

If the tendency of writing on Weimar film has been to focus on the fantastic and upon the implicit male spectator – be it the Oedipally defeated spectator of Kracauer or the poststructurally destabilized one of Thomas Elsaesser – a counterweight has been thrown into the balance recently in the form of Patrice Petro's *Joyless Streets: Women and Melodramatic Representation in Weimar Germany*. Petro's perspective is feminist and deeply indebted to Laura Mulvey, but the precise aim of her book is unclear; for although she claims that she is not seeking "to 'correct the balance' of film historiography, as it were, or simply to provide an account of the female subject to match existing accounts of the male subject during this period" (p. xxiv), her choice of films undermines this claim, for she brings to the fore melodrama – a term whose ambiguities she never discusses – and the *Dirnentragödie:* A canon appealing primarily to female spectators is placed under analysis. Despite Petro's apparent wish to overthrow Kracauer's master narrative, all her selection does is indicate his failure to tell *the whole story.** A truly radical attempt to overturn the male bias Petro discerns

* In fact, Kracauer's book tells more of the story than many critics admit, focusing as they mostly do on its 1919–24 section, in which the Caligari-to-Hitler thesis is developed. Kracauer's primary strategy for establishing the degree of unity of the period's film production involves tracking the recurrence and transformation of certain motifs – from the figure of the authoritarian leader to the image of the spiral. There are, of course, many less frequent ones (e.g., the use of the ruin in *Nosferatu* and *M*), and Kracauer's focus on the most common creates an effect of monotony enhanced by his greater interest in repetition than in transformation. Moreover, if – as he argues – film's close correspondence to the wishes of the populace renders it the best sociological gauge of the movement of moods across the period, it is surely strange that his narrativization of Weimar film history should take as its keywork an art movie that enjoyed little popular success (*The Cabinet of Dr. Caligari*). His postulate would also seem to require that he accord far more attention to the specifics of spectator reaction than he does. A teleological fatalism vitiates the thesis: Once the filmic mold has been set by *Caligari*, nothing can break it; and when it *does* break, it is only to release Caligari into reality, as Hitler – like a negative version of the old Faust's liberation from Mephisto's mirror in Murnau's film. There is thus a sense in which everything that follows the 1919 – 24 section forms an enormous parenthesis to the governing thesis, with even apparent alternatives (e.g., *Whither Germany?* [*Kuhle Wampe*]) incorporated into the inevitable flow.

in Weimar film historiography would address the films on which the accepted critical narrative of Oedipal defeat has been based: *The Student of Prague, Caligari, Nosferatu, Waxworks, Metropolis,* and so on. To be fair, Petro does indeed discuss *Caligari,* but her reading is vitiated by a perverse rejection (justified only by "I believe" [p. 148]) of the feminist scenario Elsaesser proposes as one of the several fluctuating throughout the film. Petro's primary contribution to the interpretation of *Caligari* is the application to it of Linda Williams's comparison of the structures of perception of women in patriarchal film in general to those of the monster in the horror film (not just in "early horror film," as Petro has it, the alteration surreptitiously cementing the link between Williams's hypothesis and her own concerns): Both woman and monster are stigmatized on account of their difference. Petro consequently perceives a resemblance between Cesare and Jane:

To begin with, both Cesare and Jane are perceived as powerfully different from others: Cesare, the somnambulist, inspires the fear and dread of virtually everyone who sees him, while Jane, the only female character in the film, attracts and threatens Francis with an equally trancelike passivity. Cesare is literally the instrument of Caligari, the odd sideshow spectacle who is induced to act out his master's murderous intentions and desires. Jane, too, is constituted as a spectacle, most obviously when she visits Caligari's tent and is made to confront Cesare's hypnotic stare. (p. 148)

To describe Jane as exhibiting a threatening trancelike passivity akin to Cesare's is extraordinary. But if Petro's final statement seems particularly implausible (after all, it is Cesare who is being displayed leeringly by Caligari), it is because of her failure to note how the scene's composition causes us to focus on Jane, and because of the vagueness of the reference to "spectacle": The object of the joint gaze of Caligari and Cesare, Jane's dark head, contrasts strongly with the white background, a fact that combines with its placement on the right (the side toward which the "reading eye" naturally travels) to draw our attention. She is not constituted as akin to the monster, however, but as distraught victim. Jane and Cesare may indeed move somnambulistically (or at least the Jane of the framing device may move thus), but that is hardly sufficient reason to state "that Cesare seems to recognize her vulnerability and difference as similar to his own may indeed account for the strange sympathy that he later demonstrates for her" (ibid.). Cesare's motives are unclear, as Petro's "seems" and "may" concede, but they can be accommodated within Elsaesser's Freudian model: The creature shares his master's impotence vis-à-vis women, and cannot insert the phallic knife. The ease with which he had killed men suggests latent homosexuality between him and Caligari – think of the latter's extreme grief on viewing his dead body, or his surreal, mothering feeding of the creature – in which case his decision to spare Jane would mark the discovery of a heterosexuality he is unable to sustain: the flight into nature, into natural desire, ends in collapse and is never really possible – nature is merely a set. Merely a shadow, Cesare mimics an artificial tree and crumples. In the attempted murder scene, however, Jane's vulnerability is strangely powerful: Her prone image dominates it; and when Cesare appears in the background he is tiny, as if infantile. When he carries her off across the rooftops, the fact that he is clearly bearing a dummy may make one wonder if he is no more able to capture "the real Jane" than Francis is to keep watch on "the real Cesare," as he gazes at a replica while the real one roams free. (Cesare's freedom here is a sign of the body's liberty to wander during dreams. This may help one solve the narrative conundrum of how Caligari can work at the fair and not be missed as asylum director: He is probably at the fair *in his dreams*.)

Cesare and Jane do indeed resemble one another in certain respects – the beast who spares beauty is himself beautiful, lithe in his leotard and bearing in the final scene a deathly lily that renders him as virginal as she – but the resemblance does not allow one to term either "a monster." The dualism on which the horror film is based is in fact absent from *Caligari*: It does not exploit us–them mechanisms, but sympathizes at points with Caligari (his treatment by the town clerk). Instead there is a complex web of implicit and explicit doubling in which *all* the characters partially resemble one another or can be seen to act on another's behalf (Cesare, the disavowed agent of Francis's will to exclusive possession of Jane, kills Allen; while the Allen–Francis bonding doubles that of Caligari and Cesare, and so on). Doubling brings the monster back home, showing him (and her) to be "one of us," a protagonist in the Oedipal family romance centered on the unattainable (and, in this film, unrepresentable) mother. If the film represses the mother (present, perhaps, as the womblike interior in which all events unfold?), it is surely because of the danger she poses in the Oedipal scenario; but the repressed returns through her daughter. For Jane too is unattainable, a status that places her as it were at the center of the spoked pattern of the asylum courtyard: Claimed by all, she can be held by none. To hold her is to die – as does Cesare in the framed story. Jane's unattainability stuns the elements of suspense and desire in the narrative into near-static tableaux. Partly code for her unspeakable possession by the father, that *other* Doctor, it justifies the disembodiment of the cinematic look.

Elsewhere, Petro contends that the "unstable identification" Elsaesser discerns in *Pandora's Box* is "bound to a male spectator position"

(p. 17). I would argue, however, that the emergence of cinema in a period of intense questioning of male–female roles and relationships renders somewhat dubious the theory of the gendered spectator – a theory whose apparent validity where the most sexist of Hollywood films are concerned becomes problematic when one considers that even *Gentlemen Prefer Blondes* has supported feminist readings. If Petro is right to question Elsaesser's contention that Pabst's achievement in *Pandora's Box* "is to have presented sexuality *in* the cinema as the sexuality *of* the cinema" ("Lulu and the Meter Man," p. 33), it is less because of any lack of cogency in the suggestion than because of the gnomic manner of its formulation, which elides the link between "in" and "of." That link lies in the impossibility of aligning the camera's point of view with the viewpoint of any one person – an impossibility that is constitutive of cinema, and which classic Hollywood films strive to conceal by creating an *apparent* identity, belying the fact that even when we see what the character sees we virtually never see it as he/she sees it, with the exception of moments (or even whole films that are "moments" in film history, e.g., *The Lady in the Lake*) codified as "excessive." The resultant slipperiness of subject positions generates an ambisexual (albeit often an *unconsciously* ambisexual) viewer. Petro appears to believe that every female spectator is all woman, and every male one all man: a belief that is somewhat too prevalent in feminist scholarship.

In the light of Petro's use of melodrama as a "woman's form," to be accorded a privileged position in feminist film histories, it may be worthwhile devoting some space here both to a general characterization of the form and to one film that falls under this category. (The film I have chosen is *La Habañera,* which is of interest as the last film made in Germany by Douglas Sirk, then known as Detlef Sierck, and as one of the films watched by Maria and Pauline in Reitz's *Heimat.*)

Music (*melos*) may be a defining component of melodrama, but it should not be confused with the tragedy that was born of the spirit of music. Melodrama is set clearly apart from tragedy through its dependence on the sensation of shock – and on shock to induce sensation per se. In tragedy all the reversals and catastrophes grow logically out of the original dramatic material. In melodrama, however, they arrive unexpectedly: Disaster is not precipitated by profoundly rooted character traits (hamartia) or the deep structures of reality (myth and the workings of the gods) but by purely fortuitous events. The paradigm is perhaps the way Tess's letter in Hardy's *Tess of the D'Urbervilles* slides under the door – and then under the carpet. If tragic events unfold with the appearance of inevitability, the accidental nature of melodramatic occurrences implies that things could always have been different. This sense of possible difference is not Musil's *Möglichkeitsdenken,* however, but the culture industry's willingness to overhaul the product to render it more salable. Melodrama does not draw the modernist conclusion from the unforeseeable nature of events in the contemporary world – it does not juxtapose the alternatives with one another – but keeps them in reserve to tantalize the public (who shot J. R.?). It torments one with an excruciating sense of "if only *this* had not happened." One of the consequences of melodrama's lack of inevitability is its potential endlessness. The author of a melodrama is not restricted to the material with which he begins, which imposes its own logic, but is able to throw in extraneous matter as and when he likes. Thus the melodrama is an expansionist form – the form of a Balzac or Dickens – founded on serial accumulation. This expansionism is most apparent in the compulsive additiveness of nineteenth-century melodrama, a concomitant of the perennial additions being made to the world by science, colonialism, and capitalism. If tragedy is the expression of a closed society, melodrama embodies the modern ideology of endless growth. In the soap opera, the degraded descendant of melodrama, this endlessness takes the form of successive permutations of a basic set of characters, none of whom can die, whose varying fortunes ultimately become absurd or grotesque. The endlessness of the serial is due to the fundamentally dualistic nature of characterization in the melodramatic form, which forbids any resolution: Good and Evil are split in perpetuity, and so the possibility of closure offered by tragedy – the moment of ironic realization that good and evil can be one, the dissonant synthesis that ends the plays of Sophocles or Racine – is no longer available. The melodrama's form is dictated by insatiability. Here the ancestor of melodrama proves to be the panlogism of *Clarissa*. Clarissa and Lovelace can never be one, only fall away from one another continually toward their opposed destinations: heaven and hell. For much of the time, Samuel Richardson's novel seems to be in free fall, with the apparent endlessness of the later melodramatic serial, but in the end it does concede the presence of death. As *Clarissa* draws near to its close, the melodrama is infiltrated mysteriously by tragic accents. Richardson realizes that only through the death of his characters can he prevent them from coalescing. Melodrama is compelled to admit the tragic principle of death so as to preserve its own dualism. Its most sincere tears are over the necessity of its own demise.*

---

* The defining feature of melodrama is often seen to be a lurid clash of extremes. I hope it will not add still further particles to the semantic cloud orbiting the term if I distinguish between a melodrama that is natural (even "realistic"), and one that is unnatural. In societies lacking a strong middle class, life has a natural extremism and violent chiaroscuro. Where the reality an artist confronts lacks such contrasts, he or she will be

The absolute dualism characteristic of melodrama pervades *La Habañera* and indicates that, although Goebbels may have favored indirect propaganda over the explicit agitation found in the Soviet cinema (the subtlety of indirection testifying to the "higher" nature of German culture, as well as rendering the propaganda more insidious), the form's dualism helps disseminate the us–them psychology that placed the German psychic economy on a war footing. (It is piquant that Sirk himself should have described it as "an anticapitalist film" [*Sirk on Sirk*, p. 50].) *La Habañera* stars Zarah Leander as Astree, a Swedish girl visiting Puerto Rico with her aunt; she is enchanted by the island's paradisical nature and struck by the impromptu bullfighting of a local grandee, Don Pedro de Avila. When the two women are due to leave the island, Astree jumps ship at the last minute and marries Don Pedro. Ten years later, however, she is deeply discontented. Her aunt, the patroness of a Swedish medical foundation, despatches Doctor Nagel – an old flame of Astree's – on a double mission to Puerto Rico: to discover a vaccine for the Puerto Rico fever and to rescue Astree. Don Pedro's opposition to both these enterprises (if Puerto Rico is known to harbor fever, the effects on the economy will be disastrous, and his Spanish temperament forbids him from freeing his wife) is frustrated when he is struck down by the fever, having ordered the destruction of the antidote Nagel had devised. As *La Habañera* plays, its instrumentation showing that the song has again been engulfed by the lush exoticism of the island, the ship leaves, bearing Nagel, Astree, and the very blond son of her defunct marriage.

*La Habañera* is a treatise on relations with the foreign. The foreign is in a sense brought by the wind, which crosses borders unchecked. The song that first enchants Astree begins "Der Wind hat mir ein Lied erzählt" ["The wind has told me a song"]: The story it tells is one of natural freedom. Astree is appalled at the thought of losing herself amid the starchy mores and faces of Stockholm, and chooses wild paradise instead. Later, when she remarks that paradise has become hell, the wind has turned around; it is now the hot wind that brings *fever*. The film identifies Puerto Rico with oppressive heat, and Sweden with inviting snow: When the aunt first consults with Nagel, the camera is unable to resist the snow's invitation and passes out of the window;

virtually compelled to create them – lest his or her work seem tedious. Thus in the English and French nineteenth-century novelistic tradition melodrama becomes the converse of realism – even though it may then be inserted into it, as galvanizing spark, soul into body. In societies such as nineteenth-century Russia or Germany, however, the absence of a strong middle class renders melodrama "natural." (It begins to be artificial in Germany with the tentative rise of the middle class: whence the strain underlying the expressionist use of stylistic chiaroscuro to impose – i.e., *preserve* – contrast.) Between these extremes, of course, lies the divided artist: aristocratically "free," but only in imagination; impecunious and oppressed, yet imaginatively unconstrained.

on a white rug that recalls snow, Astree playacts sledding with her son Juan; and when Nagel visits her household, it is clear that he and Astree are likeminded, for he sleds down the steps with Juan (being a male he is of course more adventurous). The ten years that elapse before Astree's rescue may remind the 1937 viewer of 1927: of the *Systemzeit,* when Germany was "lost," wild, un-Germanic. (The film's obsession with leaping numbers – e.g., 200 to 200,000 – recalls a propensity of interwar German ideology Canetti links to the twenties experience of inflation.) Hence it is hardly surprising that when celebrating his triumph over the fever – a victory an earlier American team had failed to win, as the film pointedly underlines – Nagel's manic air should be proto-SS. Astree's status as Swedish rather than German shows the subtlety of the film's ideological workings. Swedish, of course, is Nordic too – so she is "one of us."*

In making Astree a Swede, the film is able to argue that Germany is not xenophobic (giving Nagel a Brazilian companion reinforces this argument): We may dislike Puerto Ricans (mongrel versions of the Spanish we supported in 1936 – just the previous year), but then so do the Swedes, who are noted for their neutrality (i.e., objectivity). The inference that we are in fact tolerant of the foreigner upon our doorstep (the Swede) masks Germany's intention of going to war with its neighbors – concealing it even from the German population, even as it prepares for it subliminally. It is surely significant that the Swedish doctor should have a German surname. (Crossing the borders of another country will be simply supplying "fraternal aid.") The pseudoscientific vocabulary in the scenes of the clandestine hotel-room assault on the fever bacillus flatters the audience with pseudoknowledge and reiterates a common topos of paranoid Nazi propaganda, which underscored the danger of invisible germs. (They are no more invisible to the doctor than the Jews trying to pass for Aryans are to the commentator's voice that enlightens us in *The Eternal Jew:* The doctor peers through his microscope and comments that the bacteria are not invisible at all.) The fever is not only wind-borne but is carried by the rats the Nazis identify with the Jews. In contrast to Puerto Rico, the Nordic countries are clinically snow white. To succumb to Latin Romanticism is to allow oneself to be feminized (i.e., to watch a "woman's picture"), to be a woman, an Emma Bovary who wants to "live a novel" (as Don Pedro says Astree is capable of doing, early on in the film). Fortunately there are German men who have kept themselves pure, who have tended the old flame of devotion, and

* Like her near-namesake *Asta* Nielsen, also from the North – the audience may make little distinction between Denmark and Sweden – who acted in twenties German films; and so Zarah Leander becomes by association an actress as great as Nielsen.

can rescue the lost love and the son who is so blond as to be eminently worth reclaiming. Zarah Leander may sing *La Habañera* one more time near the end, before we know of the imminent happy ending, resplendent in full Spanish regalia, but this is a final fling for the viewer. To underline the point, the song is played again as the ship leaves, with native instrumentation and rhythms. It is clear that no self-respecting Nordic would find it alluring any longer. It has been contaminated and must be abandoned: It is only melody, stripped of the German words and Zarah Leander voice that allowed us – like Astree herself – to succumb to its seduction. We can go home happy to be us, glad that they inhabit the faraway places. (And so when Maria and Pauline attend this film in *Heimat,* the pleasure it offers is by no means the innocent one Reitz suggests.)

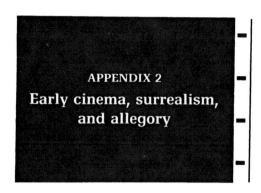

# Early cinema, surrealism, and allegory

Early cinema is an art of allegory; and it is due to the profoundly rooted modern (post-Romantic) opposition to allegory that its displacement was inevitable. Its primary allegorical feature is its location of writing and image on the same plane. In *The Origin of German Tragic Drama*, Walter Benjamin quotes Schopenhauer's condemnation of allegory, which nevertheless shows a grasp of its complicity with writing:

When, therefore, an allegorical picture has also artistic value, this is quite separate from and independent of what it achieves as allegory. Such a work of art serves two purposes simultaneously, namely the expression of a concept and the expression of an Idea. Only the latter can be an aim of art; the other is a foreign aim, namely the trifling amusement of carving a picture to serve at the same time as an inscription, as a hieroglyphic. . . . It is true that an allegorical picture can in just this quality produce a vivid impression on the mind and feelings; but under the same circumstances even an inscription would have the same effect. For instance, if the desire for fame is firmly and permanently rooted in a man's mind . . . and if he now stands before the *Genius of Fame* (by Annibale Carracci) with its laurel crowns, then his whole mind is thus excited, and his powers are called into activity. But the same thing would also happen if he suddenly saw the word "fame" in large clear letters on the wall. (*Origin of German Tragic Drama*, pp. 161–2; ellipses by Benjamin)

Benjamin remarks that the last comment comes close to touching on the essence of allegory; it is also prescient of the mechanism of silent film, in which intertitle and image are interchangeable. The silent screen does not simply display in the form of intertitles the writing that was to vanish from the cinema until Godard's Brechtian devices restored it; it also uses rhetorical gestures and mime, which stand in for words and indicate that the intertitles are not "foreign matter" troublingly inserted into the "realist illusion," but have been solicited into the work by its images' mimesis of language. If Benjamin failed to perceive that the allegory he thought dead was really alive in early cinema, it may have been because of an instinctive awareness of the death sentence hanging over it: of the manner in which the accusation of "rootlessness" was to underlie the killing both of the Jews and of silent cinema, dissociated as the latter was from the real world in which people *speak*. Was not the rejection of silent cinema a rejection of *the immigrant* and the otherness of his or her silence? (Cf. "Realism, Totalitarianism, and the Death of Silent Cinema" in Chapter 1.)

As silent cinema is about to die, however, it seeks support in the only allegorical hermeneutic compatible with the bourgeois world: that of psychoanalysis. It is a psychoanalytic hermeneutic destabilized, rendered ultimately self-destructive, by its employment to dissolve the ego rather than to reinforce it, as Freud had intended. Hence surrealist cinema gives one the *silent*, rather than the talking, cure. Its silence is a refusal to admit the necessity of any other cure than the madness itself. Rather than translate the image into an allegory, to be deciphered by reason, it transforms it into a fetish: As an allegory that denies its own allegorical status, it simulates the presence of an object that is in fact absent: for Freud, the penis whose absence from the female anatomy generates castration anxiety in the male. Surrealism, in taking psychoanalysis as its fetish, reveals psychoanalysis itself to be a form of fetishism: fetishism being in fact the fundamental form of all allegorical reading, which expresses an attachment to something history has displaced by both recognizing and disavowing that displacement. The model for this is the simultaneous displacement and fulfillment of the Old Testament by the New: History is dialectically preserved and canceled. Thus allegorical thinking is a dialectical thinking that is also double think: The object is thought as both present and absent, intrinsically valuable and valueless. Such thought is born of crisis: An old order has been displaced so violently that its afterimage persists in the minds of those unhabituated as yet to the definitive nature of its departure. Allegory is thus an attempt to cope with history conceived as the catastrophe of sudden loss. (A fixation on the Sublime, meanwhile, values only the new and sees the ruin of the old as positive.) The dream, the fetish of the surrealists, is present inasmuch as its condensations and displacements anticipate those of the surrealist artwork, but *absent* inasmuch as that work is merely the simulation of a dream. Here surrealism reveals its role as the antagonist of psychoanalysis, its hostile double: Whereas the latter seeks to restore order to chaos by means of allegory, the former idealizes chaos as the sublime liberation of the libido. This chaos can only be idealized, however, for so long as its name remains unknown, *unspeakable*. Only as the unknown, the unnamable, is it Sublime. When it takes on a name, it ceases to subvert history and becomes instead an active force within history. After the naming that betrays them, the surrealist dreams of the dissolution of the bourgeois individual leave chaos behind and become part of a new order: the order of *fascism*.

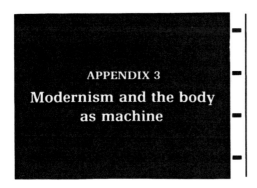

# Modernism and the body as machine

If several modernists present men transformed into animals or insects, even more depict them as having become machines. Even *The Metamorphosis* suggests a link between the two forms of transformation: Gregor's shell is described as *panzerartig*, like armor, and the donning of armor is a rudimentary form of mechanization of the body. This interest in the body as automaton had been manifest in the work of Hoffmann, but only with the advent of modernism does it become a widespread theme. In some cases the identity of man is fused completely with that of the machine: Eliot's Tiresias throbs waiting like a taxi, while the typist whose seduction he has witnessed "smoothes her hair with automatic hand, / And puts a record on the gramophone" – her hand passing across her hair with the automatism of the record player's hand jerking across to land on the record's outer rim. In the works of other modernists man is either the ghost within the machine or exists in dual form, as both man and machine. In each case, the native softness of the human body is opposed to its potential hardness.

Broch's Joachim von Pasenow can be seen to exemplify the former alternative. Soft and vulnerable within the hard shell of his uniform, he is an *emotional* creature whose expressions of feeling are nevertheless firmly corseted by his other identity as social machine, cog in the Prussian Junker order. He is correspondingly divided between two women: Ruzena, the girl from Bohemia, whose imperfect mastery of German corresponds to Joachim's own inability to express himself, and Elisabeth, the landowner's daughter he is expected to marry, a feat he achieves with heroic self-delusion. Pasenow's uniform is a refuge from the perils of civilian life, with its continual imperative to act and choose for oneself; it cocoons his nakedness and prevents him from dissolving, jellylike, into the amorphous mass of longing that constitutes his innermost self. The uniform was to be a fatal refuge to the Germans of Broch's own generation, of course, and to that extent his novel – written between 1928 and 1931 – is trenchantly prophetic. Pasenow's father, however, is entirely a machine, with a machine's angularity (stressed repeatedly in the descriptions of his exterior) and ruthlessness. His son Joachim is incapable of breaking out of the shell that constrains him, for if its hard machinelike exterior were removed he would deliquesce.

If Broch depicts in Pasenow an uneasy ghost within a machine, Musil is interested in the body as a dual entity: both soft, feminine, artistic, and emotional on the one hand, and masculine, scientific, a concatenation of muscles and chemical reactions on the other. Hence on the one hand there is Diotima, with her nineteenth-century notions of art and spirituality; and on the other there is Ulrich (and, by implication, Musil himself), for whom, as for Brecht, art is tonic, akin to sport. The double body – the body as both soul and mechanism – can only become a unity through hermaphroditism, the utopian state that is the goal of Musil's attempt to unite the sexes, the separate languages of art and science, and stitch back together a divided world. This double body can be found again in Fritz Lang's *Metropolis,* in the two incarnations of Maria, both priestess of reconciliation and robot likeness preaching revolt. In both Musil and Lang, the doubling of the body entails a splitting of consciousness that arouses apocalyptic fears – though Lang dishonestly resolves the issue where Musil leaves it, and his novel, open. (It is very apt that the central conceit of *The Man without Qualities* should be that of the *Parallel* Action, since a parallel is a duality whose components meet only in the endlessly deferred place known as infinity.)

Perhaps the main reason for this interest in the body as mechanism during this period is the growth of materialism, which deemed life an exclusively this-worldly enterprise. But if the soul was to disappear – its destination having evaporated – what was to prevent the human body becoming simply a thing among other things, primus inter pares perhaps, but objectlike all the same? The threat was all the greater, since society's transformation into an increasingly efficient totalitarian, centralized machine required the individual to identify with it. As new vehicles emerged to provide new forms of transportation, people wondered about the nature of the relationship between them and the creature they enclosed. Was it one of homology or symbiosis? Was the body an alien entity within the machine (as soft as the jelly at the center of the Daleks)? Was the machine simply an artificial extension of human capacities? Or was human consciousness being changed by its changing world? If one was an object among objects, a reified statistic, how could one tell people from objects, or be distinguished from a thing by one's neighbor? The image of the robot begins to haunt the imagination, all the more so as film emerges and presents human beings as pure exteriority, their inner lives corroded or absent. To return to *Metropolis:* How can one tell the two Marias apart? Lang himself shirks the issue: The robot Maria is eliminated; the ultimate regressiveness of the film, its failure to work through the themes it initially conjures, can be seen to be inherent in its iconography, specifically – in the traditional thatched dwelling, beneath the futuristic city, inhabited by the scientist Rotwang, which is the regressive heart beating below the film's modernist surface. In recent art however such evasiveness has proved impossible. For Thomas Pynchon, for instance, men have become indistinguishable from machines, as artificial intelligence mimics human consciousness and behavior to the point of indistinguishability. Pynchon documents the symbiosis with cool irony: Consciousness has become so self-alienated, so blinded by ideology to its true position in this society and on this earth, that it finally consents to alienation from its first seat, the human body. The object acquires its status as fetish by vampirically absorbing consciousness from the adjacent humans (who then become humanoid). This apocalypse has none of Lang's melodrama: It is the steady state of homogenization we currently inhabit, mistaking computerized patterns for the music of the spheres.

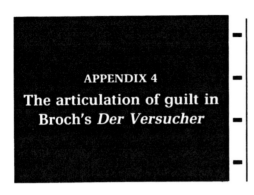

# The articulation of guilt in Broch's *Der Versucher*

*Der Versucher* (*The Tempter*; otherwise known as *Die Verzauberung* and *Der Bergroman*) tells of the fatal influence exerted upon a mountain community by a gold-obsessed charismatic leader, who persuades it to reinstitute human sacrifice; narrated by a doctor who is a precursor of Mann's Serenus Zeitblom, the book is Hermann Broch's allegory of the workings of National Socialism. Set in the heartland of the *Heimat-film*, it was the first major German literary text to dramatize the relationship between the *Heimat* ideology and National Socialism. The work's ultimate failure may reflect the difficulty of establishing the mediations between country and city in a land only recently unified – a difficulty Edgar Reitz utilizes to virtually sever the links and cut the countryside free of responsibility for the Third Reich – and may also demonstrate that the mountain is too central a totem of German literature for the self-reflexive effort to critique the ideology associated with it to succeed. Now that *Heimat* ideology seems to be resurgent in the German-speaking countries – Reitz's *Heimat* itself having been extended into a second installment – Broch's work of the mid-thirties has acquired a new timeliness.

*Der Versucher* – the unified version of the fragmentary *Bergroman* assembled following Broch's death by the editors of the Zurich edition – is a fascinating text: Consciously opposed to National Socialism, it nevertheless carries a clear imprint of a Heideggerian rhetoric of Being that constituted, as it were, the high cultural legitimation of *Blut und Boden* ideology – what Adorno has termed "the jargon of authenticity." Unity is possessed by nature, the mountains that tower above the village and harbor wisdom and perhaps gold: such mountains of course formed a keystone of proto-Nazi and Nazi ideology. Nature's unity symbolizes the possibility that all the multiple forms into which the modern self has disintegrated can knit together again. Broch's narrator is obsessed both with nature and with unity, on which he meditates in lengthy, hymnic ruminations. It can be argued that it is this obsession that cripples his effort to combat the deadly purpose of the villagers, inspired by the roving outsider Marius, which culminates in the sacrifice of the willing Irmgard at a Celtic mountain stone. As the youthful followers of Marius – blood kin of the *Hitlerjugend* – advance with devilish masks and pitchforks to prepare the sacrifice, the return of the old gods becomes a claustrophobic nightmare. (One may compare D. H. Lawrence's near-contemporary *Plumed Serpent*, where the gods' return is simply wishful thinking, so the consequences of their real resurrection – consequences Broch himself had seen in actuality – do not have to be faced.) At the same time, the long-windedness of Broch's narrator is somehow comfortable, distanced. His distance does not suggest the obtuseness of Mann's Zeitblom, for Broch's own style (except in his earliest, most expressionist works) is comfortable in an analogous fashion: Broch becomes a metaphysical Matisse, calmly stroking the vague big themes of Time, Nature, and Death, losing sight of the reality in which the characters confront their dilemmas. A frequent motif in Broch's works is the linkage of the characters by the air they breathe, which seems to issue from the lungs of the narrator: It removes them from the dangerous, fragmented modern world, with its individualism, to a preindividual, *prenovelistic* condition. (In Broch's works, unlike the *Ulysses* he so admired, myth is not a stage from whose depths the characters are separated and upon which they walk, but one with multiple trapdoors through which they all fall.) When the dance that precedes the sacrifice is likened to the dance of the mountains ("so tanzen die Berge," p. 450), the specific sense of social menace dissolves in metaphysical wonder, as the narratorial camera draws back from the scene and frames it in beauty. Describing how the assembled crowd roared for the sacrifice, the doctor adds that he too may have screamed for it ("Es mag sein, dass auch ich mitgeschrien habe," p. 461). Is he striving to suppress the memory of his participation, or does he genuinely not remember? His amnesia is prophetic of an all-too-widespread German reaction to the aftermath of the Third Reich.

*Sein* – that Heideggerian keyword – is a key one in *Der Versucher* also. The preoccupation with Being can allow one to forget that the peasant's greater intimacy with the elemental forces of nature is bought at the price of a greater brutality than characterizes such one-time city dwellers as the persecuted Wetchy, or the doctor himself. The problem in the novel lies in the degree to which Broch's own preoccupation with the fragmentation of modern city experience is ascribed to the doctor. Thus the doctor posits a need for a new religion to replace an etiolated Christianity: Only thus can the idea of community be (re-) established. (This concern for the recovery of a sense of belonging in a community is surely one reason why *eingebettet* should be among Broch's favorite adjectives.) But whereas the old religion allowed a ram to be sacrificed instead of Isaac, the new one requires the father to kill his daughter (an acceptable sacrifice for patriarchy?). The doctor half-expects a ram to appear in the thicket and render unnecessary the death of Irmgard (p. 463). The only animal to manifest itself is the "vielköpfige Tier" [multiheaded beast] of the peasant community, dancing in unified obedience to Marius; all are parts, and so no one is responsible. Just before the sacrifice begins, the text switches to the present tense, heightening the mood of excitement to implicate the reader also in the scene at which he or she has become present. The account of the sacrifice includes a moment of irony rare in Broch – the doctor reflects that he is urging this mock-primitive sacrifice while wearing machine-made clothes (p. 462) – but the overall tonality is febrile. Once the sacrifice has been consummated, the doctor concludes his rueful afterthoughts with the words that it was "sinnvoll doch" [meaningful nevertheless] (p. 479). He too has been fused into the murder he sought to refuse.

The next chapter of the work begins with reflections on the ultimate transience of suffering, which becomes "unerkennbar in der Ganzheit" ["unrecognizable in the whole"] (p. 480).* A glib metaphysical afflatus justifies forgetting. And because its tone is so close to that of Broch himself, be it in his essays or in the reflections he interjects into *Die Schlafwandler* (surely his finest novel), it brings one up short. One may wonder how much sarcasm is intended by a later title such as *Die Schuldlosen (The Guiltless)*. It is as if Broch's characters are indeed guiltless, because no more than corporeal machines, presented with studied exteriority. *Die Schuldlosen* contains a meditation on the way in which individual voices blend into the insectlike hum of a collectivity: This is not, however, the collectivity of a particular time, place, or ideology – of a *Zeitgeist,* for instance – but "das Chorhafte des Seins" ["the choral quality of Being"] (p. 240). The Heideggerian "Sein" is surely a danger signal – for how can "Being" be guilty? Its realm antedates individuation and choice.

Elsewhere in *Die Schuldlosen* the regressiveness of the philosophy of Being has a counterpart in the literary regressiveness of the treatment of the old beekeeper, the "steinerner Gast": He is depicted using a Dickensian device, that is, long before his name is given, a reference to the bees associated with him allows us to identify him and identify with the text that allows us to congratulate ourselves on our prophetic powers after having tantalized us with the possibility that we might be wrong. The implicit reader of such prose is more knowing than the

---

* The text's movement here may be reminiscent of one of the implicitly Nazi montages in Riefenstahl's *Olympia (Olympische Spiele)*, which moves by stages from an individual athlete to the mass ornament of the surrounding group, dissolving separate selfhood in the community.

characters, but less so than the narrator, with whom he is allowed in the end to identify as a special privilege. The complacency of this device indicates Broch's loss of the mordant angularity his prose possessed at its youthful best (e.g., in *Pasenow*). Characters gradually blur into a metaphysical unity that banishes isolation, and with it the sense of sin. As Richard Hieck, the mathematician hero of Broch's early *Die unbekannte Grösse* had noted, "das Isolierte ist sinnlos und sündig zugleich" ["the isolated is senseless and sinful at one and the same time"] (p. 110). Broch's later works dispense guiltlessness. If he disapproves of the doctor's absorption into the brutal community of *Der Versucher*, his disapproval is inarticulate, for his voice dissolves into that of the doctor: His loss of himself is a successful fulfillment of the doctor's unrequited longing for self-loss in the country community. Broch's feelings are thus very much of a piece with those of the Germans who felt that because language belonged to the community, opposition to the Nazi order was bound to remain dumb, inarticulate; and so the potential for resistance to Hitler was never activated, for the germs of revolt were rammed so deep into the frozen soil of isolation and silence that they could never pierce the surface of awareness. The individual who views his own isolation as sinful is unable to use private convictions as a basis for political opposition. The only guiltless option is to lose oneself in *Innerlichkeit* or inner emigration. In Broch's world, to be in a minority of one is to be insane. His embrace of the world-as-totality renders him unwittingly sympathetic to totalitarianism.

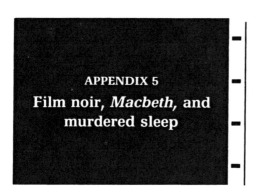

**APPENDIX 5**

Film noir, *Macbeth*, and
murdered sleep

Is there any significance in the fact that the two finest Western directors to have made versions of *Macbeth* – Polanski and Welles – should
also have made a film noir piece (*The Lady from Shanghai* and *Chinatown*) about the same time as their *Macbeth*? Or that these two films
noirs lack many of the traditional elements of the genre, while retaining what to my mind is the keystone of noir ideology, the image of the
threatening female – an image that also dominates *Macbeth*? These
may be merely random thematic and biographical echoes. But are
they?

The fundamental noir scenario is one in which a wife plots with her
lover to murder her husband, who is usually a much older man: *Double Indemnity* and *The Postman Always Rings Twice* are the prototypes, fused in pastiche in Kasdan's *Body Heat*. This scenario is only
tangentially present in *The Lady from Shanghai* and *Chinatown*; the
reason, I suspect, being that Welles and Polanski had already filmed
an alternative version of it, *Macbeth. Macbeth* has every appearance of
being a garbled account of a myth of kingly succession in a matriarchal society: The Queen disposes of the old priest-king (Duncan), who
is no longer referred to as her consort since he can in fact no longer
satisfy her, and she appoints a younger man to take his place (the *rite
de passage* he undergoes to prove his suitability for this role is the
murder of the old king). Whereas in many cultures it is the wife who
is discarded as she ages and becomes unable to bear further offspring
(hence the great irrelevant question posed by L. C. Knights, "How
Many Children Had Lady Macbeth?" is of paradoxical *relevance*), this
underlying scenario projects the male's fear of suffering the same fate
himself: If the wife can be discarded as barren, he in turn may be rejected because unable to satisfy her. Since the female position during
the sexual act is one of reception, the male may imagine her to possess a capacity for endless orgasm the periodicity of his erections forbids him to satisfy. Whence his paranoia, the paranoia of film noir.
This may also be a source of the image of the floating dagger in *Mac-*

*beth:* The mirage of a perennial erection, of an infinite capacity for performance to satisfy a female demand postulated as infinite, hovers before Macbeth.

Both Welles and Polanski tend to act in their own films, and although Polanski does not act in his own *Macbeth*, he *does* appear with a knife in *Chinatown*. The real power, however – as they well know – lies elsewhere, behind the camera they also wield. In placing themselves before the camera also, they betray a sense of helplessness that belies the euphoria of apparent directorial power. For Macbeth is only the instrument in a play whose course is really directed by someone else, with whom he is consubstantial in name: Lady Macbeth. Perhaps it would be more accurate to say: by Woman – woman in the threatening, multiplied form of the weird sisters, who foretell his fate but omit to add that, since prophecies always come to pass, there is no need for his hasty agency to secure the desired crown: It would otherwise fall into his lap. They omit to say this to ensure the consummation of the ritual murder of the old priest-king. (The link between the weird sisters and Lady Macbeth is their transgression of the normal womanly order: Both are "unsexed.") The source of the male paranoia that underlies this play is the power woman wields over man, so he too is unsexed: The phallic dagger floats away from its rightful owner, and Lady Macbeth has to complete the deed. Only the man not born of woman – the one who is totally independent of them – can escape this fatality. Macbeth himself is clearly born of woman (and of Elizabethan/Jacobean worries about the succession): "Mac" = son and "Beth" is part of "Elizabeth." So, on the one hand, Shakespeare suggests an illegitimacy in James's succession to Elizabeth. (He is no Tudor; Macbeth kills Duncan.) But on the other he legitimizes it. (Macbeth = "son of Beth," and so the rightful heir.) The matriarchal descent inscribed in his name legitimizes him.

It is high time, the reader is doubtless thinking, that we returned to film noir. Its dominant feature is the demonization of a strong woman, which may be a mystification of the child's seduction by the mother (who incites him to take the place of the absent/impotent father), but is also a response to the growing power of women in the forties wartime economy: The dominant feature of a genre is always overdetermined. The sense of paranoia felt by the male protagonist reflects the fact that he is being used: The real controlling force lies elsewhere – with mother, who 's pulling the strings. (So noir and *Macbeth* too are, among other things, about the subordinate position of the actor – a position awakening fears of latent homosexuality.) Noir does indeed put the blame on Mame (*Betrayed by Rita Hayworth*), along with so many other vulgar Freudian movies of this period. In this context, *Psycho* reveals itself as the true epitaph of film noir, exploiting for pastiche the generic cycle *Vertigo* had completed. In it the evil Godmother who imposes an Oedipal role on the child of the West reveals her identity as death's head, as Fate. As in *Macbeth,* the phallic knife is alienated from the male and placed in the hands of "Mother." The feel of nightmare in film noir is male terror of matriarchal engulfment.

"Macbeth hath murdered sleep" is the voice Macbeth hears upon killing Duncan. In murdering sleep, Macbeth has destroyed the barriers that keep nightmares out of the realm of day; and so for the rest of the play, they will enshroud the daylight. The murder of sleep deprives consciousness of any refuge from the ache of its pain. In films noirs, whenever the detective stretches out on his bed it is not to sleep but to indicate sleep's impossibility. He stares at the ceiling and watches the neon lights come on. Perennially threatened, he cannot sleep: The place of sleep has been destroyed, and nightmares roam the earth (unleashed by World War II). Existentialism and film noir coincide in their nonrecognition of the unconscious. For Sartre, for instance, to speak of the unconscious is to engage in bad faith, to shirk responsibility for one's actions; it is, as it were, bad for morale. In the first-person world of existentialist fiction, which is as hard-boiled as that of film noir, of the Chandler and Hammett scenarios from which it derives, the responsibility is one for the persistence of reality: If the I closed, the world it registers would disappear too. The detective may yearn for repose, but his world-saving conscience will make sure he stays insomniac.\* Unable to sleep, the detective cannot dream of alternatives to the present; the machinery of the dream work is appropriated and reprogrammed for the elaboration of hypotheses. The end product of this machine's labors is not a dream but a developed picture of the primal scene of the crime that occurred before the book began, during the sleep he dare not sleep again, lest the offense be repeated. The final collapse of consciousness ends the book, permitting another crime, and the inevitable sequel.

---

\* The insomnia of the lover, the other primal protagonist of film noir, is the result of insatiable female sexuality – in *Body Heat* he limps with the effects of her desire.

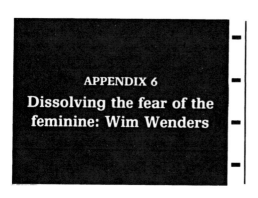

APPENDIX 6
Dissolving the fear of the
feminine: Wim Wenders

Perhaps the best point at which to begin a consideration of Wenders's itinerary, of the road that led him to *Wings of Desire,* is in medias res – with *The State of Things* (*Der Stand der Dinge*), the most self-referential of all his fiction films. *The State of Things* was made during an interval in the tortuous shooting of *Hammett* and showed a film crew stranded on the location of their science fiction film when the money ran out and the director was compelled to visit Hollywood to seek supplementary finance from his American backers (who turned out to be a Mafia group none-too-pleased to have bought into a barely saleable black-and-white European art picture). It was a smoldering meditation on Wenders's own experiences with *Hammett,* the entrée into the American market sought by so many European directors – particularly those who cherish a childhood association of Hollywood with cinema and believe that only if one makes it in America can one be said truly to have arrived. As Wenders watched editors impose a more conventional narrative shape on the abstracted rhythms of his work, his illusions peeled away one by one: They fall languidly like slow-motion apple peel in his short *Reverse Angle.* Wenders perhaps had more illusions to lose than most European directors: In his earlier films the man in a cowboy hat on Hamburg's streets had represented the American colonization of the unconscious of young Germans growing up in the ghost town of their own culture. When Wenders arrived in "Hollywood," of course, he did not encounter the assembly line empire of the studio days. Nevertheless, the largesse offered by one of the new moguls – Coppola – proved to have strings attached, as one would expect with one of the new godfathers of West Coast production. The Coppola–Lucas-financed *Kagemusha* could succeed on Kurosawa's own terms, his affinity with American cinema having long been apparent from the proliferation of Hollywood plagiarisms of his work. But only the director interested in action will find his software compatible with the American marketing hardware. Wenders and the new moguls were patently mismatched: Wenders stands closer to Ozu than

249

to Kurosawa; and until recently his films, slow burns around fetish-ized Americana, have been loving, self-defeating meditations on the impossibility of action, of translating into actuality the male icons of past American cinema (because that cinema is past, because it is American). The rhythms of his sensibility were so clearly alien to those of American narrative, with its kinetic efficiency, that the *Hammett* project can be seen as the final extension of his preoccupation with masochism.

*The State of Things*, with its ink-and-silver images, is a profoundly uncanny circling of the grave of a ruined narrative. If the uncanny sign is one that suggests the existence of another world, but is unable to reveal that world, it becomes possible to understand another apparent anomaly in Wenders's career, *The Scarlet Letter* (*Der scharlachrote Buchstabe*). Hawthorne's brooding worldly otherworldliness is of a piece with the atmosphere of Wenders's work: His signs, like Haw-thorne's, are two-dimensional – the sign that most interests the Puri-tan desirous of the wealth that will indicate divine favor being, in the end, the billboard. If Wenders's *Scarlet Letter* is a disaster, it is per-haps because at this stage of his career he was unable to link his fas-cination by two-dimensional signs – signs whose lack of resistance to decipherment seems too good to be true, so they give one pause even though it seems somehow otiose to spend time on them – to an inter-est in woman as icon. In the early films woman is removed from the work's center, either by murder (*The Goalie's Anxiety at the Penalty Kick* [*Die Angst des Tormanns beim Elfmeter*]), repression (*Kings of the Road*) [*Im Lauf der Zeit*]), splitting (*Wrong Movement* [*Falsche Bewegung*]), or diminution (*Alice in the Cities* [*Alice in den Städten*]). The focus instead is on men looking at signs whose emptiness is partly due to the absence from them of the women who ought to in-habit them: The films' enigma is that of a vacuum that does not wish to be filled.

If narrative can be said to work out the consequences of a pairing (a coupling, a transgression), then early Wenders knows no narrative. There is no desire in these early films, no Oedipal goal or scenario, only the pure passage of time itself, a river bearing no freight. What-ever crises the films present occur at the beginning (Wilhelm leaves home in *Wrong Movement*, Bloch kills the girl in *The Goalie's Anxiety*, the VW flies into the water in *Kings of the Road*); thereafter the work simply marks time. And yet it feels a certain vague anxiety over this: Wilhelm feels that his every movement is false. The fatalism is that of the goalie facing the penalty in the knowledge that whichever way he dives he is almost certain to be wrong. Wenders may speak of his af-finity with Ozu, but the early films emanate repressed disquiet over their own mere drifting. In retrospect it seems almost inevitable that the river of time would flow into that of the unconscious, propelling the protagonist into the Western world of desire. Before considering how and when this happened, however, I would like to look more closely at *Wrong Movement*, whose underestimated density embodies the strengths of early Wenders.

*Wrong Movement* is based on *Wilhelm Meister,* that prototypical *Bildungsroman*. Wenders, however, is clearly determined to subvert the form's goal-oriented linearity: Wilhelm does not develop at all. The degree to which the film is of a piece with the other early works is apparent from words Wilhelm utters in his sleep, "Im Laufe der Zeit" ["in the course of time"], the German title of *Kings of the Road*. The work is an anthology of moments as rich and strange in import as those that stud Bertolucci's *Conformist* – the difference being that whereas Bertolucci dramatizes these moments, Wenders deliberately allows them to congeal, stunning the impulse to decipher them. Thus, before leaving home, Wilhelm looks out onto the town square from an upper floor and smashes the window as a blind man and a blond girl pass below. The couple anticipate Laertes and Mignon as blind man and companion at a subway station, yet the rhyme is off-key, for the film will oppose the adolescent darkness of Mignon to the blond sexuality of Therese. Smashing the window breaks down the dichotomy between looking and acting, but movement is already associated with blindness. The blindness refers also to the potentially Oedipal subtheme in the antagonism between Laertes and Wilhelm, who is aware of the former's Nazi past, but any hint that Wilhelm might have to engage in a struggle with Laertes for the mother figure is short-circuited by the fact that his sole property is the asexual Mignon: It is as if Wenders sets up the Oedipal theme so as to undermine it. The relationship between Mignon, Wilhelm, and Therese is shown with tantalizing obliquity and is riddlingly unresolved. (The subversion of Oedipal elements extends into a refusal to resolve enigmas.) The relationship begins as Wilhelm is leaving his home town for Bonn; driven by unrest, he departs to become a writer. As he sits in the train, he catches sight of some specks of blood on the opposite seat, and thinks someone must have had a nosebleed. We then see the adolescent Mignon (Nastassja Kinski – identified as Nastassja Nakyszynski in the credits) seated at an angle to him on the other side of the train's gangway. The cut from the blood to her glance in Wilhelm's direction suggests that in thinking of a nosebleed as its cause Wilhelm has repressed the possibility of female sexuality: Visible at the seat's edge, the blood could also have been menstrual. She herself glances at the blood, and he looks out of the window as she looks at him. Landscapes fade into her face, and Wilhelm reads to himself the beginning of Eichendorff's "Aus dem Leben eines Taugenichts" about waking up.

The explicit evocation of waking indicates just how dreamlike all that has preceded it has been. And yet it seems as if the blood really has come from the nose of Laertes (this is the explanation offered by waking consciousness). On boarding another train at Hamburg/Altona, Wilhelm finds himself accompanied by Mignon and Laertes, whose fare he has to pay. As the new train leaves the station, he looks out of the window and sees a blond girl enter the train on the other side of the platform and then look out of *her* window in his direction. Laertes identifies her as Therese Farner, an actress. "You'd like to know why my nose is bleeding," he adds: "it comes from remembering." We are not told what he is remembering, as he mentions the frozen blood of Saint Januarius, which liquefies annually on his death day.

The implications of this succession of moments are staggeringly complex, and could legitimately generate a psychoanalytic treatise of some length. They clearly hint at problems of sexuality and its displacement – onto the opposite side of a railway carriage or platform; onto a nose that is itself a displaced image of the phallus – of memory, waking and forgetting. The specter of the repressed and its return is linked to the return of the Nazi past and the father Wilhelm lacks. There is also the question of speech and talking in one's sleep: The sequence is almost entirely silent, reminding one of Wilhelm's remark at the film's start: "It's as if I had no tongue; I haven't spoken for two days – except in my sleep I keep talking, says my mother." (The tongue is the mother tongue, relayed back by her to the son whose own lack of a tongue symbolizes castration, implying that writing is castrated speech.) The repression of sexuality is bound in with an inability to use words, perhaps because the liquid flow of ink is identified with a blood flow – of a diabolic pact? Reading the words of another replaces writing: Eichendorff offers the utopian possibility of being good for something, for writing, despite being "good-for-nothing."

For Wenders, the multiformed movement the film records is itself false: Traveling by train through the German landscape, Therese keeps wanting to stop. Movement is false because there is in fact nowhere to go, particularly for the artist: The flickering TV set indicates the emptiness of the available images. Thus the film lacks the lengthy discussion of past artworks that pervades Goethe's novel. Here, as in other respects, its relation to Goethe's original seems closely akin to that between Goethe's Wilhelm and many of the novel's other characters: Repeatedly people will appear whose commission of actions Wilhelm is considering dissuades him from actually acting (partly because he sees his imagined deeds' consequences, partly because the other's prior right to these actions makes them no longer "his"). "The road not taken" might be an appropriate alternative title: Again and again scenes are cut before the action they depict is resolved (e.g., Mignon in

Wilhelm's bed). In the scene in which the characters tell one another their dreams, Wenders disavows the dreamlike quality of his own work. When Therese confesses that her "dream" of skating on frozen ice (cut to a reaction shot of Wilhelm, to whose frigid aloofness she is referring) was devised consciously, the existence of the unconscious is mocked. Dreams become as ridiculous as the confessional art of Bernard Landau's poems, as worthless as the politics Laertes embodies. The American cinematic alternative that so fascinates Wenders elsewhere is interdicted, and present only as interdiction: When Wilhelm meets Therese on the town square, an American tourist's voice barks at him to get out of the line of the camera.

If *Wrong Movement* is a film whose thematics and imagery are astonishingly dense, one senses an urge on Wenders's part to frustrate the viewer's efforts to interpret it: It is the existentialist's dislike of the psychoanalysis that reveals the partiality of his control over the project of his life. It is a blocked film about writer's block. At the end, when Wilhelm looks out over the railings at the mountains opposite and speaks of how, at every moment of his life, he has been missing out, he also speaks for the viewer.

Where *Wrong Movement* leaves the source of Wilhelm's malaise unclear (is it sexual? writer's block? the German past?), the later Wenders would ascribe it to his suspension between Therese and Mignon. Deciding that the problem of selfhood may go away if ignored, recently Wenders has shifted the focus of his cinema from self to the female Other. His interest is no longer in the possibility or impossibility of identification with American directors or themes: Such identification means death, either artistic (*Hammett*) or personal (*Lightning over Water*). Instead, Europe (particularly France) becomes an object of attraction (*Paris, Texas* facilitates the transition). Wenders is less concerned now with the subject of cinema than with its object. The earlier films had hinted at an affinity between woman and cinema – women sell tickets to films to the protagonists, and near the opening of *Wrong Movement* Wilhelm's hometown girlfriend is shown asking a projectionist if he has an evening show – but not until *Paris, Texas* is the connection explicitly thematized, in the peep-show sequence with Nastassja Kinski. Wenders's newfound interest in woman-as-image can be seen as a thinking through of the consequences of what Lacan calls the mirror stage, in which the self is alienated from itself in order to form an awareness of itself as an image for others. That sense of the self reflected in others' eyes is, of course, inescapable for women in our society. The early Wenders, seeking a near-autistic authenticity of the pure, unrelated self, avoided women because they indicated the impossibility of his project. Like the goalie Bloch, who is fearful perhaps of impotence, the early Wenders erases the image of woman.

Two films in particular comprise the turning point in Wenders's representation of women: *Lightning over Water* and *Paris, Texas*. The former poses the alternative of relationship with a father figure or with a woman; the father figure's death means that only the woman is left. Woman herself then becomes the object of quest in *Paris, Texas*. If Travis nevertheless finally abandons Jane, it is because she cannot fulfill the expectations aroused by the female images of a billboard culture. (One recalls an earlier scene with Travis and Walt standing next to the overpowering billboard image of a woman.) *Wings of Desire*, in a form of special pleading that requires the virtual elimination of billboard images, will argue that in Europe the relative attenuation of American culture makes relationships possible again. Whereas in *Paris, Texas* the French woman is defeated – Anne loses Hunter – and the title mocks Parisian dreams, in *Wings of Desire* Alekan's circus is seen as home.

*Lightning over Water* dramatizes, and then rejects, the temptation to accord primacy to relationship with a father figure. The most obvious reason for rejecting the temptation is fear of the guilt that accompanies Oedipal rivalry: Wenders voices his fear that by turning his camera on Nick Ray, he is helping to kill him. He sabotages his own representation of Ray by doubling his film version with a video version shot by Tom, thus diluting his own responsibility for his images. He criticizes the film he himself shoots as false in its beauty; the video versions of certain scenes match this falsity with the falsity of their own excessive roughness: The video camera swings at abrupt angles as if it were in the hands of a crowd-jostled *vérité* reporter, rather than those of a seasoned practitioner working in an apartment in which all the set-ups can be carefully planned. Its deliberate chaos rings deliberately untrue. Wenders sets up a scene between Ray and Ronee Blakley only to destroy it in his mind's eye as he watches it: As she sits at Ray's bedside in reality, he imagines a scenario from which she has disappeared, and Ray is no longer lying on his bed (his potential deathbed) but beside it, talking to Wenders himself, whose occupation of the dreamer's position signals the sequence's status as wish-fulfillment. As he lies on the bed, he seems to be seeking at the last minute to save the father's image by putting himself in its place, to save himself from the reproach of having killed the father – be it through the oppressive attentions of his camera, or through neglecting him for his own wife. If the making of the film was an attempt to give Ray a shot in the arm (an addition to his filmography, for instance: The closing credits describe the film as directed by Nick Ray and Wim Wenders) the substitution at this point is a desperate final transfusion. "When you haven't made up your mind what you want to do, you try to do it beautifully," Wenders had remarked to Ray. If the film ends with a

beautiful image – suggested by Ray himself, a Chinese junk, sails bel-
lying, on the Hudson – its beauty is canceled as useless. By including
a sequence of the film crew partying after Ray's death, Wenders underlines his contempt for his own work: Following the studied, agonized
piety of all that has gone before, the lack of piety shocks. Wenders
himself finally arrives at the point at which Wilhelm found himself at
the beginning of *Wrong Movement:* without a father.

*Wrong Movement* begins with Wilhelm's inability to speak. It is no
surprise that *Paris, Texas* should open with a man similarly afflicted.
*Paris, Texas* allows one to guess at a possible source of Wilhelm's suffering: Mignon was virtually presexual. It takes advantage of the
happy fact that Nastassja Kinski has grown up in the meantime. In its
use of suspense, it breaks with the early work from the very start: The
lingering guitar notes may seem simply to mark time, but we are
clearly meant to ask ourselves if and when Travis will start to talk,
and whether or not he will know and wish to discuss where he has
been. It is as if Wenders wishes to demonstrate that he can tell a
story, albeit on his own terms, before departing the scene of the fiasco
of *Hammett.* The remoteness of the object of desire is shown to result
from an unnamable disaster, the fire that stands for the force that separated Travis and Jane as irrationally as it had held them together up
to that point. It is as if the glass between Jane and Travis has been
interposed to preserve the sexes from their mutual destructiveness.
Placed behind a screen, woman can be associated with cinema. With
the death of Nick Ray, the image of cinema becomes detached from the
image of the father, and so can be reattached elsewhere. It was almost
an accident that this occurred during the filming of *Paris, Texas.*
Sheila Johnston notes in her review of the film that

according to an interview with Wenders reproduced in the press notes, the
character of Jane was initially supplanted by Travis and Walt's father. "I had
already wanted to call John Huston to ask him if he would play the father. At
the last minute I didn't do it...I would have had to drop the idea of Jane. It
would have become a role of no importance.... I understood more and more
that we needed to...make her a real character. Everything we had tried before
had been a way of avoiding her character. A way of not having to define her,
by pushing the responsibility for the story onto someone else." (Johnston,
*Monthly Film Bulletin,* no. 607, p. 228.)

Instead, Huston became "Houston" (where Travis meets Jane) and
John, "Jane." The difference that made the difference was remarkably
small: The old attachment to the father figure is so displaced and con-
densed in the name "Houston" that it has the revealing status of the
key detail in a dream. (Is the use of another place name in the title a
form of repression?)

If the formula of *Paris, Texas* was partly fortuitous, its enormous success provided a sound reason for its repetition in *Wings of Desire*. Initially condemned to a bleak world of monochrome in which flight is no miracle, the angel Damiel discovers that it is wondrous when a mortal defies gravity, as does the trapeze artiste Marion. For all their apparent similarity, however, the gestures of the two films are radically different. The one stands at the end of a relationship with a woman and simply ties up the loose ends required for its closure. (Travis returns Hunter to Jane.) The other can be optimistic about the future liaison between Marion and the ex-angel, for no memories of trauma and obsession scar it. The film steps back from the unattainable image of cinema (America; Jane on the other side of the glass) to a Europe in which the object of desire is tangible and near: The movement from cinema to circus is echoed by the passage from the eerie detachment from this world in the monochrome sequences to the color that stands for the here-and-now. Yet there is something fatally willed about the film's affirmations: Only a man without a past – a man become a child – can so idealize woman. Thus it is only the required fulfillment of a schematic pattern that lends any plausibility to the film's argument: One pole dialectically summons its opposite, from timelessness to time, from male to female, from intellectuality to the body, from black-and-white to color, from detachment to populism, from eternity to her (to reverse the title of the song sung by Nick Cave and the Bad Seeds, "From Her to Eternity"). Because we are given no inkling of what may lie in Damiel's past, his attraction to Marion has none of the complexity of Heurtebise's love for Eurydice in Cocteau's *Orphée*. Damiel is in a sense a positive Travis. The alienation that pervades the film's first hour is utterly convincing: Total freedom of movement betokens total exclusion. (The constrictions that once attended movement in Berlin make it ironic that the angel's freedom is bought with an alienation as profound as that of any Berliner hemmed in by the Wall.) Damiel is like an omniscient narrator – a filmmaker perhaps – who wants to become a character, to step into his own dream. As he tunes in and out of the thoughts running through people's heads, he is like a man adjusting a radio dial in search of the right station. One has a crushing sense that the world's airwaves are pervaded by messages going nowhere. But Damiel's escape from alienation is unconvincing, and the identification of color with liberation banal. It is amusing to note how many critics refer to Rilke or Benjamin when writing of a film that persuades itself to prefer Frank Capra.

Wings of Desire, like *The State of Things*, was shot by Henri Alekan. In each work Wenders seems to be engaged in a chimerical search for the "ideal form" of film. In *The State of Things* it is the black-and-white that is strangely more realistic than color; in *Wings of Desire* color is seen as film's ultimate destination. (Wenders's identification with the movement of film history is one key to the film's popular success.) In a sense Wenders's dilemma regarding the choice of film stock – which is also a question of the degree to which the art film can swim with the mainstream – resembles Coppola's shuffling of styles in his recent work: It is almost fitting that the two should have worked together on *Hammett*. Coppola, however, accepts the vision of film history as an array of interchangeable styles with a lobotomized blandness that contrasts with Wenders's agonizing. Is monochrome the sign of alienation, or of realism? Wenders asks himself. As *Wings of Desire* moves into color – a few splashes at first, turning into a shower – it bears out the identification of monochrome with realism, as it swaps the symbolist intensity of its black-and-white for laid-back fairy tale. The impotence of adult thought gives way to childish omnipotence. The demands of American film are seen as redemptive – Peter Falk is hawk by name but dove (Columbo) by nature – rather than destructive, as they had been in *The State of Things*. Salvation lies in children and the feminine principle. So although there is wit in Wenders's film (at one point we glimpse an *Engelhardt* beer sign, *Engel* being German for "Angel"; the World War II footage is *in color*), it is not enough to arrest its slide into kitsch. The pigtailed, overcoated angels could have swept decoratively out of a U2 video. Wenders's Road Movies company should be renamed Yellow Brick Road Movies.

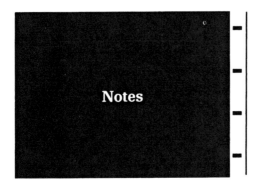

# Notes

Works listed in the Selected Bibliography are cited here using abridged bibliographical data.

### Introduction: The uncanny and the gorgon's gaze

**1.** Sigmund Freud, *"The Uncanny,"* in *Collected Papers,* vol. IV, pp. 389–90.
**2.** Ibid., p. 397.
**3.** Ibid., p. 386.
**4.** Ibid., pp. 384–5.
**5.** E.g., in my *The Realist Fantasy,* pp. 193–208, and in *New Left Review,* December 1986, pp. 122–8.
**6.** Freud, "The Uncanny," pp. 265–6.
**7.** Cf. S. S. Prawer, *Caligari's Children,* 1980, pp. 119–20.
**8.** *"Lenz,"* in Georg Büchner, *Werke und Briefe,* mit einem Nachwort von Fritz Bergemann, p. 84.
**9.** From *Werke und Brief,* p. 76 (hereafter *WuB*) and Michael Hamburger's translation of "Lenz" in *Leonce and Lena, Lenz, Woyzeck* (Chicago and London: University of Chicago Press, 1972), p. 51 (hereafter *LL*).
**10.** German: *WuB,* p. 77; English: *LL,* p. 52.
**11.** Ibid.
**12.** Ibid.
**13.** German: *WuB,* pp. 81–2; English: *LL,* p. 58.
**14.** German: *WuB,* p. 82; English: *LL,* p. 58.
**15.** German: *WuB,* pp. 82–3; English: *LL,* p. 59.
**16.** Siegfried Kracauer, *From Caligari to Hitler,* illustration 22.
**17.** German: *WuB,* p. 81; English *LL,* p. 57.
**18.** *WuB,* p. 80.
**19.** Particularly in *The Realist Fantasy, The Story of the Lost Reflection,* and *The Double and the Other.*
**20.** Tobin Siebers, *The Mirror of Medusa.*
**21.** German: *WuB,* p. 72; English: *LL,* p. 46. Further reflections of relevance on the sexual significance of the Medusa's head may be found in Freud's *Medusa's Head,* 1922 (*Collected Papers* vol. V, pp. 105–6), and in Philip Slater's *The Glory of Hera.*
**22.** *The Realist Fantasy,* pp. 61–2.

**23.** T. W. Adorno, *Negative Dialektik*, p. 364.
**24.** Pauline Kael, *"Metaphysical Tarzan."*
**25.** Friedrich Schiller, *Ueber das Erhabene*, 1801, in *Werke*, vol. II (Munich and Wiesbaden: Emil Vollmer Verlag, n.d.), p. 761.
**26.** Susan Sontag, *On Photography*, pp. 41–2.
**27.** Ibid., p. 41.
**28.** Ibid., p. 33.
**29.** Ibid., p. 40.

## I. Silent cinema and expressionism

**1.** For Irzykowski's views on psychomime, see *"The Tenth Muse (Excerpts),"* *New German Critique* (no. 42) (Fall 1987), 121–7.
**2.** Bela Balázs, *Theory of the Film*, p. 63.
**3.** Ibid., pp. 70–1.
**4.** Fredric Jameson, "Imaginary and Symbolic in Lacan: Marxism, Psychoanalytic Criticism, and the Problem of the Subject," in *Literature and Psychoanalysis: The Question of Reading: Otherwise*, edited by Shoshana Felman (Baltimore and London: Johns Hopkins University Press, 1982).
**5.** Ibid., p. 361.
**6.** Balázs, *Theory of the Film*, p. 75.
**7.** Thomas Elsaesser, "Film History and Visual Pleasure: Weimar Cinema," p. 74.
**8.** Rudolf Hoess, *Commandant of Auschwitz* (Toronto: Popular Library, 1959, p. 83).
**9.** T. W. Adorno, "Ein Titel," in pp. 654–7.
**10.** Siegfried Kracauer, *From Caligari to Hitler*, p. 73.
**11.** Hans Schwerte, *Faust und das Faustische: Ein Kapitel deutscher Ideologie* (Stuttgart: Ernst Klett Verlag, 1962), pp. 7–26.
**12.** This is one of the main themes of Thomas Elsaesser's fine "Primary Identification and the Historical Subject: Fassbinder and Germany." Victor Klemperer also writes of the pleasure derived from feeling the eye of the state upon one.
**13.** Appendix to Maas's *"Als der Geist der Gemeinschaft seine Sprayche fand."*
**14.** Alexander and Margarethe Mitscherlich, *Die Unfähigkeit zu trauern*, pp. 13–85.
**15.** Janet Bergstrom, "Sexuality at a Loss: The Films of F. W. Murnau," pp. 195–6.
**16.** Miriam Hansen, "Pleasure, Ambivalence, Identification."
**17.** Jo Leslie Collier, *From Wagner to Murnau*, p. 110.
**18.** Kracauer, *From Caligari to Hitler*, p. 71.
**19.** Wilhelm Worringer, *Abstraction and Empathy*, p. 199.
**20.** Thomas Elsaesser, "Social Mobility and the Fantastic," p. 18.
**21.** E.g., Lotte Eisner, *The Haunted Screen*, p. 232, or Rudolf Arnheim, *Kritiken und Aufsätze zum Film*, pp. 184–6.
**22.** Patrice Petro, *Joyless Streets*, pp. 26–7.
**23.** Thomas Elsaesser, "Innocence Restored," *Monthly Film Bulletin 51* (no. 611), 363–6.

24. Lotte Eisner, *Fritz Lang,* p. 83.
25. Andreas Huyssen, "The Vamp and the Machine."
26. C.f. Leonore Davidoff's "Class and Gender in Victorian England."
27. Kracauer first drew attention to the film's employment of crowds as "mass ornaments" (*From Caligari to Hitler,* pp. 91–5). His *Das Ornament der Masse* contains an exposition of the device's significance for National Socialism (pp. 50–63).
28. Elias Canetti, *Crowds and Power,* p. 181.
29. Ibid., p. 184.
30. Ibid., p. 375.
31. Ibid., p. 388.
32. Thomas Elsaesser, "Lulu and the Meter Man," pp. 17–20.
33. Ibid., p. 17.
34. Josef von Sternberg, "Preface" to *The Blue Angel* (screenplay), p. 13.
35. *Minima Moralia,* pp. 45–6.
36. Peter Baxter, "On the Naked Thighs of Miss Dietrich," in *Movies and Methods II,* edited by Bill Nicholas, pp. 557–65.
37. Ibid., p. 562.
38. Ibid., p. 564.
39. Ibid.
40. Ibid., p. 563.
41. Gilles Deleuze, *Sacher-Masoch,* pp. 50–60.
42. Gaylyn Studlar, "Masochism and the Perverse Pleasures of Cinema" (*Movies and Methods* II), p. 610.
43. Kracauer, *From Caligari to Hitler,* p. 218.

## II. The sleep of reason: Monstrosity and disavowal

1. Siegfried Kracauer, *From Caligari to Hitler,* p. 30.
2. T. W. Adorno, *Minima Moralia,* p. 115.
3. William Shakespeare, *Macbeth,* Act I, scene v, line 51.
4. Linda Williams, "When the Woman Looks," in: *Re-Vision: Essays in Feminist Film Criticism,* edited by Mary Ann Doane, Patricia Mellencamp, and Linda Williams (Frederick, Md.: University Publications of America, 1984), p. 87.
5. Ibid.
6. René Girard, *Violence and the Sacred,* p. 160.
7. The analysis of *Invasion of the Body Snatchers* is an abbreviated version of the one found in my *The Double and the Other,* pp. 66–8.
8. Franco Moretti, "Dialectic of Fear," in his *Signs Taken for Wonders,* p. 93.
9. Ibid., p. 104.
10. *Minima Moralia,* p. 110.
11. Kracauer, *From Caligari to Hitler,* p. 79.
12. Dudley Andrew, "The Turn and Return of Sunrise," p. 30.
13. Gilles Deleuze, *Cinema I: L'Image-mouvement,* pp. 158–66.
14. Tzvetan Todorov, *The Fantastic: A Structural Approach to A Literary*

*Genre* (Cleveland/London: The Press of Case Western Reserve University, 1973), p. 89.

15. Robin Wood, "An Introduction to the American Horror Film," in *Movies and Methods II*, edited by Bill Nichols, pp. 215–17.
16. Sergei Eisenstein, "The Structure of the Film," in *Film Form and the Film Sense*, pp. 170–1.

## III. Memory and repression in recent German cinema

1. Hayden White, *Metahistory*, p. 148.
2. The omission of the image of blood in Weimar cinema is noted by Paul Monaco in *Cinema and Society*, pp. 130–3. Kracauer notes "the omission of death in the German war films" of World War II in *From Caligari to Hitler*, p. 305.
3. Alexander and Margarethe Mitscherlich, *Die Unfähigkeit zu trauern*, pp. 44–57.
4. Jameson's theory is expounded in his "Postmodernism, or the Cultural Logic of Late Capitalism." The parody–pastiche distinction is enunciated on pp. 64–5.
5. Anton Kaes, *Deutschlandbilder*, pp. 135–70.
6. The quotation from Pollock is given as translated in the English version of the Mitscherlichs' *Die Unfähigkeit zu trauern* (*The Inability to Mourn*), p. 46.
7. Sigmund Freud, *Mourning and Melancholia*, in *Collected Papers* IV, pp. 158–9.
8. Ibid., pp. 159–60.
9. Susan Sontag, "Syberberg's Hitler," pp. 164–5.
10. Ibid., p. 158.
11. Jean-Pierre Oudart, "Séduction et terreur au cinema," p. 9.
12. Paul de Man, *Blindness and Insight*, p. 207.
13. Heinrich von Kleist, *Ueber das Marionettentheater*, p. 321.
14. Hans-Jürgen Syberberg, *Parsifal: Ein Filmessay*, pp. 56–7.
15. *Parsifal*, pp. 173–84.
16. Sigmund Freud, *The "Uncanny,"* in *Collected Papers* IV, pp. 373 and 375.
17. See in particular the interview with Reitz in *Cahiers du cinéma 366* (December 1984), 38–41.
18. Michael E. Geisler "*Heimat* and the German Left," esp. pp. 41–66.
19. Thomas Elsaesser "*Lili Marleen*: Fascism and the Film Industry," p. 132.
20. Umberto Eco, "The Structure of Bad Taste," in *Italian Writing Today* (Harmondsworth: Penguin, 1967), p. 119.
21. Hermann Broch, "Zum Problem des Kitsches," pp. 117–32.
22. *The Art of the Novel*, pp. 163–4.
23. A scathing denunciation of "nostalgia film" is to be found in Jameson's "Postmodernism," pp. 66–8.
24. The dependence of German identity on the confirmatory look of the Other has been the theme of much of Elsaesser's work; see in particular his "Primary Identification and the Historical Subject: Fassbinder and Germany."

## IV. Expressionism in America

1. Franz Kafka, *Der Prozess*, p. 187.
2. Michel Foucault, *The History of Sexuality*, vol. I, p. 85.
3. Stephen Heath, "Film and System: Terms of Analysis."
4. Ibid., p. 68: "No film is more obvious than *Touch of Evil*..."
5. Ibid., p. 41.
6. Ibid., p. 73: "Citizen Cane."
7. Jean Cocteau, *Cocteau on the Film*, p. 101: "My moral gait is that of a lame man, with one foot in life and the other in death."
8. John Stavrianos, a student of mine, has made some acute comments on this aspect of Welles's work in an unpublished paper entitled "The Grotesque Body and Castration Anxiety in *Touch of Evil*."
9. Heath, "Film and System," pp. 72–7.
10. Mikhail Bakhtin, *Rabelais and His World*, p. 26.
11. Kael, *The Citizen Kane Book*, p. 2.
12. T. W. Adorno, *Minima Moralia*, p. 46.
13. Fredric Jameson, "Postmodernism, or the Cultural Logic of Late Capitalism," p. 67.
14. Laura Mulvey, "Visual Pleasure and Narrative Cinema," in *Movies and Methods* II, edited by Bill Nichols, pp. 303–15.
15. Tania Modleski, *The Women Who Knew Too Much*, p. 87.
16. Ibid., p. 90.
17. Ibid., p. 99.
18. Ibid., p. 100.
19. Mulvey, "Visual Pleasure," p. 313. (All further extracted quotations in this section, ibid.)
20. Donald Spoto, *The Art of Alfred Hitchcock*, p. 309.
21. Personal communication, Queen Elizabeth's Hotel, Montréal, February 25, 1989, during his visit to Canada.
22. *Coincidence* is of course the title of one of Kieślowski's finest films (*Przypadek*); I analyze it in my "Exile and Identity: Kieślowski and His Contemporaries," in the forthcoming *Before the Wall Came Down*.

## V. Elective affinities and family resemblances: For Margarethe von Trotta

1. Paisley Livingston, *Ingmar Bergman and the Rituals of Art*, p. 57.
2. Jarosław Marek Rymkiewicz, *Umschlagplatz*, pp. 221–23.
3. E. Ann Kaplan, "Discourses of Terrorism, Feminism and the Family in Von Trotta's *Marianne and Juliane*," p. 66.
4. Julia Kristeva, *Powers of Horror*, p. 17.
5. Thomas Elsaesser, *New German Cinema*, p. 250.
6. Kristeva, *Powers of Horror*, pp. 2–4.
7. Some of the feminist misgivings concerning the film are summarized in Ellen Seiter's "The Political Is the Personal: Margarethe Von Trotta's *Marianne and Juliane*." The objections to classicism are strongest in Elsaesser ("Mother Courage and Divided Daughters"), whose sole excuse for a condescending as-

similation of Von Trotta to Hollywood practices is the ambiguity of the term "classicism," particularly in contemporary film theory ("classic Hollywood").

**8.** Kristeva, *Powers of Horror,* p. 5.

**9.** Heinrich Böll, *Billard um halbzehn,* p. 74.

**10.** Kaplan, "Discourses of Terrorism," p. 63.

**11.** Karena Niehoff, "Der Weg der Gewalt": "Jetzt übernimmt Ismene die Rolle der Antigone...."

**12.** See the chapter on *Heimat* in Anton Kaes, *Deutschlandbilder.*

**13.** For some of the problems raised by the aesthetic of *Shoah,* see my "A Ghetto in Babel: Claude Lanzmann's *Shoah,*" or Pauline Kael's review, "Sacred Monsters," in the *New Yorker.*

**14.** For a sensitive assessment of its effect upon *Heimat*'s reception, see Michael E. Geisler's "*Heimat* and the German Left."

**15.** Margarethe Von Trotta, "Rebellin wider eine bleierne Zeit," interview with Reiner Frey and Christian Göldenboog, p. 35.

**16.** Margarethe Von Trotta, *Die bleierne Zeit* (screenplay), p. 111.

**17.** Kaplan, "Discourses of Terrorism," p. 61.

**18.** Elsaesser, "Mother Courage," p. 178.

**19.** Seiter, "The Political Is the Personal," p. 109.

**20.** Kaplan, "Discourses of Terrorism," p. 67.

**21.** Daniel Cohn-Bendit, "Verdrängen oder verarbeiten: zu Margarethe Von Trottas Film *Die bleierne Zeit*" (*Die Tageszeitung,* August 25, 1981).

**22.** Interview with Franz Rath, in Von Trotta, *Die bleierne Zeit* (screenplay), pp. 100–1.

# Selected bibliography

## Primary texts

Baudelaire, Charles. *Les Fleurs du Mal*. Paris: Livre de poche, 1972.
Böll, Heinrich. *Billard um halbzehn*. Munich: DTV, 1987.
Broch, Hermann. *Die Schlafwandler*. Zurich: Rhein Verlag, 1931/2.
—. *Die Schuldlosen*. Zurich: Rhein Verlag, 1954.
—. *Die unbekannte Grösse*. Zurich: Rhein Verlag, 1961.
—. *Der Versucher*. Zurich: Rhein Verlag, 1953.
Büchner, Georg. *Werke und Briefe*. Munich: DTV, 1975.
—. *Leonce and Lena, Lenz, Woyzeck*. Chicago and London: University of Chicago Press, 1972.
Chandler, Raymond. *The Big Sleep*. New York: Ballantine, 1973.
Comito, Terry (ed.). *Touch of Evil*. New Brunswick, N.J.: Rutgers University Press, 1985.
Diederichs, Helmut H. (ed.). *Der Student von Prag*. Stuttgart: Focus Verlagsgemeinschaft, 1985.
Hochhuth, Rolf. *Eine Liebe in Deutschland*. Reinbek: Rowohlt, 1978.
Kafka, Franz. *Der Prozess*. Frankfurt a.M.: Fischer Taschenbuch, 1976 (1960).
—. *Sämtliche Erzählungen*. Frankfurt a.M.: Fischer Taschenbuch, 1976.
Kleist, Heinrich von. *Werke in zwei Bänden*. Berlin and Weimar: Aufbau-Verlag, 1976.
Lang, Fritz. *Metropolis*. London: Villiers Publications, 1973.
Lanzmann, Claude. *Shoah: An Oral History of the Holocaust*. New York: Pantheon, 1985.
Levi, Primo. *If This Is a Man; The Truce*. London: Abacus, 1987.
—. *The Periodic Table*. New York: Schocken, 1984.
Mann, Heinrich. *Professor Unrat*. Reinbek: Rowohlt, 1969.
Mann, Klaus. *Mephisto: Roman einer Kariere*. Munich: Nymphenberger Verlagshandlung, 1969.
Mann, Thomas. *Doktor Faustus*. Frankfurt a.M.: Fischer Taschenbuch, 1977.
—. *Mario und der Zauberer*. Leipzig: Reclam, 1977.
Racine, Jean. *Theatre Complet*. Paris: Garnier Flammarion, 1965.
Reitz, Edgar, with Peter Steinbach. *Heimat: Eine deutsche Chronik*. Nördlingen: Greno, 1985.
Rymkiewicz, Jarosław Marek. *Umschlagplatz*. Paris: Instytut Literacki, 1988.

Shelley, Mary. *Frankenstein, or the Modern Prometheus*. London: Oxford University Press, 1969.

Sternberg, Josef von. *The Blue Angel*. London: Lorrimer Publications, 1968.

Stoker, Bram. *Dracula*. Toronto, New York, London, Sydney, Auckland: Bantam, 1981.

Syberberg, Hans-Jürgen. *Hitler, a Film from Germany*. New York: Farrar, Straus, Giroux, 1982.

Harbou, Thea von. *Metropolis*. Frankfurt a.M., Berlin, Vienna: Ullstein, 1984.

Trotta, Margarethe von. *Die bleierne Zeit*. Frankfurt a.M.: Fischer Taschenbuch, 1985.

Wedekind, Frank. *The Lulu Plays*. Greenwich, Conn.: Fawcett, 1967.

**Main secondary sources**

*Books*

Adorno, T. W. *Aesthetische Theorie*. Frankfurt a.M.: Suhrkamp, 1974.

—. *In Search of Wagner*. London: Verso, 1984.

—. *Jargon der Eigentlichkeit*. Frankfurt a.M.: Suhrkamp, 1974.

—. *Minima Moralia: Reflections from Damaged Life*. London: New Left Books, 1974.

—. *Negative Dialektik*. Frankfurt a.M.: Suhrkamp, 1966.

Adorno, T. W. with Max Horkheimer. *Dialektik der Aufklärung*. Frankfurt a,.M.: Fischer Taschenbuch, 1986.

Arnheim, Rudolf. *Kritiken und Aufsätze zum Film*. Edited by Helmut H. Diederichs Frankfurt a.M.: Fischer Taschenbuch, 1979.

Atwell, Lee. *G. W. Pabst*. Boston: Twayne, 1977.

Aust, Stefan. *Der Baader-Meinhof Complex*. Hamburg: Hoffmann und Campe, 1986.

Bakhtin, Mikhail. *Die Aesthetik des Wortes*. Frankfurt a.M.: Suhrkamp, 1979.

—. *Rabelais and His World*. Bloomington: Indiana University Press, 1984.

Balázs, Béla. *Schriften zum Film I: Der sichtbare Mensch, Kritiken und Aufsätze*. Munich: Carl Hanser, 1982.

—. *Theory of the Film: Character and Growth of a New Art*. London: Dennis Dobson Ltd., 1952.

Benjamin, Walter. *Illuminationen*. Frankfurt a.M.: Suhrkamp, 1977.

—. *The Origin of German Tragic Drama*. London: Verso, 1985.

Boa, Elizabeth. *The Sexual Circus: Wedekind's Theatre of Subversion*. Oxford: Blackwell, 1987.

Bordwell, David, Staiger, Janet, and Thompson, Kristin. *The Classical Hollywood Cinema: Film Style and Mode of Production to 1960*. New York: Columbia University Press, 1985.

Broch, Hermann. *Die Idee ist ewig: Essays und Briefe*. Munich: DTV, 1968.

Bredow, Willfried von, with Rolf Zurek. *Film und Gesellschaft in Deutschland: Dokumente und Materialien*. Hamburg: Hoffmann & Campe, 1975.

Brooks, Louise. *Lulu in Hollywood*. New York: Praeger, 1982.

Canetti, Elias. *Crowds and Power*. London: Gollancz, 1962.

—. *Die gespaltene Zukunft*. Munich: Carl Hanser, 1972.

Coates, Paul. *The Double and the Other: Identity as Ideology in Post-Romantic Fiction.* London: Macmillan; New York: St. Martin's, 1988.

—. *The Realist Fantasy: Fiction and Reality Since "Clarissa."* London: Macmillan; New York: St. Martin's, 1983.

—. *The Story of the Lost Reflection: The Alienation of The Image in Western and Polish Cinema.* London: Verso, 1985.

Cocteau, Jean. *Cocteau on the Film.* New York: Dover Publications, 1972.

Collier, Jo Leslie. *From Wagner to Murnau: The Transposition of Romanticism from Stage to Screen.* Ann Arbor and London: UMI Research Press, 1988.

Corrigan, Timothy. *New German Film: The Displaced Image.* Austin, Tex.: University of Texas Press, 1983.

Deleuze, Gilles. *Cinema I: L'Image-mouvement.* Paris: Les Editions de Minuit, 1983.

—. *Cinema II: L'Image-temps.* Paris: Les Editions de Minuit, 1985.

—. *Sacher-Masoch.* London: Faber and Faber, 1971.

De Man, Paul. *Blindness and Insight: Essays in the Rhetoric of Contemporary Criticism.* Minneapolis: University of Minnesota Press, 1983.

Dolezel, Stephen, with K. R. M. Short. *Hitler's Fall: The Newsreel Witness.* London, New York, Sydney: Croom Helm, 1988.

Eder, Klaus (ed.). *Syberbergs Hitler-Film.* Munich and Vienna: Carl Hanser, 1980.

Eisenstein, Sergei. *Film Form and Film Sense.* Edited and translated by Jay Leyda. Cleveland and New York: Meridian Books, 1963.

Eisner, Lotte. *The Haunted Screen.* Berkeley and Los Angeles: University of California Press, 1969.

—. *Fritz Lang.* New York: Oxford University Press, 1977.

—. *Murnau.* London: Secker & Warburg, 1973.

Elsaesser, Thomas. *New German Cinema: A History.* New Brunswick. N.J.: Rutgers University Press, 1989.

Foucault, Michel. *Discipline and Punish: The Birth of the Prison.* London: Penguin, 1977.

—. *The History of Sexuality,* vol. I. London: Allen Lane, 1979.

—. *Madness and Civilization: A History of Insanity in the Age of Reason.* New York and Toronto: Mentor, 1967.

Freud, Sigmund. *Collected Papers,* 5 vols. Edited by James Strachey. Translated under the supervision of Joan Rivière. London: The Hogarth Press and the Institute of Psychoanalysis, 1950.

—. *Totem und Tabu.* Frankfurt a.M. and Hamburg: Fischer Bücherei, 1964.

Friedländer, Saul. *Kitsch und Tod: Der Widerschein des Nazismus.* Munich and Vienna: DTV, 1986.

Geist, Kathe. *The Cinema of Wim Wenders: From Paris, France, to Paris, Texas.* Ann Arbor: UMI Research Press, 1988.

Girard, René. *Violence and the Sacred.* Baltimore and London: Johns Hopkins University Press, 1984.

Grafe, Frieda, with Enno Patalas, Hans Helmut Prinzler, and Syr. *Fritz Lang.* Munich and Vienna: Carl Hanser. 1976.

Grant, Barry (ed.). *Planks of Reason: Essays on the Horror Film*. Metuchen, N.J.: Scarecrow Press, 1984.

Hayman, Ronald. *Fassbinder: Filmmaker*. New York: Simon & Schuster, 1984.

Hilton, Julian. *Georg Büchner*. New York: Grove Press, 1982.

Hoess, Rudolf. *Commandant of Auschwitz*. Toronto: Popular Library, 1959.

Insdorf, Annette. *Indelible Shadows: Film and the Holocaust*. New York: Cambridge University Press, 1989.

Irzykowski, Karol. *X Muza: Zagadnienia estetyczne kina*. Warsaw: Wydawnictwo Artystyczne i Filmowe, 1977.

Jenkins, Stephen (ed.). *Fritz Lang: The Image and the Look*. London: BFI, 1981.

Kaplan, E. Ann. *Women and Film: Both Sides of the Camera*. New York: Methuen, 1983.

—. *Women in Film Noir*. London: BFI, 1978.

Kael, Pauline. *The Citizen Kane Book*. St. Albans: Paladin, 1974.

Kaes, Anton. *Deutschlandbilder: Die Wiederkehr der Geschichte als Film*. Munich: edition text und kritik, 1987.

—. *Kino-Debatte: Literatur und Film 1909–1929*. Tübingen: Niemeyer, 1978.

Klemperer, Victor. *LTI*. Leipzig: Reclam, 1982.

Kogon, Eugen. *Der SS-Staat: Das System der deutschen Konzentrationslager*. Munich: Kindler, 1974.

Korte, Helmut. *Film und Realität in der Weimarer Republik*. Munich: Carl Hanser, 1978.

Kracauer, Siegfried. *Die Angestellten: Aus dem neuesten Deutschland*. Frankfurt a.M.: Suhrkamp, 1971.

—. *From Caligari to Hitler: A Psychological History of the German Film*. Princeton, N.J.: Princeton University Press, 1974 (1947).

—. *Das Ornament der Masse*. Frankfurt a.M.: Suhrkamp, 1977 (1963).

—. *Theory of Film: The Redemption of Physical Reality*. New York: Oxford University Press, 1960.

Kristeva, Julia. *Powers of Horror: An Essay on Abjection*. New York: Columbia University Press, 1982.

Kuhn, Annette. *The Power of the Image: Essays on Representation and Sexuality*. London and Boston: Routledge & Kegan Paul, 1985.

Kundera, Milan. *The Art of the Novel*. New York: Grove Press, 1986.

Kurtz, Rudolf. *Expressionismus und Film*. Berlin: Verlag der Lichtbildbühne, 1926.

Livingston, Paisley. *Ingmar Bergman and the Rituals of Art*. Ithaca and London: Cornell University Press, 1982.

Maas, Utz. *"Als der Geist der Gemeinschaft seine Sprayche fand": Sprache im Nationalsozialismus*. Wiesbaden: Westdeutscher Verlag, 1984.

Malson, Lucien. *Wolf Children and the Problem of Human Nature*. New York and London: Monthly Review Press, 1972.

Metz, Christian. *The Imaginary Signifier: Psychoanalysis and the Cinema*. Bloomington: Indiana University Press, 1982.

Mitscherlich, Alexander, and Mitscherlich, Margarethe. *Die Unfähigkeit zu trauern: Grundlagen kollektiven Verhaltens.* Munich and Zurich: R. Piper, 1977 (1967). Translated by Beverly R. Placzek as *The Inability to Mourn: Principles of Collective Behavior.* New York: Grove, 1975.

Modleski, Tania. *The Women Who Knew Too Much: Hitchcock and Feminist Theory.* New York: Methuen, 1988.

Möhrmann, Renate. *Die Frau mit der Kamera: Filmemacherinnen in der Bundesrepublik.* Munich and Vienna: Carl Hanser, 1980.

Monaco, Paul. *Cinema and Society: France and Germany during the Twenties.* New York, Oxford, and Amsterdam: Elsevier, 1976.

Moretti, Franco. *Signs Taken for Wonders.* London: Verso, 1983.

Nash, Mark. *Dreyer.* London: BFI, 1977.

Newton, Judith L., ed., with Mary P. Ryan and Judith R. Walkowitz. *Sex and Class in Women's History: Essays from "Feminist Studies."* London and Boston: Routledge & Kegan Paul, 1983.

Nichols, Bill, ed. *Movies and Methods II.* Los Angeles and Berkeley: University of California Press, 1985.

Nietzsche, Friedrich. *The Birth of Tragedy and The Genealogy of Morals.* Garden City, N.Y.: Doubleday, 1956.

—. *Richard Wagner in Bayreuth, Der Fall Wagner, Nietzsche Contra Wagner.* Stuttgart: Reclam, 1973.

Petley, Julian. *Capital and Culture: German Cinema 1933–45.* London: BFI, 1977.

Petro, Patrice. *Joyless Streets: Women and Melodramatic Representation in Weimar Germany.* Princeton, N.J.: Princeton University Press, 1989.

Polan, Dana. *Power and Paranoia: History, Narrative, and the American Film, 1940–50.* New York: Columbia University Press, 1986.

Prawer, S. S. *Caligari's Children: The Film as Tale of Terror.* Oxford: Oxford University Press, 1980.

Reik, Theodor. *Myth and Guilt: The Crime and Punishment of Mankind.* New York: George Braziller, 1957.

Rentschler, Eric. ed. *German Film and Literature: Adaptations and Transformations.* New York and London: Methuen, 1986.

Rosen, Charles. *Schoenberg.* London: Fontana/Collins, 1976.

Rosenberg, Alfred. *Die Spur des Juden im Wandel der Zeiten.* Munich: Zentralverlag des NSDAP, 1937.

Rosenfeld, Paul. *Musical Impressions.* London: Allen & Unwin, 1970.

Roud, Richard. *Straub.* London: Secker & Warburg/BFI, 1971.

Sandford, John. *The New German Cinema.* London: Oswald Wolff, 1980.

Sartre, Jean-Paul. *Anti-Semite and Jew.* New York: Grove Press, 1962.

—. *Baudelaire.* Paris: Gallimard, 1963.

Schrader, Paul. *Transcendental Style in Film: Ozu, Bresson, Dreyer.* Berkeley, Los Angeles, and London: University of California Press, 1972.

Schwerte, Hans. *Faust und das Faustische: Ein Kapitel deutscher Ideologie.* Stuttgart: Ernst Klett, 1962.

Siebers, Tobin. *The Mirror of Medusa.* Berkeley, Los Angeles, and London: University of California Press, 1983.

Silver, Charles. *Marlene Dietrich.* New York: Pyramid, 1974.

Sirk, Douglas, with Jon Halliday. *Sirk on Sirk*. London: Secker & Warburg/BFI, 1971.

Slater, Philip E. *The Glory of Hera: Greek Mythology and the Greek Family.* Boston: Beacon, 1968.

Sontag, Susan. *On Photography*. New York: Delta, 1977.

Spoto, Donald. *The Art of Alfred Hitchcock*. New York: Doubleday, 1976.

—. *The Dark Side of Genius: The Life of Alfred Hitchcock*. New York: Ballantine, 1983.

Sternberg, Josef von. *Fun in a Chinese Laundry*. London: Secker & Warburg, 1966.

Sudendorf, Werner (ed.). *Marlene Dietrich: Dokumente, Essays, Filme*. Munich: Carl Hanser, 1977.

Sullivan, J. W. N. *Beethoven: His Spiritual Development*. London: Unwin, 1972.

Syberberg, Hans-Jürgen. *Parsifal: Ein Filmessay*. Munich: Wilhelm Heyne, 1982.

—. *Syberbergs Filmbuch*. Frankfurt a.M.: Fischer, 1979.

Szondi, Peter. *Theorie des modernen Dramas (1880–1950)*. Frankfurt a.M.: Suhrkamp, 1974.

Thomson, David. *A Biographical Dictionary of the Cinema*. London: Secker & Warburg, 1980.

—. *America in the Dark*. New York: Morrow, 1977.

Virilio, Paul. *War and Cinema: The Logistics of Perception*. London and New York: Verso, 1989.

Völker, Klaus, ed. *Faust: ein deutscher Mann*. Berlin: Verlag Klaus Wagenbach, 1981.

Weil, Claudius, with Georg Sesslen. *Kino des Phantastischen*. Munich: Roloff & Sesslen, 1976.

White, Hayden. *Metahistory: The Historical Imagination in Nineteenth Century Europe*. Baltimore and London: Johns Hopkins University Press, 1973.

Wilson, Colin, with Robin Odell. *Jack the Ripper: Summing Up and Verdict*. London: Bantam Press, 1987.

Wood, Robin. *Bergman*. London: Studio Vista, 1970.

—. *Hitchcock's Films*. London: Zwemmer; Cranbury, N.J.: A. S. Barnes, 1965 (rev. 1969).

Wood, Robin, with Ian Cameron. *Antonioni*. London: Studio Vista, 1970.

Worringer, Wilhelm. *Abstraction and Empathy: A Contribution to the Psychology of Style*. London: Routledge & Kegan Paul, 1967 (1908).

*Articles, essays, reviews*

Adorno, T. W. "Auf die Frage: was ist deutsch?," in *Schriften 10.2, Kulturkritik und Gesellschaft II*, pp. 691–701. Frankfurt a.M.: Suhrkamp, 1977.

—. "Aufarbeitung der Vergangenheit," in *Schriften 10.2, Kulturkritik und Gesellschaft II*, pp. 555–72. Frankfurt a.M.: Suhrkamp, 1977.

—. "Die auferstandene Kultur," in *Schriften 20.2, Vermischte Schriften*, pp. 453–64. Frankfurt a.M.: Suhrkamp, 1986.

—. "Zur Bekämpfung des Antisemitismus heute," in *Schriften 20.1, Vermischte Schriften I*, pp. 360–83. Frankfurt a.M.: Suhrkamp, 1986.

—. "Erziehung nach Auschwitz," in *Schriften 10.2, Kulturkritik und Gesellschaft II*, pp. 674–90. Frankfurt a.M.: Suhrkamp, 1977.

—. "The Musical Climate for Fascism in Germany," in *Schriften 20.2, Vermischte Schriften*, pp. 430–40. Frankfurt a.M.: Suhrkamp 1986.

—. "Ein Titel" and "Unrat und Engel," in *Schriften 11. Noten zur Literatur* pp. 654–60. Frankfurt a.M.: Suhrkamp Taschenbuch, 1981.

Andrew, Dudley. "The Turn and Return of *Sunrise*," in his *Film in the Aura of Art*, pp. 28–58. Princeton, N.J.: Princeton University Press, 1984.

Andrews, Nigel. "Hitler as Entertainment," *American Film 3* (no. 6) (April 1978), 50–3.

Bayer, Eva-Suzanne. "Schwestern oder die Bilance der Identität," *Stuttgarter Zeitung*, March 20, 1981.

Bergstrom, Janet. "Sexuality at a Loss: The Films of F. W. Murnau," *Poetics Today 6* (nos. 1–2) (1985), 185–203.

Buchka, Peter. "Ein deutsches Familienalbum," *Süddeutsche Zeitung*, October 2, 1981.

Burch, Noël, with Jorge Dana. "Propositions," *Afterimage* (no. 5) (Spring 1974), 40–66.

Burnett, Ron. "Lumière's Revenge," in *History On / and In / Film*, edited by Tom O'Regan and Brian Shoesmith, pp. 140–66. Perth: History and Film Association of Australia, 1987.

Christie, Ian (ed.). "The Syberberg Statement," *Framework 11* (no. 6), 12–18.

Coates, Paul. "Anatomy of a Murder," *Sight and Sound 58* (no. 1), (Winter 1988–9), 63–4.

—. "From 'Clarissa' to 'Dynasty,' " *The World and I 4* (no. 6) (June 1989), 182–7.

—. "The Cold Heaven of the Blue Angel: Dietrich, Masochism, and Identification," *Social Discourse/Discours social 2* (nos. 1–2) (Spring–Summer 1989), 59–67.

—. "Exile and Identity: Kieślowski and His Contemporaries," in *Before the Wall Came Down*, edited by Graham Petrie (forthcoming).

—. "A Ghetto in Babel: Claude Lanzmann's *Shoah*," *Encounter 69* (no. 1) (June 1987), 59–61.

—. "Karol Irzykowski: Apologist of the Inauthentic Art," *New German Critique* (no. 42) (Fall 1987), 113–15.

—. "The Monster and His Double," *The World and I 4* (no. 10) (October 1989), 262–7.

—. "Sartre, Shakespeare and Film Noir," *The World and I 3* (no. 6) (June 1988), 242–6.

—. "You Can't Go Home Again: Thomas Brasch's *The Passenger*," *The World and I 3* (no. 10) (October 1988), 234–37.

Cohn-Bendit, Daniel. "Verdrängen oder Verarbeiten," *Die Tageszeitung*, September 25, 1981.

Comolli, Jean-Louis, with François Géré. "La Réal-fiction du pouvoir," *Cahiers du cinéma* (no. 292) (Sept. 1978), 24–7.

Davidoff, Leonore. "Class and Gender in Victorian England," in *Sex and Class in Women's History: Essays from "Feminist Studies,"* edited by Judith L. Newton, Mary P. Ryan, and Judith R. Walkowitz, pp. 19–30. London and Boston: Routledge & Kegan Paul, 1983.

Delorme, Charlotte. "Zum Film, *Die bleierne Zeit* von Margarethe von Trotta," *Frauen und Film* (no. 31) (1982), 52–5.

Elsaesser, Thomas. "A Cinema of Vicious Circles," in *Fassbinder*, edited by Tony Rayns, pp. 24–36. London: BFI, 1976.

—. "Film History and Visual Pleasure: Weimar Cinema," in *Cinema Histories, Cinema Practices*, edited by Patricia Mellencamp and Philip Rosen, pp. 47–84. Frederick, Md.: University Publications of America, 1984.

—. "Werner Herzog: Tarzan Meets Parsifal," *Monthly Film Bulletin 55* (no. 652) (May 1988), 132–4.

—. "*Lili Marleen*: Fascism and the Film Industry," *October* (no. 21) (1982), 115–40.

—. "Lulu and the Meter Man: Louise Brooks, Pabst and *Pandora's Box*," *Screen* 24 (nos. 4–5) (October, 1983), 4–36.

—. "Memory, Home and Hollywood," *Monthly Film Bulletin 52* (no. 613) (February 1985), 48–51.

—. "Mother Courage and Divided Daughters," *Monthly Film Bulletin 50* (no. 594) (July 1983), 176–8.

—. "Murder, Merger, Suicide," in *Fassbinder*, 2d ed. edited by Tony Rayns, pp. 37–53. London: BFI, 1979.

—. "Myth as the Phantasmagoria of History: H. J. Syberberg, Cinema and Representation," *New German Critique* (nos. 24–5) (Fall/Winter 1981–2), 108–54.

—. "The Post-War German Cinema," in *Fassbinder*, edited by Tony Rayns, pp. 1–16. London: BFI, 1976.

—. "Primary Identification and the Historical Subject: Fassbinder and Germany," *Ciné-Tracts* (no. 11) (Fall 1980), 43–52.

—. "Secret Affinities," *Sight and Sound 58* (no. 1) (Winter 1988–9), 33–9.

—. "Social Mobility and the Fantastic: German Silent Cinema," *Wide Angle 5* (no. 2) (1982), 14–25.

Faye, Jean-Pierre. "Faust, Teil III" (translation of *Le troisième Faust*), in *Syberbergs Hitler-Film*, edited by Klaus Eder, pp. 33–5. Munich and Vienna: Carl Hanser, 1980.

Foucault, Michel. "Die vier Reiter der Apokalypse und die alltäglichen kleinen Würmchen" (translation of conversation with Bernard Sobel), in *Syberbergs Hitler-Film*, edited by Klaus Eler, pp. 69–73. Munich and Vienna: Carl Hanser, 1980.

Geisler, Michael E. "*Heimat* and the German Left: The Anamnesis of a Trauma," *New German Critique 36* (Fall 1985), 25–66.

Hansen, Miriam. "Dossier on *Heimat*," *New German Critique 36* (Fall 1985), 3–24.

—. "Pleasure, Ambivalence, Identification: Valentino and Female Spectatorship," *Cinema Journal 25* (no. 4.) (Summer 1986), 6–32.

Heath, Stephen. "Film and System: Terms of Analysis," *Screen 16* (nos. 1–2), 7–77. 91–113.

Huyssen, Andreas. "The Vamp and the Machine: Technology and Sexuality in Fritz Lang's *Metropolis*," *New German Critique* (nos. 24–5) (1981), 221–37.

Jameson, Fredric. "Imaginary and Symbolic in Lacan: Marxism, Psychoanalytic Criticism and the Problem of the Subject," in *Literature and Psychoanalysis: The Question of Reading: Otherwise*, edited by Shoshana Felman, pp. 338–95. Baltimore and London: Johns Hopkins University Press, 1982.

—. " 'In the Destructive Element Immerse . . .'," in *October* (no. 17) (Summer 1981), 99–118.

—. "Postmodernism, or the Cultural Logic of Late Capitalism," *New Left Review 146* (July–August 1984), 53–92.

Johnston, Sheila. "*The German Sisters*," *Films and Filming* (no. 334) (July 1982), 25–6.

—. "*Paris, Texas*," *Monthly Film Bulletin 51* (no. 607), 227–8.

Kael, Pauline. "A Devil without Fire," *The New Yorker*, May 17, 1982.

—. "Metaphysical Tarzan," *The New Yorker*, October 20, 1975.

—. "*Persona*," in *Kiss Kiss Bang Bang*, pp. 171–2. London: Calder and Boyars, 1970.

—. "Sacred Monsters," *The New Yorker*, December 30, 1985.

Kaplan, E. Ann. "Discourses of Terrorism, Feminism and the Family in Von Trotta's *Marianne and Juliane*," *Persistence of Vision 1* (no. 2) (Spring 1985), 61–8.

Lardeau, Yann. "L'Art du deuil: *Hitler, un Film d'Allemagne*," *Cahiers du cinéma* (nos. 292) (September 1978), 15–23.

Lobeck, Rolf. "Unruhige Träume, traurige Gesichter," *Deutsche Volkszeitung*, October 29, 1981.

Nave, Bernard. "Margarethe von Trotta, ou le réfus de l'oubli," *Jeune cinéma* (no. 138) (November 1981), 19–33.

Niehoff, Karena. "Der Weg der Gewalt: Margarethe von Trottas Film *Die bleierne Zeit*," *Der Tagesspiegel*, September 26, 1981.

Oudart, Jean-Pierre "Séduction et terreur au cinema: Notes de mémoire sur *Hitler*, de Syberberg," *Cahiers du cinéma 294* (November 1978), pp. 5–15.

Pym, John. "Home and the World," *Sight and Sound 54* (no. 2) (Spring 1985), 126–8.

—. "Syberberg and the Tempter of Democracy," *Sight and Sound 46* (no. 4) (Autumn 1977), 227–30.

Ranvaud, Don. "Edgar Reitz in Venice," *Sight and Sound 54* (no. 2) (Spring 1985), 124–6.

Reichert, Manuela. "Bilder? Beweise: was man sieht, und was man ist," *Deutsches Allgemeines Sonntagsblatt*, October 4, 1981.

Rhode, Carla. "Schwestern des Unglücks," *Der Tagesspiegel*, April 5, 1981.

Ruf, Wolfgang. "Die Begegnung der beiden Schwestern," *Deutsches Allgemeines Sonntagsblatt*, October 23, 1981.

Sansom, Gareth. "Fangoric Horrality: The Subject and Ontological Horror in a Contemporary Cinematic Sub-Genre," *Social Discourse/Discours social 2* (nos. 1–2) (Spring–Summer 1989), 163–73.

Schlüpmann, Heide. "*Je suis la solitude: Zum Doppelgängermotiv in Der Student von Prag*," *Frauen und Film* (no. 36) (1984), 10–24.

Schneider, Peter. "Hitler's Shadow: On Being a Self-Conscious German," *Harper's Magazine 275* (no. 1648) (September 1987), 49–54.

Schulz-Gerstein, Christian. "Vom Abtanzball zu El-Fatah," *Der Spiegel,* September 14, 1981.

Schwarze, Michael. "Zwei Schwestern," *Frankfurter Allgemeine Zeitung,* September 14, 1981.

Scott, Jay. *"Marianne and Juliane,"* in *Midnight Matinees,* pp. 191–2. Toronto: Oxford University Press, 1985.

Seiter, Ellen. "The Political Is the Personal: Margarethe Von Trotta's *Marianne and Juliane,"* in *Films for Women,* edited by Charlotte Brunsdon, pp. 109–16. London: BFI, 1986. Reprinted from *Journal of Film and Video 37* (no. 2) (Spring 1985).

Skasa-Weiss, Ruprecht. "Olle Kamelle und Goldener Löwe," *Stuttgarter Zeitung,* September 25, 1981.

Sontag, Susan. "Bergman's *Persona,"* in *Styles of Radical Will,* pp. 123–45. New York: Farrar, Straus & Giroux, 1969.

—. "Syberberg's *Hitler,"* in *Under the Sign of Saturn,* pp. 137–65. New York: Vintage, 1980.

Syberberg, Hans-Jürgen. "The Abode of the Gods," *Sight and Sound 54* (no. 2) (Spring 1985), 125.

—. "Aus keinem meiner Filme wird man jemanden hinausgehen sehen, der taumelt," interview with Reiner Frey and K. L. Baader, *Filmfaust* (no. 22) (April/May 1981), 3–16.

—. "Form Is Morality," *Framework* (no. 12) (1980), 11–15.

Trotta, Margarethe von. "Rebellin wider eine bleierne Zeit," interview with Reiner Frey and Christian Göldenboog, *Filmfaust* (no. 24) (1981), 29–36.

Wajda, Andrzej. Interview with Dan Yakir, *Film Comment 20* (no. 6) (November–December 1984), 24–8.

Witte, Karsten. "Im Transit: Thomas Braschs neuer Film," *Die Zeit,* June 6, 1988.

Wood, Robin. "Burying the Undead: The Use and Obsolescence of Count Dracula," *Mosaic 16* (nos. 1–2) (Winter–Spring 1983), 175–87.

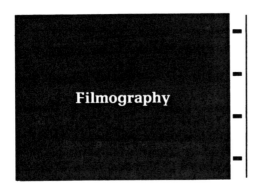

# Filmography

*Alice in the Cities* (*Alice in den Städten*), dir. Wim Wenders (W. Germany, 1973)

*Amour fou, L'*, dir. Jacques Rivette (France, 1968)

*Andalusian Dog, An* (*Un Chien Andalou*), dir. Luis Buñuel (France, 1929)

*Angi Vera*, dir. Pal Gabor (Hungary, 1978)

*Another Way* (*Egymásra nézve*), dir. Károly Makk (Hungary, 1982)

*Battleship Potemkin* (*Bronenosets Potemkin*), dir. Sergei Eisenstein (U.S.S.R., 1925)

*Berlin Alexanderplatz*, dir. Rainer Werner Fassbinder (W. Germany, 1980, for TV)

*Big Sleep, The*, dir. Howard Hawks (U.S., 1948)

*Birds, The*, dir. Alfred Hitchcock (U.S., 1963)

*Blackmail*, dir. Alfred Hitchcock (Great Britain, 1928)

*Blow-Up*, dir. Michelangelo Antonioni (Great Britain, 1966)

*Blue Angel, The* (*Der blaue Engel*), dir. Josef von Sternberg (Germany, 1930)

*Body Heat*, dir. Lawrence Kasdan (U.S., 1981)

*Bolweiser*, dir. Rainer Werner Fassbinder (W. Germany, 1977)

*Boule de Suif* (*Pyshka*), dir. Mikhail Romm (USSR, 1934)

*Cabinet of Dr. Caligari, The* (*Das Kabinett des Dr. Caligari*), dir. Robert Wiene (Germany, 1919)

*Carrie*, dir. Brian de Palma (U.S., 1976)

*Cat People*, dir. Jacques Tourneur (U.S., 1942)

*Céline and Julie Go Boating* (*Céline et Julie vont en bateau*), dir. Jacques Rivette (France, 1974)

*Chinatown*, dir. Roman Polanski (U.S., 1974)

*Citizen Kane*, dir. Orson Welles (U.S., 1941)

*Coincidence* (*Przypadek*), dir. Krzysztof Kieślowski (Poland, 1982)

*Conformist, The* (*Il conformista*), dir. Bernardo Bertolucci (Italy–France–W. Germany, 1970)

*Creature from the Black Lagoon*, dir. Jack Arnold (U.S., 1954)

*Cries and Whispers* (*Viskningar och rop*), dir. Ingmar Bergman (Sweden, 1973)

*Dark Corner, The*, dir. Henry Hathaway (U.S., 1946)

*Day of Wrath* (*Vredens Dag*), dir. Carl Theodor Dreyer (Denmark, 1943)

*Death by Hanging* (*Koshikei*), dir. Nagisa Oshima (Japan, 1968)

*Despair* (*Eine Reise ins Licht*), dir. Rainer Werner Fassbinder (W. Germany, 1977)

*Deutschland Erwache!*, dir. Erwin Leiser (W. Germany, 1968)

*Diary of a Lost Girl* (*Das Tagebuch einer Verlorenen*), dir. G. W. Pabst (Germany, 1929)

*Dirty Harry*, dir. Don Siegel (U.S., 1975)

*Dishonored*, dir. Von Sternberg (U.S., 1931)

*Double Indemnity*, dir. Billy Wilder (U.S., 1944)

*Dr. Mabuse, the Gambler* (*Dr. Mabuse, der Spieler*), dir. Fritz Lang (Germany, 1922)

*E.T. – The Extraterrestrial*, dir. Steven Spielberg (U.S., 1982)

*Elephant Man, The*, dir. David Lynch (U.S., 1980)

*Eraserhead*, dir. David Lynch (U.S., 1976)

*Eternal Jew, The* (*Der ewige Jude*), dir. Ministry of Propaganda of the Third Reich, under supervision of Fritz Heppler (Germany, 1940)

*Everything for Sale* (*Wszystko na sprzedaż*), dir. Andrzej Wajda (Poland, 1968)

*Exorcist, The*, dir. William Friedkin (U.S., 1973)

*Fanny and Alexander* (*Fanny och Alexander*), dir. Ingmar Bergman (Sweden, 1982)

*Fatal Attraction*, dir. Adrian Lyne (U.S., 1987)

*Faust*, dir. F. W. Murnau (Germany, 1926)

*Fear Eats the Soul* (*Angst essen Seele auf*), dir. Rainer Werner Fassbinder (W. Germany, 1973)

*Fearless Vampire Killers, The* (a/k/a *Dance of the Vampires*), dir. Roman Polanski (U.S.–Great Britain, 1977)

*First Blood*, dir. Ted Kotcheff (U.S., 1982)

*Foolish Wives*, dir. Erich von Stroheim (U.S., 1921)

*Frances*, dir. Graeme Clifford (U.S., 1982)

*Frankenstein*, dir. James Whale (U.S., 1931)

*Gentlemen Prefer Blondes*, dir. Howard Hawks (U.S., 1953)

*Germany in Autumn* (*Deutschland in Herbst*), dir. Alf Brustellin, Rainer Werner Fassbinder, Alexander Kluge, Maximiliane Mainka, Edgar Reitz, Katja Ruppé, Hans Peter Cloos, Berhard Sinkel, Volker Schlöndorff, Margarethe von Trotta (W. Germany, 1978)

*Goalie's Anxiety at the Penalty Kick, The* (*Die Angst des Tormanns beim Elfmeter*), dir. Wim Wenders (W. Germany–Austria, 1971)

*Godfather, The*, dir. Francis Ford Coppola (U.S., 1972)

*Great Dictator, The,* dir. Charles Chaplin (U.S., 1940)

*Habañera, La,* dir. Douglas Sirk (Germany, 1937)

*Hammett,* dir. Wim Wenders (U.S., 1982)

*Heimat,* dir. Carl Frölich (Germany, 1938)

*Heimat,* dir. Edgar Reitz (W. Germany, 1985)

*Hitlerjunge Quex (Unsere Fahne Flattert Uns Voran),* dir. Hans Steinhoff (Germany, 1933)

*Holocaust,* dir. Marvin Chomsky (U.S., 1978, for TV)

*Hour of the Wolf (Vargtimmen),* dir. Ingmar Bergman (Sweden, 1968)

*In a Year with Thirteen Moons (In einem Jahr mit dreizehn Monden),* dir. Rainer Werner Fassbinder (W. Germany, 1978)

*In the Realm of the Senses (Ai no corrida),* dir. Nagisa Oshima (Japan, 1976)

*Invasion of the Body Snatchers,* dir. Don Siegel (U.S., 1956); remake dir. Philip Kaufman (U.S., 1978)

*Jetée, La,* dir. Chris Marker (France, 1962/4)

*Kagemusha,* dir. Akira Kurosawa (Japan, 1980)

*Karl May,* dir. Hans-Jürgen Syberberg (W. Germany, 1974)

*King Kong,* dir. Merian C. Cooper and Ernest B. Schoedsack (U.S., 1933); remake dir. John Guillermin (U.S., 1976)

*Kings of the Road (Im Lauf der Zeit),* dir. Wim Wenders (W. Germany, 1976)

*Kriemhild's Revenge (Kriemhilds Rache),* dir. Fritz Lang (Germany, 1924)

*Lady from Shanghai, The,* dir. Orson Welles (U.S., 1948)

*Lady in the Lake,* dir. Robert Montgomery (U.S., 1946)

*Lady Vanishes, The,* dir. Alfred Hitchcock (Great Britain, 1938)

*Last Laugh, The (Der letze Mann),* dir. F. W. Murnau (Germany, 1924)

*Lightning Over Water (Nick's Film),* dir. Wim Wenders (U.S., 1981)

*Lili Marleen,* dir. Rainer Werner Fassbinder (W. Germany, 1980)

*Little Shop of Horrors, The,* dir. Frank Oz (U.S., 1986)

*Lost Honor of Katherina Blum, The (Die verlorene Ehre der Katherina Blum),* dir. Margarethe von Trotta and Volker Schlöndorff (W. Germany, 1975)

*Love in Germany, A (Ein Liebe in Deutschland),* dir. Andrzej Wajda (France–W. Germany, 1984)

*Love of Jeanne Ney, The (Die Liebe der Jeanne Ney),* dir. G. W. Pabst (Germany, 1927)

*Ludwig – Requiem for a Virgin King (Ludwig – Requiem für einen jungfräulichen König),* dir. Hans-Jürgen Syberberg (W. Germany, 1972)

*M (M, Mörder unter Uns),* dir. Fritz Lang (Germany, 1931)

*Macbeth,* dir. Orson Welles (U.S., 1948)

*Macbeth,* dir. Roman Polanski (Great Britain, 1971)

*Magician, The* (*Ansiktet*; a/k/a *The Face*), dir. Ingmar Bergman (Sweden, 1958)

*Maltese Falcon, The*, dir. John Huston (U.S., 1941)

*Man Hunt*, dir. Fritz Lang (U.S., 1941)

*Man Like Eva, A* (*Ein Mann wie Eva*), dir. Radu Gabrea (W. Germany, 1983)

*Man of Iron* (*Człowiek z żelaza*), dir. Andrzej Wajda (Poland, 1981)

*Man of Marble* (*Człowiek z marmuru*), dir. Andrzej Wajda (Poland, 1978)

*Marianne and Juliane* (*Die bleierne Zeit*; a/k/a *The German Sisters*), dir. Margarethe von Trotta (W. Germany, 1981)

*Marriage of Maria Braun, The* (*Die Ehe der Maria Braun*), dir. Rainer Werner Fassbinder (W. Germany, 1978)

*Mattei Affair, The* (*Il caso Mattei*), dir. Francesco Rosi (Italy, 1972)

*Mephisto*, dir. István Szabó (Hungary, 1986)

*Merchant of the Four Seasons, The* (*Der Händler der vier Jahreszeiten*), dir. Rainer Werner Fassbinder (W. Germany, 1971)

*Metropolis*, dir. Fritz Lang (Germany, 1926); reedited by Giorgio Moroder (U.S., 1984)

*Mildred Pierce*, dir. Michael Curtiz (U.S., 1945)

*Mirror, A* (*Zerkalo*), dir. Andrei Tarkovsky (USSR, 1975)

*Mr. Arkadin* (*Confidential Report*), dir. Orson Welles (Great Britain, 1955)

*Mystery of Kaspar Hauser, The* (*Jeder für sich und Gott gegen alle*), dir. Werner Herzog (W. Germany, 1974)

*Night and Fog* (*Nuit et brouillard*), dir. Alain Resnais (France, 1955)

*Night Moves*, dir. Arthur Penn (U.S., 1975)

*Nosferatu, the Vampire* (*Nosferatu – Eine Symphonie des Grauens*), dir. F. W. Murnau (Germany, 1922); remake (as *Nosferatu – Phantom der Nacht*), dir. Werner Herzog (W. Germany, 1979)

*Not Reconciled* (*Nicht versöhnt oder Es hilft nur Gewalt, wo Gewalt herrscht*), dir. Jean-Marie Straub (W. Germany, 1965)

*Okoto and Sasuke* (*Okoto to Sasuke*), dir. Yasujiro Shimazu (Japan, 1935)

*Olympia* (*Olympische Spiele*), dir. Leni Riefenstahl (Germany, 1938)

*Omen, The*, dir. Richard Donner (U.S., 1976)

*Ordet* (*The Word*), dir. Carl Theodor Dreyer (Denmark, 1955)

*Orphée*, dir. Jean Cocteau (France, 1950)

*Our Hitler, A Film from Germany* (*Hitler. Ein Film aus Deutschland*), dir. Hans-Jürgen Syberberg (W. Germany, 1977, in four parts)

*Pandora's Box* (*Die Büchse der Pandora*), dir. G. W. Pabst (Germany, 1928)

*Paris, Texas*, dir. Wim Wenders (U.S., 1984)

*Parsifal*, dir. Hans-Jürgen Syberberg (W. Germany, 1981)

*Passenger, The* (*Pasażerka*), dir. Andrzej Munk (Poland, 1963)
*Passion of Joan of Arc, The* (*La Passion de Jeanne d'Arc*), dir. Carl Dreyer (France, 1928)
*Persona*, dir. Ingmar Bergman (Sweden, 1966)
*Phantom*, dir. F. W. Murnau (Germany, 1922)
*Picture of Dorian Gray, The*, dir. Albert Lewin (U.S., 1944)
*Postman Always Rings Twice, The*, dir. Tay Garnett (U.S., 1946)
*Psycho*, dir. Alfred Hitchcock (U.S., 1960)
*Querelle*, dir. Rainer Werner Fassbinder (W. Germany, 1982)
*Red Desert* (*Deserto rosso*), dir. Michelangelo Antonioni (Italy, 1964)
*Reverse Angle – New York City, March 1982*, dir. Wim Wenders (U.S., 1982)
*Ritual, The* (*Riten*), dir. Ingmar Bergman (Sweden, 1969)
*Rope*, dir. Alfred Hitchcock (U.S., 1948)
*Sacrifice, The* (*Offret*), dir. Andrei Tarkovsky (Sweden, 1986)
*Sawdust and Tinsel* (*Gycklarnas afton*), dir. Ingmar Bergman (Sweden, 1953)
*Scarface*, dir. Brian de Palma (U.S., 1983)
*Scarlet Letter, The* (*Der scharlachrote Buchstabe*), dir. Wim Wenders (W. Germany–Spain, 1972)
*Schneider von Ulm, Der*, dir. Edgar Reitz (W. Germany, 1978)
*Seventh Seal, The* (*Det sjunde inseglet*), dir. Ingmar Bergman (Sweden, 1957)
*Sheer Madness* (*Heller Wahn*), dir. Margarethe von Trotta (W. Germany, 1983)
*Shoah: An Oral History of the Holocaust*, dir. Claude Lanzmann (France, 1985)
*Short Film about Killing, A* (*Krótki film o zabijaniu*), dir. Krzysztof Kieślowski (Poland, 1987)
*Sid and Nancy*, dir. Alex Cox (U.S., 1986)
*Silence, The* (*Tystnaden*), dir. Ingmar Bergman (Sweden, 1963)
*Singing Detective, The*, dir. Jon Amiel (Great Britain, 1986, for TV)
*Sisters, or The Balance of Happiness* (*Schwestern oder Die Balance des Glücks*), dir. Margarethe von Trotta (W. Germany, 1979)
*Solaris* (*Solyaris*), dir. Andrei Tarkovsky (USSR, 1972)
*Song of Love, The*, dir. Clarence Brown (U.S., 1947)
*State of Things, The* (*Der Stand der Dinge*), dir. Wim Wenders (W. Germany, 1982)
*Stranger, The*, dir. Orson Welles (U.S., 1946)
*Strangers on a Train*, dir. Alfred Hitchcock (U.S., 1951)
*Student of Prague, The* (*Der Student von Prag*), dir. Stellan Rye (Germany, 1913); remake dir. Henrik Galeen (Germany, 1926)
*Summer Interlude* (*Sommarlek*), dir. Ingmar Bergman (Sweden, 1951)

*Summer with Monika* (*Sommaren med Monika*), dir. Ingmar Bergman (Sweden, 1953)

*Sunrise: A Song of Two Humans*, dir. F. W. Murnau (U.S., 1927)

*Texas Chainsaw Massacre, The*, dir. Tobe Hooper (U.S., 1975)

*Thousand Eyes of Dr. Mabuse, The* (*Die Tausend Augen des Dr. Mabuse*), dir. Fritz Lang (W. Germany, 1960)

*That Obscure Object of Desire* (*Cet Obscur Objet du désir*), dir. Luis Buñuel (Spain–France, 1977)

*Threepenny Opera, The* (*Die Dreigroschenoper*), dir. G. W. Pabst (Germany, 1931)

*Throne of Blood* (*Kumonosu-jo*), dir. Akira Kurosawa (Japan, 1957)

*Through a Glass Darkly* (*Såsom i en spegel*), dir. Ingmar Bergman (Sweden, 1961)

*Touch of Evil*, dir. Orson Welles (U.S., 1958)

*Trial, The*, dir. Orson Welles (U.S., 1962)

*Triumph of the Will* (*Triumph des Willens*), dir. Leni Riefenstahl (Germany, 1935)

*Vampyr*, dir. Carl Theodor Dreyer (Germany, 1932)

*Variety* (*Variété*), dir. E. A. Dupont (Germany, 1925)

*Vertigo*, dir. Alfred Hitchcock (U.S., 1958)

*Waxworks* (*Das Wachsfigurenkabinett*), dir. Paul Leni (Germany, 1924)

*Welcome to Germany* (*Der Passagier*), dir. Thomas Brasch (W. Germany, 1988)

*Wetherby*, dir. David Hare (Great Britain, 1985)

*Whither Germany?* (*Kuhle Wampe*), dir. Slatan Dudow (Germany, 1932)

*Wild Child, The* (*L'Enfant sauvage*), dir. François Truffaut (France, 1969)

*Wild Strawberries* (*Smultronstället*), dir. Ingmar Bergman (Sweden, 1957)

*Wings of Desire* (*Der Himmel über Berlin*), dir. Wim Wenders (W. Germany, 1987)

*Winter Light* (*Nattvardsgästerna*), dir. Ingmar Bergman (Sweden, 1963)

*Woman Alone, A* (*Sabotage*), dir. Alfred Hitchcock (Great Britain, 1936)

*Woyzeck*, dir. Werner Herzog (W. Germany, 1979)

*Written on the Wind*, dir. Douglas Sirk (U.S., 1956)

*Wrong Movement* (*Falsche Bewegung*), dir. Wim Wenders (W. Germany, 1974)

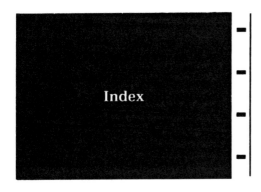

# Index

9 780521 063364